Britain in the
European Union today

Third edition

Duncan Watts and Colin Pilkington

Manchester University Press

Manchester and New York

distributed exclusively in the USA by Palgrave

First edition published 1995 by Manchester University Press
Second edition published 2001 by Manchester University Press

This edition published by
Manchester University Press
Oxford Road, Manchester M13 9NR, UK
and Room 400, 175 Fifth Avenue, New York, NY 10010, USA
www.manchesteruniversitypress.co.uk

Distributed exclusively in the USA by
Palgrave, 175 Fifth Avenue, New York,
NY 10010, USA

Distributed exclusively in Canada by
UBC Press, University of British Columbia, 2029 West Mall,
Vancouver, BC, Canada V6T 1Z2

British Library Cataloguing-in-Publication Data
A catalogue record for this book is available from the British Library

Library of Congress Cataloging-in-Publication Data applied for

ISBN 0 7190 7179 8   *paperback*
EAN 978 0 7190 7179 9

This edition first published 2005

14 13 12 11 10 09 08 07 06 05   10 9 8 7 6 5 4 3 2 1

Typeset in Photina
by Northern Phototypesetting Co. Ltd, Bolton
Printed in Great Britain
by Biddles Ltd, King's Lynn

Contents

Tables and boxes

Tables

Boxes

Preface to the
second edition

When I wrote the preface to the first edition of this book in November 1991 I stated quite categorically that British involvement in the European Union was one of that handful of subjects, present in all political science syllabi, that are inadequately dealt with, in that it is an area about which students are mostly ill informed. Apathy and ignorance of European issues on the part of both students and teachers are two important factors, but of even greater importance is the lack of correctly targeted information, for the teacher as much as for the student.

At that time there were a number of text books dealing with the European Community itself, but for the most part they either concentrated on the history and institutions of the Community or they discussed the economic or constitutional aspects of the Community in a very technical sense, and without any specific British dimension. That situation has changed to a certain extent in that there is an increasing number of resources available to those seeking basic information about the European Communities, not least the availability now of the massive Europa website on the Internet. On the other hand, it still remains difficult to keep up to date on European issues if the intention is to retain a clear, objective picture of what is involved. Too many of the words that have been written about Europe take the form of polemic argument, with a partisan agenda either for or against (but mostly against) the idea of European integration. As for the British press, it is so eurosceptic in its outlook that most newspapers only publish as many negative aspects of the European Union as they can find, while totally ignoring anything that might be held to be positive.

The European dimension is of increasing importance in British politics, affecting all the many different aspects of British legislation and decision making. There is also no doubt that the long debate over economic and monetary union has raised the profile of European issues considerably, especially over the question of sovereignty. Nor can we ignore the impact Europe is having on the political parties, a divisive issue comparable with the effects of the Corn Laws or Home Rule in the past.

A knowledge of the relations between the UK and Europe has been useful to candidates for some time, but now, with the increased emphasis on European issues in recent years, examiners are likely to lay even more stress and importance on this aspect of a candidate's answer. This is applicable to all students who are following a course in government or politics at school, college or university – which makes my point about the paucity of basic, objective source material even more relevant than it was in 1994. Hence this second and almost completely re-written edition of a book in which my aim has been to write a clear, concise and accessible account to cater for all politics students, as well as to members of the general public looking for clarification over British membership of the European Union.

At this point I feel I should make a disclaimer about my own personal position. I have tried, throughout my writing of this book, to retain a detached and unbiased view of Europe and of issues such as sovereignty. Readers, however, may detect a slight leaning towards pro-Europeanism on my part. I have to say that this is less because of a strong ideological belief than it is the result of the overwhelming euroscepticism of most British commentators, especially in the tabloid press, that have forced me to argue the pro-European position as a sort of devil's advocate in order to overcome their vicious and often inaccurate anti-European arguments.

I should like to thank Dr Bill Jones, the series editor, and Richard Purslow, then the commissioning editor for Manchester University Press, both for the trust and confidence they showed when they commissioned me to write the first edition of this work and for the help and encouragement they provided during the writing process. For later assistance at MUP, leading up to this second edition, I am indebted to Nicola Viinikka, who took over from Richard Purslow, and to Pippa Kenyon who kept me on the straight and narrow. As always, I owe a great deal to the team involved in examining politics at AQA-NEAB, in particular Dennis Harrigan and Cliff Jones, for making suggestions that were mostly useful. A relatively tame headteacher of my acquaintance, Dr Rob Gibson, spurred me on to greater efforts by showing, through his questions to me on behalf of his sixth form, just which areas most needed to be covered. A grateful acknowledgment is also due to many members of the Politics Association, but I am particularly indebted to Glynis Sandwith of PARC.

I also have to say that I received much useful guidance as to what students actually need from those candidates whose work was submitted to me as examiner. Indeed, I should like to pay tribute to one student in particular. For his highly competent and merciless evaluation of the worth, usefulness and readability of resource material about the European Community I salute the work of Matthew Forrester, then a student at Leftwich County High School in Northwich, Cheshire. Matthew was only sixteen and a year eleven student when he wrote his critique, but his conclusions were very logical, incisive and mature, such as to give this academic writer considerable pause for thought as to how far what he had to say had any relevance or meaning for the average student for whom he was supposed to be writing.

We are in the midst of a period of major changes to the European Union and the next few years will see us plunged into a fresh round of growth and development. I trust that this book might help students to understand just what is happening in Europe and what impact that is having on the British political scene.

Colin Pilkington

Preface to the third edition

The second edition of *Britain in the European Union today* appeared in 2001, the text having been revised in late 1999. Since it was written, a number of important developments have occurred, in a relatively short time. Among them are the signing and ratification of the Treaty of Nice; the total elimination of national currencies in the countries belonging to the eurozone; the British assessment of its five tests for entry into the same; disunity in Europe concerning the war with Iraq; the search for agreement on the European constitution drafted by the Convention; a fifth enlargement; and a further round of European elections. The European Union (EU) had fifteen members in 2001, in 2004 it had twenty-five and it is due to expand to twenty-seven in 2007. The expansion has led to changes in the size of EU institutions and provoked considerable discussion and contention about the development of EU policies (not least the Common Agricultural Policy) and the way in which decisions are made.

The developments outlined above and a number of others have all highlighted the need for a third edition. Colin Pilkington's preface to the second one pointed to the need for 'correctly targeted information' about an issue that was and remains of growing importance in national and international politics. This information is also of very considerable importance to the many examinees who are increasingly expected to know something of the growth and workings of the EU, either as part of a course in British government and politics or one more specifically about the EU.

Sadly, Colin died in 2002. His death seriously depleted the ranks of those writers who possess the gift of explaining sometimes difficult issues with accuracy and clarity. It has fallen to me to assume the mantle and take over the tasks of revising and updating this work. Some parts of the second edition remain as applicable today as when Colin wrote them, notably the historical material up to 1999, the debates concerning sovereignty and decision making, and much more besides. However, the developments refered to above make a new version desirable and necessary.

Where possible, I have left the original untouched, apart from carrying out discreet, and in many cases, minor editing of the text. Some other chapters required more extensive attention, to take account of recent events and perspectives, or – in the case of the Introduction – to provide greater clarity about the key terms employed in studying moves to integration. In addition, two new chapters have been added. The role and operations of pressure groups in the EU previously received short treatment, as part of a section of material on policy and decision making. A much extended coverage has been accorded them, in the light of the increasing recognition of their role and importance, as national groups make more and more use of EU institutions as an outlet for their lobbying activities. Also, at the end of the book, the position of Britain in Europe has been reviewed, to bring together various references in the book, draw conclusions about the way in which Britain has worked with its European partners and explain some of the difficulties that have arisen.

Throughout the editing and rewriting of the text, an attempt has been made to present evidence and arguments fairly, without any overt leanings towards either europhilism or euroscepticism being allowed to emerge. The nature of the subject makes it difficult to eliminate all bias, not least because of the reason given by Colin in his last preface:

> Readers, however, may detect a slight leaning towards pro-Europeanism on my part. I have to say that this is less because of a strong ideological belief than it is the result of the overwhelming euroscepticism of most British commentators, especially in the tabloid press, that have forced me to argue the pro-European position as a sort of devil's advocate in order to overcome their vicious and often inaccurate anti-European arguments.

By the end of this book it is hoped that readers will be in a better position to make up their own minds about the attitudes and performance of British governments and politicians from all sides on matters relating to the European Union. At that point, it may be possible to reach some judgement on whether Britain has been a 'reluctant', if not at times 'awkward' European.

Duncan Watts

Glossary

Acquis communautaire   A French term meaning 'the Community as it is', here meaning the rights and duties shared by member states of the EU. The *acquis* includes all past EC/EU treaties, laws, resolutions, agreements and Court decisions that collectively have shaped the development of the EU. All accession states have to accept the *acquis* before being allowed to join and incorporate it into their own national legislation. 'Accepting the *acquis*' therefore means accepting the EU as they find it: its principles, laws and practices.

Cohesion   Action to reduce regional differences within the EU, brought about by structural funds to boost living conditions.

Common Market   Original name for the tariff-free area of the Six.

Communautaire   Supportive of the principles of the EU.

Convergence   The idea that the economic performance of EU nations must be brought more closely into line before full economic and monetary union can be achieved.

Democratic deficit   A situation in which there is a deficiency in the democratic process, usually where a governing body is insufficiently accountable to an elected institution. The term often refers to the lack of democracy and accountability in the decision-making processes of the EU and to the obscurity and inaccessibility of its difficult legal texts. The EU is seeking to overcome these deficiencies via simpler legislation and better public information, and by allowing organisations representing citizens a greater say in policy making. But these measures do not address the demands of those who wish to see a more powerful Parliament and maybe an elected Commission.

Enlargement   The process by which new members join the EU. The six original members have now become twenty-five, as a result of successive enlargements. Two more nations are due to join in 2007.

Enhanced co-operation   Any arrangement allowing some countries to work together on a particular project or in a particular area, even if the other EU countries are unable or unwilling to join in – on the basis that they can join in later on. There are several forms of such flexibility or 'differenti-ated integration'. All refer to any set of arrangements that represents a departure from the notion that all member states must proceed towards the same objective at the same time and at the same speed.

Europe des Patries   A Europe made upon of independent nation-states which co-operate for purposes of mutual benefit: the Gaullist/Thatcherite vision of how Europe should develop.

Europhile   A euro-enthusiast: someone who admires the EU and broadly supports its aims, policies and practices. A committed integrationist.

Europhobe   A person who strongly dislikes and distrusts the EU, its aims, policies and practices, especially as they impact upon Britain. Many euro-phobes would like to see Britain quit the EU.

Eurosceptic   The term that became fashionable in the 1990s for a person who is opposed to European integration and is sceptical of the EU, its aims, policies and practices. Usually, eurosceptics wish to try and reverse the tide of integration and often they talk of 'repatriating' powers to the UK.

Eurosclerosis   A period of stagnation and disappointment, when the Community/Union seemed mired in difficulties.

Eurozone or euroland   The nickname used to denote the euro area, com-prising member states that have adopted the single currency – the euro.

Factortame   The famous case that arose when a number of companies, largely Spanish-controlled, sought a judicial review of certain provisions of the British Merchant Shipping Act 1998. Spanish fishermen had been evad-ing an agreement on fishing quotas by using British-registered vessels to fish in British waters. The Thatcher government responded by laying down a strict definition of what made a vessel qualify as British. The Spanish fisher-men alleged the provisions to be discriminatory. In the judgement made by the Court of Justice, the British Act was ruled to be invalid, for it conflicted with the EU's Common Fisheries Policy. This was the first time that a British law was effectively set aside by the Court of Justice and made many people understand that the sovereignty of the British Parliament had suffered a serious blow. The case served to underline the primacy of Community law over national law.

Federalism   Strictly speaking, a division of responsibility in which power is divided between one central authority, which tackles some issues such as defence and foreign policy, and several states or provinces, which deal with other matters. In a EU context, British politicians often use the term as a description for policies leading in the direction of closer European integration. Post-war European federalists believed in a swift movement to complete political unification. They were inspired by Churchill's rhetoric about a 'United States of Europe', and their vision enthused the post-1945 generation.

Founding fathers   The pioneers of the modern EU who – in the years after the Second World War – had a vision of how the continent should develop as a united entity, committed to peace and friendship. Monnet and Schuman are prime examples of founding fathers.

Four freedoms The term sometimes used to cover the frontier-free approach of the EU's single market, which allows for free movement of goods, people, services and money.

Integration The process of making a community into a whole, by strengthening the bonds between its component parts. In this case, building unity between nations on the basis that they pool their resources and take many decisions jointly, thereby leading to a deepening of the ties that bind the EU.

Intergovernmentalists Those who favour co-operation between governments for their mutual advantage. They want to retain as much national sovereignty as possible – see Europe des Patries. Theirs is an essentially practical rather than a visionary approach.

Qualified majority voting The most widely adopted method of voting in the Council of Ministers, involving the allocation to each member state of a 'weighting' very broadly reflecting its population.

Schengen Agreement The agreement, originally signed in 1985 by France, Germany and the Benelux countries, that refers to the 'gradual abolition of controls at the common frontiers'. Some measures taken under Schengen referred to short-term issues (visa regulations, etc.); others were long term ones (strengthening external frontiers, duty free allowances, etc.). Its more sensitive provisions cover questions such as control of drugs, control of firearms, extradition, etc.

Subsidiarity A description of a political system in which the functions of government are carried out at the lowest appropriate level for efficient administration; the idea that each level of government has its suitable geographical level. Subsidiarity is believed to enhance democracy. Germans would portray it as the very essence of federalism, but Majorite Conservatives saw it as a means of fending off a more deeply integrated Europe.

Supranationalism The transfer of some national sovereignty to a multinational organisation which acts on behalf of all the countries involved – for example from Britain to the EU.

Transparency Opening up institutions to the public gaze: more openness in decision making and improving access to information and documents.

Treaty of Rome The treaty establishing the European Economic Community, signed in March 1957.

Two-speed Europe An approach that would allow a core group of EU countries to move faster than the others towards European integration. As such, it is one of the forms of flexibility designed to ensure that the process of integration can move forward, even if not all states feel ready to participate.

Variable geometry A model of integration in which states can decide whether or not they wish to participate in any particular policy, subject to them taking part in a basic core of activities.

Abbreviations

The European Union is littered with acronyms that exist for the various institutions, treaties, agencies, political groupings, etc. The following is a glossary of the acronyms used in the text of this book. Readers may be puzzled when the initials of a supposed acronym do not agree with the meaning given, but as an explanatory example European Standardisation Committee is given to the initials CEN, although the acronym actually stands for Comité Européen de Normalisation.

ACP	African, Caribbean and Pacific countries associated with the EC
BBQ	British budgetary question (1979–84), also known as the bloody British question
CAP	Common Agricultural Policy
CEN	European Standardisation Committee (non EU body)
CFP	Common Fisheries Policy
CFR	Charter of Fundamental Rights
CFSP	Common foreign and security policy (one pillar of the TEU)
Coface	Confederation of Family Organisations in the EC
COPA	Committee of Professional Agricultural Organisations in the EU
COR	Committee of the Regions
Coreper	Committee of Permanent Representatives of Member States
DG	Directorate-general of the Commission (there are twenty-three, differentiated by Roman numerals, e.g. DGVI, directorate-general for agriculture)
DTI	Department of Trade and Industry (UK)
EC	European Community (created by the merger of EEC + ECSC + Euratom, 1967)
ECB	European Central Bank
Ecofin	Economics and finance (Council of Ministers)
ECSC	European Coal and Steel Community (Treaty of Paris 1951)

ECU	European Currency Unit (used as a currency of account before the adoption of the euro)
EDC	European Defence Community (aborted in 1954)
EDD	Europe of Democracies and Diversities (group in the EP)
EEA (1)	European Economic Area (the free-trade area of eighteen countries, including those of the EU and the EFTA countries other than Switzerland)
EEA (2	European Environmental Agency
EEC	European Economic Community (the original Common Market, founded in 1957)
EFA	European Free Alliance
EFTA	European Free Trade Area (rival to EEC, founded in 1959)
EIB	European Investment Bank
EIF	European Investment Fund
ELDR	European Liberal, Democrat and Reform Party
EMS	European Monetary System
EMU	Economic and monetary union
EP	European Parliament
EPC (1)	European Political Community
EPC (2)	Eropean Political Co-operation
EPP/ED	European People's Party (Christian Democrat) and European Democrats
ERM	Exchange Rate Mechanism, within the EMS
ESC	Economic and Social Committee
ESCB	European System of Central Banks
ETUC	European Trades Union Confederation
EU	European Union (made up of EC plus defence and security pillars)
Euratom	European Atomic Energy Community (Treaty of Rome 1957)
Europol	European Police Office
FCO	Foreign and Commonwealth Office (UK)
GATT	General Agreement on Tariffs and Trade
GUE/EUL/NLG	Group of the European United Left/Nordic Green Left
IGC	Intergovernmental conference
IMF	International Monetary Fund (of the United Nations)
MEP	Member of the European Parliament
NATO	North Atlantic Treaty Organisation
OECD	Organisation for Economic Co-operation and Development
OEEC	Organisation for European Economic Co-operation
PES	Party of European Socialists
QMV	Qualified majority voting (in the Council of Ministers)
RRF	Rapid Reaction Force
SCA	Special Committee on Agriculture (like Coreper but for agriculture)

SEA	Single European Act of 1987
TEN	Trans-European network
TEU	Treaty on European Union (Maastricht 1992)
UKREP	United Kingdom Permanent Representation
UNICE	Union of Industrial and Employers' Confederations of Europe (employers' group).
WEU	Western European Union (defence arm of the Council of Europe)
WTO	World Trade Organisation

Introduction

Early in the nineteenth century the great Austrian statesmen Metternich, faced with rampant Italian nationalism, remarked contemptuously, 'Italien ist ein geographischer Begrift' – that is to say, 'Italy is no more than a geographical expression'. And yet the term 'Italian' was always rather more than merely geographical. The concept of being Italian may not have been a statement of nationality, but it did make a statement about an entire people's culture, language and way of life, even though there was no cohesive political entity called Italy at that time.

What was true for Italy in the first half of the nineteenth century was equally true of Europe in the first half of the twentieth – the term 'European' gave an indication of geographical origin and could also be a statement of cultural identity, but had very little meaning other than that. Latter-day sceptics dismiss the idea of European integration with as much contempt as Metternich showed for Italian nationalism. Nevertheless, despite Metternich's dismissal of the idea, Italians overcame their internal differences and did achieve political union. Similarly, throughout the twentieth century, there have been those who ignored the sceptics and, through their personal vision of a European identity, have sought ways in which Europe might be encouraged to develop its own political and economic union, just as the fragmented states of Italy and Germany had achieved unification in the late nineteenth century. As Walter Hallstein, the first president of the European Commission, said in his memoirs:

> Europe shares a sense of values: of what is good and bad; of what a man's rights should be and what are his duties; of how society should be ordered; of what is happiness and what disaster. Europe shares many things such as its memories that we call history.[1]

Themes and perspectives to be explored

While this book is about Europe and is about politics, it is not necessarily about European politics. Aimed at the student of British government and politics, the intention is primarily to study the impact that the movement towards European integration as it has developed since 1945 has had upon the British peoples, on the British political system and on the constitution of the UK. However, in the process of such an exploration, there will inevitably be a need to explain what was happening in Europe so that British developments, motives and policies can be compared to those of other member states.

This first section of the book provides an opportunity to introduce a number of problems and terms involved when studying the European Union (EU). One factor that emerges very clearly from any consideration of the EU's history and present structure is that the debate over Europe has not been primarily about membership or non-membership, but about the sort of co-operation in which member states wish to share with their partners and the sort of Europe to which they wish to belong.

To the casual and uninformed onlooker the impression is sometimes given that the only argument over Europe is whether Britain or any other country should ever have joined. In fact, although there always has been, and continues to be, a strong (if relatively small) anti-European body of opinion in this and other countries of the EU, the real arguments that have influenced development over the years, and which continue to dominate discussions, concern different views as to the nature of EU membership. Over the years there have been differing perspectives that govern attitudes towards what is seen as European co-operation. These sometimes diametrically opposed approaches thread themselves through the historical development, lay constraints upon the functions of European institutions and determine the degree of British commitment to the European ideal.

The labels given to these conflicting attitudes and ideas are terms that will be used throughout this study, so it is useful to clarify their meaning at this point. Broadly, there are three views of how integration in Europe has come about and what it involves, two of which have the same broad ultimate goal:

Federalists

A federation is a form of political organisation characterised by a division of responsibility between a central authority and component parts (usually known as states, regions or provinces). The distribution of power between the centre and the component parts in any federal structure varies from case to case and over time, but the essential framework is normally embodied in a constitution.

Federalist ideas inspired many pioneers of European integration in the 1940s and 1950s, for the Second World War had highlighted the dangers of the nation-state as a basis for sound international relations. Federalists shared, either explicitly or implicitly, the aim of creating a full political and economic union of Europe, with considerable powers in the hands of a central or federal government. Post-war enthusiasts such as the Italian Altiero Spinelli believed in a swift movement to complete their grand design: political unification. Federalists were impressed when Churchill spoke of a 'United States of Europe'.

Federalists continue to believe that the national interests of component states should be subordinated to the general good of the EU as a whole and want to see policies leading in the direction of an ever closer EU. In the words of Hugo Young: 'To be a "fed" is merely to be on the pro-Union side of the argument. To be against the "federal" is to propose oneself as a valiant upholder of the unchanging nation-state'.[2] Used as a pejorative term by opponents, the 'f-word' is sometimes replaced by the term 'eurocentrism' to suggest the overthrow of national liberties by authoritarian centralisation in Brussels.

Functionalists

Functionalist theories began to flourish in the inter-war years. The idea was that because in many areas the needs of different countries overlap, the best means of making progress on such issues was to act in a way that cut across national boundaries. In the words of David Mitrany, it was 'not a matter of surrendering sovereignty, but merely of pooling so much of it as may be needed for the joint performance of the particular task'.[3] There would be a shared agency that would have supranational authority over the specific policies included within its orbit.

The schemes put forward after 1945 reflected a development of this approach. More cautious than committed federalists, functionalists preferred to work for unification sector by sector, as seemed necessary and appropriate. They favoured practical co-operation for the more efficient working of different economic and state functions and were willing to hand over power to a supranational body where this was the best way forward. They understood that once countries went down the route of sectoral co-operation, this inevitably had an effect on relations between them as they found themselves becoming increasingly interdependent. Indeed, some later theorists of post-war co-operation such as Ernst Haas wrote about 'neo-functionalism', arguing that closer integration would come about as a result of 'spillover'.[4] The more co-operation there was in one area, so would spillover impact in other areas, for few policies operate entirely in isolation. Decisions in one area tend to have repercussions elsewhere.

Functionalists always had an end goal in view and it was a federal one; thus Martin Holland has referred to 'functionalist principles with a political objective'.[5] Haas and fellow neo-functionalists stressed that the process of co-operation was leading in the direction of ultimate federation. In their view, the creation of supranational institutions and policies in economic policy would ultimately lead to greater political unity that would come about by essentially secretive means. Two other analysts of neo-functionalism, Robert Keohane and Stanley Hoffmann, noted that change in Europe often came about not as a result of 'heady idealism', but more because of 'a convergence of national interests'.[6] Member states 'seek to attain agreement by means of compromises' rather than by vetoing proposals unconditionally. In the view of Keohane and Hoffman, such a bargaining process at conferences is a prerequisite to spillover. The more agreement that can be reached, the better the chances of spillover occurring. In other words, spillover is not enough to explain the process of integration. It requires, among other things, what Holland calls 'the bargaining process characteristic of intergovernmentalism'.

Intergovernmentalists

Intergovernmentalists have always favoured co-operation between governments for their mutual advantage. This is an essentially pragmatic rather than a visionary approach. Intergovernmentalists emphasise the importance of national interests. They feel that for all the grandiose talk of the merits of co-operation and the dreams of the founding fathers, the main reasons for co-operation have derived from individual states pursuing their own advantage. On occasion – in fact rather often in Western Europe – there has been an obvious value in countries working together.

The notion of intergovernmentalism has been remarkably resilient and at different moments has asserted itself strongly. Yet in spite of attempts to safeguard national interests, the EU has not only established itself, but has moved more closely together – to the extent that fundamental thinking has been required about the course of future development.

It is important that these perspectives are borne in mind while reading this book because the behaviour of those involved whether individuals, parties or governments, and whether in the past or today – can only be properly understood in relation to their stance on the nature of Europe. But it must be stressed that positions on these matters do not always follow a consistent pattern: they tend to shift according to the political climate or economic realities of the moment. At different times, idealism and pragmatism have both been prominent features of the post-war era.

For many countries in the EU, the two main impulses of federalism and intergovernmentalism have often gone hand in hand. Large and powerful members of the EU such as France and Germany have been strongly integrationist members, but have usually been able to reconcile national and European interests. A minority, sometimes of only one or two countries, has been anxious about the pace of development and wished to call a halt to further moves to integration. They see merit and perhaps necessity in developing co-operation of an intergovernmental type, but are deeply sceptical about any loss of national sovereignty and independence. Britain, often Denmark, and France in the years of de Gaulle's primacy, have usually fallen into this category. Rather than a 'United States of Europe', they prefer a Europe des Patries, with states co-operating on the basis of mutual advantage.

Klaus Dieter-Borchardt has attempted to distinguish between the two camps by labelling them as the confederalists and the federalists, the former favouring interstate co-operation and the latter integration. As he puts it:

> Essentially, the confederalist approach means that countries agree to cooperate with each other without ceding any of their national sovereignty. . . . The . . . principle underlies . . . the second and third pillars of the European Union [see the details relating to Maastricht, pp. 48–51] . . . . This does not . . . rule out the possibility of progress towards closer integration in these areas at some stage in the future.
>
> The federalist aims to dissolve the traditional distinctions between nation states. . . . The result is a European federation in which the common destiny of its peoples . . . is guided and their future assured by common (federal) authorities.[7]

As we have already seen above, one other word often occurs in the debate concerning the federalist and intergovernmental approaches: supranationalism. Supranational institutions are the bodies favoured by federalists. Officials staffing the institutions are encouraged to think of themselves as loyal only to the EU, ignoring their former national loyalties. The policies they advocate are in the interests of all and take precedence over national positions. The Commission, Parliament and Court of the EU are supranational institutions. In contrast are the intergovernmental institutions in which members discuss and negotiate as representatives of their national governments, retaining their national loyalties. Intergovernmentalists see these institutions as places where they can defend their national interests against the encroachment of federalism. The Council of Ministers and European Council are intergovernmental bodies.

While considering vocabulary, it is useful to consider the use of the terms 'European Union' and 'European Community'. The European Community is the older term and is taken to refer to the three original communities established by the Treaty of Rome and merged in 1967. The European Union, as established by the Maastricht Treaty with its defence and security 'pillars', is the wider of the two. All citizens of member states making up the European Community are *de jure* citizens of the European Union. But all the institutions we think of as European, from the Commission and European Parliament to the Court of Justice, belong to the European Community rather than to the European Union. When the alternative terms 'Union' or 'Community' are used in this book there is a very subtle distinction of meaning between them but, as far as the reader is concerned, they both essentially refer to the same thing and should be regarded as interchangeable. The same apparently indiscriminate use of both labels is to be found in literature produced by the EU institutions themselves. Broadly, the pattern adopted is to employ the word 'Community' in the period up to the implementation of the Maastricht Treaty and 'Union' when referring to events of the last decade or so.

Finally, although technically Britain does not include Northern Ireland, the terms 'UK' and 'Britain' have been used interchangeably, folowing modern usage.

Notes

1 W. Hallstein, *Europe in the Making*, Allen & Unwin, 1972.
2 H. Young, *The Guardian*, 10 September 1991.
3 D. Mitrany, 'The functional approach to world organisation' in C. Cosgrove and K. Twitchett (eds), *The New International Actors: the UN and the EEC*, Macmillan, 1970.
4 E. Haas, *The uniting of Europe: Political, Economic and Social Forces, 1950–57*, Stanford University Press, 1964.
5 M. Holland, *European Integration: From Community to Union*, Pinter 1994.
6 R. Keohane and S. Hoffmann, 'Conclusions: Community politics and institutional changes' in W. Wallace (ed.), *The Dynamics of European Integration*, Pinter, 1992.
7 K. Dieter-Borchardt, *European Integration: The Origins and Growth of the European Union*, European Commission, 1995.

Part 1

History and structure of the European Union

1

The origins and growth of the European Community, 1945–85

In 1929 Jean Monnet, a young Frenchman working for the League of Nations, drew up the Briand Plan for a Federal Union of European States, named in honour of the then French foreign minister. The plan was presented to European governments in 1930 but came to nothing at a time of rampant and growing nationalism. However, the idea sparked off something in the mind of that same Jean Monnet who, thirty years later, became known as one of the 'fathers of Europe'.

Another key figure in the growth of a European identity was Winston Churchill. In a famous speech in Zurich in September 1946 he claimed that the best way to counter the threat of a third and atomic world war was through the unity of the 'European family', adding that the key to that unity would be reconciliation between France and Germany: 'The fighting has stopped; but the dangers have not stopped. If we are to form the United States of Europe, or whatever name or form it may take, we must begin now.'[1]

More sceptical politicians of the new millennium might find it difficult to appreciate the enthusiasm with which this speech was received by the growing European movement at that time. They tend to overlook the intense war-weariness that permeated a Europe that had suffered the destructive impact of two world wars since 1914. In 1946 there was a burning determination that Franco-German rivalry should never again force the countries of Europe into war. Churchill's Zurich speech was enthusiastically received because he articulated an as yet imperfectly constructed belief and understanding that the peace of the continent and of the world depended on a Franco-German rapprochement within some form of European union.

Those who welcomed Churchill's speech and believed that he meant Britain to lead the growing European movement read far more into it than the former prime minister had ever intended. It is true that Churchill had a clear vision of what Europe might become, but that vision did not include Britain. What Churchill had said in 1930 was a truer reflection of his views: 'We see nothing but good and hope in a richer, freer, more contented European commonalty', he observed. 'But we have our own dreams and our own task. We are with Europe but not of it.'[2]

In 1949 Churchill repeated this sentiment in a speech about the newly founded Council of Europe:

> The French Foreign Minister, M. Schuman, declared in the French Parliament this week that 'without Britain there can be no Europe' . . . our friends on the Continent need have no misgivings. Britain is an integral part of Europe, and we mean to play our part.
>
> But Britain cannot be thought of as a single state in isolation. She is the centre of a worldwide Empire and Commonwealth. We shall never do anything to weaken the ties of blood, of sentiment and tradition and common interest which unite . . . the British family of nations.[3]

Churchill was a federalist as far as Europe was concerned, as were many other leading political thinkers at a time when 'federalism' did not have a pejorative sense. But his view of federalism did not necessarily see Britain forming part of that federation. In Churchill's eyes, Britain had a unique role in the Cold War as the only nation to occupy the space where three important and interlocking political groupings in the non-Soviet world all overlapped. Britain had to maintain a central position in all three of the intersecting circles, as part of:

- an Atlantic Alliance linking North America to Europe;
- Europe itself;
- the British Commonwealth.

In his study of Britain's relationship with Europe, Hugo Young points out that Churchill was not only a 'father of Europe' but also the 'father of British misunderstandings about Europe'.[4] Churchill still believed completely in the greatness of Great Britain and shared with the British people a misguided complacency about the wealth and power of a country that had won the war. The British people could see why devastated countries of continental Europe would need to band together for mutual support, but Britain was different: one of the 'Big Three', ranking alongside the USA and the Soviet Union as a world power. According to that perspective, Britain did not need Europe.

That attitude was shared by everyone with power and influence, not least by the foreign secretary of the post-war Attlee government, Ernest Bevin. A man of instinctively Churchillian opinions, Bevin spoke in friendly tones about European unity and Britain's role in that Europe. But he meant simply that Britain should act as a friend and supporter of any new developments, rather than as a participant. A sentiment often expressed in the late 1940s was that Europe had been fatally damaged by the war and that Britain should avoid 'chaining itself to a corpse'.[5]

The Benelux Agreement and the Treaty of Brussels

In March 1947 Belgium, the Netherlands and the Grand Duchy of Luxembourg agreed to form a common market. This was not new, since an informal agreement on economic co-operation had been in force before the war, but it was the first concrete move towards integration between European states. Economic union for the three countries came into force in October 1947, followed by a customs union, with a common external tariff, in January 1948.

Alongside this Benelux Agreement came hints of a wider European customs union and negotiations began in 1947, at the suggestion of the Americans. Ultimately Britain squashed the plan and ensured that it was forgotten until the Treaty of Rome, ten years later. The sticking point for British ministers was a suggestion that the customs union should have a supervisory council or supranational assembly whose remit might diminish the sovereignty of member states.

And here we have the dilemma which has plagued Britain's attitude towards Europe since the 1940s and which continues to dominate any debate about Europe today. First seen in the attitude of Bevin towards customs union in 1947, it finds obvious parallels in the attitude of eurosceptics towards monetary union in 1999:

- On the one hand there is a recognisable economic argument for support, co-operation and integration between nations in the face of the global market.
- On the other hand there is the political argument of national sovereignty, pushing in the opposite direction. 'Any union, in Bevin's view, had to be between sovereign governments, with no power ceded to a supranational body.'[6]

After 1948 attitudes towards European union were affected by evidence of Soviet expansionism, including the Greek Civil War, the Berlin blockade and the *coup d'état* against Jan Masaryk in Czechoslovakia. The integration of Western Europe came to be seen as a necessary safeguard against this expansion. Also, as the Cold War intensified, the need emerged for some kind of third world force, interposed between the superstates of the USA and USSR.

In January 1948 Ernest Bevin made an important speech to the House of Commons calling for an alliance of the nations of Western Europe to resist the encroachment of the Soviet bloc. This speech led directly to the Treaty of Brussels, signed in March 1948 by Britain, France and the Benelux countries. Basically it was a treaty of mutual assistance in the event of any one of the signatories being attacked. But the signatories went beyond this defence agreement and examined the idea of a future unified defence policy and military alliance for the non-communist countries of Europe, to be known as the Western European Union (WEU). And, while creating this defence community, they also explored the possibility of economic and political co-operation, with an assembly or 'parliament' to provide some form of co-ordination and democratic control.

For a time Britain seemed to favour the idea, with even prime minister Attlee speaking of 'pooling some degree of authority' for the sake of the WEU. The Foreign Office, however, at Bevin's behest, made it very clear that the community was for defensive purposes only. While Britain was happy to see a political union in Europe, that union would stop short at the English Channel. The parliamentary idea was strangled at birth and the suggested assembly was replaced by a largely ornamental Permanent Consultative Council.

When, in October 1954, full sovereignty was restored to West Germany, permitting German rearmament, the UK with France and the Benelux countries resurrected the Treaty of Brussels, admitting Italy and West Germany to the treaty and restructuring the WEU by creating a common assembly with the Council of Europe. At the time it seemed a major step forward in the process of European integration but, on the whole, the WEU had very little importance until the signing of the Maastricht Treaty for European Union (TEU) and discussion of a growing defence and foreign affairs role for the European Union (EU). Within that role the WEU has come to be seen as the military arm of the EU and it played a not insignificant role in the troubles of the former Yugoslavia.

The Truman Doctrine, Marshall Aid, the OEEC and NATO

In 1947 the post-war recovery of Europe faltered. Countries that had tried to rebuild their economies too rapidly failed to meet the cost of imports, resulting in massive balance of payments crises and deficits in European gold and dollar reserves. Britain was particularly affected because of its insistence on its role as a world power – which a country impoverished by six years of war found it hard to sustain in the face of so many threats to peace as then existed. The economic crisis began to affect the ability of European countries to defend themselves. Early in 1947 the British government – worried by signs of communist subversion in Europe – appealed to the USA for economic and military aid, pointing out the danger that otherwise the continent might fall victim to Soviet meddling.

In President Truman's reply in March, he promised full support and assistance to 'those free peoples who are resisting attempted subjugation by armed minorities or by outside pressures'. This declaration became known as the Truman Doctrine: a clear statement of the case for containment of communist aggression, wherever it be found. In June 1947 the secretary of state, George Marshall, proposed a programme of financial aid to Europe in what was to become known as the Marshall Plan. The proviso was that countries accepting any aid must work together in planning its use and distribution. In July 1947 representatives of eighteen non-communist European countries met in Paris to formulate the European Recovery Program (ERP) and devise the institutions to execute that programme. By April 1948, with the beginning of Marshall Aid, a body had been set up to administer the ERP known as the Organisation for European Economic Co-operation (OEEC). This was an intergovernmental organisation, guided by a council that had one representative from each member state. Beneath the council was a network of committees and agencies whose task was to prepare reports for council decisions.

The OEEC was very successful, achieving its main objectives in three years and then building on its success so that, by the mid-1950s, it had completely transformed the economic situation in Western Europe and Britain. The complex organisation involved in setting up and administering the OEEC was an inspiration to European federalists, showing just what could be achieved by co-operative effort. The French, with American backing, wanted to give the OEEC its own secretariat, with an executive and decision-making capability, thereby forming a putative European governing institution. The European enthusiasts even chose their own candidate to run the OEEC – the Belgian Paul-Henri Spaak, whose appointment would be almost guaranteed to make the OEEC a major force for European integration. However, Bevin and the Foreign Office, finding federalist enthusiasms 'embarrassing', not only opposed any attempts to make the OEEC supranational, but also vetoed Spaak's nomination as OEEC chairman in favour of a safe, anti-federalist 'mandarin' from Whitehall, Oliver Franks.

Always intergovernmental in scope and organisation, and with strong links to the USA, the OEEC belonged more to the Atlantic community than to Europe. In 1960 its international nature was recognised by the admission of the USA and Canada to membership and by a change of name to Organisation for Economic Co-operation and Development (OECD). In 1964 the membership extended beyond the Atlantic community with the entry of Japan. Since then, other members such as Australia and New Zealand have joined, making the OECD into a fully international body, albeit one with a formative influence on European development.

The other organisation to emerge from the Truman Doctrine was fully international from the start, even though its headquarters and zone of operation were located in Europe. Hopes in 1945 that the Soviet Union would be a useful ally in the peaceful reconstruction of Europe had been dashed by Soviet expansionism. The onset of the Cold War made it clear that the Russians were never going to be true partners and it became a matter of some urgency to re-engage the USA in the concerns of Europe. The Marshall Plan provided one way in which this was done, and the North Atlantic Treaty Organisation (NATO) was the other.

The membership of NATO was made up of the five signatories of the Treaty of Brussels together with Denmark, Iceland, Italy, Norway and Portugal in Europe, and the USA and Canada in North America. Created to provide collective security in a treaty signed on 4 April 1949, NATO's purpose was to defend Western Europe against any Soviet threat. However, although obviously part of a common European defence structure, NATO covered the Atlantic community as a whole, rather than Western Europe alone.

The attitude taken by Britain towards Europe and European matters towards the end of 1948 can still be observed today. Britain may claim to want to be 'at the heart of Europe', but any hint of integration usually leads to rejection and active counter-measures. During 1948 three of the events mentioned above exemplified the typical British response to European unification:

- the suppression of moves towards a European customs Union;
- the refusal to accept a 'parliament' or assembly for the WEU;
- the refusal to accept the OEEC as a supranational institution and the rejection of Paul-Henri Spaak in favour of Oliver Franks.

The Council of Europe

The International Committee of the Movements for European Unity, better known as the European Movement, was formed in December 1947. Based on an idea of Winston Churchill's, the Committee proposed that a forum should be created within which European nations could discuss their problems and difficulties, thereby beginning to break down centuries of distrust through the open exchange of views.

On 7 May 1948 663 delegates from sixteen European states attended a Congress of Europe in The Hague, delegates including such luminaries of the European Movement as Monnet, Alcide de Gasperi and Paul-Henri Spaak. A keynote and reportedly very moving speech by Churchill was delivered to a gathering containing eight former prime ministers and twenty-eight former foreign ministers. Significantly, Churchill's speech to the Congress put the strongest arguments yet heard for a partial surrender of national sovereignty in order to create 'that larger sovereignty which can also protect their diverse and distinctive customs . . . and national traditions'.[7] This concept of 'pooled sovereignty', much used by advocates of European unity in the 1950s and 1960s, might have soothed the doubts of future eurosceptics if it had been adopted as the British position from the first. But Churchill was again being ambivalent, advocating European unity for all European countries – except Britain.

The substance of what Churchill was actually proposing in his visionary remarks to delegates at The Hague was not entirely clear, being vague and difficult to interpret, but the resolution finally adopted was more precise. It urged the creation of an assembly to debate European issues, guided by a council of ministers. Within weeks, the suggestion was taken up by the French government, which also offered the proposed council a home in Strasbourg. Within a year the idea had progressed so far that, with the initial agreement of ten governments – Belgium, Denmark, France, Ireland, Italy, Luxembourg, the Netherlands, Norway, Sweden and the UK – the Statute of the Council of Europe was signed in London in May 1949. It stated that:

The aim of the Council of Europe is to achieve a greater unity between its Members for the purpose of safeguarding and realising the ideals and principles that are their common heritage and facilitating their economic and social progress: This aim shall be pursued through the organs of the Council by discussion of questions of common concern and by agreements and common action in economic, social, cultural, scientific, legal and administrative matters and in the maintenance and further realisation of human rights and fundamental freedoms.[8]

Convened in Strasbourg in August 1949 under its first president, Spaak, the Council consisted of an assembly of 150 members, together with a guiding Council of Ministers who met in closed session twice a year. In 1952 this guiding council, largely made up of foreign ministers, appointed permanent deputies who would provide continuity between meetings of the ministers themselves.

The Council of Europe played an important role in the development of European institutions but was never central to integration. Its structure and purpose was always intergovernmental and although it remains useful for airing important European issues, its decisions are not binding. It remains very much a powerless talking shop. As one British MP nominated to the Assembly said: 'The Council of Europe was a body with a high moral content, inclined towards the passing of resolutions in favour of good causes . . . it carried little weight'.[9]

The Council of Europe does have one important success to its credit. In 1950 the European Convention of Human Rights was produced, modelled on the United Nations Declaration of Human Rights. It defined those civil and natural freedoms that should belong by right to the citizens of Europe. The Convention was signed by all member states and enforced by the European Court of Human Rights in Strasbourg, to which citizens of all Council of Europe members have the right to appeal, as an independent legal forum superior to the national courts of the member states. However, the Convention of Human Rights can serve as something rather more than a superior court of appeal, for it has been incorporated into the national law of many countries. Following the election of the Blair government in 1997, a Human Rights Act was passed in 1998 to integrate the Convention into British law, thus in effect creating a ready-made bill of rights, operative from 2000.

Within the context of this book it is important that the Council of Europe should not be confused with the European Council, which is the major legislative institution of the EU. Nor should the European Court of Human Rights in Strasbourg be confused with the European Court of Justice in Luxembourg: the latter being concerned with constitutional and institutional matters relating to the EU.

At the time of the creation of the Council of Europe in 1949, and in the following years, the position adopted by British governments was as equivocal as ever. Whereas in opposition Churchill and his colleagues were at least giving the impression that the Conservative Party favoured a united Europe, Labour sounded thoroughly sceptical in its attitude towards such developments in mainland Europe. It had not encouraged its members to attend The Hague gathering (twenty-six did so) and in response to the resolutions at The Hague Ernest Bevin, always fiercely anti-federalist, sounded a cautious note: 'I feel that the intricacies of Western Europe are such that we had better proceed . . . on the same principle of the association of nations that we have in the Commonwealth'. He also referred to 'the process of constant association, step by step, by treaty and agreement, and by taking on certain things collectively instead of by ourselves'. He favoured a series of bilateral agreements in which Britain formalised relations with Europe one country at a time. In answer to a suggestion for strengthening the Council of Europe, Bevin made a much-quoted statement that splendidly mixed his mythological allusions: 'If you open that Pandora's box, you never know what Trojan 'orses will jump out'.[10] Government policy was to remain one of co-operation with Europe, but it was to be a very limited form of co-operation.

The Schuman Plan and the role of Jean Monnet

In 1949 Monnet was the most prominent supporter of the drive towards ultimate unity in post-war Europe. He rejected 'mere co-operation' as favoured by contemporary intergovernmentalists. His eventual goal was 'a federation of the West', as he later acknowledged: 'The Community we have created is not an end in itself. It is a process of change. I have never doubted that one day this process will lead us to the United States of Europe; but I see now point in trying to imagine today what political form it will take.'[11]

At the time, Monnet summed up the position vis-à-vis European integration by declaring that 'a start would have to be made by doing something both more practical and more ambitious. National sovereignty would have to be tackled more boldly and on a narrower front'. His plan of action involved a 'sectoral strategy', tackling one economic sector at a time, until the various sectors meshed together into an integrated whole, because 'the everyday realities themselves will make it possible to form the political union'.[12] This was in reality the incremental approach of a practical visionary.

According to Monnet the first sector to be tackled should be heavy industry, rationalising economic recovery in France and West Germany by forming a common market in basic industrial materials. He had in mind the creation of a European Coal and Steel Community (ECSC). Explicitly this would be a pragmatic agreement in the economic interests of member countries, but Monnet made it clear that economic integration was merely the 'narrower front' of which he had spoken. The implicit and more visionary purpose was ultimately to be political integration. The choice of coal and steel was symbolic in that the principal product of heavy industry has always been armaments. To place heavy industry under joint Franco-German control would have the implied effect of ruling out the future possibility of war between the two countries.

Monnet was a bureaucrat rather than an elected politician. He operated best on the periphery, influencing rather than initiating the action. However, his ideas in relation to heavy industry were taken up and promoted by a practical politician, Robert Schuman, French foreign minister since 1948. At a press conference on 9 May 1950, he set out his Plan (sometimes known as the Schuman Declaration), announcing the establishment of a Franco-German Coal and Steel Community. He observed that: 'the pooling of coal and steel production will immediately provide . . . common bases for economic development as a first step in the federation of Europe . . . The solidarity thus achieved will make it plain that any war between France and Germany becomes not only unthinkable but naturally impossible.'

Originally, the proposed community comprised only France and West Germany who would go ahead in any case, but Schuman insisted that any other country was welcome to join them. Both he and Monnet made it clear that, quite apart from any economic benefits, the main purpose of the agreement was to create the first stage of political union. It is primarily because of this explicitly supranational objective that Britain so decisively rejected the offer when an invitation to join the negotiations was extended in 1950. As the Memorandum of 27 May stated: 'If the French Government intend to insist on a commitment to pool resources and set up an authority with certain sovereign powers as a prior condition to joining the talks, His Majesty's Government would reluctantly be unable to accept such a condition'.

Moreover, Europe was not a priority, for the Attlee government thought in terms of Britain as a world power. Bevin was lukewarm publicly and, according to Acheson, the former American secretary of state, he 'bristled with hostility to Schuman's whole idea'. The chancellor of the Exchequer, Sir Stafford Cripps, expressed the ministerial reservations very clearly in a parliamentary debate in June 1950. Noting the French view that the proposal was 'the first concrete foundation of the European federation', he argued that:

> This approach involves the other partners in the scheme not only in commitments in regard to the coal and steel industries, but also in commitments in regard to the future political framework for Europe. In our view, participation in a political federation, limited to Western Europe, is not compatible either with our Commonwealth ties, our obligations as a member of the wider Atlantic community or as a World Power.[13]

There were other reasons peculiar to Britain – and to a Labour government in particular – that led to the British rebuff. In 1950 the long-awaited nationalisation of the British coal and steel industries, a fundamental plank of party policy since Labour's foundation, had just been completed. Labour ministers, having finally realised that long-term goal, were not going to hand over these two key industries to international regulation. For them, any pooling of resources would lessen the opportunities for socialist planning of the economy.

Above all, as we have seen, Labour had wider objections. It was sceptical of any moves in the direction of a unified Europe. Although a few individuals were well-disposed, the bulk of the party wanted nothing to do with integration, even though fellow socialists in mainland Europe were much involved in the early moves. In his introduction to a pamphlet on party history, Attlee expressed a Labour approach that was widely felt at the time: 'The Labour Party is a characteristically British production, differing widely from continental socialist parties. It is a product of its environment, and of the national habit of mind.'[14] And, although the Conservative government that took office in 1951 was elected in time to reverse its decision on ECSC membership, it failed to do so. Churchill and his colleagues had been more enthusiastic about British involvement in the talks, but they were in reality little more enthusiastic than many in the Labour Party about committing an important area of the British economy to that of the continental states in the manner proposed. As for the larger objective of European federation, most Conservatives shared the misgivings outlined by Sir Stafford Cripps and quoted above.

The Treaty of Paris, establishing the ECSC, was signed in April 1951 by representatives of six countries – France, West Germany, the Benelux countries and Italy – without the participation of the UK. The Community had its headquarters in Luxembourg and Monnet was appointed its first president. He saw the institutions of the ECSC as significant, for 'only institutions grow wiser: they accumulate collective experience'. Four were established by the Paris Treaty:

- **The High Authority**, the principal body of the ECSC. Supranational in character, it comprised nine experts appointed by the member countries, with at least one representative from each country. They were to be completely independent in the performance of their duties and with Monnet's presence at their helm would ensure that 'the neo-functional supranational character objectives were honoured and enhanced at every opportunity'.[15]
- **The Council of Ministers**, with one minister representing each member country. In his original proposals, Monnet made no provision for the inclusion of such an intergovernmental body. Its creation was a concession to the principle of national sovereignty, and a recognition of the anxieties of some of those who took part in the discussions that led to the signing of the Treaty. Over the years, the Council of Ministers gained strength and influence at the expense of the supranational High Authority. Even at this stage, there were tensions inherent in the approach to co-operation: should it be supranational or intergovernmental?
- **The Assembly**, with members nominated by national parliaments rather than elected. This consultative body had few powers and was largely advisory.
- **The Court of Justice**, made up of seven independent judges, which dealt with any disputes between member states or community institutions. Its role was to interpret ECSC law, a task that enabled it to determine the parameters of supranational integration.

In forming the ECSC, a constitutional pattern was established for all later communities. All of them, down to the post-Maastricht EU, have been characterised by the four basic institutions of High Authority (later the Commission), Council of Ministers, Assembly (later the Parliament) and Court of Justice. Although supranational machinery had been established, member states had ensured – via the creation of the Council of Ministers, that they would retain the final say in decision making. In the debates surrounding the writing of a constitution for the EU in late 2003, the same battle to protect 'essential' national interests was still being waged.

One other episode occurred in the early 1950s that also illustrated the sometimes faltering process towards closer co-operation in Europe and the attitude of Britain towards any new initiative. This was the publication of the Pleven Plan, proposed by another Frenchman even before the Treaty of Paris was actually signed. This proposed the pooling of forces from national armies into a common European army, in which West German units could be integrated. Britain again gave grudging encouragement, but made it clear that there was no intention to participate. A European Defence Community (EDC), backed by a parallel European Political Community (EPC), would have represented a major step towards European federation. For Europeans, the initiative seemed an obvious and logical development of the functional approach, for it was an expansion of co-operation sector by sector. However, in this case the plan proved to be unsuccessful, for an adverse vote in the French National Assembly scuppered the idea.

The prospect of British involvement in an EDC might have encouraged the French to go ahead, but this was never on the cards. Ministers again had doubts about the supranational element involved, especially in such a sensitive and important area as defence and foreign policy. So the British reaction was 'all support short of membership'. With the failure of the Pleven Plan, British ministers tended to assume that progress towards European co-operation had stalled. In this, they were mistaken. The ECSC was proving a definite success, and the six nations involved moved ahead with their plans for a common market.

The Treaty of Rome: from the European Economic Community to the European Free Trade Area

According to the softly-softly strategy of Monnet and Schuman, a long process of step-by-step economic integration was the best way to achieve political union. In 1955, as part of just such a process, the Benelux countries suggested that the ECSC consider extending the customs union created by the Benelux Agreement of 1948. The idea was referred to the next meeting of the ECSC Council of Ministers, which opened in Messina, Sicily, in June 1955. And the Messina Conference put into words the goals towards which Monnet, Schuman and the federalists had been working for so long. The Messina Resolution stated that:

The governments of Belgium, France, the Federal Republic of Germany, Italy, Luxembourg and the Netherlands consider that the moment has arrived to initiate a new phase on the path of constructing Europe. They believe that this has to be done principally in the economic sphere and regard it as necessary to continue the creation of a united Europe through an expansion of joint institutions, the gradual fusion of national economies, the creation of a common market, and the gradual co-ordination of social policies. Such a policy seems to them indispensable if Europe is to maintain her position in the world, regain her influence, and achieve a steady increase in the living standards of her population.[16]

On the basis of this resolution, a working party was set up, chaired by the Belgian, Paul-Henri Spaak. The project conceived at Messina and developed by the study group was always going to be more than a common market, although that was the label best understood by the public. Spaak was later to inform the Council of Europe in 1964 that 'those who drew up the Treaty of Rome . . . thought of it as a stage on the way to political union'.[17]

At the time, negotiations were complicated by national interests such as the French need for an agricultural policy, but determination and compromise on the part of the negotiators achieved success within a year. Meeting in Paris in February 1957, the prime ministers of the six countries agreed the two treaties that were to be signed in Rome on 25 March 1957. The more important, the Treaty of Rome, established the European Economic Community (EEC) – popularly known as the Common Market – while a second treaty set up the European Atomic Energy Community (Euratom). Once ratified by all six states, the Treaties of Rome came into force in January 1958.

The institutions of the EEC were essentially those created for the ECSC:

- **The Assembly and Court of Justice**. The existing institutions of the ECSC became the Assembly and Court of the combined communities of the EEC, ECSC and Euratom.
- **The Commission**. The executive of the EEC, this had two commissioners each for France, Italy and West Germany, and one each for the other three.
- **Council of Ministers**. The legislature of the EEC, this was normally made up of the six foreign ministers, who could be replaced by the relevant ministers when any specific topic was discussed – agriculture, trade, etc.
- **The Assembly**. The members were nominated rather than elected, usually being chosen from members of the national parliaments. However, the Assembly had very little power and its role was a consultative one. It lacked legislative authority, but had a degree of budgetary control.

Britain had not attended the Messina Conference since it was a meeting of the ECSC, to which Britain did not belong, but Britain was pressed hard to appoint a representative to the Spaak Committee. Harold Macmillan, the foreign secretary, was enthusiastic and wanted the British representative to be an active participant rather than an observer. But Eden and Butler, as prime minister and chancellor, were less keen and appointed an official rather than a politician. An under-secretary at the Board of Trade, Russell Bretherton was sent to Brussels without plenipotentiary powers, in the firm belief that the Spaak Committee would collapse with nothing achieved. The position adopted by the British government towards the Spaak Committee was similar to that taken towards monetary union forty years later: the British government did not rule out 'joining eventually' but meanwhile 'reserved its position' and would 'wait and see what happened' – fully expecting the venture to fail.

Bretherton soon realised that the working party had achieved far more positive results than the British government had expected, but his response was limited by his watching brief. In November 1955 there was a confrontation in the Spaak Committee about which there are conflicting stories. One version says that Bretherton stormed out of the meeting, allowing others to claim that Britain walked out of the Common Market before it even existed. In another version, it was Spaak himself who threw Bretherton off the committee because of his negative attitude, ruling out any British participation in the Treaty of Rome. Probably neither story is true. Either way, neither Bretherton nor any other British representative took any further part in the deliberations of the Spaak Committee after the meeting of 7 November 1955.[18]

The British hoped that they might be able to lure the Six (members of the EEC) into joining them in a wider association of countries that could then work towards customs-free trade in industrial goods. Once the details of the EEC were agreed, Conservative ministers concentrated on pressing a scheme involving all OEEC members. Britain submitted ideas on how a free trade area might operate, containing safeguards such as the maintenance of special rights for the Commonwealth and the absence of any initiative concerning agriculture. At a NATO Council meeting in December 1956, the foreign secretary, Selwyn Lloyd, outlined this counter-proposal in the 'Grand Design'. This alternative plan would create a low-tariff common market, without any political or integrationist implications.

To continental Europeans, this all seemed like a spoiling tactic to undermine the Six in their bold venture. When talks on the proposals got underway in 1958, they quickly ran into difficulties. The coming to power of General de Gaulle in June of that year had an important effect, for he was unsympathetic to any dilution of the ECC's negotiating position. The French announced to the press in November 1958 that no agreement was possible, and the other five nations acquiesced. The British attempt to secure a wider consensus had failed and it was apparent that within a few years the Six would be imposing a common external tariff against non-members.

The UK, together with Portugal, Norway, Sweden, Denmark, Austria and Switzerland, did build on Lloyd's suggestion by creating the European Free Trade Area (EFTA) at the Stockholm Convention of July 1959. Intergovernmental in character, the new organisation was a loose free trade association committed to the removal of duties on industrial goods over ten years. Its founders hoped that it might work alongside the EEC, but hopes of such bridge building were a delusion. The aims and practice of the two bodies were very divergent, as Monnet later pointed out in his observation that: 'the Community is a way of uniting peoples and the Free Trade Area . . . is simply a commercial agreement'.[19]

In the architecture of the new Europe, there were therefore two rival bodies: the inner Six and the outer Seven. It soon became apparent to British ministers that EFTA, made up as it was of nations peripheral to the continental mainland, was no match for the fast-growing economies of the EEC. Britain had excluded itself from the decisive events taking place on its doorstep. Its isolation was to force it into a reappraisal of its stance, for the Six were going from strength to strength.

In the long term, the battle of the sixes and sevens was won decisively by the EEC. As the EU, it continues to flourish and expand, in spite of periodic disputes between member states over the degree of integration that membership entails. By 2004 most of the original or early EFTA members were part of the EU (Austria, Denmark, Ireland, Portugal, Sweden and the UK); another (Norway) had twice contemplated membership (only to see the bid to join rejected in a national referendum on each occasion) and three of the present four members (Iceland, Liechtenstein, Norway, but not Switzerland) are associated with the EU via the European Economic Area. Through their membership of the EEA, the three EFTA/EEA members have the benefits of the single market and also participate in a wide range of other EU programmes including research and development, environmental matters, and education and training.

EEC – the first phase

The EEC set itself several targets on the route to integration, agreeing that they would be achieved by 1970. They included:

- the removal of internal tariffs and trade restrictions, so forming a common market;
- the creation of a common external tariff, so that imports from outside the Community pay duty according to the same tariff, regardless of the importing country;
- legislation to outlaw practices preventing free competition between members;
- the free movement of goods, persons, capital and services;
- the development of a common agricultural policy.

With the fulfilment of these objectives, there would be a 'common market' comprising three elements: the ECSC, the EEC and Euratom. The term 'common market' is in a sense misleading, for it has a narrow focus, implying a customs union plus a greater degree of internal market freedom than that achieved simply by removing tariff barriers. While this was certainly established by the Rome Treaties, the concept of economic unity underlying it was a broader one. As Article 2 explained, the Six were aiming for 'a harmonious development of economic activities, a continuous and balanced expansion, an increased stability, an accelerated raising of the standard of living, and close relations between its member states'.

The Common Market was a means to this end, not the end in itself. The aim of the Rome Treaty was economic unity. It does not directly mention political unity, but it is quite impossible to divorce economics from politics in this context. Governments are by their nature political and decisions on economic matters cannot be made without taking political considerations into account. The founding fathers of the EEC were well aware of this, and knew that there were clear political implications in the treaty they had signed. Yet on this occasion their language was rather less grandiloquent than it was in the Treaty of Paris. There was no talk of 'merging interests' or 'sharing destiny', although according to the preamble the Six 'were determined to lay the foundations of an ever closer union among the peoples of Europe'. A few years later, the president of the EEC Commission pointed the way forward, when he observed: 'The rest is for the future and by the rest I mean common foreign and defence policies and, in addition, the crowning of all our endeavours by a political arrangement that will embrace them all.'[20]

The establishment of the EEC was in many respects a decisive moment in post-war history. The Six had continued with their earlier resolve to create integration along the lines of supranational activity, and in creating the new organisation they were on this occasion covering a much wider area of policy than in the ECSC. Clearly, within the countries involved there was developing a momentum for greater co-operation, and this was based firmly upon the strong axis linking France and West Germany. The historic discord between the two nations, which British policy makers had always taken for granted, was at an end.

Over the following years, progress was ahead of schedule, for members recognised that there was less likelihood of success if they all pursued divergent economic policies. A Common Agricultural Policy (CAP) was agreed in 1962, all customs duties between the Six were eliminated in 1968, and by then a common external tariff was applied to goods from outside the Community. In other fields, such as transport, industrial and social policies, progress was less impressive. However, by the late 1960s/early 1970s, discussions began on ways of moving towards political and monetary union, though they were at this stage inconclusive.

Quickly, 'big businesses' and especially large, multinational corporations benefited, and many mergers took place. In the first five years, the gross national product (GNP) of the EEC rose 27 per cent, as compared with 18 per cent for the USA and 14 per cent for Britain, and statistics for industrial production were similarly impressive. American investment in Europe, especially in technology, quickly developed, and trade within the EEC was considerably expanded. In fact, the years up to the early 1970s were good ones for the Six. During that time, industrialists benefited from the large market of about 170 million people, and West Germany, especially, prospered via its membership.

In April 1965 the three communities – the EEC, the ECSC and Euratom – were brought together when the members signed the Merger Treaty. This established a single Commission and a single Council for the three communities which already shared a common Assembly and Court of Justice. The Merger Treaty took effect in June 1967, the merged communities becoming known as the European Community (EC).

In the early 1960s Charles de Gaulle, the French president, sought to establish his country's hegemony over the institutions of the communities by fully exploiting the intergovernmental nature of the Council of Ministers. In the Council a unanimous vote of all six members was required for new structural measures, meaning that a single adverse vote became a national veto. De Gaulle repeatedly used that veto to force through measures that were in the interests of France and to block any measure he believed was against French interests. Most notably that veto was used by de Gaulle to refuse Britain's entry into the EEC – twice.

Britain – the first application

EFTA came into force in April 1960. Europe was thereby divided into two rival trading camps or, according to the contemporary press, was 'at sixes and sevens'. Britain claimed to admire the 'economic and commercial freedom' of EFTA as against the 'political straitjacket' of the EEC. And yet, within a year, the Macmillan government was to change its mind and contemplate British membership of the Six.

Many factors changed the attitude of the British government, the following being the most important:

- The Suez affair in 1956 led Britain to realise that its days as a world power were over. The press began to write about Britain having 'suffered a crisis of identity' and 'needing to find a new world role'. For many people that new role would seem to be in Europe.
- While the late 1950s and early 1960s were boom years in Britain, growth was even healthier elsewhere and economic commentators asked what was wrong with Britain when, in comparison, EEC members had almost doubled their standard of living inside ten years.
- British politicians watched the EEC create a series of political and economic institutions while building a ring fence against outsiders. It was felt that, if one day it became necessary to join the European communities, Britain would have to face a Europe formed without any British input. In 1959 Harold

Macmillan observed that: 'For the first time since the Napoleonic era the major continental powers are united in a positive economic grouping . . . which, though not directed against the United Kingdom, may have the effect of excluding us both from European markets and from consultation on European policy'.[21]

- Britain assumed that the so-called 'special relationship' between itself and the USA would ensure that, in trading with Europe, the Americans would favour EFTA with its British connections. However, President Kennedy privately informed Macmillan that he was irritated by Europe's divisions. If the USA was forced to choose between EEC and EFTA, the USA would choose the more important EEC.

In July 1961 Prime Minister Macmillan announced Britain's application for EEC membership. Three other countries applied at the same time: the Republic of Ireland, whose currency (the punt) was pegged to sterling, and Norway and Denmark because they depended on British trade. In November 1961 Edward Heath was appointed to negotiate Britain's entry and talks began in earnest. Almost immediately they became bogged down over protectionism for British trade links with the Commonwealth. De Gaulle saw this as a British plot to destroy the EEC's agricultural policy, claiming in his memoirs that Britain had only applied to join in order to wreck the EEC: 'Having failed, from the outside, to prevent the birth of the Community, they [the British] now plan to paralyse it from within'.[26]

Ironically, if there were anyone intent on wrecking the EEC, it was de Gaulle himself. Not only did the French president fear that Britain would be too powerful a partner, he also looked askance at the three smaller countries of Denmark, Ireland and Norway. While he could manipulate a Community of six nations, he was less sure of controlling ten. Above all else, however, the French president distrusted all things Anglo-Saxon. In his thinking, Britain was a Trojan horse – part of the USA's plan to gain control of European affairs. He told an audience in Paris of his fears in a speech in shortly before his application of the veto:

> It must be agreed that the entry first of Great Britain, and of [other] states, will completely change the series of adjustments, agreements, compensations and regulations already established between the Six. We would then have to envisage the construction of another Common Market which . . . would without any doubt no longer resemble the one the Six have built . . . in the end, there would be a colossal Atlantic Community under American domination.[27]

In December 1962 de Gaulle told Macmillan that he intended to veto Britain's application unless Britain broke with the American alliance. In response Macmillan took the opposite path, flying to a meeting with President Kennedy in the Bahamas. The resulting Nassau Agreement secured an increased stake

Box 1.1
The Macmillan approach to Europe and European developments

Macmillan was an internationalist whose thinking had been profoundly affected by his experiences of the suffering he witnessed when fighting in the First World War. After World War Two he was Churchillian in his vision of a united continent: he was in favour of the Council of Europe and a European army, and an enthusiast for the European Movement. In office after 1951 he was – unlike the prime minister – sympathetic to membership of the ECSC and circulated a memorandum attacking the attitudes of his colleagues who wanted to maintain the traditional British aloofness from European involvement. In a private letter to Churchill, he lamented the Foreign Office line and, according to his biographer, came near to resigning over the issue.[22]

History and geography inclined Macmillan to a Europeanism that was much in advance of most members of his party. But like his colleagues, he was also committed to the Commonwealth, which enabled ministers to think of themselves as global players. As foreign secretary, he failed to grasp the importance of the Messina Conference, suggesting that in some respects he, too, was a prisoner of conventional ministerial thinking. At this time, he was – in Hugo Young's description – 'a tormented and indecisive' European, unwilling to participate in the fulfilment of the initiative taken by the Six.[23] Indeed, on becoming prime minister, he sought to outflank the signatories of the Rome Treaties, in his capacity as the prime mover of the EFTA alternative. He viewed this as a European option that paid due regard to the British position as the foremost European nation.

The lack of support among the Six for the British proposal and the division of Europe into two economic groupings left Macmillan acutely aware of the dangers inherent in the British position. Noting that the Common Market was likely to be around for 'at least the foreseeable future', he sensed that any continuous attempt to disrupt it would displease the Americans, play into the hands of the Russians and 'unite against us all the Europeans who have felt humiliated during the past decade by the weakness of Europe'.[24]

Macmillan concluded that it was inevitable that Britain should seek to join the EEC. But the approach he adopted to European affairs was pragmatic rather than idealistic. It was based firmly upon a perception of British interests, and was not easily swayed by the rhetoric of continental pioneers of unity such as Monnet and Schuman. In his memoirs, he provided an explanation of the differing mindsets of the British and the Europeans:

> The difference is temperamental and intellectual. It is based on a long divergence of two states of mind and methods of argumentation. The continental tradition likes to reason a priori from the top downwards, from the general principles to the practical application . . . The Anglo Saxon likes to argue a posteriori from the bottom upwards, from practical experience.[25]

The 1961 Cabinet Papers contain Macmillan's thirty-seven-page memorandum 'The Grand Design', a frank, far-sighted analysis of the decline in British world power. In this and other documents, the reasons for British application to the EEC were stated as being primarily political:

> The countries of the Common Market, if left to develop alone under French leadership, would grow into a separate political force in Europe . . . Eventually, it might mean that the Six would come to exercise greater influence than the United Kingdom, both with the United States and possibly with some of the independent countries of the Commonwealth ... our interests would be better served by working for a wider European association in which we could play a prominent part.

The same issues of loss of sovereignty and a federal/confederal future were being discussed by ministers then as they have been more recently, but it was clearly accepted by Macmillan that 'we shall become more and more Europeans'. To persuade General de Gaulle to accept British membership of the Common Market, he was even prepared to share nuclear secrets, and provide France with bombs and technical know-how.

for Britain in NATO's nuclear programme by the USA's offer of the Polaris missile. Macmillan returned from Nassau in triumph, having renewed the 'special relationship', and was able to dismiss as irrelevant the press conference in January 1963 at which de Gaulle confirmed his veto.

Throughout these negotiations, Britain's position was not helped by British attitudes towards Europe. Instead of adopting the position of humble supplicant in applying to join the Communities, Britain gave the impression of doing Europe a favour by the application. As one political commentator has recently said: 'It was in many respects as if Britain had decided that the EEC was worthy of British membership, and not the other way around.'[28] It is an attitude that has pervaded Britain's relationship with Europe ever since and which was certainly the position adopted by Margaret Thatcher in her relations with the EC.

Britain – the second (unsuccessful) and third (successful) applications

In Britain the Labour Party narrowly won the election of 1964. Traditionally Labour was hostile towards Europe, or at best lacking in interest. Under Hugh Gaitskell's leadership the sentiment was expressed that for a Labour government to join Europe would be 'turning one's back on a thousand years of history'. However, while the party's grassroots remained hostile, over the three years between 1964 and 1967 the leadership and parliamentary party began to change their minds for a number of reasons:

Box 1.2
The failure of the first British bid

When de Gaulle exercised his veto in January 1963 and the British attempt to join the Common Market failed, it was easy to blame the French leader. The imperious way in which de Gaulle ended the bid ensured that general and informed opinion was critical, and contemporary opinion polls showed that only 17 per cent of those questioned held the British government culpable for the setback. Macmillan has been absolved of any serious criticism in most assessments. Some more recent studies have dissented from this view, and a German one has actually suggested that Macmillan knew that de Gaulle would block British entry even before the formal application was made. Others have criticised Macmillan's personal diplomacy with de Gaulle and Chancellor Adenauer of West Germany, in particular the failure to persuade them or offer any incentives in order to obtain their support.

In particular, Piers Ludlow[29] has detected three flaws in the British approach:

1 **The conditional nature of the bid.** Britain was concerned to find out the terms on which entry might be possible. As the negotiations continued, more and more requests for concessions for the Commonwealth, EFTA and the British farmers were made.

2 **Domestic reticence.** Ministers were reluctant to confront critics of their new policy head-on, and to sell the decision to join. The prime minister was too gentle with the eurosceptics of his day, for they were all people with a substantial following and power-base within the party. In August 1961 *The Economist* was moved to observe that the application was covered in a 'bower of ifs and buts'.

3 **Flawed bilateral diplomacy.** Macmillan believed that skilful handling of the European leaders in bilateral discussions would overcome any difficulties. However, Adenauer saw France as a more useful partner, finding particular comfort in de Gaulle's strong backing for German interests in Berlin at a time when the Cold War was still a key fact of European life. De Gaulle had serious reservations about British membership, and did not believe that Europe would be strengthened by British participation. He felt that Britain was too close to the USA and was not as yet ready to be a 'good European'. From a French perspective, France had little to gain and much to lose. As Ludlow explains:

Alone with de Gaulle or with Adenauer, the British prime minister had little to offer and was confronted by two determined leaders who he could neither browbeat nor cajole . . . The delusion that direct intervention with Europe's principal statesmen would obviate the need for painful concessions in Brussels . . . distracted Macmillan for too long. In May 1962, for instance, the British Prime Minister's attention was directed almost entirely at his forthcoming encounter with de Gaulle . . . Little

> high-level attention was by contrast given to the first signs of advance in the tech-
> nical negotiations . . . The Prime Minister's time would have been much more fruit-
> fully spent in clearing the way for further concessions on Commonwealth trade and
> agriculture, rather than in pondering implausible nuclear bargains with the
> French.
>
> Whatever the real reasons for failure, publicly blame was heaped on de Gaulle's
> shoulders and Britain's own hesitations and miscalculations were all but forgot-
> ten. This made Edward Heath's task in 1971–72 easier than otherwise might
> have been the case. If Britain's first bid had ended in a technical impasse, or –
> much worse – a parliamentary rejection of the terms, renewed negotiations
> would have been more difficult.

- As more and more former colonies gained their independence, trade with the Commonwealth was rapidly declining.
- The economies of Europe, especially West Germany, were booming, while Britain's growth was weak.
- Trade between Britain and EEC member countries was at a near standstill because of Britain's exclusion.
- The special relationship with the USA was damaged by the USA's involvement in Vietnam.
- Harold Wilson had won two elections on slogans involving the term 'technological revolution', but research and development work in major technological industries such as aerospace was so expensive that it needed international joint funding. Projects such as Concorde were undertaken in association with the French, and there were similar projects with other members of the EC such as Italy and West Germany.

In 1967 the Wilson government reopened negotiations for EC membership. On this occasion de Gaulle acted after just five months. As before he neither consulted his fellow members nor did he go through the correct channels. He simply held a press conference at which he announced 'it would be impossible to bring the Great Britain of today into the Common Market as it stands'.

Unlike in 1963 the other five members of the EC let their displeasure at de Gaulle's attitude and actions be known. It was made clear to Britain, Denmark, Ireland and Norway that their applications would be left in place, with the understanding that, while the application could not proceed while de Gaulle remained in power, the days of the General were numbered. In fact, shaken by the student protests of 1968, de Gaulle resigned in 1969. Within the year, the new French president, Georges Pompidou, had met the new British prime minister, Edward Heath, and a rather broad hint was dropped that France would no longer oppose British membership.

The good personal rapport between Pompidou and Heath undoubtedly eased the relationship between Britain and France. Pompidou had no deep-rooted objection to British membership of the EC. Moreover, amidst fears of growing German power and independence within France, he understood that Britain could prove a useful counterweight within the EC.

Edward Heath (see Box 1.3) was probably the only prime minister Britain has had who truly believed 100 per cent in the European ideal. Under his guidance, the negotiations conducted by Geoffrey Rippon went smoothly and remarkably quickly. Britain was able to sign the Treaty of Accession in Brussels on 1 January 1972.

Britain's fellow applicants were also accepted, but all three announced that they would consult the people by holding referendums on the subject. In Ireland, voting in May 1972, 82 per cent of those voting said 'yes': in Denmark, voting in October 1972, those in favour were 63 per cent. In Norway, however, there was a bitter argument about membership terms. In the Norwegian referendum, in September 1972, only 46 per cent voted 'yes', as against 54 per cent voting 'no'. Norway withdrew from membership.

Accession and after

There could hardly have been a worse time for Britain to join the EC. The oil crisis of 1973 quadrupled the price of oil, producing a world recession and slowing down economic growth. Britain joined the EC in an attempt to share in the economic growth of the 1960s, only to find in the 1970s that there was no longer any growth to share. Without economic growth, the less attractive aspects of EC membership, such as the CAP, became more evident and arguments in favour of British membership were much harder to sustain. During the recession there was a slowing down of EC development and the problems of the period came to bear the nickname 'eurosclerosis'.

In 1974 the Labour Party very narrowly defeated the Conservatives in both the elections of that year. Since its rejection in 1967 Labour had reverted to a policy of outright opposition to Europe, and it fought the February 1974 election on a commitment to a 'fundamental renegotiation of the terms of entry'. By that time, Britain had been a member of the EC for fourteen months, but the omens for continued membership did not look good as ministers signalled their hostility to the EC and its doings. In Young's words, foreign secretary James Callaghan set about his task of engaging in the euroworld 'with a notable brutality of purpose'.[33]

However, faced once more with the 'realities of office' Wilson found that it would be very difficult to break with Europe. He wanted Britain to 'stay in', though the objective was pursued through 'dense veils of hostile obfuscation'.[34] Too save face and avoid too blatant a volte face, he announced that Labour was not opposed to Europe in principle but only to the unsatisfactory

Box 1.3
The Heath approach to Europe and European developments

Described by Hugo Young[30] as being the 'nodal' figure in the history of the post-war British relationship with Europe, Edward Heath was by background and instinct a convinced European. He had an unwavering commitment to the cause of British entry into the EC and pursued this goal with exceptional determination and single-mindedness.

Brought up in Broadstairs, Heath's childhood was spent in a town that looked outwards towards mainland Europe. In her position as a maid, his mother often travelled to France and beyond and as a young man Heath often crossed the Channel. During his university years, his love of classical music meant that he was familiar with European composers, and he developed a more general taste for European culture in his regular sorties to Germany and elsewhere.

The Second World War threatened that civilisation of which Heath had first-hand knowledge and experience, and after it was over he found himself absorbed by the issue of Britain's involvement with the continental powers. Following his election to the House of Commons in 1950 and a tour of Germany, his maiden speech was supportive of the Schuman Plan and thereafter he was committed to British membership of the ECSC. 'Coming from his heart as well as his head, [his speech] was the first piece of the political platform that launched him and his country, twenty years later, into the Common Market'.[31]

Heath's later experiences as Macmillan's negotiator gave him a knowledge and mastery of the European scene, as well as an impressive range of European acquaintances. At his first meeting in the negotiations, he emphasised that he did not regard the British approach as merely an enquiry about the possible terms of entry. Rather, it was 'a turning point in our history, and we take it in all serious-ness'. After the first de Gaulle veto, he was disappointed but not to be put off from his mission. As his brief statement explained: 'We are part of Europe by geogra-phy, tradition, history, culture and civilisation. We shall continue to work with our friends in Europe for the true unity and strength of this continent'.[32]

During his spell as Opposition leader after 1965, Heath developed and out-lined his thinking on Europe in a series of Harvard lectures in the summer of 1967. His views were distinctive, preparing the ground for a break with the tra-ditional party foreign policy, based on Churchill's three circles. It became clear that while not specifically anti-American, he was more lukewarm and less senti-mental about the 'special relationship' than were his immediate predecessors. As for the Commonwealth, he lacked the emotional bonds for the white Common-wealth felt by many kith-and-kin Conservatives. Neither did he have much of a rapport with the black African nationalist leaders whose style of oratory and emotional approach sometimes irked him.

After his election victory in June 1970, negotiations over entry into the EC began without delay. British accession was to be the policy that has given Heath an enduring place within the history books. However, to eurosceptics and euro-phobes, his role is more problematic. They regard him as the person who misled the country about what membership really entailed and denied them the oppor-tunity of a vote specifically on the issue.

terms obtained by Edward Heath. Wilson proposed that the terms should be renegotiated and that the government would then do what Heath should have done in 1972. It would place the revised terms before the people in a referendum, the result of which would be accepted by the government, whatever the verdict might be.

In due course, renegotiator James Callaghan came back from Brussels with what he claimed were improved terms, although to many even sympathetic observers the changes were merely cosmetic. The referendum was held in June 1975 and the outcome was a positive result for the government. In a turnout of 64 per cent, 66 per cent of those who voted said 'yes', as against 34 per cent who said 'no'.

Britain and Europe in 1979

Very little changed in the wake of the referendum. The remaining Labour years under Wilson and Callaghan were passed in the midst of a domestic economic crisis that had begun with the dramatic oil price increase in 1973 and which occupied the government's thinking to the exclusion of such issues as Europe. As the global economic crisis affected both Europe and Britain to an equal extent, the EC remained sunk in eurosclerosis and Britain seemed to suffer all the negative aspects of EC membership without reaping any of the positive benefits. But, at the end of the Labour period in office, three events made 1979 particularly significant:

1 The European Monetary System (EMS) came into operation, representing the first step in a process intended to lead to economic and monetary union.
2 The first direct elections to the European Parliament took place, a move towards greater democracy in a Community not known for carrying the peoples of Europe along with it.
3 The British general election produced a Conservative government that would have a major effect on relationships between Britain, the Conservative Party and Europe.

The EC in 1979 was the antithesis of everything advocated by the new British prime minister, Margaret Thatcher. Ironically, Roy Jenkins, a former Labour minister and the then president of the Commission, originally believed that Margaret Thatcher would be more amenable towards Europe than the previous prime minister, James Callaghan. Like many other politicians, Jenkins misread Thatcher. She had declared often enough that she was opposed to compromise and would remain committed to her chosen policies, but no one believed her, dismissing it as a political stance she would readily abandon when faced with the experience of office.

As it was, Thatcher had been prime minister for two or three years before the realisation dawned that she meant exactly what she said. As part of her governing approach, she:

- despised committees;
- was very reluctant to agree to any compromise or consensus;
- would not, without a real struggle, do any deal which detracted from her demands;
- believed in her own judgement – her position in any argument was that she was right and everyone else was wrong.

This was so contrary to the way in which the EC operated that Britain's European partners were in turn shocked, repelled and alienated. Thatcher may have had right on her side but she also adhered to the view of British superiority to Europe (see p. 9). There is little doubt that her behaviour in successive European Council meetings throughout the 1980s led to a growing isolation of Britain in Europe. Her relationship with the EC is clearly described by Roy Jenkins in his account of her first European Council meeting at Dublin in 1979, a meeting which defined the ways in which she would invariably deal with her fellow European leaders:

> Towards the end Mrs Thatcher got the discussions bogged down by being too demanding. Her mistake . . . arose out of her having only one of the three qualities of a great advocate. She has the nerve and determination to win but she does not have a good understanding of the case against her . . . her reiterated cry of 'It's my money. I want it back' strikes an insistently jarring note. She lacks also the third quality . . . of not boring the judge and jury . . . She only understood four out of the fourteen or so points on the British side and repeated each of them twenty-seven times during the evening.[35]

The British budgetary question

The question of Britain's contribution to the European budget arose at Thatcher's first European Council meeting and dominated discussions in the Council for five years, much to the despair of Jenkins, the Commission and the rest of Europe. The issue was known in Brussels as 'the BBQ', which, according to Jenkins, meant 'the British budgetary question', but was more usually referred to as 'the bloody British question'.

The point was that, despite economic difficulties, Britain was making net contributions to EC funds quite as large as those being paid by West Germany. Overall, it was paying into the EC vastly more than it got out of it. At the time, nearly three-quarters of the EC budget was being used to support agriculture. Britain did not greatly benefit from this, for its agriculture was smaller and more efficient than that in most of Europe. Payments to Britain out of CAP funds were comparatively so low that efficient farmers in Britain were heavily subsidising inefficient farmers in France. To make matters worse, EC rules forced Britain, which imported more food from outside the EC than the others, to pay a much higher import levy than they did. What would have helped Britain was assistance for its ailing regions and for the modernisation of traditional industries. But compared to the 74 per cent of the EC budget spent on farming, only 4 per cent was spent on the Regional Fund whose purpose was to make grants to areas of low income, chronic unemployment or declining population.

Soon after her election Thatcher instructed an under-secretary at the Treasury, Peter Middleton, to discover the exact size of Britain's contribution to the European budget, and to estimate just how much Britain ought to be paying. As a result of these investigations, Thatcher presented her first European Council in Dublin, November 1979, with the exact amount by which she wanted British contributions to be reduced – £1 billion. The EC offered a reduction of £350 million, which Thatcher rejected out of hand.

At this point Thatcher succeeded in shocking both her European colleagues and her own advisers. Repeated demands for what she called 'her money' made it clear that the sum she wanted was not negotiable and she would do no deals. The British commissioner, Christopher Tugendhat, reported that she accused other European states of the outright theft of British money, an accusation that horrified Foreign Office advisers who knew the rules of the European game.[36] Under those 'rules', negotiations would improve on the £350 million offered by some deal on oil, or fishing rights, or the price of lamb.

However, there was to be no deal. Experienced negotiators were lost in what for them was an unprecedented situation. Among Britain's partners there were many who, while originally sympathetic, were subsequently alienated by such behaviour. As Roy Jenkins said, 'on the merits Mrs Thatcher had right broadly on her side although she showed little sense of proportion, some of her favourite arguments were invalid and her tactical sense was as weak as her courage was strong'.[37] Thatcher continued to demand her money throughout dinner and after. The Europeans retaliated – President Giscard d'Estaing of France ignored her, Chancelor Schmidt of Germany pretended that he was asleep and Jørgensen, the Danish prime minister, shouted insults. The complete breakdown of the Council was only prevented by postponing a decision on the BBQ until the next year.

That Dublin meeting set the tone for Britain's relationship with Europe throughout the Thatcher years. Her behaviour was deplored by the other EC members and indeed, at one point, would lead the French prime minister, Jacques Chirac, to call for Britain's expulsion from the EC. Attitudes towards Thatcher rubbed off on to Britons in general. Even the europhile Roy Jenkins found that his colleagues in the Commission were treating him and Christopher Tugendhat as potentially hostile.

Over the winter of 1979–80 the Commission worked for a resolution of the BBQ. The answer it came up with was that Britain should get a rebate on budgetary contributions to the value of one billion ecus (£700 million). Efforts were then made on the one hand to persuade other members to agree to this, and on the other to persuade Thatcher to accept what she insisted on regarding as only two-thirds of what was rightfully hers.

At Luxembourg in April 1980 all seemed more promising. Thatcher was less strident, Schmidt duly made the agreed offer to Britain and Giscard added that they were willing to increase that rebate to 2,400 million ecus over two years. Everyone confidently expected that this would settle the matter but, at 5.00 in the afternoon, after a full day's discussion, Thatcher rejected the offer outright. She wanted a permanent agreement, not one for two years, and she wanted her demands paid in full. 'We must look after British interests', she said.[38]

Matters were then left in the hands of the Council of Ministers and the Foreign Office. Thatcher herself had nothing more to do with the negotiations, which were entrusted to Lord Carrington, supported by Sir Ian Gilmour. Negotiations in Brussels were long and hard, culminating in an eighteen-hour session that continued through the night of 29–30 May 1980. Ironically, the agreement, when it came, was almost identical to that rejected by Thatcher in Luxembourg. When Carrington and Gilmour took the news to the prime minister at Chequers they were shouted at for three-and-a-half hours. Gilmour describes her as 'incandescent' and believes she would have rejected the agreed terms had he not leaked the story to the press, so that she was faced with the fait accompli of tabloid headlines praising her 'success' in extracting such good terms from Europe.[39]

BBQ – the issue resolved

The immediate problem of Britain's over-payment was resolved by the agreement of May 1980, but the cause of the problem would not go away. Britain may have got a rebate, but that did not alter the fact that it was paying too much in the first place. As Thatcher said to a dinner given for Members of the European Parliament (MEPs) in Strasbourg in 1984, 'I am tired of this being described as a British problem, the problems are Europe-wide. I want an agreement but I don't want to paper over the cracks. I want to get rid of the cracks. I want to rebuild the foundations'.[40]

When she reopened negotiations in 1983, Thatcher's two main opponents had changed. The new West German chancellor, Helmut Kohl, and the new French president, François Mitterand, did not as yet have the experience or sense of close partnership that typified the Schmidt–Giscard axis of 1979–81. Even so, the process dominated no fewer than four European Council meetings in a twelve-month period. A complication was that, following the example set by de Gaulle, Britain made it clear that no agreement on any other problem such as the CAP would be allowed until the BBQ had been settled to Britain's satisfaction.

At Stuttgart in June 1983 the European Council passed a vague resolution on European union but nothing else. At Athens in December there was not even a final communiqué; the first time that this had happened. In March 1984, at a European Council meeting held in Brussels, French and British officials working together had put together a practical formula. In the event, the Germans put forward an impossible alternative, the Irish walked out, Thatcher resumed her hectoring stance and the Council ended in mutual recriminations. Jacques Chirac, the French prime minister, wanted the EC to expel Britain. Although this was unlikely to happen, people were beginning to talk about a 'two-speed' Europe in which those countries prepared to progress would go ahead without the others.

The Fontainebleau Summit of June 1984 began as though it would also fail but, as is often the case in Council crises, there was an eleventh-hour agreement under which Britain would receive a permanent rebate worth 66 per cent of the difference between what Britain paid into the EC and the amount Britain got back from the EC. The same agreement increased EC resources by raising the levy on value-added tax (VAT) from 1 per cent to 1.4 per cent. The matter was finally settled after five years and Britain could be said to have 'won' – and indeed was said to have 'obtained much more than was reasonable'.[41] The agreement, however, was only achieved at considerable cost to future relations between Britain and Europe. The insistent demands made by Thatcher, and her domineering and insulting treatment of her supposed partners, had at times almost turned Britain into a pariah in European circles.

Summary – developments up to 1985

The late 1970s saw something approaching stagnation as far as moves towards European integration are concerned. It was a time when some EC mechanisms, particularly the CAP, were questioned and there was a serious delay in creating a Common Fisheries Policy. Yet the twentieth anniversary of the Treaty of Rome was marked with a sense of solid achievement.

Out of the vague aspirations towards a new Europe that marked the immediate post-war period sufficient strands had emerged to show that European co-operation and integration had become a permanent feature of international relations. Such initiatives as NATO and the OEEC ensured that, at least in the fields of defence and the economy, some surrender of national sovereignty to ensure mutual benefits was seen as both necessary and possible. The Council of Europe, with its important European Convention on Human Rights, also required states to surrender aspects of sovereignty for a greater good.

Thanks to the sectoral strategy developed by Monnet and Schuman, the growth of the EC had been an evolutionary rather than a revolutionary process. The step-by-step approach to integration and enlargement avoided the disruption of major change and created a Community strong enough to survive such strains as the position adopted by France under de Gaulle. In the 1970s the EC emerged as 'a geographically significant, economically powerful and politically durable unit'.[42]

The nature of the EC was changing, as was inevitable with enlargement. In 1973 the Six had become nine with the addition of the UK, Ireland and Denmark. With the late 1970s came the prospect of increasing to twelve, given the applications of first Greece and then Spain and Portugal. Each enlargement altered the balance between federalists and functionalists with, generally speaking, the larger states – particularly France and Britain – in favour of intergovernmental perspectives, while the smaller states – such as the Benelux countries – tended to look more favourably on the supranational viewpoint.

The stance adopted by Britain in this developmental period was anomalous and often contradictory. Despite the original impetus given to European integration by Churchill's Zurich speech and the commitment of a few enthusiasts such as Edward Heath, the British proved to be very reluctant Europeans. The interesting lesson to be learned from the history of these early years is to discover just how long-standing is Britain's ambivalent attitude – wishing to seem to be a major part of Europe without wanting actually to take part. In one sense, the problem with the confrontational attitude adopted by Margaret Thatcher was that it had proved to be so successful over the issue of the budget rebate. For some time after Fontainebleau, Thatcher went on believing that her success on this one issue meant that she could control and guide her European colleagues along lines favourable to British interests on all matters. It was only later, in the rapid resolution of the Single European Act, that the façade began to crumble. In Hugo Young's words, 'there began to emerge the unsettling sense that she didn't know what she was doing'.[43]

Notes

1   Churchill's Zurich speech, quoted in M. Gilbert, *Never Despair: Winston S. Churchill 1945–1965*, Heinemann, 1988.
2   W. Churchill, quoted in the *Saturday Evening Post*, 10 February 1930.
3   Speech of 28 November 1949, quoted in M. Gilbert, as in 1 above.
4   H. Young, *This Blessed Plot*, Macmillan, 1998.
5   A view expressed in contemporary foreign office documents and quoted by H. Young, as in 4 above.
6   The episode of the customs union is described by H. Young, as in 4 above.
7   Much quoted by a wide range of sources, including H. Young, as in 4 above.
8   Article 1 of the Statute of the Council of Europe, 1949.
9   J. Critchley, *A Bag of Boiled Sweets*, Faber and Faber, 1994. As a Conservative MP, Critchley served as a nominated member of the Assemblies of the Council of Europe and the WEU between 1972 and 1979.

10 Ernest Bevin, Speech in the House of Commons, 13 November 1950.

11 J. Monnet, *Memoirs*, Doubleday & Co., 1978.

12 J. Monnet, quoted in M. Holland, *European Integration: From Community to Union*, Pinter, 1994.

13 Sir Stafford Cripps, speech in the House of Commons, 10 June 1950.

14 C. Attlee, quoted in K. Harris, *Attlee*, Weidenfeld & Nicolson, 1982.

15 J. Monnet, as in 12 above.

16 Text of the Messina Resolution, quoted in N. Nugent, *The Government and Politics of the European Union*, Palgrave, 2003.

17 P-H. Spaak, quoted in M. Holland, as in 12 above.

18 The full story of Russell Bretherton and the Spaak Committee can be found in H. Young, as in 4 above.

19 J. Monnet, as in 11 above.

20 W. Hallstein, *European Community*, European Commission pamphlet, 1966.

21 A letter from Harold Macmillan to Selwyn Lloyd, December 1959, quoted by H. Young, as in 4 above.

22 A. Horne, *Macmillan*, vol. 2, Macmillan, 1989.

23 H. Young, as in 4 above.

24 H. Young, as in 4 above.

25 H. Macmillan, *At the End of the Day 1961–1963*, Harper Row, 1973.

26 C. de Gaulle, *Memoirs of Hope*, Weidenfeld & Nicolson, 1971.

27 C. de Gaulle, quoted in P. Ludlow, 'Historical aspects of Britain's relationship with Europe', paper delivered to PSA Conference, University of Glasgow, April 1996.

28 A. Jones, 'UK relations with the EU, and did you notice the elections?', *Talking Politics*, Winter 2000.

29 P. Ludlow, as in 27 above.

30 H. Young, as in 4 above.

31 H. Young, as in 4 above.

32 H. Young, as in 4 above.

33 H. Young, as in 4 above.

34 R. Jenkins (Lord Jenkins), *European Diary 1977–1981*, Collins, 1989.

35 R. Jenkins, as in 34 above.

36 C. Tugendhat, *Making Sense of Europe*, Pelican, 1986.

37 R. Jenkins, as in 34 above.

38 Reported in H. Young, *One of Us*, Macmillan, 1989.

39 Lords Carrington and Gilmour related the story in a television programme, *Thatcher, The Downing Street Years* (part one), shown on BBC Television, autumn 1993.

40 A conversation of March 1984, quoted in H. Young, as in 38 above.

41 A view expressed by the secretary-general of the EC, Emile Noel, during an interview with H. Young and quoted in H. Young, as in 4 above.

42 G Minshull, *The New Europe – into the 1990s*, Hodder & Stoughton, 1990.

43 H. Young, as in 4 above.

2

From the single market to the constitution, 1985 to the present day

In the decade or so after Britain joined the EC, there was little sign of further progress towards the goal of promoting closer co-operation between the member states. In this period of eurosclerosis, many pro-Europeans expressed their disappointment at the stagnation of the EC and some were gloomy about its future prospects. On its cover in one edition in March 1982, *The Economist* depicted a tombstone on which were inscribed the words: 'EEC born March 25th 1957, moribund March 25th 1982. Capax imperii nisi imperasset' ('It seemed capable of power until it tried to wield it').

It is true that the problems created by the British budgetary issue consumed an enormous amount of time and the EC failed to progress while the matter remained unresolved. The broader questions of enlargement and the future shape of the EC received comparatively little attention. Yet there were some areas on which progress was made during the first half of the 1980s, even if it was mainly tentative in nature. The more important developments can be summarised as follows:

- Greece became the tenth member of the EC in January 1981, while work continued on applications from Spain and Portugal.
- The EC signed the second Lomé Convention with fifty-eight ACP (Africa, Caribbean and Pacific) countries, mostly former British or French colonies.
- In 1983 a Common Fisheries Policy (CFP) was agreed, establishing members' national areas within 20 km of their own shores and acting in the interests of conservation by fixing allowable catches, divided into national quotas. The quotas would prove controversial.
- The Stuttgart Council in June 1983 issued a declaration on European union and, in February 1984 the European Parliament (EP) approved a draft treaty for such a union.
- The EMS was working towards convergence between the economies of EC members with the ultimate goal of economic and monetary union. An important element of the EMS was the Exchange Rate Mechanism (ERM), by

which EMS members undertook to keep their currencies pegged within fairly narrow bands, only a limited degree of divergence being allowed before intervention to maintain parities was invoked.

The Fontainebleau Summit (1984) finally resolved the budgetary problem and enabled European leaders to move on from their endless squabbles and think in more strategic terms about the future direction of the EC. The Germans and Italians, among others, were active in devising new initiatives to carry the EC forwards into a closer union with distinctly political objectives. By the mid-1980s, its future was under serious consideration once more, and during the Luxembourg presidency in the second half of 1985 a conference was held to discuss possible amendments to the Treaty of Rome. It was here that arrangements were to be agreed for the next major step towards European integration – the introduction of an internal market via the Single European Act.

The Thatcher government had circulated a paper at the meeting entitled 'Europe: the future', in which it urged the creation of a genuine single market as part of a bid to enshrine Thatcherite beliefs in European practice. In 1985 the new president of the Commission, Jacques Delors, took up the idea with enthusiasm. It would be the 'big idea' that might propel the EC forward as part of a new drive towards integration.

The Delors presidency and the SEA between them generated momentum not only for the creation of the internal market but also for the moves to closer co-operation to be resolved at Maastricht in 1991.

The Delors presidency

Jacques Delors, a French socialist and ardent European, assumed office in 1985. He was to retain his post as president of the Commission for a record ten years. His was an appointment that had a considerable effect, not only on the speed with which the EC began to move towards union, but on the relationship with Europe of both major political parties in Britain. From the start there were those who were highly critical of Delors because, as Nugent says:

> [Delors] has the requirement of a forceful personality, but he has also displayed traits and acted in ways which, many observers have suggested, have had the effect of undermining the team spirit of his Commission: he has indicated clear policy preferences and interests of his own; he has made important policy pronouncements before fully consulting with his colleagues in the Commission; and he has sometimes appeared to give more weight to personal advisers than to Commissioners.[1]

A committed social democrat, Delors was dedicated to the social and welfare dimension in the EC and was to produce the Community Charter of the Fundamental Social Rights of Workers (later known more simply as the Social Chapter) in 1989. Early in his presidency Delors visited Britain as a guest of the Trades Union Congress (TUC) and made a speech to the Labour Party at a time when, under Neil Kinnock, it was reassessing its policies. Thwarted as they were by the attitudes and actions of the Conservative government, both the Labour Party and the TUC found a meeting of minds with Delors. It led to a change of approach by the Labour movement and the development of a markedly more pro-European stance.

On the other hand, given that Delors was a Catholic, socialist, intellectual Frenchman, 'it is difficult to think of a collection of attributes less calculated to appeal to Mrs Thatcher'.[2] This conflict of attitudes led to a situation where Delors 'became, in the European context, the enemy Mrs Thatcher often seemed to need for the successful prosecution of the politics of battle'.[3] It is ironic that Delors was only appointed because France's first choice as president of the Commission, Claude Cheysson, had been eliminated by Thatcher's use of the veto in the European Council. Delors, on the other hand, was initially very popular with the British government, which believed that he 'began imposing our policies as a finance minister after our own hearts'.[4]

The Single European Act

The relaunching of Europe after its period of stagnation was largely based on the attempt to complete the single internal market. This had been its aim since the Treaty of Rome and many statements in support of the idea had been issued by the Council, Commission or Parliament at regular intervals from 1970 onwards. But it was only after 1985 that progress towards the goal was speeded up.

The Commission's White Paper on the issue was presented to the Council of Ministers in June 1985 by the British commissioner, Lord Cockfield, a former civil servant who had been chief executive of the Boots drug company before being appointed secretary of state for trade. He was a man much favoured by both Delors and Thatcher, both of whom admired his drive. His proposals listed 297 legislative measures necessary for the creation of the single market. He worked so quickly that a Single European Act (SEA), proposing the creation of a 'Europe without frontiers' by 1992, was drawn up in time for the December 1985 European Council in Luxembourg. During the following year the proposed act was ratified by the various national parliaments, the British bill being steered through Westminster by Sir Geoffrey Howe. The SEA became law in July 1987; the single market becoming operative on 1 January 1993.

In the light of its importance for the future development of an integrated EC, it is worth noting the ease with which the SEA was accepted by Thatcher, the Conservative Party and the British Parliament. The bill ratifying the act took a mere six days to pass through the Commons in April 1986 while, on the third reading, less than 200 MPs voted on the motion – 149 in favour, with 43 against.

The market is essentially based on what are known as the 'four freedoms' – the freedom of movement for goods, people, capital and services without the restrictions of internal borders or customs regulations. The aspect that most obviously affected the general public was a relaxation on the amounts of tobacco and alcohol that could be purchased in other member states of the EC, a relaxation that led to a boom in cross-Channel shopping. But the SEA also affected the public through a reduction in administrative costs, both in the movement of goods and through minimal passport controls. However, details surrounding the SEA concerned more than just the single market. In what was essentially a tidying-up operation, the act produced fundamental changes in the constitution and operation of the Community and represented the most far-reaching moves towards European integration that there had been since 1957. For example, the SEA:

- included many changes to the EP, increasing its role in the legislative process and requiring its assent for such things as enlargement of the EC;
- increased the legislative and decision-making powers of the Council of Ministers;
- extended the ability of the Council to make decisions by a qualified majority vote (QMV);
- limited the power given to larger member states by the national veto;
- gave legal recognition to the twice-yearly European Council summit meetings, for the first time since they began in 1975.

At that time, it has to be stressed, all these measures were purely bureaucratic in nature because they were not incorporated by treaty. It was for that purpose that the EC later moved on to consider a treaty on European union.

One can only assume that Mrs Thatcher accepted the SEA because she was so pleased to be within reach of fulfilling her two main aims in Europe – the reform of the CAP and the formation of a single internal market – that she ignored the supranational nature of that to which she was agreeing. Speaking some years later about Britain's acceptance of the SEA, Michael Heseltine was to say that Thatcher was responsible for 'the biggest transfer of sovereignty undertaken in any period of our history'.[5] In 1991 Lady Thatcher (as she had then become) was to claim that she had not understood the SEA when she signed it and, furthermore, that she would not have signed it if she had understood.

This attempt to plead ignorance, however, is rather questionable. Ten years later, Sir Michael Butler, for a long time Britain's permanent representative in Brussels, was to say on television: 'I never remember an occasion in the six years when I worked for her when she negotiated something without knowing exactly what it was she was talking about'.[6] His views are substantiated by the recall of David Williamson, her then head of the Cabinet Office's European Secretariat, who later observed:

I was present in No.10 Downing Street on one occasion when Mrs Thatcher came down the stairs and said to me: 'I have read every word of the Single European Act'. She certainly knew from the start that there were two competing visions of Europe, but at that stage felt that our vision of a free enterprise Europe des Patries was predominant.[7]

Perhaps Thatcher was most guilty of misreading the character of Lord Cockfield. Originally a close confidante of Edward Heath, he had proved an ardent convert to Thatcherism very shortly after she had taken over as party leader. Misled by his enthusiasm into thinking him a committed loyalist, Thatcher did not see that his opinions could change again, every bit as quickly, 'effecting as swift a transfer from the Thatcher project to the Delors as he had from the Heath to the Thatcher'.[8]

By the time she wrote her memoirs, Margaret Thatcher[9] herself was able to look back with 'the wisdom of hindsight . . . sadly denied to practising politicians' upon the years 1983–87 as what Hennessy has termed 'the watershed for European policy'.[10] As she put it:

It is now possible to see my second term as Prime Minister as that in which the European Community subtly but surely shifted its direction away from being a Community of open trade, light regulation and freely co-operating sovereign nation-states towards statism and centralism'.[11]

The Bruges speech

Jacques Delors soon proved that he was a euroenthusiast and a federalist. In particular, he made it abundantly clear that he favoured two specific measures that were alien to beliefs held by the Conservative government in Britain:

- European political and monetary union;
- a social dimension to all EC policies and legislation (ultimately to find expression in the Social Chapter).

Nothing could be more opposed to Thatcher's view of Europe: everything Delors said and did confirmed her in the belief that the EC was imposing socialism on to Britain 'through the back door'. In June 1988 Jacques Delors was entrusted with studying how the EC could move towards economic and monetary union (EMU). The move, which ignored all her own statements on the subject, infuriated Mrs Thatcher.

In September 1988, during a speech to the College of Europe in Bruges, the prime minister vented her anger on integrationist tendencies in Europe, saying that she had not spent nine years rolling back the frontiers of the state in Britain in order to allow that work to be overset by the manoeuvres of European

Box 2.1
The Thatcher approach to Europe and European developments

In an article written in 1998, Lady Thatcher, as she had by then become, reviewed the role of Europe in British politics. 'In my lifetime', she declared, 'Europe has been the source of our problems, not the source of our solutions. It's America and Britain that saved the world'. However, as she conceded, it 'did not seem like that at the time [when she was prime minister]'.[12] Nonetheless, during her premiership, she 'gave it the loudest place on her agenda'.[13]

Margaret Thatcher's approach to matters European was in certain respects in line with the attitudes expressed by some of her predecessors. Admittedly her rhetoric and style were distinctive, so that she seemed markedly more hostile than many of those around her. Yet faced with thorny issues such as the budgetary issue, her instinct was to assert traditional British interests. Like Wilson and Callaghan, she was wary of any schemes that smacked of supranationalism. Arguably, she was unlucky that the later period of her premiership happened to coincide with another in a series of periodic spurts of enthusiasm within the EC that pushed Europe further towards integration. She was therefore the person whose task she believed it was to resist the integrationist tide.

In the same way that Attlee had turned down the chance of British involvement in the ECSC, so Thatcher found the idea of a single currency unacceptable. A common currency she could accept, for this might exist alongside national currencies. But a single one was a step too far, associated as it was with moves towards closer integration. She preferred the policy of countries uniting in a trading organisation, in the same way that in the late 1950s British ministers had established EFTA as an alternative to the EEC. Indeed, she had supported membership of the EC for such reasons, believing it to be, in Geddes' words, 'little more than a glorified free trade area'.[14]

Whereas Heath 'lived and breathed the air of Europe', Thatcher's approach to European issues was pragmatic rather than idealistic. She had backed membership at the time of the first and second Heath negotiations; indeed, she was wholeheartedly in favour of it. But she actually made little contribution to the referendum debates shortly after becoming leader. The idea of standing on the same platform as her political opponents had no appeal and seemed an affront to the partisan politics she espoused.

In her early years as Opposition leader and then premier, Margaret Thatcher saw European unity as necessary at a time when the Cold War was still a major factor in international relations. To her, this was more important than any talk of a European Idea or other 'absurd aspirations'.[15] She felt that there were sound reasons for being in Europe and genuinely believed that it would have been foolish to leave the EC. Her pragmatism about the issue was evident in her remarks to the 1981 Conservative annual conference, in which she reviewed the state of British membership:

> It is vital that we get it right. Forty three out of every hundred pounds that we earn abroad comes from the Common Market. Over two million jobs depend on our trade with Europe, two million jobs which will be put at risk by Britain's withdrawal [the policy Labour was then advocating]. And even if we kept two thirds of our trade with the Common Market after we had flounced out – and that is pretty optimistic – there would be a million more to join the dole queues.

> Thatcher was impressed by the idea of a single European market, for this was a reflection of her attitude in domestic policy. Deregulation and liberalisation were the essence of Thatcherite economic policy and on these and other issues she shifted the political battleground at home and similarly wished to do so on the continent also. As part of a meaningful single market, she could be persuaded of the merits of a common currency. This seemed like a practical and attainable one, in the British tradition. But it was not what most of her fellow European leaders wanted, for it was not rooted in the federal ideas to which many of them sub-scribed. The goal of greater unity in Europe was an adventurous journey on which they were happy to embark.

> Thatcher had no interest in the so-called European Idea, and was unim-pressed by talk of federalism or any 'United States of Europe'. Perhaps this helps to explain her approach to the SEA. Because it did a number of things of which she approved, she felt able to gloss over the sections of the Preamble that spoke of furthering the European Idea, protecting common interests and 'laying the foun-dations of an ever closer union among the peoples of Europe'. In her view, this was federalist verbiage and at the time she regarded its inclusion as an irritation, rather than a problem. Thus language was not addressed with the seriousness that Britain's continental partners felt that it deserved.

bureaucrats. The speech marked a decisive turning point. Thatcher's attitude changed from a reluctant acceptance of Europe to one of outright hostility, opposed to anything that might place a restraint on the independence of the component nation-states. The greatest impact of the Bruges speech was, of course, on the Conservative Party itself as it moved from a mild form of euroen-thusiasm to one of euroscepticism – a sea-change of attitude that will be con-sidered in more detail in Chapter 8.

The Delors Plan

Economic union for the EC was first proposed in 1969, but it was 1978 before anything concrete emerged in the form of the EMS, which was intended to create monetary stability within the EC. The EMS had three bases:

Box 2.2
The Bruges speech, 1988

The broad outlook of Margaret Thatcher on European issues was perhaps most clearly expressed in her Bruges speech of 1988. Having reviewed the British contribution to Europe over the centuries and denounced the idea of a 'European superstate', she pointed out that – contrary to its pretensions – the EC 'was not the only manifestation of European identity . . . We shall always look on Warsaw, Prague and Budapest as great European cities'. She went on to express her own preferences:

> Willing and active co-operation between independent sovereign states is the best way to build a successful European Community . . . Europe will be stronger precisely because it has France as France, Spain as Spain, Britain as Britain, each with its own customs, traditions and identity. It would be folly to try to fit them into some sort of identikit European personality.

She ended on a high note, which she would see as far from anti-European:

> Let Europe be a family of nations, understanding each other better, appreciating each other more, doing more together, but relishing our national identity no less than our common European endeavour. Let us have a Europe which plays its full part in the wider world, which looks outward not inward, and which preserves that Atlantic Community - that Europe on both sides of the Atlantic - which is our noblest inheritance and our greatest strength.

If she lacked enthusiasm for the hopes that inspired some fellow European leaders, Lady Thatcher would deny that she was a Little Englander. She was interested in widening the EC so that the countries of Central and Eastern Europe might be brought into its orbit, for as she remarked on another occasion: 'Europe is older than the European Community. I want the larger, wider Europe in which Moscow is also a European Power'.[16] In her memoirs, she makes it clear that a supranational EC had little to offer to meet the 'aspirations and needs' of 'those millions of Eastern Europeans [then] living under communism'.

Ultimately her vision was of an EC which was open to all, and which preserved 'the diversity and nationhood of each of its members'. In the words of Lynton Robins:

> What Mrs Thatcher was seeking, like three out of her four predecessors, was a looser, outward-looking partnership of European nations, which was not opposed to Atlanticist ties, and which was intergovernmental in character rather than based on the proto-federalist institutions of the Community.[17]

Such a vision was not markedly dissimilar to that of Wilson and Callaghan before her, even if the tone in which it was expressed was considerably more shrill. Her distaste for European union was in line with theirs, but in her case it was thrown into negative relief when matched against the idealistic statements from the continent.

1 **The European Monetary Co-operation Fund** (EMFC), which was intended to buy and sell EC currencies, minimising or eradicating major fluctuations in exchange rates.
2 **The European Currency Unit** (ECU), used for accountancy purposes only and based on a weighted basket of currency values.
3 **The ERM**, as an agreed parity of exchange rates within which the rates of one member country would not diverge more than 2.25 per cent from those of any other member.

Britain did not join the EMS at first. Nor did Margaret Thatcher's new euroscepticism augur well for British acceptance of the proposed EMU that was advocated by Jacques Delors in 1989. This proposal, arising from the negotiations which created the single market, was just part of a programme sometimes known as the Delors Plan, the mere mention of which could produce a mood of near-incandescent rage in Thatcher.

In April 1989 the committee chaired by Jacques Delors, which had been examining possible ways forward to achieve EMU, produced its report. This envisaged a three-stage progression towards EMU:

1 Increasingly co-ordinated economic policies between EC members, within the ERM.
2 The foundation of an independent European Central Bank (ECB), using the US Federal Reserve Bank as a model.
3 The introduction of a single European currency.

Thatcher went to the European Council meeting of June 1989 in Madrid determined not to accept the Delors proposals for monetary union. As she said in a newspaper interview: 'The Delors proposals would not command the support of the British Cabinet'.[18] On the other hand, she was accompanied to Madrid by two members of her Cabinet who did wish to accept the Plan – foreign secretary Geoffrey Howe and chancellor of the Exchequer Nigel Lawson. Lawson had been in favour of the ERM for some years and, although he was regularly and repeatedly denied permission to join, he had been attempting unofficially to shadow the German currency, maintaining the value of the pound at around DM3.

In Madrid, Howe and Lawson combined against the prime minister and threatened to resign if she did not agree to the Delors Plan. Furious at what she regarded as betrayal, Thatcher was forced to sign the agreement; although she did manage to lay down four fairly stringent preconditions before Britain could join the ERM:

• Internal market arrangements must be completed.
• All exchange controls should be abolished.
• There should be a free and open market in financial services.
• There must be a strengthening of competition policy.

After returning from Madrid Thatcher had her revenge for what she saw as her humiliation. The following month Geoffrey Howe was demoted from foreign secretary and replaced by Thatcher's protegé, John Major. In October Nigel Lawson also felt that he, too, was being undermined and he resigned, to be replaced in his turn by John Major. And it was John Major, on 5 October 1990, who finally took Britain into the ERM, albeit at what many people felt at the time was a dangerously high rate of DM2.95 to the pound.

From the fall of Thatcher to Maastricht

At Strasbourg in December 1989 the European Council accepted Delors' Social Chapter and agreed to set up an intergovernmental conference (IGC) on economic and monetary union, decisions that were confirmed at the Dublin Councils in April and June 1990. On all three occasions Britain was the only country opposed to the Delors proposals and an isolated Margaret Thatcher was again voted down by eleven votes to one.

In October 1990 the Italians, who held the presidency, called a special European Council in Rome to prepare for the official Council meeting which would set up the all-important IGC in December. Thatcher had been highly critical of the way in which Italy was conducting the presidency and now the Italian prime minister, Bettino Craxi, had his revenge by calling a simple majority vote on stage two of the Delors Plan, despite warnings from both Delors and Chancellor Kohl of Germany not to isolate the British. Irritated by Thatcher's confrontational style, the other European leaders lined up behind Craxi to vote against her and, inevitably, Britain found herself alone against the other eleven. Mrs Thatcher was furious at the turn of events and particularly over the decision that the EC would aim to have a single currency in place before the end of the century.

In her statement to the House of Commons about the Rome Council of 15 December 1990 (at which two IGCs had been convened, one on economic union and the other on political union) Thatcher adopted a reasonable attitude at first. She was still opposed to a single currency but she was quite prepared to consider a common currency of account. The breaking point came when Neil Kinnock, as leader of the Opposition, described a different view of the Delors proposals put forward by Sir Leon Brittan, once a close political ally of Thatcher but now one of Britain's European commissioners. At this point the prime minister failed to stay calm and almost exploded with the pressure of her own frustrated anger. Declaring herself firmly against the integrative tendencies of the EC, she departed from her prepared answers to savage both the EC and the Labour Party:

> Yes, the Commission wants to increase its powers. Yes, it is a non-elected body and I do not want the Commission to increase its powers at the expense of the House, so of course we differ. The President of the Commission, Mr Delors, said at a press conference the other day that he wanted the European Parliament to be the

democratic body of the Community. He wanted the Commission to be the Executive and the Council of Ministers to be the Senate. No. No. No.

Perhaps the Labour party would give all those things up easily. Perhaps it would agree to a single currency and abolition of the pound sterling . . . What is the point of trying to get elected to Parliament only to hand over sterling and the powers of this House to Europe?[19]

It was his repudiation of this speech that led to the resignation of Sir Geoffrey Howe. His own resignation speech played an important part in the downfall of Margaret Thatcher. In it, he explained that 'the Prime Minister's perceived attitude towards Europe is running increasingly serious risks for the future of our nation. It risks minimising our influence and maximising once again our chances of being once again shut out'.[20]

The Maastricht Treaty

The IGCs convened in Rome formulated amendments that needed to be made to the treaties establishing the European Communities, if economic and political union were to be achieved. Measures proposed by the IGCs, as amended by Britain and others, were agreed by the European Council that met at Maastricht in the Netherlands in December 1991. The IGCs reconvened in February 1992 to draw up an actual treaty embodying what had been decided. This treaty, known as the Treaty on European Union (TEU) and presented in its final form on 7 February 1992, created a major landmark on the long road of European unification. The treaty would come into force on 1 January 1994, at which point the Communities covered by the treaty would become known as the European Union (EU). The principal aim of the treaty, as set out in Article A, was to bring about 'a new stage in the process of creating an ever closer union among the peoples of Europe'.[21]

The new EU was to comprise three pillars. The second pillar was for foreign policy and defence (the common foreign and security policy), and the third was for policing and immigration (justice and home affairs), neither of which had been dealt with by any of the original treaties. The first and main pillar finally established the EC in law by incorporating the provisions of the SEA into the Treaty of Rome. There were also attempts to reduce the so-called 'democratic deficit' in the EC, modifying some of the more bureaucratic aspects of the SEA:

- The Council of Ministers acquired a greater freedom to act by the use of qualified majority voting.
- Increased powers were given to the European Parliament.
- Enhanced powers were given to the European Court of Auditors.

In the year that had followed Margaret Thatcher's departure, the new prime minister, John Major, had managed to stifle debate on Europe, concentrating his efforts on achieving an outcome in the IGC that would more or less satisfy all the varying British attitudes. In particular, there were two proposals in the treaty to which Britain could not agree and John Major negotiated at length for the treaty to be amended by the addition of two protocols. One of these protocols removed the need for Britain to move towards EMU, while the other dealt with those social policies that require members to work towards improvements in the proper use and development of human resources, including employment and working conditions. This second protocol (the Social Chapter) was binding upon eleven members of the Community, but the UK was specifically excluded for as long as the Conservatives remained in power. Indeed, this remained until the policy was reversed in the Amsterdam Treaty of 1997.

The forward momentum of first the SEA and then the Treaty on European Union had been so swift and relatively trouble free, transforming the entire European venture from head to toe in little more than seven years, that there were those who labelled the mood of the time as 'europhoric'. Yet, as soon as agreement was reached at Maastricht things began to go wrong. Lady Thatcher and right-wing Conservatives, now totally opposed to the Delors proposals, campaigned vigorously for the British people to be allowed to vote on Maastricht in a referendum along the lines of the two member countries – Denmark and Ireland – who were constitutionally required to hold referendums prior to ratification.

John Major ruled out the idea of such a thing for the UK, but elsewhere the referendum issue began to cause problems. In the referendum of June 1992, Denmark rejected the Maastricht proposals by a margin of 40,000 votes. Two weeks later the pendulum may have swung the other way when Ireland voted very positively, with 68 per cent of those voting saying 'yes', but the damage had been done. The Community was faced with the need to renegotiate Danish terms for the treaty and these in turn had be submitted to another referendum. Further political problems arose when France also decided to hold a referendum and a French rejection began to seem quite possible. In fact, when the referendum was held in September, the vote was for acceptance, but only by the very small majority of 51 to 49 per cent. One commentator could write:

> Public disquiet about the Treaty, expressed in the EC's *Eurobarometer* opinion polls, and in the Danish and French referendums, lends support to the claim that European integration is an élite-led process, viewed with indifference or hostility by the peoples of Europe.[22]

German reunification and a British exit from the ERM

In mid-September 1992 serious flaws within the ERM began to appear. Since 1979 the ERM had largely maintained parity between currencies, mostly because of a strong Deutschmark and the controlling hand of the Bundesbank.

When economic union was first mooted, a necessary precondition of membership was satisfying 'convergence criteria', by which the economies of at least seven members had to sustain a stable parity of currencies over a period. Until then interim members only allowed exchange rates and levels of inflation and growth to diverge within very narrow limits, correcting any drift by fiscal measures such as interest rates. The strength of the German economy meant that the Deutschmark and Bundesbank formed the main reference points for regulating the European economy.

Between 1989 and 1990 the Soviet bloc collapsed, the Berlin Wall came down, the communist government of East Germany (DDR) fell and Germany was reunited by redesignating the DDR provinces as Länder of the Federal Republic. Economic problems associated with the DDR were made worse by Chancellor Kohl's insistence that the exchange rate between east and west versions of the deutschmark should be on a one-for-one basis. The vast sums of money expended in this currency exchange combined with other factors to throw the German economy into crisis.

Many countries in the EC slumped into recession and, during the summer of 1992, the weaker currencies within the ERM – the pound sterling, the Italian lira and the Spanish peseta – proved to be overvalued in comparison with the Deutschmark and came under heavy pressure from currency speculators. The mechanisms of the ERM demanded that the EC central banks should intervene and buy those currencies under threat. But rigid anti-inflationary measures introduced by Germany to ease reunification meant that the Bundesbank could not provide the necessary support. A crisis developed:

- In September 1992, the adverse Danish and French referendums created uncertainty in the money markets and there was a massive movement out of weaker currencies into the Deutschmark.
- Over the weekend of 13–14 September Italy devalued the lira by 6 per cent and pressure increased on the pound and French franc.
- On 16 September (Black Wednesday) desperate measures raised the British interest rate twice in the same morning, taking it to an astonishing 15 per cent. At the same time, the Bank of England intervened on the money markets and spent millions of pounds in an attempt to prop up its value. In the afternoon the British government bowed to the inevitable, cut interest rates to where they had started and withdrew from the ERM. On the same day, Italy also 'temporarily suspended' its ERM membership.

For Britain the value of the pound fell rapidly to find its true level and the crisis was over. There was talk of returning to the ERM when conditions were better but, unofficially, most people said that they could not envisage conditions becoming right in the foreseeable future. On 1 August 1993 an emergency meeting of EC finance ministers agreed that ERM constraints should be relaxed and fluctuation of 15 per cent allowed.

Debating Maastricht

The currency crisis was inextricably entwined with negotiations over Maastricht, as witness two European Council meetings during the British presidency in the second half of 1992. An emergency meeting was held in Birmingham in October to resolve the Danish crisis. In the event, the ERM dominated the Birmingham Council and the Maastricht Treaty was carried forward to Edinburgh in December. At that meeting Major achieved most of what he wanted: Denmark gained an opt-out on EMU like that obtained by Britain, concessions were made on the defence and security pillar, and other adjustments were made in advance of the second Danish referendum of May 1993 – adjustments which ensured that the Danes accepted Maastricht by 56.8 to 43.2 per cent.

As a counterweight to any suggestions of federalism or centralism embodied in the Maastricht Treaty, Major promoted subsidiarity at Edinburgh. Subsidiarity meant that:

- proposals by the centre in Brussels should be implemented according to the decisions of national or regional government;
- no major policy decision should be made in Brussels if it is more properly the concern of national or regional government.

Article A of the Maastricht Treaty now reads, 'creating an ever-closer union among the peoples of Europe, in which decisions are taken as closely as possible to the citizen'.

The debate on Maastricht that now resumed in the British Parliament was not strictly necessary for ratification and was much more about internal Conservative policies than about Europe (and will be discussed more closely in Chapter 8 on party attitudes). The process took up 204 hours of debate, 163 of these in one 23-day Committee of the whole House. It also involved 70 divisions, one of which was lost by the government, and another of which became a vote of confidence. It was 2 August 1993 before the UK could ratify the treaty, although Germany was actually the last to ratify, in October 1993. Despite the problems, the treaty became operational as planned on 1 January 1994: the European Community thereby becoming absorbed within the European Union.

Enlargement

A major factor affecting Europe in the 1990s was that the process of enlargement seemed to be accelerating, with an increasing number of countries applying to join, carrying the potential membership to between twenty-five and thirty. This was a very different situation from the first thirty years, which is how long it took for membership to increase from six to twelve.

The first enlargement of the EC by the UK, Ireland and Denmark was delayed by de Gaulle. It has been claimed that the second and third enlargements of the 1980s, involving the admission of Greece, Spain and Portugal, were delayed by the fact that all three countries were somewhat less than democratic when they first became eligible for membership; Greece was then ruled by a military junta and the other two had fascist dictators. In fact, the real cause of delay in processing the Greek, Spanish and Portuguese applications was probably less to do with democracy than because all three countries had weaker economies than the existing members. In particular, a lot of complex negotiations proved necessary in order to extend the CAP to countries with a Mediterranean agriculture.

After the accession of Spain and Portugal in 1986 the movement toward enlargement gathered additional momentum, until there were three groups of would-be members.

1 **Turkey** (which applied in 1987) **and the islands of Malta and Cyprus** (both of which applied in 1990). In December 1989 the Commission advised the Council of Ministers to reject the Turkish application, in part because of doubts over human rights violations. The applications of Cyprus and Malta remained on the table but were elbowed to one side by other developments.
2 **Former members of the Soviet bloc**. Most of these negotiated 'Europe Agreements' with the EU, giving them favourable trade terms. The countries most enthusiastic for membership were the Czech Republic, Hungary and Poland. After the accessions of 1995, these three countries, together with Slovakia, Bulgaria, Romania and Slovenia, became the focus of attention.
3 **Former EFTA countries**. These countries, concerned at the implications of the single market and freed from fears for their neutrality by the end of the Cold War, applied first for associate status and then for full membership. The applicants were Austria, Finland, Norway, Sweden and Switzerland, who would initially join the single market to form a European Economic Area (EEA). Britain was very keen on these five applicants because: enlargement might help to dilute the federalist tendencies within the EU. In addition, all five countries were wealthy and potential net contributors to the Community budget, easing the strain for existing ones.

As a result of a referendum in December 1992 Switzerland withdrew its application to both the EEA and EU. However, Austria, Sweden and Finland pressed ahead and opened negotiations in February 1993, with Norway following in April. Negotiations were rapid, agreement on Finnish and Swedish entry being reached by 28 February 1994 and the Austrian application following the next day, while negotiations with Norway extended for a further week. All was settled by early March 1994 and accession for the four countries was fixed for 1 January 1995.

At this point Britain, with some backing by Spain, demanded that there be no change to majority voting procedures in the Council of Ministers. The dispute threatened a serious delay because, unless the position could be resolved quickly, the accession treaties could not come before the EP prior to its dissolution for the June 1994 elections. This was another round in the Conservative Party's internal argument over Europe and was less about European voting rights than about keeping face in the eyes of party critics at home. The British position, however, was non-sustainable – concessions were made at the eleventh hour and a compromise agreed.

Once the dispute over voting rights had been settled, the accession of the four applicants could proceed, although the applicant countries still had to seek the approval of their own citizens. Referendums in Austria, Finland and Sweden approved the accession agreements, although by very small majorities in the latter two cases. Then, on 28 November, the people of Norway voted against membership, as they had done in 1972. Norway joined Switzerland, Leichtenstein and Iceland in being the only Western European countries not belonging to the EU, retaining the trading benefits of EEA membership but lacking any power to influence decisions of that body.

Norway is often cited by eurosceptics as an example of a country that manages to reap the trading benefits of EEA membership, without the adverse factors of EU membership. The suggestion is that such an arrangement would make an ideal solution for Britain. However, as Hugo Young has pointed out, the idea that Norway has all the advantages of membership without any of the disadvantages is the reverse of the truth:

> The entire apparatus of EU rules on immigration, transport, manufacture and trade in goods and services applies in Norway. Norway's courts and companies live under law as interpreted by the European Court in Luxembourg. This is the precondition for Norway's trade with the EU, unmediated, however, by the presence of any Norwegian ministers at the political table.[23]

Appointment of the Santer Commission

The main business of the European Council held on the island of Corfu in June 1994 was the election of a new president of the Commission to succeed Jacques Delors. According to tradition, the presidency of the Commission is held alternately by someone coming from a large member country and someone from a small country, by someone on the left and someone on the right. As the Commission had been headed by a French socialist from a large country, it therefore followed that the new president should be a centre-right politician from one of the Benelux countries.

The most obvious candidates were Ruud Lubbers, the Dutch prime minister, and Jean-Luc Dehaene, prime minister of Belgium. Unfortunately, Lubbers had upset Chancellor Kohl in a dispute between Germany and the Netherlands and, at a meeting in early June, Chancellor Kohl and President Mitterrand of France had decided that the post should be given to Dehaene. Several EC members, particularly the Dutch, Italians and Spanish, were unhappy at this Franco-German manipulation and were prepared to vote against Dehaene on the first ballot, although knowing they would ultimately have to accept the majority choice.

Not so John Major. Supported by Douglas Hurd, he stated bluntly that, if he could not have the British commissioner, Leon Brittan, he might settle for Ruud Lubbers. He would never accept Jean-Luc Dehaene and would be prepared to use the British veto to prevent the Belgian from becoming president. The British stressed that there was nothing personal in their rejection of Dehaene: the objection, said Douglas Hurd, was the way in which Kohl and Mitterrand had done a secret deal that the rest were supposed to accept without question.

The other members interpreted Britain's stance as due to Major's need to look tough and resolute in the eyes of the eurosceptics in his own party at home. However, they assumed that, having proved his virility by waving the big stick, Major would back down and accept Dehaene. Instead, the British prime minister stuck to his threat and duly employed the veto. It was a significant moment in Britain's relations with the EU because, by using the ultimate weapon of the veto for party political purposes, John Major had just broken the unwritten rules of the EU club.

Once the Germans had taken over the presidency of the EU from the Greeks in July, intensive discussions ensured that, by the time the ministers met in Brussels, they only needed to rubber-stamp a previously determined choice in Jacques Santer, prime minister of Luxembourg. On 20 July the EP, newly elected in June, chose to exercise the right granted to the Parliament by the Maastricht Treaty, and voted on whether to accept the nominee for Commission president. As it was, Santer was accepted by a mere twenty-two votes and the crisis was over. But the chain of events that began in Corfu highlighted three important points:

- John Major's use of the veto may have restored his personal standing with the Conservative Party but it weakened Britain's standing in Europe.
- In the aftermath of the Delors era, the Council of Ministers was perfectly willing to see the Commission weakened and marginalised.
- The EP now had real powers for the first time, and intended to use them.

Another legacy of Corfu was that, for the two-and-a-half dying years of the Major government, eurosceptics in the Conservative ranks seized on the national veto as the last bastion of sovereignty, while majority voting was something to be resisted. Tory ministers represented the right of a British minister to block the wishes of other member countries as the last ditch defence of British sovereign rights. As part of its strategy to force Europe to abandon the ban on British beef in 1996, the British government made great use of its veto to block any decision making by the Council of Ministers. This conduct merely ensured that the BSE crisis continued to the year 2000 and beyond.

New Labour in office

Maastricht had laid down a timetable for monetary union, with the first wave of members joining in 1998, as well as establishing those convergence criteria which member countries would have to satisfy before being allowed to join. At the time of Maastricht, Britain had won an opt-out clause in the treaty so that it did not have to join the EMU. At that time of economic recession in Britain, it seemed that Britain could never satisfy the convergence criteria, so no one worried overmuch about an issue which might never arise. As the British economy improved, however, the possibility of Britain joining EMU in the first wave became ever more real, making eurosceptics demand even more stridently that membership of EMU should be ruled out, at any time and under any conditions.

Europe therefore became a major issue in the 1997 general election, but not in the way that anyone might have expected:

- The debate on Europe was initiated by eurosceptics in the Conservative Party, and encouraged by the tabloid press. But later Labour introduced the topic, knowing that a mere mention of Europe provoked a Tory response that was both self-destructive and self-defeating.
- Discussions concerning Europe were almost exclusively about the single currency, about which the general public had no firm opinion. Other European issues like fish quotas and beef bans, both of which really were of some concern to the electorate, were largely ignored.
- There is no evidence that the British people are as europhobic as elements in the right-wing of the Conservative Party think they are. Some British people may dislike foreigners, particularly the Germans and French. They do not like the idea of 'losing the pound' and they can get very annoyed with the 'nit-picking' bureaucracy of Brussels. However, abstract arguments over concepts such as national sovereignty come a very poor second to bread-and-butter election issues like taxation or education.

In contrast to the increasingly europhobic position adopted by the Conservative Party in opposition, the re-establishment of Britain's position in Europe was one of the first priorities of the Blair government after the 1997 victory.

Within days of becoming foreign secretary, Robin Cook had committed the British government to signing the Social Chapter and agreed to extensions of majority voting. Doug Henderson was appointed as the first specifically European minister at the Foreign Office and it was made clear that in future intergovernmental talks Britain would be represented by Henderson as a minister, rather than by a civil servant as had been the case under the Conservatives – thus bringing UK procedures into line with other member states. Within a month, Robin Cook had gone further than any British minister had gone before by appointing an MEP as his European parliamentary private secretary to handle liaison with the EP.

These concessions, together with a willingness to negotiate and accept compromises rather than seek confrontation, sent out hints to Europe that Britain would henceforth be far less obstructionist than had been the case in recent years. This change in relations between Britain and the EU may have been more a difference of style and attitude than one of substance, but it proved acceptable to the other member states, and Tony Blair's first European Council meeting in Noordwijk seemed bathed in goodwill. The prime minister was still basking in the glow of European approval when he faced his first summit meeting at Amsterdam in July, where issues considered by the IGC set up to succeed Maastricht were to be resolved.

The Amsterdam Summit and Treaty

In negotiations to draw up the Amsterdam Treaty the new mood of give and take meant other member states were more ready to accommodate British positions on contentious issues. The Amsterdam Council was hailed as a triumph for Blair and his government in that, without surrendering a tough negotiating stance, the Blair team showed a willingness to listen to arguments, an ability to compromise when required and a reluctance to employ the British veto.

At the intergovernmental conference in Amsterdam:

- Agreement was reached on a range of internal security measures, including freedom of movement, immigration, political asylum and harmonisation of civil laws such as divorce.
- Britain gave up its solitary opt-out on the Social Chapter.
- Strong measures were introduced against discrimination on the grounds of gender, race, religion, sexual orientation or age.
- Policing remained with national governments, but a supranational Europol was inaugurated.
- Britain and Ireland, as island members with a terrorist problem, were allowed to retain their external border control.
- Plans by France and Germany to make the Western European Union into the defence arm of the EU were blocked by Britain, Finland, Sweden and Ireland, leaving NATO as the safeguard of European defence.
- New anti-unemployment measures were introduced across Europe. The European Investment Bank would make £700 million available to underwrite pan-European job creation schemes and an employment chapter was to be written into the revised Treaty on European Union.[24]

The Amsterdam Council failed to agree on new constitutional structures for the EU prior to current applicants for membership being accepted into the EU. There was a feeling that a general willingness to allow for Blair's inexperience led the other leaders to give the prime minister an easy ride, giving ground on a number of controversial areas, as well as defence and security. The result was a bland treaty that left unresolved quite a few of the issues carried forward from Maastricht.

To continue the examination of these unresolved issues, Jacques Santer went before the EP on 16 July 1997 to outline the Commission's strategy for strengthening and widening the EU in the early years of the twenty-first century. This strategy is known as Agenda 2000.

The document submitted by the Commission was 1,300 pages long and made a detailed assessment of what needed to be done in the wake of the Maastricht and Amsterdam Treaties. It stressed the need to concentrate on five broad aspects:

1 the enlargement of the union through the accession of new member states, with initially five serious contenders;
2 a more proactive role in foreign affairs;
3 further institutional and constitutional reform;
4 effective action to create employment and reduce unemployment;
5 further reform of the Common Agricultural Policy.

The British presidency and the People's Europe

At the heart of New Labour's approach to the problems facing the EU was the need to reform EU institutions and procedures in order to meet the issues created by a wider union. Very shortly after his election victory, Tony Blair announced that, just as he had modernised his party and created New Labour, he now wanted to create a new kind of Europe: a People's Europe that would empower its own citizens. And Blair stressed the central role he wanted Britain to take in the creation of this new Europe.[25]

In the first half of 1998 the UK assumed the presidency of the EU, taking office at a critical time since, within the six-month period of the presidency:

- The outcome of the Amsterdam IGC had to be finalised and assessed, completing work begun at Maastricht.
- The go-ahead for monetary union (EMU) had to be given.
- The Central European Bank had to be established.
- The nature and number of member states willing and qualified to become members of EMU had to be determined.
- Moves had to be made with regard to the enlargement of the EU, with eleven states competing for accession, many of them with serious problems over meeting the conditions for entry.

With all that to do, the British government was aware that it had been in power for little more than seven months when it took over the presidency and could

Box 2.3
The Blair approach to Europe and European developments

On becoming leader, Tony Blair soon made it clear that he wished Britain to play a constructive role in Europe. He had not always been so enthusiastic. Indeed, at the time when he entered politics, Europe had – in Hennessy's words – passed through its 'inspirational phase'.[27] A decade of membership in which membership was downplayed by Wilson and Callaghan, had made the issue seem humdrum and rather 'a functional extension of the business of governing'. It was not an issue about which the ambitious young Blair felt it worth making a challenge to the party line. It did not seem to be a defining issue, even if he had private misgivings about his party's approach. When he entered the House of Commons in 1983, like other new Labour entrants, he absorbed the official position espoused by Michael Foot and advocated British withdrawal from the EC.

But although in 1983 Blair said he was against membership, he did enter the caveat in his personal manifesto 'unless fundamental changes are effected'. He was not Bennite in his opposition to the EC, but noted that it removed Britain's freedom of manoeuvre in economic policies. Perhaps he was in reality never as lukewarm about Europe as his public stance indicated. After all, back in 1975, he had voted for Britain to remain in the EC. Even if he lacked crusading zeal on the subject, his choice seems to mark him out as broadly pro-European.

In his heart, Blair had probably never had much of a problem with membership, but it was rather risky to come out and say so in the early 1980s. But over the next decade, along with many other Labour members, he came to see how positively beneficial Europe might be in reviving the fortunes of social democratic politics. He did not need to decide in detail what he did believe about the issue, but watched with growing pleasure the turmoil it caused in Tory ranks. He was keen to see Labour a step ahead of his opponents. He was alarmed by the 'drift towards isolation in Europe', and wanted to see instead 'constructive engagement'.

Describing himself as a 'passionate European' by the time he became leader in 1994, he was alarmed by the xenophobic tone of the tabloid press. He wanted to see the country 'at the centre of Europe', and fulfil its destiny on the continent and its 'historical role in the world'. Without being active within the Union, Britain would forfeit any chance of global influence; Europe must be 'our base'.[28]

As Opposition leader, Blair sounded positive about Europe, but this did not mean that he was wildly idealistic. Indeed, he advocated reform of European institutions and of the CAP. But while he was intent on safeguarding national interests and ensuring that Britain extracted its best possible deal from the EU, he was not in favour of the 'impotent posturing' of the then prime minister.

On the single currency, he sounded more sympathetic than John Major. He felt that if it could be made to work, it would be a good thing, and noted its practical advantages, such as greater stability, lower transaction costs and lower interest rates. His only anxiety was whether it could operate effectively when there were serious economic discrepancies between the different regions of the EU. The approach was 'watchful EMU-readiness' – not very different from the approach of pro-Europeans in the then Conservative government, who wanted to 'prepare and decide'.

therefore be considered as totally inexperienced. The Blair governmen
only to lead the EU through a series of vitally important decisions but ...
so while simultaneously proving its own European credentials in the wake of
an outgoing government that was ambivalent about Europe to say the least.
Most interestingly and paradoxically, Britain had to negotiate and administer
the start of monetary union while retaining its opted-out determination not to
join in the first wave of participants.[26]

Monetary union

At Maastricht, progress towards EMU moved into phase two of the Delors Plan.
Under the guidance of the Economic and Finance Council (Ecofin) of the EU,
EMU would create three institutions:

1 **The European Central Bank** (ECB), to operate monetary policies such as the
   setting of interest rates for the EMU as a whole.
2 **The European System of Central Banks** (ESCB), made up of the fifteen central banks of EU member states, in conjunction with the ECB, and intended
   to be the overall co-ordinating body determining monetary policy for EMU.
3 **A common currency**, the euro, its value initially based on the ECU basket of
   currencies.

Of all the integrationist measures proposed for Europe, this is the one most distrusted by the eurosceptics. Emotionally, British sceptics use patriotism to
argue against monetary union, refusing to 'give up the pound' in favour of
some alien imposition. However, the retention of the pound is largely irrelevant. The valid political argument of those opposed to EMU is that the existence of a European central bank would mean that the British government
would lose control of the British economy, forfeiting the right to set budgetary
measures such as tax and interest rates.

Denmark and Britain both had opt-outs from monetary union and were
joined by Sweden after its accession. From 1995 onwards, British ministers
were pleased that they could wait and see what was on offer before deciding on
whether to join or not. After Labour's 1997 victory, government policy officially remained the same, because Tony Blair broadly accepted Major's wait-
and-see approach, but gave it a more positive slant of 'prepare and decide'.
According to the Labour government, Britain would not join EMU with the first
wave of countries in 1999, but would make a decision regarding entry at a later
date 'when the time was right'; the chancellor, Gordon Brown laid down five
tests to assist in deciding when the moment was opportune (see pp. 158–9).
Should the Labour government decide that entry was appropriate, the issue
would be put to the country in a referendum.

It has long been accepted that Tony Blair is theoretically in favour of EMU.
Yet he would not press the issue. He and most other ministers remained

strangely reticent, possibly for fear of sceptics in the tabloid press such as *The Sun* (owned by Rupert Murdoch), and a suspicion that to advocate European unity was to court electoral rejection. 'Now, by sidelining EMU from immediate decisions, he [Blair] was pre-empting a Murdoch onslaught which, he feared, might undercut his prospects of a second term'.[29] It was also widely rumoured that the chancellor and his Treasury team was more sceptical about entry than the prime minister. Gordon Brown would have to be won round, for he would be the arbiter of whether or not the conditions were right.

As far back as the 1950s when the Treaty of Rome was proposed, eurosceptics have comforted themselves with the thought that any movement towards unity could never happen. In 1995–97 the same sceptics were confidently predicting that not more than one or two countries would be able to meet EMU convergence criteria. As recently as May 1997, the europhile Kenneth Clarke was saying that EU members were in such economic difficulty that the single currency would probably never happen. This was, however, whistling in the wind. On 1 May 1998 the European Monetary Union was created at an Ecofin meeting in Brussels. Only one country that wanted to join – Greece – failed to meet the convergence criteria. Despite being qualified to join, Denmark and Sweden decided to side with Britain and opted out of EMU for the moment, so that eleven countries actually signed the May agreement. One irony of the situation was that, with Britain holding the EU presidency at the time, Gordon Brown had to take the chair for the actual ceremony creating monetary union. He then had to withdraw from the room while the ESCB members of Ecofin discussed matters relating to the euro, which Britain was barred from discussing.

The government's stance over the euro disappointed the impatient euro-enthusiasts in all parties and many members of the business community. They yearned to see ministers take a more active role in educating the country to accept the euro and were disappointed that the glittering launch of the 'Britain in Europe' campaign was not followed up by more obvious governmental action.

Developing problems with the EU

It was obvious that the initial honeymoon effect would wear off and Europe would become more critical of Blair and his government, but such criticism was markedly less than that engendered by the Thatcherite tactics typical of the later Conservative years. There were issues that forced the Blair government on the defensive, most notably when the German finance minister and prominent member of the Social Democrats, Oskar Lafontaine, outlined proposals for tax harmonisation in the EU. His initiative, supported by other spokespersons in the German administration, offered a slice of candour of just the type from which John Major routinely suffered and which Margaret Thatcher tended to relish. Both Tony Blair and Gordon Brown made it clear that they would use the veto to reject any attempt to harmonise or expand European taxation. Not for the first time in Britain's often-turbulent relations with the other member states, ministers were forced on to the defensive as France and Germany seemed to be racing ahead towards another distant Euro-goal. That drive towards integration has been a consistent one ever since the two countries buried their national differences back in the 1950s, even if there have been periods when it has been placed on the back burner.

The British tabloid press was vehement in its denunciation of the Lafontaine plans and Lafontaine soon became a 'European from hell' in the writing of several journalists. In the face of such hostility in the media to 'unwanted' European initiatives, ministers adopted a more anti-European style of rhetoric that played well at home. But there were some continental partners who thought that the British response was too reminiscent of that which they had seen from earlier administrations.

Meanwhile, much of the press coverage about Europe was negative and the Conservatives had taken up the eurosceptic cause. As Opposition leader, William Hague developed this approach, backed by a parliamentary party whose membership contained a higher proportion of 'hostile' MPs than there were in the previous Parliament. He was personally responsible for the slogan adopted by the party in the run-up to the 1999 European elections, 'In Europe, but not run by Europe'. The party continued to snipe at ministerial 'surrenders' to continental partners after every summit and were buoyed up by the increasing level of euroscepticism apparent in opinion-poll findings.

Hague felt vindicated by the outcome of the European elections when, on a remarkably low turnout, his party scored 35.8 per cent of the vote and won a handsome victory. The new unity of the Shadow Cabinet over Europe and these signs of popular support strengthened his determination to place the Blair government at a disadvantage. This encouraged him to oppose the Nice Treaty, which he pledged to renegotiate if the Conservatives returned to office.

The Treaty of Nice

At Nice in June 2000, the assembled heads of government were concerned to achieve the changes necessary as a result of the next enlargement. It was agreed that the institutional and policy foundations of a Union of fifteen would be inadequate when the EU had perhaps another ten members. In the event, the major governments won the important arguments and confirmed their unassailable dominance. The summiteers seemed more concerned with national interests than the cause of integration. The treaty:

- capped the size of the Commission and the number of seats in Parliament; larger countries would each lose one Commissioner to accommodate representatives of the new entrants;

- [as a quid pro quo] gave those larger countries a favourable reweighting of votes in the Council of Ministers, ensuring that the interests of the main players in the EU would be preserved as majority voting became more common;
- continued the movement towards qualified majority voting, permitting it in some twent-three policy areas;
- allowed for the establishment of a Rapid Reaction Force (see p. 191).

In Britain, there was relief that the prime minister had succeeded in preserving the 'red lines' that he had pledged to defend – in other words, there was to be no majority voting on indirect taxation and social security. Tony Blair had got what he wanted, with headlines reading 'Nice one at Nice' and 'Nice one, Tony'. He came home able to talk of victories, having handled the summit with considerable skill. He was able to turn the issue of Europe to his advantage in the Commons, as a stick with which to beat the Conservatives.

The treaty was signed in 2001 and ratified following a second Irish referendum in October 2002 (after the voters in the first one had rejected the agreement).

The 2001 election and after

In the 2001 election British voters were more concerned with issues such as education and health than they were about Europe. Although the Conservative leader tried to make Europe a major campaign theme and spoke in alarmist terms of 'ten days to save the pound', it did not register as a decisive theme. This was despite an untimely intervention by the president of the Commission, Romano Prodi, who on 29 May issued a call for a more centralised European economy. He also toyed with the idea of an elected president for the EU and further development of EU competence in matters of taxation. Ministers quickly repudiated these suggestions. They proclaimed that the battle against an over-centralised EU would best be won by the effective negotiating of committed Europeans operating within the councils of Europe, rather than by the vocal criticism of those with an anti-European agenda.

Since the 2001 election, there have been four other developments of significance in assessing Britain's relationship with the EU: the issue of the single currency, a further stage in the process of enlargement, the divisive issue of policy towards the Iraqi regime of Saddam Hussein, and the attempt to reach agreement over a constitution for Europe.

Britain and the eurozone

The national currencies of members of the eurozone disappeared in January 2002, the single currency becoming the sole basis of all transactions. At that time, Greece was allowed to join with the other eleven countries, leaving three countries outside. On behalf of the British government, in June 2003 Gordon Brown produced his assessment as to whether the conditions for entry were favourable and decided that four of the five criteria had not been fulfilled (see p. 159).

A further review was promised prior to the next election, but the likelihood was that ministers would not contemplate embarking upon such a contentious policy as membership without seeing greater signs of support in the country. Although Euro-enthusiasts were disappointed that a government twice elected with an overwhelming majority and led by a self-confessed pro-European was unable to take Britain into euroland, non-participation found a surprising ally in Jacques Delors[30]. The former president of the Commission expressed the view in early 2004 that Britain had good reason to feel content outside the euro and would probably steer clear of the currency for several years. He was critical of the way in which the EU had lost its way and not taken advantage of its single currency, noting that EU leaders (including his fellow Frenchman, Jacques Chirac) had failed to heed his warning that monetary union must be matched with close co-ordination of economic policies and arguing that consequently the euro was less attractive than it otherwise might have been. He recognised that: 'Since we have not succeeded in maximising the economic advantages of the euro, one can understand the British . . . saying: "Things are just fine as they are. Staying out of the euro hasn't stopped us prospering"'.

Enlargement

In 1995 the EU had become an organisation of 15 members in what was the fourth enlargement to the original six member Community. But by then its leaders were already having to grapple with the unexpected and unprecedented opportunity to extend European integration into the countries of Central and Eastern Europe that were formerly members of the Soviet Union. In the aftermath of the collapse of the Berlin Wall in 1989, several 'new democracies' had been created. At first they had association agreements with the EU, but at the Copenhagen meeting of the European Council in December 2002 it was agreed that ten more countries should accede to the EU in May 2004 (the Fifth Enlargement) A prolonged process of preparation and negotiation culminated in the entry of the Baltic states of Estonia, Latvia and Lithuania, Hungary, Poland, Slovakia, Slovenia, the Czech Republic and the two Mediterranean islands of Malta and Cyprus. The process of enlargement is due to be taken further in 2007, with the accession of Bulgaria and Romania, and there is even a possibility that Croatia might be fast-tracked to join at the same time.

Britain has long been a supporter of enlargement. Ministers of both parties have recognised that, having thrown off the deadening grip of the old Soviet Union, the new member states were unlikely to favour any irksome interference from Brussels. These new member states mostly believe in open markets, but are less enthusiastic about state intervention and undue central interference. Their entry is likely to bolster the EU's liberal economic credentials and affirm support for the idea that the EU should be an association of nation-states rather than evolve into a giant superstate of the type feared by many British Conservatives. The model they favour is not the traditional Franco–German integrationist project. Rather, shunning the idea of any monolithic entity, they are nearer to the pragmatic British and Scandinavians, in their preference for a looser, more varied and multispeed EU.

Table 2.1　*The growth of the EU*

Enlargement	Date	Countries joining
	1951	Original members: Belgium, France, Italy, Luxembourg, Netherlands, West Germany
First	1973	Denmark, Ireland, UK
Second	1981	Greece
Third	1986	Portugal, Spain
Fourth	1995	Austria, Finland, Sweden
Fifth	2004	Cyprus, Czech Republic, Estonia, Hungary, Latvia, Lithuania, Malta, Poland, Slovakia, Slovenia
Proposed sixth	2007	Bulgaria, Romania; Croatia has an outside chance of being 'fast-tracked' at the same time

Note: Greenland is as yet the only territory to have voted to leave the EC, as it then was. A large and autonomous Danish island, it voted to reject continued membership in 1982 and officially left in January 1985. Many Greenlanders were unhappy about the impact of EC fisheries policy and felt remote from the 'Brussels bureaucracy'.

Policy over Iraq

The idea that the EU should speak with one voice in world affairs is a long-standing one, almost as old as the post-war process towards greater unity itself. However, despite repeated attempts to galvanise the issue, the EU has made much less progress in forging a common foreign and security policy than it has in creating a single market and a single currency.

The difficulties of achieving any breakthrough were highlighted by the deep divisions among EU member states in early 2003 over whether or not the United Nations Security Council should authorise the American-led war on Iraq (see pp. 188–90). In the event, the British government gave strong endorsement to the US position and thus reaffirmed its traditional transatlantic ties. Britain had the backing of Spain and some of the countries then awaiting entry into an enlarged Union, but found itself on the opposite side of the fence to France and Germany. As one of the permanent members, France would not support the war in the Security Council and had the backing of Russia for the stance it adopted. EU member governments once again found it difficult to reconcile the cause of Union solidarity with their own national preferences.

The Convention and proposed constitution

Meanwhile, a Convention on the Future of Europe chaired by former French president, Giscard d'Estaing, was engaged in devising a constitution for the enlarged EU. The Convention comprised parliamentarians from all present and future EU member countries, representatives of national governments, Members of the European Parliament and two European commissioners. It was hoped that this varied membership could produce a draft treaty that would be adopted in its entirety by the heads of state and government. Their work last for eighteen months and culminated in a gathering in Brussels, in December 2003.

The Convention's mandate, when it was set up in late 2001, was to prepare the EU's institutions and workings for the forthcoming expansion to twenty-five member states. Its task was not so much to revise the current constitutional structure of the European Union, but more to clarify and modernise it. This mandate was reflected in the most visible achievement of the Convention, the merging of all previous treaties (with the exception of the Euratom Treaty) into a single text. It was primarily this desire to codify and consolidate which led many of the Convention's members to conceive of their work as devising a constitution. The term was a technically accurate designation of what they believed they were producing. While their proposed Constitutional Treaty contained some innovations, the overwhelming majority of its text was already to be found in the existing treaties.

At the December gathering in Brussels, the British representatives had certain key 'red lines' that they felt must not be crossed. Ministers wished to retain the national veto on tax, social security, defence and foreign policy, and protect British interests in other sensitive areas. They were under pressure from the Conservative Opposition and elements in the tabloid press to stand firm and resist any integrationist moves that might be written into any agreement. By inclination, they were not enthusiastic about the necessity for a treaty. Indeed, four years earlier Tony Blair had contended that given the sheer diversity and complexity of the EU, its constitution (like the British one) would continue to be found in treaties, laws and precedents. There was, he had observed, a case for 'a statement of principles', a 'charter of competences', that would be a political rather than a legal document, one that was 'simpler and more accessible to Europe's citizens'. Clearly the proposed constitution was more than this, and it had definite legal implications. Nonetheless, in early 2004 the prime minister tended to downplay it as a mere tidying up exercise. The Conservatives claimed that it was much more sinister. They saw such a document as unnecessary and undesirable.

Negotiations finally foundered on the specific question of voting weights in the enlarged EU for two countries, Spain and Portugal. These two countries articulated the fears of smaller member states that they were in danger of being bullied by the major countries in the EU and were holding out for better protection in majority votes than they were being granted. The proposal would have meant that in order to succeed a majority vote would require the backing of 50 per cent of members, these countries representing at least 50 per cent of the EU's population.

British ministers seemed relaxed about the collapse, since they were sure that there was plenty of time to reach agreement. Foreign Secretary Jack Straw noted that if it did not come about, then the EU had contingency plans to deal with enlargement and that these did not expire until 2009. However, during the six months Irish presidency that began in the following January, the Irish Taoiseach Bertie Aherne was anxious to achieve a settlement of the issues on which the December Council had failed to reach agreement.

From the beginning, it was always likely that there was going to be a compromise. However, all the national leaders gathered in Brussels had to 'talk tough' in order to create the impression to their electorates back home that they were holding out in sturdy defence of their countrys' positions. Several of the same issues reappeared on the agenda that had been debated previously and there was a similar desire among the smaller nations to ensure that their wishes were not overridden by the heavyweights, France and Germany. Austria, Finland and most of the ten new members opposed plans to scale down the size of the Commission and wanted to retain their representation. The Netherlands wanted greater powers for the same body in policing eurozone budget deficits and again the issue of voting rights in the Council was contentious, with the Taoiseach seeking to persuade the Polish and Spanish representatives to surrender the disproportionately generous and complex voting powers they had won at Nice four years previously.

For Tony Blair the already high stakes had been raised by the unprecedented eurosceptic gains in the European-elections held on 10 June 2000. He argued that a deal was desirable and in Britain's interests, but was determined to defend the red lines that really mattered as he attempted his political rehabilitation after a year in which his reputation had been seriously tarnished over Iraq. Whereas some leaders could afford to be seen to have yielded in some areas in the cause of reaching a settlement, his room for manoeuvre was strictly limited.

Opponents felt that the treaty was far more than a mere tidying up exercise. If it was so, then in their view it seemed odd that ministers should be so concerned to emphasise their spirited and determined resistance over red lines. Critics suspected that integrationist tendencies in the EU would be allowed to creep in by the back door, even if they were not overtly stated in the treaty. As *The Economist* put it (19 June 2004):

> The British have done dogged and effective work to pare back the more federalist aspects of the constitution. But it still has a number of legal and institutional innovations, including the Charter [of Fundamental Rights], the creation of a single legal personality for the EU, more majority voting, the establishment of a foreign

minister and a full-time president of the European Council. Combine them, and assume that the European Court of Justice puts a federalist spin on them, and the potential for a big increase in EU power is clear.

The Conservative attack echoed several of these concerns. Shadow Foreign Secretary Michael Ancram claimed that 'the constitution was a gateway to a country called Europe . . . it's going to be a constitution which has supremacy over our constitution, over our laws and this is something which we believe is highly damaging to the interests of this country'.

Yet again, the imperatives of British politics, fear of the tabloids and a rising tide of euroscepticism were unhelpful influences on British negotiators. The requirements of national politics meant that the story presented in this next stage of the European saga was of them against us, a British Daniel in the European lion's den, St George against the Brussels dragons, and fighting over red lines – were not actually in the proposed treaty.

In the event, the key red lines were broadly held. Broadly the agreement was about defining and clarifying who does what. Most of the EU powers were already in existence, although there was a modest extension of majority voting in some areas. In all sensitive new areas, such as justice and home affairs or social security, Britain cannot be outvoted. There is only one new area where the EU has the power to act (jointly with other governments): energy. Again, even on this issue, the EU already had some role through its environmental policy. The British position and the level of success achieved in the negotiations at Brussels are summarised in the Box 2.4. For further discussion of the implications of the proposed constitution for the future of Britain in Europe, see pp. 283 and 286 in the concluding chapter.

Also under discussion in Brussels was the question of a successor to Romano Prodi, widely seen as a lacklustre president of the Commission. The preferred choice of France and Germany was Guy Verhofstadt, the Belgian federalist who had the additional disadvantage in British ministerial eyes of being anti-American in his rhetoric. British ministers had hopes that its outgoing Conservative commissioner Chris Patten, might be chosen, but the French were equally unwilling to accept this candidate. Out of the stalemate emerged a compromise choice, the Portuguese prime minister, José Manuel Durão Barroso. As a free marketeer, moderniser and pro-American who backed the war in Iraq, he was acceptable to the British government, which hoped that his appointment might prove helpful in its bid to influence the orientation of the future EU. He was confirmed as the new president at a special summit in Brussels at the end of June 2004. Though consensus is the preferred route to nomination, a formal vote in the Council of Ministers still has to be taken. Barroso was chosen by a clear majority in the QMV. If France or Germany had tried to block him, then they risked an embarrassing defeat in the newly enlarged Europe.

Box 2.4

Key elements of the British negotiating stance in Brussels, June 2004

Crime and immigration

- **Proposals in draft treaty**. Common asylum and immigration position to operate under QMV, so that Britain could be outvoted on border control, treatment of asylum seekers and immigrants.
- **British government position**. Britain was a traditional advocate of action against organised crime, illegal immigration and terrorism. However, Labour wished to hang on to the symbolic control of border entry; it also opposed the creation of an EU prosecutor.
- **Outcome**. Britain was forced to concede some ground by allowing the introduction of majority voting on cooperation over crime, but it will have an opt-out clause on anything it finds unacceptable. This would not stop other nations from going ahead. All nations would have to agree to establish a European public prosecutor who would help combat fraud. Britain also has an opt-out on border policy and retains the right to police its own frontiers.

Foreign and defence policy

- **Proposals in draft treaty**. EU competence would cover 'all areas of foreign policy and all questions relating to the Union's security, including the progressive framing of a common defence policy, which might lead to a common defence'.
- **British government position**. Ministers wanted to ensure that member states and the intergovernmental Council of Ministers (not the supranational Commission) retained responsibility for foreign and security policy. Britain was willing to see the EU given a single voice in foreign policy matters, where there was a shared policy (although it would have preferred the title 'external representative' to foreign minister), but resisted any defence structure duplicating NATO.
- **Outcome**. Britain insisted on no common defence policy that would undermine NATO, which remains the mutual defence organisation for the Atlantic Alliance of Europe and North America. Initial strategy decisions will be taken by all twenty-five states, but majority voting will suffice on the ground implementation. The position of foreign minister was created, but without a seat on the UN Security Council; neither is Britain's permanent seat there under threat from the EU. There is no mutual defence pact: EU nations simply promise to help each other if they suffer a terrorist attack or natural disaster.

The Social Chapter and labour laws

- **Proposals in draft treaty**. A last-minute red-line issue, based on the fear that the proposed Charter of Fundamental Rights (CFR) would allow British unions to challenge labour laws dating from the Thatcher era that impose secret ballots for strikes and elections, as well as banning secondary picketing.

- **British government position**. Ministers claimed to be relaxed about the CFR, which they portrayed more as a political than a legal declaration. However, they were very aware that labour laws were much discussed in the tabloid press: the Murdoch papers portrayed the CFR as a document already being granted legal force by the Court of Justice.
- **Outcome**. Ministers insisted that the right to strike should not be enshrined in the constitution, so as not to undermine British trade union laws. The CFR does not create any new employment rights and the document was given a cautious initial welcome by the Confederation of British Industry (CBI).

Tax harmonisation and social security

- **Proposals in draft treaty**. The national veto would be removed over social security for migrant workers. The draft did not dilute the British opt-out from the single currency.
- **British government position**. Ministers were committed to the right of member states to determine their own tax policies, which was seen as a key element of national sovereignty. They were determined to uphold the British veto and the very different traditions of social security systems and workers' rights.
- **Outcome**. The EU does not have the right to levy taxes and the treaty will not grant the EU any new powers over tax. Britain blocked an end to the national veto on fiscal policy, and concerns that there would be majority voting on measures to tackle cross-border tax fraud were allayed (ministers had feared that this would allow the EU into the domestic tax arena by the back door). Britain argued that national social support systems were so complex and particular to individual countries that a unanimous vote should accompany all change. It secured an 'emergency brake' compromise to allow Britain to opt out should it disagree with the majority.

Voting systems and EU efficiency

- **Proposals in draft treaty**. Pragmatists argued that the constitutional treaty was essentially a tidying up measure of forty years of EU treaties, in order to streamline decision-making in an era in which twenty-five countries had national vetoes. Efficiency was said to require a president of the Council to be elected, for a maximum of two five-year terms, by fellow heads of government. Each state would no longer be entitled to at least one member of the Commission and there would be changes in voting rights to curb blocking minorities from thwarting action.
- **British government position**. As one of 'big four', Britain saw the changes as strengthening its power to drive the EU agenda. It realised the potential for opposition of smaller states to create deadlock over the issue of voting rights, but if the talks failed on this issue then ministers would have been relaxed.
- **Outcome**. There was a compromise over voting rights whereby for any majority vote to succeed it would need the support of 55 per cent of members, and these countries should represent at least 65 per cent of the EU's population. This presented no problem for Britain, which welcomed the changes.

Conclusion

From this account of British attitudes to and involvement in first the European Community and then the European Union, two continuous threads emerge. First, it is apparent that euroscepticism in Britain has a long history and that because of this Europe has been a difficult and often divisive issue for British politicians David Butler and Martin Westlake have elaborated on this theme, pointing out that:

> If there is a European 'problem', it is not restricted to one British political party, but more generally diffused throughout the British political and administrative establishment . . . In truth, virtually every postwar British prime minister has been in a similar position and played a similar role, from Attlee to Churchill and Eden, from Macmillan to Wilson, and from Callaghan to Major and Thatcher.[31]

All prime ministers have found the British relationship with mainland Europe an uneasy one and – however pro-European their inclinations – have often found themselves responding to the initiatives of other heads of government who wish to see the pace of integration move along more swiftly. Often, Britain has been in the slower lane, sometimes trying to halt or delay advance, some-times opting out of the developments taking place elsewhere. The last half cen-tury or so has been a period in which Britain has struggled – in the words of Hugo Young – to 'reconcile the past she could not forget with the future she could not avoid'. As he elaborated:

> At the beginning . . . with a world war barely over, Winston Churchill first placed on record the outline of a new, united Europe. At the end of it, an agreement was signed, under the collaborative eye of Prime Minister Blair, who was at the time the chairman of what we mean by 'Europe', to create a single currency for the European Union. There was an uneasy continuity between these two moments of creative apotheosis. Both Mr Churchill and Mr Blair, at their different times and from their own vantage-points, were spectators rather than actors in a continen-tal drama from which Britain, the island nation, chose to exclude herself.[32]

Second, two forces have been at work in the evolution of the Community, now the Union: intergovernmentalism and integration. At different times over the last forty years, one set of ideas has gained the ascendancy, as different thinkers and political leaders have pressed their particular viewpoint. The dispute is still at the heart of the controversy within the EU about the way it has developed and the future direction it should take. The notion of intergovernmentalism has been remarkably resilient and Britain has been a strong exponent of an approach that shuns talk of federalism or supranationalism and prefers instead the rhetoric of safeguarding national interests and the benefits to be derived from states working together for their mutual benefit. Yet in spite of the

attempts made by British and on occasion other political leaders to be pragmatic rather than idealistic, and to emphasise practical co-operation rather
than a more visionary approach, the process of integration on the continent
has moved forward. The EU has not only established itself as an important
player on the international scene; its members have also moved more closely
together.

Notes

1 N. Nugent, *The Government and Politics of the European Union*, Palgrave, 2003.
2 A. Watkins, *A Conservative Coup*, Duckworth, 1992.
3 H. Young, *This Blessed Plot*, Macmillan, 1998.
4 Lord (Geoffrey) Howe, speaking on *The Last Europeans*, Channel 4 Television, July 1995.
5 M. Heseltine, interview in *The Independent*, 10 October 1989.
6 Sir M. Butler, speaking on *The Last Europeans*, Channel 4 Television, July 1995.
7 P. Hennessy, *The Prime Minister*, Allen Lane, 2000.
8 H. Young, as in 3 above.
9 M. Thatcher, *The Downing Street Years*, Harper Collins, 1993.
10 P. Hennessy, as in 7 above.
11 M. Thatcher, as in 9 above.
12 M. Thatcher, interview in 'Changing the face of Britain. But at what cost?', *Saga* magazine, September 1998.
13 H. Young, in 3 above.
14 A. Geddes, *The European Union and British Politics*, Palgrave, 2004.
15 H. Young, as in 3 above.
16 M. Thatcher, as in 9 above.
17 L. Robins, *Talking Politics*, Spring 1997.
18 *The Times*, 27 June 1989.
19 Margaret Thatcher to the House of Commons, 30 October 1990.
20 G. Howe, *Conflict of Loyalty*, Pan, 1995.
21 The full text of the Maastricht Treaty is published in English by the Office for Official Publications of the European Communities, Luxembourg, 1992.
22 P. Lynch, 'Europe's post-Maastricht muddle', *Politics Review*, November 1993.
23 H. Young, as in 3 above.
24 Taken from the communiqué detailing agreements reached at Amsterdam, published by the Council of Ministers and to be found on the EU website: www.europa.eu.int.
25 C. Pilkington, 'Europe', in S. Lancaster (ed.), *Developments in Politics*, vol. 10, Causeway Press, 1999.
26 Material presented to those attending 'People's Europe 98', a conference of non-governmental organisations held at the London School of Economics, 5–7 June 1998.
27 P. Hennessy, as in 7 above.
28 H. Young, as in 3 above.
29 H. Young, as in 3 above.

30 J. Delors, interviewed in *The Guardian*, 17 January 2004.
31 D. Butler and M. Westlake, *British Politics and the European Elections 1994*, Macmillan, 1995.
32 H. Young, as in 3 above.

3

The institutions of the EU

Political institutions and their modus vivendi are not in themselves exciting. The precise details of their operation in particular circumstances can seem complex and their procedures obscure and esoteric, understood only by those who work in them or specialise in their analysis. However, the composition and powers of institutions arouse greater interest, for on occasion the range of their authority and the nature of their membership become part of the political battleground. Both are liable to change and development, and this is certainly true of the machinery of the EU. In this case, however, there is an added source of controversy. As the EU institutions evolve via successive treaty amendments, they raise the issue of the balance of power between member states and the EU.

General observations

The organisational structure of the EC was formally established by the Treaty of Rome in 1957, but the basic framework was already there in the machinery of the ECSC. Outwardly, these institutions have changed very little since then, despite the mutation of the Assembly into the European Parliament (EP). But behind the apparently unchanging façade, their underlying nature and functions has been subject to a fundamental process of amendment that continues still. In addition, new institutions have emerged over the last twenty years, such as the European Court of Auditors, the European Investment Bank, the European Ombudsman, the Committee of the Regions and the European Central Bank.

One aim of the Maastricht Summit was supposed to be the redefinition of the institutions of the EU in the light of these organisational changes, formalising the resulting amendments by incorporation in the treaty. However, in the event, it was not possible to complete a full review of the institutions at Maastricht and, like other aspects of the treaty, this was one of the tasks passed to the IGC which reported at Amsterdam in 1997. And even that was not completed. At Nice (2000), various changes were made to prepare for enlargement, although the issue of voting rights in the EU Council still remained unresolved. At the summit to discuss the draft constitution in December 2003, no agreement could be reached, for Germany and Poland were deadlocked. The Irish Taoiseach Bertie Aherne brokered a compromise over the issue at the Brussels Summit six months later, during the talks on the yet-to-be-ratified constitution.

The impact of the various treaty revisions upon the main institutions is summarised in Table 3.3 on p. 92. Two constitutional problems influence the restructuring of EU's institutions:

- The so-called 'democratic deficit' of those institutions;
- the vexed question of the rights belonging to individual member states.

Most of the bodies involved in the policy and decision-making processes of the EU are not directly accountable to the peoples of the EU. Until 1979 the Assembly was appointed rather than elected and, even after the introduction of direct elections, the EP was left with very few powers to control the Commission, and even less to control the Council of Ministers. As Neill Nugent says: 'It is the case that Community decision-makers are less directly accountable than are national decision-makers'.[1] Some constitutionalists would argue that the Council of Ministers, composed of elected ministers of the member countries, can be considered accountable in that those ministers are answerable to the electorate of their own countries. These issues are more fully discussed in the section on the 'democratic deficit', on pp. 99–102.

An issue that generates supranational versus intergovernmental arguments concerns the comparative powers of member states that are of disparate sizes and populations. Germany has a population in excess of 82 million, while Luxembourg has only 400,000 inhabitants. If each state were to have equal voting rights then Luxembourg would have an influence equal to that of a country 200 times greater. On the other hand, giving member countries an influence weighted for comparative size would mean that larger states could trample at will over the wishes of smaller countries.

The eighteenth-century solution arrived at by the Federalists drawing up the US constitution was to create two houses of Congress in which one, the House of Representatives, represents the population through constituencies of roughly equal size; while the second, the Senate, represents states' rights by having equal representation (two senators) for each state of the union. There are those in Europe who would like to replicate this system by granting full legislative powers to the EP and Council of Ministers, with the EP taking the role of the House of Representatives and the Council acting as Senate. This suggestion has, however, met with opposition from anti-federal national governments. Although the EP has gained a considerable number of additional powers and legitimacy since Maastricht, the changes have not been sufficient to remove the democratic deficit, let alone make the Parliament a true legislative body.

As we have seen, Britain has always emphasised its preference for an intergovernmental rather than a supranational approach to EU affairs. British governments have had reservations about any moves conceding greater powers to supranational elements and have become suspicious and alarmed when meetings are planned to produce constitutions in which there may be talk of federalism. If anything, they might be more enthusiastic about repatriating some power from Brussels back to the capitals of individual countries. Smaller states in particular are enthusiastic about supranationalism and more willing to concede greater powers to those institutions that are run more in the interests of the EU itself than of its component member states.

If British governments have been concerned to limit the scope of European institutions, British people have been largely ignorant about them. Surveys have revealed that they seem to know little and care even less. Data collected by *Barometer*, the EU's official polling organisation, regularly reveal that knowledge of and trust in every EU institution is lower in Britain than elsewhere.

Of the five main institutions – the Commission, Parliament, Court of Justice, Council of Ministers and European Council – three are more supranational in character and two more intergovernmental. In each case, we will examine their membership and formal powers, before giving consideration to any issues surrounding their workings. We will then more briefly describe the main details associated with the other institutions. Finally, we will assess the widely held belief that there is a serious lack of accountability and democracy within European machinery and contemplate changes that might be made to remedy the alleged defect. We will begin with the institutions that are supranational.

The Commission

The Commission is the executive arm of the EU and is sometimes perceived as the 'government' of the Community, while others see it as the 'civil service'. In fact, it is neither. In policy-making decisions the Commission differs from a civil service in that it formulates statements of policy but, unlike a government, it is powerless to control the vote on acceptance or rejection of that policy. In reality, the Commission is a unique institution, somewhere between an executive and an administrative machine. The very term 'Commission' is itself a misnomer, for the body's organisation embraces these two distinctive aspects. The executive responsibilities are carried out by the College of Commissioners (in effect, the political arm of the Commission) and the administrative ones by the bureaucracy.

Until 2004, larger countries such as France, Germany and the UK, each had two commissioners. Since the creation of the new College of Commissioners in November of that year, it has numbered twenty-five, with one representative for every EU country. The people nominated to be commissioners are experienced politicians, often having held ministerial office in their home countries before going to Brussels. They form the powerhouse of the Commission, meeting weekly to formulate and develop proposals.

The number of commissioners, having started as nine in 1957, steadily grew to twenty before the latest enlargement and thirty after it, for each of the largest five countries had two commissioners. As long ago as 1977 Roy Jenkins[2] was complaining that there were more commissioners than there were suitable portfolios for them, and that was when there were only thirteen in all. At Helsinki in 1999 it was agreed that the present Commission would be the last in which any country would have more than two commissioners. The IGC was left to resolve whether the smaller states might not have to share commissioners between themselves. At Nice, it was agreed that the Commission would have a maximum of twenty-seven members, with a rotation system that is fair to all countries to be introduced once EU membership exceeds twenty-seven states. This was confirmed in the new constitutional arrangements agreed at Brussels, as a step to ensure that the institution does not become too unwieldy.

Since January 1995 commissioners have been appointed to serve for five years, instead of the original four. This five-year term now coincides with the life of the EP, although the commissioners take office in January, six months after the June parliamentary elections. This delay is designed to allow time for the commissioners-designate to be vetted by the new Parliament before they take office.

In theory, according to the Treaty of Rome, appointment to the Commission is a collective decision of all member governments. In fact, the appointments are usually the result of nominations by individual countries. Those member states that have always had one commissioner normally appoint a member or supporter of the government or majority party. Those states that have in the past had two had their individual arrangements. The usual practice for British governments was to nominate one person each from the Conservative and Labour parties. For the Commission operative from January 2005, the British government selected Peter Mandelson.

The Commission is a supranational body and those appointed to the Commission must forget their national origins and serve only the Community. Newly appointed commissioners swear an oath of independence, undertaking that they shall 'neither seek nor take instructions from any government or from any other body'. Furthermore: 'Each Member State undertakes to respect this principle and not to seek to influence the members of the Commission'.[3] While it is only natural that commissioners maintain links with former colleagues at home and remain sympathetic to their own country's interests, the Commission cannot function if its members are too preoccupied with national loyalties. On the whole, they are community-minded, often to the despair of the governments that appointed them. Margaret Thatcher chided her commissioners for their failure to represent the viewpoint of her administrations. As a former British commissioner, Sir Leon Brittan, said: 'I may be a British Conservative but I do not agree with the Conservative government on many European questions'.[4]

Commissioners are given a portfolio, which is to say that they are placed in charge of some function of the Commission's work such as health and consumer protection or development and humanitarian aid. In that respect they are rather like government ministers, although with greater freedom. As Brittan is quoted as saying in the article referred to above: 'Commissioners do have somewhat greater personal political autonomy than a cabinet minister – you do not have to clear things with the top'.

To assist them, commissioners have a small group of aides or advisers known as a *cabinet*. The word here is used in its French sense and would be better translated into English as 'private office'. The members of a *cabinet* are mostly civil servants who have been seconded, either from the commissioner's own national civil service or from another part of the EU's bureaucracy. Members of the *cabinet* are often fellow-nationals of the commissioner, although convention expects at least one to be from another member state. One of the first moves made by Romano Prodi on taking office as president in 1999 was to state that he wanted his commissioners' *cabinets* to be truly international and not packed with officials and cronies from the commissioners' own countries. As an example, Prodi initially appointed an Irishman, David O'Sullivan, as his own *chef de cabinet*. Later, O'Sullivan was replaced by a Frenchman and then by an Italian.

The president of the Commission

The president of the Commission is appointed by the European Council after a process of bargaining between the heads of governments. These leaders will be made aware of the views of the EP on the candidates for nomination and, since ratification of the Maastricht Treaty, the EP has had to approve the choice of the president and the Commission en bloc. The Santer Commission was the first to be endorsed in this way and the same procedures applied when the Prodi Commission began its work. Recent presidents, periodically allluded to in this volume, are listed in Table 3.1.

Before Maastricht the original rules stated that a new president should be chosen from the ranks of the existing commissioners. This was never a practical possibility since the office is so important that member governments need to spend a long time in consideration of the choice: it would be impossible to wait until an entirely new Commission was in place before beginning the selection process. As it is, the process of lobbying and negotiation begins well over a year

Table 3.1   *The five most recent Presidents of the Commission since 1985*

President	Nationality	Dates in office
Jacques Delors	French	1985–1995
Jacques Santer	Luxembourgian	1995–1999
Manuel Marin	Spanish	1999 (interim)
Romano Prodi	Italian	1999–2004
José Barroso	Portuguese	2004–

in advance of appointment, the nominee traditionally being announced at the European Council held in the June prior to the January appointment. A convention has grown up over the years under which the office of president alternates between citizens of large and small countries, and between representatives of the right and left. Normally the appointment is tacitly agreed between the member states before the European Council meets to announce the appointment, but there have been two occasions when this preliminary agreement has not been reached. On both occasions, the chosen candidate was vetoed by one country, Britain. In 1984 the French candidate, Claude Cheysson, was vetoed by Margaret Thatcher (ironically enough to be replaced by Jacques Delors) and in 1994 the Belgian Jean-Luc Dehaene was vetoed by John Major. At the Brussels Council in 2004 Britain made it clear that it would not accept the preferred French and German choice (the Belgian prime minister, Guy Verhofstadt, who withdrew from the race) and France responded by taking the same view of the existing British commissioner (Chris Patten), whose name had been under discussion (see p. 67).

Although possessing limited powers, the president of the Commission is the nearest thing the EU currently has to a head of government. Probably the true head is the president of the European Council but, since that post has circulated on a six-monthly rota, the president of the Commission is a more clearly identifiable figurehead for the EU as a whole. At the summit in Brussels (2004) it was decided that the EU should have a president of the Council who is in place for at least two and a half years, so in effect would be the key figure in the EU who provides continuity to policy, chairs meetings and ensures that decisions are acted upon. Nonetheless, the presidency of the Commission remains a prestigious and potentially influential position.

The definition of the president's role is sufficiently vague as to allow a strong personality to dictate their own agenda. Delors was strong, while Prodi also came into office aiming to create a quasi-prime ministerial role for himself, heading a cabinet-style administration in which he had the powers to fire or reshuffle individual members of the College of Commissioners.[5]

The more easily identified duties of the president of the Commission are:

- to chair weekly meetings of the College of Commissioners at which proposals are adopted, policies finalised and decisions taken;
- to co-ordinate the work of the various commissioners – an even more arduous task than it might appear since they often have partisan interests and ideological positions at variance with those of the president;
- to allocate portfolios at the start of a new Commission, a process that requires all the president's skills of negotiation and political judgment since there is always a shortage of portfolios, or at least a shortage of important portfolios, compared with the number of personnel available (one of the fascinations of the Jenkins' diary[6] is the picture he paints of the months of negotiation involved in fixing jobs for the commissioners);

- to represent the Commission with other institutions of the EU, including giving an annual state of the union address to the EP, and attending and participating in meetings of the European Council (at these meetings the president has the same status as other heads of government);
- to represent the EU at international gatherings such as the G8 economic summits;
- to give a sense of direction to the supranational development of the EU: strong presidents can give a real impetus to policy initiatives, in the way that the Delors Plan would lead to the single market, monetary union and the Maastricht Treaty.

The bureaucracy

About half the staff employed by the EU serve with the Commission. Despite the public perception of a massive bureaucracy, the Commission's staff of about 24,000 people[7] is actually remarkably small, being no larger than the average government ministry in one of the member states or the administrative staff of a large municipal authority, such as Barcelona.[8] Only around 4,000 personnel are involved in policy-making positions. Many are involved in the work of translation and interpretation. Although the Commission's working languages are French and English, there are larger meetings where interpreters are required and, of course, all documents of record must be issued in all the twenty official languages of the EU – all citizens having the right to know of, and have access to, the workings of the EU. As a result, almost 3,000 staff are involved in the translation and interpreting services. A 1994 survey, conducted by a pressure group promoting Esperanto as a universal language for the EU, found that the EU generates more than three million words a day at a cost in translation and interpretation of £1.2 billion a year.

Commission staff are permanently employed and mostly appointed on merit. In the case of senior or specialised potential appointees, that merit is judged by means of a highly competitive open examination. There is a career structure and most promotions are internal, but the ever-present question of national jealousies prevents the organisation being truly meritocratic. Something in the nature of a national quota system does exist, at least for those senior administrators who can initiate legislation, and it is still not unknown for outsiders to be seconded from their national civil services into the service of the Commission in order to preserve the balance of nationalities.

The Commission administration is divided into twenty-three policy responsibilities, similar to government ministries, each headed by a director-general. These directorates-general are not known by their area of responsibility but by a Roman numeral preceded by DG for directorate-general: hence DGVI for agriculture, DGXVI for regional policy, and so on. The normal hierarchical structure divides the directorates-general into directorates and the directorates into divisions. The pattern is not uniform, however, because the size of the directorates-general varies so much: DGIX for example, which deals with budgetary matters, has a staff of more than 2,500, while DGXXII, dealing with structural policy, has a staff of less than 60. Some of the smaller directorates-general have directorates but no divisions, while others have divisions but no directorate. Each director-general is answerable to a commissioner but there is no precise match between the areas of responsibility given to the directorates-general and the portfolios given to commissioners. Liaison between the College of Commissioners and the directorates-general is through the six officials forming each individual commissioner's *cabinet* or private office:

> The Commission is the archetypal multi-organisation, with each directorate-general anxious to preserve its own territory. This produces a chronic lack of co-ordination, and plenty of jurisdictional fights. The style and attitude of directorates can vary enormously and can change over time according to the nationality and personality of the director-general.[9]

Apart from the directorates-general there is quite a sizeable section of Commission staff that is organised into twelve or more specialised service units, such as the translation and interpreting services mentioned above.

The tasks and duties of the Commission

The most important duty carried out by the Commission is the drafting of policy documents for discussion and decision by the Council of Ministers, its remit being to initiate and formulate those policies that will promote the aims for which the European Communities were founded. The Commission is not the only source of policy to be presented to the Council, but the majority of issues discussed in the latter can only be accepted if they have been framed by the former. Apart from this task, the Commission has the following responsibilities:

- It has an executive role after policy decisions have been made and will issue the regulations, directives and instructions by which Community decisions are executed in the member states. The Commission issues something like 5,000 of these legislative instruments each year, although most of them deal with very minor matters, such as price levels for a single commodity in the CAP.
- It is responsible for preparing the EU's annual budget and for the management of EU finances, including the various structural funds
- It monitors the actions of member states in obeying and carrying out Community law. In the event of non-compliance or deliberate law-breaking, it is up to the Commission to demand obedience or, if the offence continues, to prosecute the country or organisation through the European Court of Justice.

- It has the ability to determine policies and actions in some areas. As a result of certain clauses in the Maastricht Treaty, there are particular areas of responsibility such as competition, agriculture and trade policy over which the Commission is autonomous and able to take decisions without consulting the Council of Ministers.
- Commissioners and senior Commission staff must attend meetings of the EP and its committees. Commissioners must answer questions from MEPs as well as attend, and even participate in, debates which deal with the subject of the commissioner's portfolio.
- The Commission is represented and participates in the work of various international bodies such as the United Nations, the General Agreement on Tariffs and Trade, the Council of Europe and the OECD.
- It deals on behalf of the EU with diplomatic relations with non-member countries. In the same way that a country receives ambassadors from foreign countries, the Commission deals with diplomatic missions from over 125 foreign countries accredited to the EU. On the other side of the same coin the Commission itself maintains diplomatic relations with nearly a hundred non-member states. Through the Lomé Convention the Commission regulates relations between the EU and the developing countries of Africa, the Caribbean and Pacific (ACP).
- It acts as the first check on new applications for membership of the EU. On receipt of such an application the Commission is asked to conduct an enquiry into all the implications of that application. Negotiations can only begin with the Commission's approval.

In pursuance of its tasks, the Commission held some 44 meetings in 2001, presenting some 456 directives, regulations and decisions for adoption by the Council of Ministers. In addition, it presented 297 communications and reports on EU activities and produced four White and six Green Papers.[10]

The European Parliament

Until 1979 the European Parliament was composed of delegates nominated by their national governments in the same proportions as the various parties were represented in their national parliaments; many members had 'dual mandate' membership of both European and national parliaments. At the European Council in Paris (1974), it was decided to bring into force the provision for direct elections that had been written into the Treaty of Rome. This may have increased the legitimacy of the EP but it did not produce any strengthening of its powers. Indeed, throughout its life, via discussions in the Council of Ministers and the European Council, member states have sought to hold back the powers of the EP, because of their fear that any strengthening of the EP would weaken the sovereignty of national parliaments.

The EP has had three locations:

1 the Assembly Chamber for plenary sessionsin Strasbourg;
2 the committees structure in Brussels;
3 the General Secretariat in Luxembourg.

There used to be an Assembly Chamber in Luxembourg (it was the Assembly of the ECSC), but this was abandoned when the size of the EP doubled on the introduction of direct elections. The Strasbourg Chamber in turn became too small in 1994, not only because of the addition of forty-nine MEPs to allow for German reunification but also because a further increase was pending due to the accessions of new member states in 1995. Many MEPs wanted to end their nomadic existence by transferring the plenary sessions to Brussels, where there are ample facilities in the new parliament buildings. However, as was said at the time, 'this possibility is being blocked by the French government which intends to force through the construction of a new parliament building in Strasbourg for the benefit of la Gloire'.[11] The French government refused to ratify procedural matters relating to German reunification unless the EP agreed to continue meeting in the new Strasbourg buildings. It had its way and the prestigiously modern parliament building was completed and opened in time to welcome the intake from the 1999 elections.

Currently, there are 732 MEPs, a figure due to rise to 786 with the arrival of Bulgaria and Romania in 2007. An MEP spends one week of every month in plenary session and between one and two weeks in every month on committee work. The rest of the time is spent working within the political group to which they belong (see chapter 7), travelling with an EP delegation on a fact-finding mission, or consulting with EP officials in Luxembourg. Some MEPs, including the British, also do a certain amount of constituency work. In the Assembly Chamber, Commissioners deliver reports, there are debates and also a question time: the plenary session quite often votes, using electronic means to do so. Yet there seems to be little interest in the debates: the perpetual language problem means that speeches are deprived of oratory or humour, and the sessions becoming uniformly dull and boring as a result. Much of the important work is done in committee, each MEP being assigned either to one of the twenty or so standing committees or to an ad hoc specialised committee. These have an important input into the legislative process, since committee members draft reports on proposed legislation and put forward amendments.

The EP works closely with the Commission on proposed legislation but finds the Council less sympathetic. About 75 per cent of EP amendments are accepted by the Commission, whereas less than 20 per cent get past the Council into final legislation. This is part of the EP's 'democratic deficit' in that – up until now – no one has been legally obliged to listen to what the EP has to say and decisions have often been simply ignored by the Council of Ministers. A fuller account of the EP's role in the legislative process can be found in chapter 5.

Powers of the European Parliament

Parliament has several functions, the powers being supervisory (control), legislative and budgetary. In all these areas, the powers have increased, in some more than others. Key responsibilities include:

- the right to vote on the accession of new member states;
- the right to be consulted by the Council of Ministers on the granting of associate status to other countries;
- the power to reject or amend Council decisions on matters relating to the single market – a move that can only be reversed by a unanimous vote of the Council if a proposal is rejected, or by qualified majority if it is an amendment;
- [most importantly] the ability to reject the EU's budget in its entirety or to amend any part of the budget that does not relate to a provision required by treaty.

The Commission must report to the EP every month and the EP has the ultimate weapon of being able to dismiss the entire Commission (although it cannot dismiss individual commissioners) on a two-thirds majority. The Maastricht Treaty also gave the EP the right to pass a vote of confidence or non-confidence in an incoming Commission. These rights were exercised to the full during the controversy surrounding the Santer Commission in 1999 and again in October 2004 (see Box 3.1).

Box 3.1
Parliament and the Commission: the cases of Santer and Buttiglione

In 1998–99, serious allegations of fraud and impropriety against individual commissioners, including former French premier, Edith Cresson, began to surface. The resulting damage to the reputation of the College of Commissioners provoked a trial of strength between Parliament and the Commission. Individual commissioners cannot strictly speaking be dismissed. Parliament's only sanction is to dismiss the body in its entirety. Yet a vote of censure on the Commission in general was defeated by only 293–232 votes.

Following an independent review, there were further allegations of fraud and lax management 'at the highest level', implicating Santer personally in the developing scandal. An outraged Parliament demanded and obtained the resignation of the Santer Commission, *en masse*.

A further tussle between the Commission and Parliament occurred in 2004, following Italy's nomination of Rocco Buttiglione as its new commissioner. a God-fearing Christian Democrat minister, he had in the past expressed strong, contentious views on homosexuality and the role of women. He repeated some of them before the EP, when it was faced with the task of approving would-be members of the Barroso Commission. Parliament made it clear it would not endorse the Commission if Buttiglione's name was included. Barruso withdrew his nominated team, Italy withdrew the nomination and a modified list of nominees proved acceptable to Parliament.

Parliament makes the most of its limited powers. It is much derided for its weakness, critics often being disparaging about its status as a 'talking shop'. In comparison with many national parliaments, it is a weak body, having originally been only a consultative assembly. But every recent treaty change (see Table 3.3 on p. 92) has enlarged its role in EU decision making and in several areas it shares equal power with the Council in formulating legislation. Even in the 1980s, when it lacked the power of co-decision, it was able to employ procedural devices to enable it to exert greater influence than it actually possessed – in particular, the power of delay. At that time, the Council of Ministers could not vote on proposed legislation until it received Parliament's opinion. Elizabeth Bomberg and Alexander Stubb have illustrated the way in which 'the EP might suggest to the Council that an Opinion could not possibly be delivered in a timely way . . . unless, of course, the Council wished to rethink its opposition to certain amendments favoured by the EP'.[12] In other words, this is a parliament that has proved skilful in extracting maximum influence from limited formal powers.

The introduction of direct elections marked a significant step towards reducing the EP's democratic deficit, but an important contributory factor to that deficit remains – the apathy of the public in several member states. The people not only seem uninterested in the workings of the EP but they are also universally ignorant as to the function and identity of MEPs. Moreover, with the exception of those countries such as Belgium where voting is compulsory, turnout in European elections is pitifully small, while the issues on which people vote have more to do with national rather than with European factors. 'This places the EP in a legitimacy bind: it claims to represent the people of Europe, but the people of Europe demonstrate little interest in its activities'.[13] We shall return to the subject of European elections, parties and voting behaviour in chapter 7.

The European Court of Justice

The Court of Justice, based in Luxembourg, is not to be confused with the European Court of Human Rights, which meets in Strasbourg and is part of the machinery of the Council of Europe. The latter has nothing to do with the EU, even though all member states of the EU have signed the European Convention of Human Rights. The Court of Justice is exclusively concerned with the administration of Community law.

The Court is made up of twenty-five judges appointed by common agreement of the member states for a renewable term of six years: continuity over those six years is assured by a staggered replacement over a three-year cycle. Judges are nominated for appointment by the member states, those nominated being individuals whose independence is beyond doubt and who have usually either held high judicial office in their own countries or who are international jurists of a known competence. The judges choose one of their members to act as president of the Court, with a three-year term of office. The presiding judge administers the work of the Court, in particular assigning cases to specific panels of judges and appointing the individual judge-rapporteurs who will be in charge of those panels. Nine advocates general, also appointed by mutual agreement between member states, are in charge of collecting documentary and other evidence for presentation to the judges, together with their own conclusions and legal judgments.

Because of the pressure of business as the Community grew, a second court, the Court of First Instance, was introduced in September 1989 in order to deal with the consequences of the Single European Act and specifically in order to protect individual interests. This innovation allowed the Court of Justice to concentrate on the interpretation of Community law. The Court of First Instance also has twenty-five judges as members, but does not have advocates general, one of the judges acting in the capacity of advocate if required.

Cases can be brought before the Court by the institutions of the EU or by member states. Possibly the most frequent are cases brought by the Commission against member states for non-compliance with EU directives or regulations. Cases can, however, be brought by individuals or organisations who feel that their national governments are penalising them in breach of Community law, although these cases are usually held before the Court of First Instance. Many cases are referred to the European Court after they have failed on appeal in the national courts, but the Luxembourg judges emphasise that they are not a court of appeal: the only valid basis for appeal against a member state's national courts is in situations where there has been a misinterpretation of Community law by those courts.

Actual court actions, however, only form part of the Court's duties. More than half the work done by the Court arises from requests by member states for clarification or interpretation of some aspect of Community law.

Only the most important cases, involving the EU institutions or member states, are heard before a full plenary Court, for which the quorum is seven judges. Most cases are heard in chambers before a panel of three judges in most cases, or five for more complex matters. Cases in the Court of First Instance are heard before any one of five chambers, each of which has a panel of three or five judges, although plenary sessions can be held for certain important cases.

The Court of Justice has five areas of competence:

1 rulings on the treaties which form the basis of the EU – Treaty of Paris, the two Treaties of Rome, the SEA, the Maastricht, Amsterdam and Nice Treaties;
2 regulation of any international agreements made by the EU;
3 any problems arising from EU regulations;
4 any problems arising from EC directives;
5 rulings on decisions made by the Commission.

As we have seen, the Court of First Instance deals with more routine matters, including breaches of competition rules and disputes between the EU and its staff.

In a direct action, the applicant chooses the language in which the case is heard, while cases referred by a national court use the language of that national court. For clarity and to avoid errors with a possible eleven languages in use, most pleadings and submissions are initially made in writing. It is only at the end of a long written phase that cases are argued orally in open court. At the end of the hearing, it is the advocate general assigned to the case who sums up the arguments submitted, interprets the relevant law and recommends a decision. The opinion of the advocate general is not binding on the Court but it is very influential. The panel of judges consider the matter in closed session and then deliver judgement in open court. The text of the judgement includes the reasoning behind the decision and is then published in full, in all eleven languages of the EU.

Since the Court began as an institution of the ECSC in 1954, it has heard well over 9,000 cases and delivered more than 4,000 judgements. However, for the average individual or small business the Court of Justice is far too expensive (legal aid is not available) and the process is far too slow, even urgent cases taking two years to reach judgement.

The Council of Ministers

The twenty-five-strong Council of Ministers is the decision-making body of the EC with a crucial role in the legislative process, although the Maastricht Treaty increased the role of the European Parliament through the co-decision procedure. However, to use the term 'Council of Ministers' as though there was only one institution of that name would be misleading. The treaties refer to one Council, but there are, in fact, as many as twenty-five different ones, because the type of minister present varies according to the subject-matter of the meeting – transport ministers will meet to discuss transport policy, energy ministers to discuss energy, and so on. If there is such a thing as the definitive Council of Ministers it is the General Affairs Council, which is made up of foreign ministers from the member countries. It has the widest brief, dealing with general policy issues rather than foreign affairs. Another important council is the Ecofin Council, made up of the economic and finance ministers and obviously dealing with matters such as EMU. The other councils – transport, energy, etc. – are known generically as technical councils. In each case, there is one – relevant – representative from each member state.

There are Council meetings throughout the year, normally convening in Brussels, although meetings are held in Luxembourg during April, June and October. As an example of how busy the programme can be, there were eighty-four formal ministerial meetings in the year 2001. The General Affairs Council, the Ecofin Council and the Agricultural Ministers' Council accounted for thirty-

eight of them. Whereas they meet at least monthly, some of the minor technical councils may not meet more than once or twice a year. Meetings seldom last
more than one day and, even if the meeting extends over two days, it is usually
from lunchtime to lunchtime. (Of course, advisory groups and working parties
continue to operate between meetings and some groups, especially the foreign
and finance ministers, will meet informally outside Brussels, perhaps within
the context of a social weekend). In the year of the last British presidency
(January–June 1998), there were – in addition to the European Council meeting in Cardiff – forty-three meetings of the Council of Ministers. In the case of
the technical councils, some met on only a handful or less occasions.

Leadership of the Council is vested in the presidency of the EU – a position
that has in the past rotated among member states, each holding the responsibility for a period of six months (see Table 3.2). During their tenure, ministers
of the country holding the presidency called Council meetings, decided the
agenda, introduced initiatives and took the chair for all Council meetings. The
position of president is a key one in the affairs of the EU, for as Martin Westlake
observes: 'the modern presidency is at one and the same time, manager, pro-
moter of political initiatives, package broker, representative to and from the
other Community institutions, spokesman for the Council and for the Union,
and an international actor'.[14] If the changes agreed at Brussels (2004) are
implemented, the Council will no longer rotate from 2007, a more permanent
figure having been selected from among the heads of the member states.

The Secretariat and Coreper

There is a vast bureaucratic input into Council meetings from a number of
sources, including the 2,000 members of the General Secretariat. Headed by the
secretary-general, they have an important role in brokering deals and crafting
compromises. Their duties in servicing the Council involve, among other things:

- preparing for meetings
- keeping records and giving advice
- providing all the services that might be looked for in civil servants
- providing some services peculiar to the European situation, such as the need
  to translate working documents into all eleven official languages.

Table 3.2   *The rotating European presidency*

Year	January–June	July–December
2002	Spain	Denmark
2003	Greece	Italy
2004	Ireland	Netherlands
2005	Luxembourg	UK
2006	Austria	Finland

Since the responsibility for arranging meetings and agendas lies with the presidency, the Secretariat works closely with the national officials of the state holding the presidency, the numbers of such national officials seconded to Brussels always increasing substantially during the relevant six months. The size of the supporting Secretariat turns Council meetings into very large affairs. Roy Jenkins claimed that the room in which the Council of Ministers met reminded him of a crowded aircraft hangar.

Of considerable importance in the policy and decision-making processes of the Community is the body known as Coreper (Committee of Permanent Representatives of Member States). These are the diplomatic missions sent by member states to the Community. While civil servants seconded to the Commission must forget their national loyalties, and civil servants accompanying ministers to Council meetings are transient, the senior British diplomat sent to Brussels as permanent representative (UKREP) ensures the continuous representation of British national interests at all times. The permanent representative has a large staff including a delegation of up to forty officials, most drawn from Foreign and Commonwealth Office staff, but with other policy areas also represented.

Coreper was originally set up to hammer out the details written into the 1957 Treaty of Rome, meeting informally, but was recognised as an official organ of the Community by the Merger Treaty of 1965 when a definition of Coreper's duties was written into the treaty and all its subsequent amendments: 'A committee consisting of the Permanent Representatives of the Member States shall be responsible for preparing the work of the Council and for carrying out the tasks assigned to it by the Council.'[15] The committee is not only a vital part of the legislative process but is the principal channel of communication between the institutions of the Community and national governments.

Coreper has developed into one of the most powerful groups of officials in the world. Over the years the committee has begun to devolve some of its duties to specialists and, as a result, now comprises literally hundreds of officials, splitting for convenience in 1962 into two bodies, Coreper I and II. Coreper II was designated the senior, dealing with key political issues such as economic and financial policy, defence and foreign affairs. Its core membership comprises the twenty-five permanent representatives, while Coreper I became a forum for their deputies. The Council of Agricultural Ministers incidentally does not use Coreper but has its own Special Committee on Agriculture (SCA) made up of Brussels-based representatives of the member states who meet at least weekly.

The two committees into which Coreper is divided are responsible for:

- keeping the EU's institutions and the governments and bureaucracies of the member states informed of each others' work;
- ensuring that national and European policy are not at loggerheads;
- finding compromises so as not to undermine core national positions.

In practice these different functions are difficult to separate and merge into a more general aim of keeping the EU working smoothly.[16]

Westlake's analysis of the Council at work suggests that 80 per cent of its business is conducted in working parties, 10 per cent in Coreper, 5 per cent in the Council and 5 per cent in corridors. Coreper and the vast number of working groups therefore account for the bulk of the background, preparatory work.[17] This points to the importance of the corridors within the Justus Lipsius Council building in Brussels. They are a hive of activity and the location of much bargaining and compromise. They make it possible for the formal Council meetings to reach agreed decisions more easily.

Voting in the Council

There are three ways in which the Council of Ministers can vote to take a decision: by unanimous vote, by simple majority or by qualified majority. Originally, decisions of the Council needed to be unanimous, in effect giving a dissenting state the veto, a fact exploited by de Gaulle in the 1960s. The Luxembourg Compromise of 1966 reduced the need for unanimity, extending the number of issues that could be settled by qualified majority. Since then there has been a steady extension of qualified majority voting (QMV), most significantly as a result of the Single European Act.

In pillar one of the Maastricht Treaty, unanimity is still required for:

- all new policies;
- amendments to the policy issues of taxation and industry;
- matters relating to regional and social funds;
- where the Council wishes to agree or amend a policy against the wishes of the Commission.

Since Luxembourg in 1966 the member states have additionally insisted on retaining the right to veto any decision they can claim was against their national interests. However, the veto is usually regarded as being like a nuclear deterrent, held in reserve but never used. The Major government nonetheless decided that its use was justified as a result of the impasse reached over BSE (see pp. 171–3).

For the other two pillars created by the Maastricht Treaty – the common foreign and security policy (pillar two) and justice and home affairs (pillar three) – the Council has the sole right to act as decision maker and unanimity is the rule.

It is QMV that is the most contentious of the voting methods, since it is directly related to the question of states' rights and the comparative strengths of small and large states within the Community. Under QMV the member states are given so many votes each, with a token acknowledgement of the comparative size of the member states. From the start it was agreed that for a decision to be passed it would require in the region of 70 per cent of the votes, representing something like 60 per cent of the population of the Community. The votes are distributed in such a way that the large countries acting together cannot out-vote the smaller, needing the combination of two major countries and at least one more to block the decision-making process.

The weighting given to individual states is of critical importance, and has been a matter of fierce controversy whenever there was an enlargement. It has proved a vexed topic in a series of IGCs and was a major issue to be resolved before the latest increase in membership in May 2004. Under the arrange-ments painfully negotiated at Nice, the revised figures are as given in Table 3.3. A 'triple lock' operates under which any decision requires that three criteria be fulfilled:

- A QMV decision must have 71.3 per cent of the votes (74 per cent following the next enlargement to twenty-seven states).
- QMV must be supported by a majority of the member states.
- Any individual member state may require confirmation of a 'demographic test', namely that the QMV represents at least 62 per cent of the EU population.

Table 3.3   *QMV in the enlarged EU*

Countries	Number of votes
France, Germany, Italy, UK	29
Poland, Spain	27
Netherlands	13
Belgium, Czech Republic, Greece, Hungary, Portugal	12
Austria, Sweden	10
Denmark, Finland, Ireland, Lithuania, Slovakia	7
Cyprus, Estonia, Latvia, Luxembourg, Slovenia	4
Malta	3

Note: The proposed new entrants, Bulgaria and Romania, will each have 10 and 14 votes. In effect, there is currently a blocking minority of 90/321 votes; 91 after the next expansion of the EU.

In the 1990s majority voting was very seldom used by the Council of Minis-ters, even in areas where QMV is expected. The Council preferred to give the appearance of unanimity by continuing discussion overnight or over successive meetings until a compromise on a consensus decision was reached. In 1994, for example, only about 14 per cent of legislation adopted by the Council was subjected to contested voting.[18] But every new treaty has expanded the policy areas in which QMV operates, both Nice and the new constitution each adding some thirty additional issues subject to its provisions. Today, it can be applied on around three quarters of all legislation and is regarded as the norm in matters concerned with the single market and any issues related to the clarification and implementation of existing law and policies. Yet still, although any member state can call for its use, the Council prefers to seek agreement on policies. Members are aware that the taking of a formal vote can be divisive and a cause of resentment. This may make it more difficult to work together in the future.

Simple majority voting, with each state allowed one vote, is not allowed on policy or legislative proposals. Its use is mainly confined to procedural matters.

The European Council

Throughout the 1960s the heads of government of each of the member states of the EEC met from time to time in what were largely unofficial and informal summits. In the early 1970s, however, after the first enlargement, a feeling grew that there was a lack of leadership. The institutions of the EC coped well enough with detailed policy but there was no focus of authority to give direction and purpose to future developments. Following an initiative of Giscard d'Estaing and Helmut Schmidt, it was proposed at the Paris Summit in 1974 that the occasional summit meetings should be formally institutionalised.

The term 'European Council' first appeared in the Single European Act of 1986, which had just one article setting out its composition and the frequency of its meetings. At that time there was no definition of the body's functions, clarification only coming with the Treaties of Maastricht in 1993 and Amsterdam in 1999. However, since the European Union became established through these treaties, the European Council gained a particular importance as the sole body which links, co-ordinates and integrates the three separate pillars of the EU. In Article D of the Treaty of Maastricht, the role of the European Council is laid down as being to 'provide the Union with the necessary impetus for its development and shall define the general political guidelines thereof'.

The Council still does not form part of the legal framework of the EU. It cannot legislate unless it transforms itself for the purpose into an extraordinary meeting of the Council of Ministers, and decisions of the European Council are not subject to the jurisdiction of the Court of Justice. It is a political body, whose role has dramatically grown in importance. In many recent meetings, the assembled heads of state and government have resolved issues left undecided elsewhere and provided that leadership that Giscard and Schmidt had in mind. The Council sets the agenda for future developments, and the major initiatives on treaty reform, direct elections, monetary union and the creation of a Rapid Reaction Force have been set in motion at this level.

The European Council meets at least twice a year, the meeting usually being held in the final month of each six-month presidency and hosted by the country holding the presidency at that time. The meetings of the European Council have therefore come to represent a public statement on the performance of the presiding country during its half-year tenure. Since most member states now aim to satisfy some objective during their presidency, European Council meetings can be seen as passing judgement on the achievement of those objectives. During the UK's presidency in the second half of 1992 it was Britain's stated

Table 3.4   *The Treaties and institutional change*

Treaty	European Council	Council of Ministers	Commission	Parliament	Court of Justice
Rome	N/A: non-existent	Granted powers to pass legislation, appoint Commission and agree budget	Able to propose legislation, draft budget, act as guardian of the treaty	Right to be consulted on legislation and to dismiss Commission en bloc	Guardian of EC treaties and of EC law
SEA	Acquired legal status	Use of QMV in areas related to single market	Granted right of initiative in new areas, re single market	Co-operative procedure introduced, extending legislative authority	Court of First Instance created
Maastricht	Granted responsibility for determining general guidelines of the Community	Extensions to QMV; able to propose legislation under second and third pillars	Increased powers in relation to EMU and foreign policy	Co-decision introduced in limited range of policy areas: stronger role re appointment of Commission	Granted powers to impose fines on member states, but not in second and third pillars
Amsterdam	Confirmed role in EMU and strengthened its position re CSFP	Extensions to QMV and powers of co-decision with Parliament	President's role strengthened	Extensions to co-decision. Granted rights of approval over choice of president and Commission	Granted jurisdiction over third pillar (justice and home affairs)
Nice	Location moved to Brussels	Extensions of QMV, plus reweighting of votes to the advantage of larger states	President's role strengthened: changes to size of Commission, to cater for enlargement from 2005	Extensions to co-decision, plus right to place matters before Court on same basis as Council and Commission	Further sharing of tasks with Court of First Instance: more chambers created to improve judicial capacity in larger EU

Source: Adapted from E. Bomberg and A. Stubb, *The European Union: How Does it Work?*, Oxford University Press, 2003.

aim to amend the Maastricht Treaty to satisfy the doubts of countries such as the Britain and Denmark, this being accomplished at Edinburgh with the strengthening of opt-out clauses and the doctrine of subsidiarity.

Council meetings have become something of a public relations exercise for European political leaders. They provide an opportunity for those involved to gain much media publicity and are a source of excellent photo opportunities. Staging a successful Council meeting where long-standing and difficult issues are resolved or new initiatives launched, confers particular prestige on the host country. As a result, considerable amounts of time and money can be spent on the two days of the Council. The Edinburgh Summit in 1992, for example, cost the British government £9 million.[19]

In addition to the prominent politicians, many other people are 'in town' for Council meetings. Attendance at Council sessions is restricted, but the two-day gathering as a whole involves the coming together of a very large number of other people as well. Each national delegation will consist of about fifty members, not to mention the 2,000 or so journalists, television crews and photographers who wish to be on the premises. Nor should we forget the three interpreters needed for each of the eleven official languages of the EU. Accommodation is always a problem: translation booths were stacked in tiers to fit them into Edinburgh Castle in 1992, while at Fontainebleau in 1984 the typing pool was located in Marie Antoinette's bedroom.

Much of the work of the European Council takes place outside the meeting room. Some of the most important contacts are informal head-to-head meetings between individual leaders, popularly known as 'fireside chats'. Most of the work, however, is accomplished by the officials of the presiding country working alongside officials from the various national delegations. There is always far too much on the agenda for the participants to debate at length. In the months preceding the Council teams of officials will have drawn up papers which they feel will be agreed by the members of the Council. If they are successful, it is only the finer points of detail that need to be discussed in the meeting.

Other EU machinery

The Court of Auditors

The European Court of Auditors is an important institution set up to scrutinise the EC's budget and financial accounts. It has been in existence since 1977 and has increased its visibility and enhanced its reputation over the last decade. Its powers were strengthened at Maastricht, in answer to calls for greater 'transparency' in the EU.

The Court has twenty-five members – one for each member state, and all of them suitably qualified and often being members of an official audit body in their own country. Nominees have to be approved by the Council of Ministers and the EP. Appointment is initially for six years, after which time the appointment can be renewed. From among their number the Court elects one member to act as president for three years.

The duties of the Court of Auditors are quite obviously related to auditing the Community's annual budget and validating the Commission's efficiency in administering that budget. There are groups within the Court of Auditors that deal with specific budgetary questions, such as the CAP or the Regional Fund. Since being revised at Maastricht, the Court has extended its activities away from mere concern over financial rectitude and is more involved in questions of policy effectiveness. To that extent the Court both checks that the legal regulations laid down by the Community are observed and ensures that the EU is getting value for money.

Every institution and body that has access to EU funds is subject to scrutiny. The Court is not restricted to Community institutions but must examine all administrations, national, regional or local, which manage Community funds, whether or not those administrations are member states of the EU. The Court carries out on-the-spot audits in institutions, the member states or even in those countries outside the EU receiving Community funds. The Court of Auditors also produces an annual report each November. This has an important influence on the EP in its annual review of the Commission.

Box 3.2
The problem of fraud in the EU

The expanded workload of the Court of Auditors is a reflection of mounting public concern in recent years over fraud and mismanagement. There have been several examples of serious mismanagement and misconduct, with past examples of fraud including:

- cheating on the VAT payable on used cars;
- mixing illegal imports of cane sugar with legitimate imports of beet sugar;
- claiming money for the same aid project, once from the Commission and then again from member states;
- diverting aid for Kosovo;
- subsidising oranges grown on farms that do not exist;
- claiming money to develop tourist facilities in a region so remote that no tourist is ever likely to visit it.

The amount of fraud is inevitably difficult to quantify, but the EU's own figures suggest that the shortfall in revenue from agricultural levies, customs duties and VAT alone amounts to several hundred million euro per year.

The European Investment Bank

The European Investment Bank (EIB) provides long-term loans for capital investment and is controlled by a board representing all twenty-five member states. Administering a vast loan budget, the EIB is devoted to strengthening the economies of EU member states. To this end it has two principal areas of operation:

- It underpins regional development in the EU, with over half of total lending going towards investment in the less favoured regions of the EU. These loans are made in co-operation with the Commission through the EU's structural funds and cohesion fund
- It finances trans-European networks (TENs) – large-scale and long-term projects in the fields of transport, telecommunications and energy. This investment is designed to help member states strengthen their economies and competitiveness and their capacity to create new jobs to combat unemployment. To assist in the work the EIB, in association with the Commission and the EU's banking sector, has set up the European Investment Fund (EIF).

Although the EIB is principally concerned with lending within the EU, it also assists with the EU's financial involvement with non-member states. The Bank operates in more than a hundred countries, supporting development projects.

The Economic and Social Committee

The Economic and Social Committee (ESC) was written into the Treaty of Rome because it was felt that the then Assembly would not represent fairly the various sectional interests of the Community. The resulting committee has two main functions within the EU. It acts as:

- a forum for special interest groups in the exchange of views and ideas;
- a body that has a minor but integral place in the policy and decision-making process.

Originally the ESC was regarded purely as a consultative body for the Council and Commission, but successive treaties have extended the range of mandatory issues that must be referred to it. In addition, the Amsterdam Treaty allows for the ESC to be consulted by the EP as part of the decision-making process.

The 344 members of the ESC are appointed by their national governments for a renewable four-year term of office, membership being roughly proportional to the size of the member state. Membership of the national delegations can be divided into three broad socio-economic groups:

- **Employers**, of which about half represent industry, the other half being from commercial bodies or services in the public sector.

- **Workers**, i.e. representatives of trade unions.
- **Other interests**, of which about half represent protectionist groups in areas of importance to the EU, such as agriculture and transport, the other half representing special interest groups, such as the environment or consumer affairs.

Members serve as part-time representatives. The ESC meets in plenary session about ten times each year but most of its work is in sub-committee, drawing up opinions and advisory documents. Opinions are delivered each year: they are often well-researched, but may be ignored.

The Committee of the Regions

The Committee of the Regions (COR) is one of the newer Community institutions, set up in the aftermath of Maastricht in order to facilitate the doctrine of subsidiarity; it met for the first time in March 1994. It was established as part of an attempt to bridge the gap between Brussels and citizens of the EU, although anti-federalists claimed that its creation was part of a Brussels plan to undermine the nation-state.

The existence of the Committee reflects the growing importance of the regions in many member countries and, indeed, of the new relationships encouraged by cross-border regions such as the Rhine-Meuse (created from parts of Belgium, Germany and the Netherlands) and the Atlantic Islands Council (created by England, the Scottish Parliament, Welsh National Assembly, Northern Irish Assembly and the Isle of Man).

The COR must be consulted during the legislative process on any matter which it is felt has regional implications, the key issues being identified as trans-European networks, health, education, culture and economic and social cohesion. There are those who would like to see the COR become a directly elected body and form a second chamber in an enlarged and strengthened EP.

Like the ESC, the COR also has 344 members, provided by member states in exactly the same proportions and appointed for a four-year term. The criteria for appointment to the COR differ between member states, largely depending on their degree of decentralisation. As a federal state, Germany is represented by members of the Länder governments. Belgium is also virtually a federation of the Flemish and Walloon communities. Other countries, such as Italy and Spain, are highly regionalised into semi-autonomous regional administrations and these countries draw most of their COR members from the regional governments. More centralised states such as Britain have traditionally appointed COR members from the ranks of mayors of cities or chairmen of county councils. The Scottish Parliament, and Northern Irish and Welsh Assemblies each have two members.

The COR meets in Brussels for five plenary sessions a year. Again, much of its work is done through a structure of seven standing committees, covering areas such as:

- regional policy, structural funds, cross-border and inter-regional co-operation;
- agriculture, rural development and fisheries;
- urban issues, energy and the environment.

As with the ESC, members are keen to belong to it, but often lament its lack of influence. Its internal divisions and the nature of its membership (deriving from large, autonomous bodies but also smaller local councils), combine to mean that as yet it has not fulfilled all the high hopes of those who devised it. But it remains a useful channel of communication between the various units of government across the EU.

For Britain, the major significance of the COR has lain in its work for those regions such as Scotland or Wales that have gained their own devolved machinery. The COR is useful in gaining EU structural funds for the regions and can also work to exempt the regions from blanket measures aimed at national governments. For example, both Wales and Scotland wished to be treated differently from England over beef production during the BSE crisis.

The Ombudsman

The idea of appointing an Ombudsman for the EU was first mooted at Maastricht but, because of 'procedural delays', no appointment was made until 1995, when Jacob Söderman, a Finn, was appointed. The Ombudsman's purpose is to reconcile the interests of EU citizens and EU institutions, by providing for a thorough investigation of any accusation of maladministration on the part of any EU institution other than the Court of Justice. The appointee has wide-ranging powers of inquiry, the EU institutions being required to hand over all the documents and other evidence that he or she might demand of them. If maladministration is discovered, the Ombudsman:

- reports in full to the institution concerned and makes recommendations for correcting the fault;
- can also refer the case to the EP for further action.

In the first year of operation the Ombudsman and his staff dealt with nearly 700 complaints, the largest number of which came from Britain. Most, however, were ruled to be inadmissable. The number of complaints received has increased steadily year by year since the office was established.

The European Central Bank

The European Central Bank (ECB) was instituted in July 1998, at a meeting of the Ecofin Council in Brussels. Prior to that date work on monetary union had been carried out by the European Monetary Institute (EMI) supported by the combined forces of the central banks of all EU members, the European System of Central Banks (ESCB).

Based in Frankfurt, the ECB is intended to serve as a normal central bank for those countries able and willing to participate in monetary union. As such the bank has three main areas of responsibility:

1 the printing, minting, issue and administration of the new euro notes and coins, together with the ultimate withdrawal of the old currencies after the transition to a single currency, which came about on 1 July 2002;
2 the determination of fiscal policy, including the setting of interest rates, for all countries in the 'eurozone';
3 maintaining a watching brief on the suitability for entry of countries currently outside EMU.

The ECB has an executive board and governing council that should be composed solely of representatives from those member states participating in stage three of EMU. But the European Council can give special associate membership to non-participating states, with the UK being keen to maintain observer status. At the head of the ECB is a president who is appointed for eight years.

Foreign affairs, defence and internal security

The institutions described in this chapter have all been first and foremost institutions of the European Community which is only one of the three pillars of the EU, the other two pillars being a common foreign and security policy (CFSP) and a common policy relating to justice, home affairs and internal security. The only institution common to all pillars of the EU is the European Council. For the two pillars created at Maastricht, the TEU had to create new institutions, or rather to rationalise existing ad hoc institutions within a framework of intergovernmental co-operation. These are described in chapter 6 on EU policy areas.

Table 3.5   *The UK and EU institutions*

Country	Total membership	UK membership
The Commission	25	1
The Parliament	732	78
The Court of Justice	25	1
The Council of Ministers	25	1
The European Council	25	1
The Court of Auditors	25	1
The European Investment Bank	25	1
The Economic and Social Committee	344	24
The Committee of the Regions	344	24
The European Central Bank	22	0 (observer only)

The 'democratic deficit'

The term 'democratic deficit' refers to the widely-held belief that there is a lack of democratic control and accountability within the EU. This is said to prevent its institutions from acquiring political legitimacy and widespread recognition and acceptance. Former French president Giscard d'Estaing has gone as far as to suggest that 'if the EU itself applied to join the EU as a member, it would be rejected for being insufficiently democratic . . . The Community cannot continue to be governed according to procedures which are contrary to the imperative requirements it formulates itself in relation to countries which are candidates for membership'.[20]

Such a democratic deficit is not unique to EU machinery, for in most countries there are problems with establishing effective democratic control, associated with:

- falling turn-outs in elections;
- declining membership of political parties;
- a lack of interest in and a distrust of politics and politicians;
- a feeling of disengagement and alienation from the political process.

In other words, there is a developing gap between those who are governed and those who seek to govern them.

In the case of the EU, this gap is a wide one, much concerned with the way in which the Community and then Union emerged. Jean Monnet and his co-founders of the ECSC and the EEC were not primarily concerned with the issue of democratic legitimacy. Their urgent desire was to create the Communities at the earliest opportunity and to ensure that effective supranational practices were in place. Some commentators have spoken of 'rule by technocracy' in the early days.[21] Today, this approach is reinforced by the way in which decisions are agreed in a secretive Council, in the search for agreement and compromise.

In his *Memoirs*, Monnet claimed that he did always envisage a move towards democratisation. He wrote of how 'the pragmatic method we had adopted would also lead to a federation validated by the people's vote'.[22] But Monnet and others like him had a tendency towards elitism – a belief that they understood best what was good for the continent and its inhabitants. Martin Holland has shown how 'Europe was being constructed by a cohesive and remarkably small elite; while public support was welcomed, it was never a prerequisite for Monnet's Europe'.[23]

Europe has developed in a rather open-ended way. The original pioneers were federalists; some being advocates of an immediate federal solution, others being incrementalists who felt that federalism would be achieved by an onwards, step-by-step march towards ever closer integration. No clear boundaries or limits have been set down to this notion of an 'ever closer union', the term having more far-reaching implications than federalism itself, for it implies a never-ending journey in which member states ultimately seek to merge their identities. Federal at least has an end in view and involves a clear division of functions between the centre and individual states.

However, the lack of democracy within the EU is not just about low public interest, poor levels of participation, the way in which an elite imposed its vision of a united Europe upon the people, or the way the Community and then Union have developed. It is much concerned with:

- the way in which institutions operate;
- the lack of democratic control over those who have the power to make decisions.

In a speech in 1994, Sir Leon Brittan, a former British Commissioner, identified 'a widespread sense of unease about Brussels and what it stands for'.[24] He drew attention to:

- the feeling that Brussels was interfering where it should not do so;
- the absence of knowledge of what was going on in the central decision-making bodies;
- the belief that Brussels lacked sufficient democratic legitimacy.

By way of a solution, Brittan urged devolution of decision-making (subsidiarity – see p. 120), transparency (more open and accessible decision making) and more democracy (to overcome the democratic deficit). At Maastricht it was agreed that the new Union should act transparently and in a way that people can understand. Towards the fulfilment of these ends, there has been some progress in recent years. The Council has changed its rules of procedure, so that although debates and votes are held in secret, there is now more information available about the way member states reacted, along with some explanation of the events leading to the final outcome. Some open debates have been held in countries occupying the presidency and the Commission has produced more consultative White and Green Papers, establishing areas for reflection and discussion. In addition, there has been some attempt to open up access to European documentation. Yet still there are complaints about the manner in which the Council (and Coreper in particular) makes its decisions in seclusion, it being one of the few legislative bodies in the democratic world to do so. This seclusion may facilitate the process of reaching a consensual agreement, but it does nothing to reassure commentators and members of the public who are sometimes suspicious of the way in which deals are done.

Brittan's final concern was the lack of democratic legitimacy. Philip Norton, too, has referred to the democratic deficit as 'the limited input into the law-making processes of the European community by directly elected representatives of the people'.[25] To these and other analysts, it is a worrying feature that there is still no very credible system of democratic control within the EU. There is no effective accountability of the Council or Commission to either national Parliaments, or to the European one. Norton has suggested three possible approaches to the problem:

1 strengthening the powers of the European Parliament;

2 creating a new EU institution comprising elected representatives from national parliaments;

3 strengthening the role of national parliaments in the law-making process.

At different times, all three suggestions have been contemplated and they each have their advocates and detractors. As for the first, strengthening the EP, the key step forward was taken in 1979, with the onset of direct elections, although the EP still suffers from a modest turn-out on each occasion when the public has been invited to cast its judgement. There is a case to be made in favour of equipping it with more powers, as it is the only directly elected institution. Indeed in the SEA, at Maastricht and subsequently, it is a body whose power and influence have grown. No longer is it a mere talking shop, although, in Norton's phrase, it is 'still only on the edge of constituting a legislature'. It does have limited powers to exercise supervision or control over the Council, so that – for instance – its assent is required before the Council can approve the accession of new members. It has more powers over the Commission, having to approve the Council's nominee for the presidency, appoint (or not) the whole Commission and sack the entire body in a vote of censure. It has relatively little control over areas of policy such as the CAP, justice and home affairs, and security policy.

Those who strongly criticise the democratic deficit are often the very same people who are most reluctant to make the EP a more effective watchdog – British governments are often particularly keen to ensure that control is firmly maintained in Westminster hands. Any extension of the EP's current role, is therefore, highly contentious.

The creation of a new institution comprising elected representatives from national parliaments is an approach that was urged by Brittan, who believed that '. . . if voters felt their local MPs were lending a hand to the process of Euro-legislation, it would greatly strengthen the EU's democracy and enhance its credibility'.[26] One way of achieving this goal would be the creation of an upper house or senate, made up of people from either chamber in their national state. One of the problems is that this would create a rival body to the existing EP, which is still seeking to establish a greater role for itself. Any such creation might be seen to represent a dilution of the position and importance of the existing body. The outcome may be two relatively weak bodies, instead of one that is becoming more effective.

As British foreign secretary until 2003, Robin Cook[25] was concerned about the separation of European institutions from the people they are meant to represent: 'Our Parliament needs to be part of the project rather than outside of it . . . The European Parliament does a very useful job, but the missing link is tying the national parliaments with the work of Europe'.[27] He advanced an idea to remedy the problem, by involving MPs directly in the running of the EU. He proposed the creation of a second chamber in Europe, made up of MPs from national parliaments, to curb the power of Brussels. The chamber would sift through decisions made in Brussels and block any that meddle in the minutiae of British life.

As we have seen, others take a different view, and feel that the body that should hold this European executive to account is the EP. If directly elected MEPs had genuine powers of scrutiny, this would erase the democratic deficit at an instant. But Cook felt that the problem was that the EP lacks public esteem – that it is national parliaments that are respected. This may be true, but of course if MEPs were given political muscle it might be that voters would then learn to take them more seriously.

Control via national parliaments

Norton notes the view taken by the Danish government a few years ago: 'It must be recognised that a considerable part of what is known as the democratic shortfall is attributable to the fact that apparently not all national parliaments have an adequate say in the decisions at community level'.[28] The Danish chamber, the Folketing, is better placed than others in this respect. It has the reputation of keeping a watchful eye over any European initiatives. In general, the Nordic states have been more successful in devising effective scrutiny and control of the EU, via their domestic legislatures.

From the 1980s onwards, most legislatures have made greater provision for dealing with European legislation and given their MPs or deputies more opportunities to acquire specialised information. In Britain, apart from the committees which have been established in the two chambers of Parliament (for example the House of Lords European Union Committee), there are rare occasions when MEPs are invited to meet with their national colleagues in party committee meetings and informally. Yet keeping up with the burden of work coming from Brussels is a difficult task for the British Parliament, and one that has grown with the preparation for and implementation of the single market. If eventually much foreign and security policy – as well as immigration and policing – are handled in Brussels, the task will be even more daunting.

Alternative means of dealing with the deficit

In most democracies, it is of course via political parties that effective links are established between citizens and their governments. Single party or coalition governments are formed from political parties that compete with one another in periodic general elections. These parties provide a channel of communication through which voters are kept in touch with those who make decisions, for ultimately the electorate has the power to 'throw the rascals out'. Governments have an incentive to carry popular opinion with them, for fear of losing the next election if they become remote from popular aspirations and out of touch.

As yet, there is no European party system, with Europe-wide parties contesting elections, and it is unlikely that any genuinely European parties will emerge in the foreseeable future. If they existed, and had truly transnational membership and programmes, then this would encourage debate on European issues by an EU-wide electorate and provide a clearer link between individuals and those who make decisions. But there is little likelihood that the decision-making machinery of the EU will have cause to respond directly to voters' needs and wishes on an EU basis, in the foreseeable future.

One other channel of communication is via the use of referendums. These have been employed in some countries as a means of claiming popular backing for treaty developments. The problem here is that the outcome of any vote on a single issue may owe more to the standing of the government than to the merits of the case. The issue can become blurred with other factors. In any case, as some countries make little use of the device under any circumstances and have no provision for them, it is unlikely that we shall see anything like a Europe-wide referendum as a means of ascertaining popular feeling.

Conclusion

Some EU policy-making institutions are rather more open than their national counterparts in their mode of operation. But they are not perceived in that way. People detect a large gap between the elites who live in Brussels and elsewhere, and the peoples whose interests they purport to represent. The more they feel this way, the less likely they are to feel inspired to vote.

Bomberg points out that 'supranational systems of governance like the EU pose a dilemma for their citizens, as gains in performance may be at the cost of losses in democratic legitimacy'.[29] She quotes the theorist of democracy, Robert Dahl, who notes a problem affecting large organisations:

> In very small political systems, a citizen may be able to participate extensively in decisions that do not matter much, but cannot participate much in decisions that really matter a great deal; whereas very large systems may be able to cope with problems that matter more to a citizen, but the opportunities for the citizen to participate in and greatly influence decisions are vastly reduced.[30]

Notes

1 N. Nugent, *The Government and Politics of the European Union*, Palgrave, 2003.
2 R. Jenkins (Lord Jenkins), *European Diary 1977–1981*, Collins, 1989.
3 TEU, Title II (amendments to the Treaty of Rome), Article 157, Clause 2.
4 L. Brittan, quoted by John Palmer, *The Guardian*, 23 March 1994.
5 J. Coman, 'Prodi lays foundations for "United States of Europe"', *The Observer*, 11 July 1999.
6 R. Jenkins, as in 2 above.
7 No one source seems able to agree on the exact size of the Commission staff – figures quoted range from 13,000 to 24,000, with the figure chosen depending on variable factors. A. Geddes in *The European Union and British Politics* (Palgrave,

2004) gives 20,000, whereas E. Bomberg and A. Stubb in *The European Union: How Does it Work?* (Oxford University Press, 2003) opt for a lower figure of approximately 15,000. The figure I give is that officially used in literature produced by the Commission itself. It includes all administrative officials, experts, translators, interpreters and secretarial staff. This vagueness, however, does not invalidate the point that, for a busy bureaucracy with wide-ranging responsibilities, the Brussels establishment is in fact very small. Bomberg asserts that within member states the average number of civil servants per 10,000 citizens is 322. For all the EU institutions, the corresponding ratio is 0.8 civil servants per 10,000 citizens.

8 According to figures released in April 1998 the number of civil servants employed by the Department of the Environment, Transport and the Regions totalled 15,215 – almost exactly the same as the numbers given for the Commission. Even the annual budget of i97 billion administered by the Commission is only half the budget spent by the British Department of Social Security. Figures given in C. Pilkington, *The Civil Service in Britain Today*, Manchester University Press, 1999.

9 S. Mazey and J. Richardson, 'Pressure groups and the EC', *Politics Review*, September 1993.

10 A. Geddes, as in 7 above.

11 M. Engel, 'Parliament of snoozers', *The Guardian G2*, 25 January 1994.

12 E. Bomberg and A. Stubb, as in 7 above.

13 A. Geddes, as in 7 above.

14 M. Westlake, *The Council of the European Union*, Harper, 1999.

15 TEU, Title II, Article 151, Clause 1.

16 Details of Coreper are taken from an article by A. Keene in *Europa*, a discussion journal published by the European Commission, 1997.

17 M. Westlake, as in 14 above.

18 Details of voting in the Council of Ministers are taken from the web pages of the Council, to be found within the general Europa website: www.europa.eu.int.

19 A useful insight into the organisation of European Council meetings was provided by a BBC Television documentary showing the workings of the Foreign Office. This programme, *The Minister*, shown on BBC2, 28 April 1994, followed the then minister of European affairs, Tristan Garel-Jones, during Britain's tenure of the presidency in 1992.

20 G. d'Estaing, quoted in W. Nicoll and T. Salmon, *Understanding the European Union*, Longman, 2001.

21 M. Holland, *European Integration: From Community to Union*, Pinter, 1994.

22 J. Monnet, Memoirs, Doubleday & Co., 1978.

23 M. Holland, as in 21 above.

24 L. Brittan, 'Making law in the European Union', paper delivered to Centre for Legislative Studies, March 1994.

25 P. Norton, *Talking Politics*, Spring 1995.

26 L. Brittan, as in 24 above.0

27 R. Cook, Interview in *New Statesman*, 13 August 1998.

28 P. Norton, as in 25 above.

29 E. Bomberg and A. Stubb, as in 7 above.

30 R. Dahl, 'A Democratic dilemma: system effectiveness versus citizen participation', *Political Science Quarterly*, 1994.

Part II

The impact of Europe on the British political system

4

Sovereignty and constitutional change

By signing the Treaty of Accession in 1972, the British government tacitly accepted as part of British law more than 2,900 regulations and 410 directives. These were contained in some forty-three volumes of European legislation, the sum total of legislation agreed by the EC over the years since its formation. Admittedly, much of this legislation was trivial, for most regulations or directives from Brussels deal with points of detail such as intervention prices for commodities within the Common Agricultural Policy (CAP). Nevertheless, there were some major issues involved and, in any case, the triviality of certain details is unimportant compared to the basic principle that here was a solid corpus of law that became binding upon the peoples of the UK, despite that law never having been scrutinised or debated by the British parliament. It was a massive breach of the constitutional convention that holds that Parliament is the supreme, and indeed only, law-making body in the UK.

Ironically enough, this major shift in the constitutional position was hardly noticed at the time. In the early years of British membership, most complaints about Europe concerned the operational faults and absurdities of the EC. People complained that Europe was too bureaucratic, too time-wasting, too remote from the people, too undemocratic and far too expensive. Probably what most alienated many of them was the seeming irrationality of the CAP, a mechanism widely seen as costly and wasteful.

This perception of cost and waste became fixed in peoples' minds and many of the criticisms levelled at the EC in the early years were value judgements, based on preconceived ideas that often did not stand up to serious scrutiny. Such fears and criticisms were almost exclusively practical matters relating to the working of the EC. Very few people understood or concerned themselves with constitutional theory, and it was only old-fashioned parliamentarians such as Enoch Powell who gave much thought to the issue of sovereignty and the constitution at that time. It is only in recent years that increasing anxiety has been expressed as to the extent to which membership of the EU has led to a transfer of sovereignty from Westminster to Brussels.

Sovereignty

A dictionary definition of the word 'sovereignty' is 'supreme and unrestricted power residing in an individual or group of people or body'. In Britain, Parliament is held to be sovereign because no other body has the right to pass and implement laws. There is no superior body able to override the legislative or judicial decisions made for the territory over which Parliament is sovereign.

So jealously does Parliament guard the right to be the only legislative body that other governmental or quasi-governmental bodies that need to pass laws, rules and regulations, such as local government or transport undertakings, can only do so through the device known as delegated legislation. Through delegated legislation, Parliament grants to other bodies the facility to pass laws, but only laws specifically related to the jurisdiction of the authority concerned. In strict legal parlance they are not laws, but by-laws. As the nineteenth-century constitutional writer Dicey put it:

> The sovereignty of Parliament is the dominant characteristic of our political institutions . . . [Parliament] has, under the English constitution, the right to make or unmake any law whatever, and, further, that no person or body is recognised by the law of England as having a right to override or set aside the legislation of Parliament.[1]

Sovereignty is difficult to define precisely, for it has a number of aspects. In modern political theory, two types of sovereignty are distinguished:

1 **Legal sovereignty**, which – in unitary states – is usually vested in the legislature. The source of legal sovereignty in federal or supranational states is harder to define, although the general belief in the USA is that the constitution is sovereign.
2 **Political sovereignty**, which is vested in a person or persons. At one time the monarch was sovereign but in a democratic era there is a widespread belief that political sovereignty is vested in the people. Implied in this concept of the constitution is a belief that no change can be made to the nature of the state without consulting the people through a referendum or plebiscite.

In Britain sovereignty is said to be vested in 'the Crown in Parliament', conjuring up visions of the State Opening of Parliament, with the Queen enthroned in the House of Lords, surrounded by both her Houses of Parliament. In practice, the term 'Crown' no longer refers to the monarch but to the body that now exercises the royal prerogative on behalf of the monarch; in other words, the Crown equals the government. This highlights an anomaly in any dispute over the surrender of sovereignty. In the face of the ability of the government to whip its own backbenchers through the voting lobbies to support its policies, it is only fair to say that what is called by ministers 'parliamentary sovereignty' is rather more accurately 'executive' or 'governmental' sovereignty. David Judge has claimed that this is the 'contradiction at the heart of the British Constitution: of the principle of parliamentary sovereignty being used by executives to minimise their accountability.'[2]

This ambivalence over the definition of sovereignty can lead to problems in that those who believe they are arguing about sovereignty from a common basis can in fact be arguing about two quite different things: 'Sovereignty has two meanings in UK politics, whereas it has only one in other European countries . . . (therefore) . . . debating sovereignty is more difficult in the UK than elsewhere in Europe, because of its other reference to parliamentary sovereignty'.[3]

Any government which speaks about the need to preserve sovereignty is almost certainly talking about parliamentary sovereignty, and therefore about the government's fears of a curtailment of its own powers. Those opposed to Europe, however, tend to speak in terms of national sovereignty, playing upon the chauvinism inherent in the British people. Margaret Thatcher, for example, tended to wrap herself in the Union flag when speaking of Europe, hinting that the freedom of Britain was at stake. As she put it in her Bruges speech: 'Willing and active co-operation between independent sovereign state is the best way to build a successful European Community'. Some of her supporters were even more willing to play the xenophobic card to maintain national independence, often by exploiting anti-German prejudices that have lingered since the Second World War. In July 1990 there was a furore over an interview given by Nicholas Ridley, a favoured Thatcherite minister, to the *Spectator* magazine. In the midst of other anti-European remarks, Ridley went so far as to say: 'I'm not against giving up sovereignty in principle, but not to this lot. You might just as well give it to Adolf Hitler.' The implied suggestion was that the surrender of British sovereignty to the EC was akin to the Germans using the EC to fulfil the dream of world domination pursued by Hitler in the Second World War. The sense of outrage which greeted Ridley's comments, particularly in Germany, led to his resignation, but his words reawakened the natural distrust of foreigners on the part of the British, encouraging a kind of thinking that saw Europe as representing foreign, particularly German, domination.[4]

What europhobes tend to obscure in this debate is that any surrender of sovereignty that has taken place so far is only partial and that, quite irrespective of the EU, all nations in the modern world are inevitably having to surrender some aspects of their sovereignty. The multinational nature of life in the late twentieth century, particularly in the fields of defence, trade and the economy, forced most countries into a series of compromises between independence and dependency. One result is a marked decline in the nature and status of the nation-state. And, as the nation-state has declined, so too have the more chauvinistic aspects of nationalism.

The nation-state

In medieval Europe the concept of a politico-geographical entity composed of people with a common ethnicity, religion, language and culture was unknown. Everyone paid lip service to a vague concept known as Christendom, within which the emperor represented secular power and the pope spiritual dominion. Within that dual hegemony, loyalties and allegiances were personal, made up of the reciprocal oaths, duties and obligations of the feudal system. When the nation-state began to emerge, as early as the fourteenth century, it was largely due to a breakdown in feudal relationships through disputed allegiances.

The dispute between France and England over the overlordship of Aquitaine known as the Hundred Years War transformed a feudal quarrel between two kings into a bitter war between two countries, each of which developed a strong sense of national identity as a result. Early examples of nation-states came about through war, revolution or the expulsion of an alien power. England, Scotland and France discovered their national identities in fighting one another, while Spain and Portugal emerged through expulsion of the Moors from Iberia.

Although a handful of nation-states existed as early as the fifteenth century, the development of the nation-state to the point at which it was perceived to be a part of the natural order of things, is a fairly recent development. In Europe, the oppressive Austro-Hungarian and the crumbling Ottoman Empires led to the rise of liberal nationalism in the nineteenth century, leading to successes such as the independence of Greece and the unification of Italy, the latter being what Mazzini called 'a sovereign nation of free and equal beings'.

The heyday of the nation-state, however, undoubtedly came after 1918 when the collapse of the Austro-Hungarian, Russian and Ottoman Empires created several new nations. The period of decolonisation that followed the Second World War produced even more new states and a further batch followed with the collapse of the Soviet bloc in 1989:

> Between 1870 and 1914, there were only about 50 sovereign states in the world, 16 of them in Europe. The figure barely fluctuated over the period. By the end of the first world war, the community of nations had grown by 10 as new states emerged in Europe. When it was founded in 1920, the League of Nations had 42 members: its successor, the United Nations, was established in 1945 with a membership of 51. By 1960, this figure had grown to 82; by 1973 it was 135 and in 1992 it stood at 183.[5] [By 2004, the number of countries who had signed the UN Charter stood at 191.]

The supranational institution of the EU has therefore to be placed in the context of a period in which the nation-state is internationally viewed as the normal political unit. As John Major said in 1994: 'Europe's peoples in general retain their favour and confidence in the nation state . . . I believe the nation-state will remain the basic political unit for Europe. The European Union is an association of states, deriving its basic democratic legitimacy through national parliaments.'[6] Yet in the early twenty-first century, the nation-state is under threat from two separate directions: on the one hand overshadowed by supra-national and multinational organisations, and on the other undermined by the minor nationalisms of regions, religious groups or ethnic minorities.

The state survives, but it is no longer the supreme authority within a defined territory. Increasingly, it finds itself bargaining with multinational companies strong enough to play one state off against another, and sharing power with subnational provincial or regional authorities on the one hand and with the proto-federal institutions of the EC on the other. It has ceased to be the sole, or even the chief, custodian of the interests of its citizens.[7] It follows, therefore, that the use of euroscepticism to defend national sovereignty against the encroachment of an alien Europe is undermined, because – instead of reaching its apotheosis in the modern world – the nation-state is in decline in the face of international reality.

The decline of the nation-state

The impression given by the opponents of the EU is that Europe is the only threat posed to national sovereignty and that withdrawal from the EU would leave Britain once more independent of foreign influences. This is to ignore the reali-ties of the modern world and the extent to which Britain, in common with most other countries, has surrendered vital aspects of its sovereignty quite independ-ently of EU membership. In the early part of the twenty-first century it is no longer possible for a country to exist in glorious isolation. In defence, economics and the development of trade, the countries of the world are inter-dependent:

- After 1945 Britain, France and other European countries were dwarfed militarily by the superpowers of the USA and USSR. Defence in the post-war world was only possible through the collective security of international alliances such as NATO. Elements of national sovereignty were sacrificed, part of the nation's armed forces was put under international control and national defence policy was subordinated to strategic decisions made by a supranational body – in this case the North Atlantic Council for NATO.
- As far as international trade and commerce is concerned, few national economies are strong enough to survive in a world of unrestricted market forces; indeed, all nations have found that it was in their interests to subor-dinate themselves to GATT (the General Agreement on Tariffs and Trade) and its successor, the World Trade Organisation (WTO).
- In any country, a hallmark of sovereignty is the ability of the country's gov-ernment, banks and financial institutions to dictate the nature of economic

and fiscal policy within that government's jurisdiction. In 1976 the economic situation facing the Labour government became so grave that Britain was on the verge of what, for an individual, would have been called bankruptcy. To escape from its difficulties the government, in the person of the chancellor, Denis Healey, appealed to the United Nations agency, the International Monetary Fund (IMF) for help and Britain was granted a loan to extricate the country from the situation in which it found itself. But the loan came with conditions attached, one of these being that the Treasury would receive a team of advisers from the IMF which would have the power to dictate certain aspects of British economic policy. A programme of cuts in both services and public expenditure followed. It represented economic policy and legislation that was not originated by the government and which was not subject to amendment by Parliament.

- In signing the European Convention for the Protection of Human Rights and Fundamental Freedoms in 1950, and in accepting the subsequent establishment of the European Court and Commission of Human Rights, the British government acknowledged a source of law other than parliament and a final court of appeal other than the House of Lords. Since 1998 the Convention has been absorbed into British law as the Human Rights Act. But in accepting and implementing the decisions and judgments of a supranational Court and Commission for so many years, British governments voluntarily surrendered the main theoretical plank defining parliamentary sovereignty.

Bearing these factors in mind, it can be said that any surrender of sovereignty resulting from accession to the EC was merely part of a more general recognition that a modern state cannot be nationally self-sufficient and that states are now essentially interdependent. Consequently, the more enthusiastic Europeans tend not to talk of surrendering but of pooling sovereignty. In other words, the nation-state retains its separate identity in the more general sense, while sharing sovereignty with other states in certain agreed areas.

Sovereignty then, is not a timeless and unchanging concept. In the words of one British MEP: 'Sovereignty is the ability to do what we like, when we like and not be tied up with others . . . In practice, we've been trading bits of our sovereignty for bits of other people's sovereignty to make a stable world for ourselves.'[8]

At the same time as the nation-state is diminished by the pooling of sovereignty over major policy matters, it has to some extent been undermined by the growth of regional autonomy and separatist movements based on ethnic, linguistic or religious considerations. Most European countries have powerful regions or separatist movements:

- Within the UK there are Scottish and Welsh Nationalist Parties, as well as the problems of Northern Ireland that are much connected with the preference of many Catholics for a united Ireland.

- France has language-based separatist movements in Brittany and Languedoc.
- Belgium's division between Dutch and French speakers has turned the country into a de facto federal state, with separate assemblies for Flanders and Wallonia.
- In Italy, the Lega Nord was popular for a time, with a programme of federalisation through a division of Italy into North, South and Central.
- In Spain, regions such as Catalonia have become semi-autonomous, while the Basques continue to fight for independence.

The evidence suggests that the monolithic power of the nation-state, while being vigorously defended against the external threat of a federal Europe, is crumbling and fragmenting under internal pressures. This dual attack on the nature of the nation-state leads to many anomalies. National governments, in defending themselves against the centralising powers of Brussels, sometimes claim rights for themselves that they deny to those of their own regions that are seeking autonomy. The last Conservative Party administration protested at regulation from a distant and remote Brussels, but still insisted on Westminster's domination of Scotland's affairs, even though London is as remote to the Scots as Brussels is to the English.

Some of the difficulties concerning the twin pulls of centralisation and more regional self-government arise from different interpretations of the term 'federal'. For ardent adherents of the nation-state in the British Conservative Party, federalism is equated with a centralised superstate in Brussels, eating away at the independence of member nations. On the other hand, the view of committed federalists is that the federal state is a necessary prerequisite for decentralisation. In their view a federal structure provides the means by which the power to take decisions may be devolved, to national governments if need be, but equally to regional or local administrations, where that is more appropriate. As Lord Thomas said in 1994:

> It seems that when John Major talks of disliking a centralised federal Europe, he must actually be saying nothing, since the essence of the word 'federal' is that it is not centralised. If a group of states wish to act in common in some ways and, at the same time, want to preserve national identity, how can you avoid having a [federal] polity . . . There is thus a paradox if those who say they want to preserve national identity insist, at the same time, that they are against a federal solution in Europe. Surely only a federal structure can preserve the identity of peoples.[9]

The loss of sovereignty

By signing the Treaty of Accession in 1972, Britain accepted the Treaties of Rome and the other foundations of European Community law. Since then the UK government has signed the Single European Act and the Treaties of

Maastricht, Amsterdam and Nice. By so doing, ministers have accepted a diminution of sovereignty in that:

- laws enacted by the Communities are directly applicable in Britain;
- the UK Parliament is barred from passing laws in areas where Community law already exists or where national law would be inconsistent with Community law;
- British courts must accept and enforce decisions of the European Court of Justice.

As Community law states:

> On the basis of the powers thus conferred on them, the Community institutions can enact legal instruments as a Community legislature legally independent of the Member States. Some of these instruments take effect directly as Community law in the Member States, and thus do not require any transformation into national law in order to be binding, not only on the Member States and their organs, but also on the citizen.[10]

This surrender of sovereignty is not, however, all-embracing. The Community works according to the principle of the specific attribution of powers. This means that the scope and parameters of Community competence are limited and vary according to different tasks:

- Some areas are not defined in the founding treaties, where Community law has no relevance.
- In other areas Community law is directly applicable and has clear primacy over national law.
- In between are areas where Community decisions lay down the general aims of the law but where national governments are permitted considerable latitude as to how those decisions are applied.

Regardless of this, however, the argument can legitimately be advanced that sovereignty is not abandoned when Community law is made by the Council of Ministers on which all member states are strongly represented:

> The Member States have pooled certain parts of their own legislative powers in favour of these Communities and have placed them in the hands of Community institutions in which, however, they are given in return substantial rights of participation.[11]

However, those who comfort themselves with the thought that the transfer of sovereignty to Europe is limited and of no great importance are embracing false comfort. It has long been established that, if there were a conflict between

Community law and national law then, constitutionally, Community law has primacy. In one important test case in 1991 (see Box 4.1 on Factortame) the judgement clearly stated the situation: 'Under the terms of the 1972 Act, it has always been clear that it was the duty of a United Kingdom Court to override any rule of national law found to be in conflict with any directly enforceable rule of European law'.[12]

Over the forty years or so that the European Communities have been in existence there has been a succession of judgments, by both the European Court of Justice and the various national courts, that have helped to build up a formidable corpus of case law concerning the relationship between Community and national law. It is now established that:

- Member states have transferred sovereign rights to a Community created by themselves. They cannot reverse this process by means of unilateral measures inconsistent with the general interests of the Community.
- No member state may call into question the status of Community law as being a system uniformly and generally applicable throughout the Community.

Box 4.1
Factortame

Britain's legal subordination to Brussels was underlined in an important legal case, judgement in which was given in 1991 by the European Court of Justice: that involving *Factortame v. Secretary of State for Transport*.

In 1988 the Thatcher government passed the Merchant Shipping Act, designed to deal with the problem of quota-hopping by Spanish and other fishermen who were registering their vessels under the British flag and using British fishing quotas, much to the dismay of British trawlermen. The Act provided that UK-registered boats must be 75 Per cennt British owned and have 75 per cent of their crew resident in Britain.

In the Factortame judgement, the Merchant Shipping Act of 1988 was ruled invalid and therefore effectively quashed by the Court of Justice. The position was made very clear. The Act contradicted EC law because it was discriminatory in a Community committed to freedom of movement. It was therefore invalid. In the words of one journal, 'this is a historic judgement . . . it overturns the English ruling that no injunction can be granted against the Crown . . . the Europeans are rewriting our constitution'.[13]

At the time, a senior judge Lord Bridges observed that the verdict was only a reaffirmation of the supremacy of Community law, as had been recognised since 1973.[14] But it has come to be seen as a major test of the constitutional position. In the Maastricht debates, Lady Thatcher invoked it as evidence that 'European law will prevail more and more'.

- Community law, enacted in accordance with the treaties, has priority over any conflicting law of the member states.
- Community law is not only stronger than earlier national law but has a limiting effect on laws adopted subsequently.[15]

The most obvious constitutional change brought about by membership of the EU is therefore a surrender of the UK's parliamentary sovereignty to the primacy of Community law. One interesting argument put forward prior to 1972 was that advanced by Harold Wilson. In reply to the accusation that membership of the EEC would diminish British sovereignty, particularly parliamentary sovereignty, he said:

> Accession to the Treaties would involve the passing of United Kingdom legislation. This would be an exercise, of course, of Parliamentary sovereignty . . . Community law, past and future, would derive its force as law in this country from that legislation passed by Parliament.[16]

The suggestion would seem to be that the Treaty of Accession, which gave entry into the British legal system for all past, present and future Community law, was little more than an advanced form of delegated legislation. In other words, Community law can be applied in Britain without detracting from British parliamentary sovereignty because the right to apply that law was originally granted by a law passed by the British Parliament. Harold Wilson was an astute politician and a past master of sophistry but it has to be said that to see Community law as yet more delegated legislation is a delusion. The fact is that the British Parliament cannot refuse to accept Community law, nor debate it, nor repeal it, unless Britain were to cancel the Treaty of Accession and withdraw altogether from the EU.

So it must be accepted that Britain has surrendered both parliamentary and national sovereignty through the act of joining the EU. That loss of sovereignty and thereby the loss of national identity is the main complaint about membership now brought by those hostile to the European ideal, whether they are known as eurosceptics or as europhobes. However, to speak of sovereignty in such simplistic terms is to ignore a more recent perspective which would first ask whether it is real or theoretical sovereignty that is being talked about, given the extent of current globalisation.

[handwritten marginal note: lost of sovereignty parliamentary and national equals to lost of national identity as all law as well as policies will be transfer to Bruxells]

Real and theoretical sovereignty

The difference between real and theoretical sovereignty has been described Peter Anderson and Anthony Weymouth in this way: 'real sovereignty is the degree of control which a nation can exercise over its own destiny, while theoretical sovereignty can be best described as symbolic control, signifying little if any substance'.[17] Very often the loss of sovereignty that seems to cause the most concern is theoretical by nature. In their book on British attitudes towards Europe, the two writers cite two important instances where symbols of British sovereignty can be said to be theoretical rather than real.

The first of these is the so-called 'independent' nuclear deterrent, which was said to guarantee Britain's independent defence and security strategy in the post-war world. Yet, from the 1950s onward, control of Britain's nuclear arsenal was shared with the USA and it is unthinkable that nuclear weapons could ever have been used without American permission. Indeed, it is far more likely that they would have been used as a result of orders emanating from Washington. So much for Britain's independence of action: the image of Britain as a major world power with sovereign control over its own defence capabilities was in fact a fairly transparent fiction maintained simply in order to bolster British self-esteem.

The other area where sovereignty is illusory concerns the maintenance of the strength and importance of the pound sterling. The eurosceptic argument against British membership of EMU is based on the undesirability of the British government and Bank of England surrendering control of British taxation or interest rates. And it is true that a Britain within the EMU would lose the ability to deal with short-term economic issues through fiscal measures such as the exchange rate. But the fact is that the British economy lost the ability to deal alone with medium to long-term issues many years ago. The sterling crises of 1967, 1986 and 1992 had comparatively little to do with decisions made within the British economy and much more to do with global problems associated with the German, Japanese and US economies.

The sovereignty that has quite clearly been lost or surrendered to the EU is almost entirely of a theoretical nature. Anderson and Weymouth suggest that the European concept of pooled sovereignty might well mean the definite loss of theoretical sovereignty, but in reality could actually mean an increase of real sovereignty. According to this viewpoint, real sovereignty in a collective organisation like the EU is something that is open to negotiation and 'real sovereignty in some areas of governance should be traded in order to secure a greater overall level of real sovereignty'. Ironically enough, in view of her anxieties about the loss of sovereignty involved in British membership of the EU, Margaret Thatcher recognised these tactics of negotiation when she signed the Single European Act. She gave ground on the controversial issue of qualified majority voting in return for an application of market forces that was suited to the British view of the single market.

Critics of the EU seem to concentrate on the loss of British sovereignty as though no other member state of the EU had sovereignty to lose. Yet every country has its own particular interests that are often in conflict with the interests of other countries. Those countries that have derived the greatest benefits from membership of the EU are those that have realised from the start that some aspects of real sovereignty must be surrendered at the negotiating table in return for gains in other aspects within the EU's pooled sovereignty. The history of Britain's relationship with Europe has been all too often one of delaying membership until after all the negotiations are over. Perhaps British fears of a constant draining away of sovereignty derive from the fact that Britain was never there in the early stages of forming the Community, when participating members were trading-off some aspects of sovereignty in return for others.

There are elements of paranoia and pessimism in the eurosceptic view of things. In arguing against British participation in EMU and the common currency, the sceptics say that it is undesirable in that it would give a measure of control of the British economy to other countries – and Germany is usually meant. They do not consider the reverse of that position and the possibility that, if Britain had been involved from the start at the negotiating table, then rather than simply seeing it as Germany controlling the British economy it could be represented as equally true that Britain might have a certain measure of control over the German economy.

That view, however, has not gained much ground and much of the development of Britain's place in Europe over the past few years has been coloured by the Major government's determined efforts to counter or ameliorate the degree to which the Community could impinge upon the country's independence of action.

Defending the national identity

As prime minister, Margaret Thatcher first expressed the government's determination to defend British national independence and oppose federalism, which she stigmatised as 'centralisation'. Yet the irony is that by signing the Single European Act she made a loss of sovereignty inevitable. As Philip Norton has pointed out, the acceptance of QMV meant that British law could be changed by Brussels directives, even though the British might oppose them.[18] What had been a national veto over proposals was removed in certain areas of policy at a stroke. Moreover, as a prominent student of the EU stated: 'If you remove internal barriers, you let illegal as well as legal substances cross Europe. If you want to police that, you have to have co-operation and this will affect the law-making authority of individual countries.'[19]

When John Major succeeded Margaret Thatcher as prime minister, he spoke of Britain's place 'at the heart of Europe'. Nevertheless, it was not long before his government, faced with the opposition of eurosceptics on the Tory bankbenches, became just as opposed to European integration as its predecessor had been. From being mildly euro-enthusiast in his views, John Major became what Hugo Young called 'a pragmatic eurosceptic'.[20] In November 1992 the Foreign and Commonwealth Office published a pamphlet to mark Britain's presidency of the EC. Called *Britain in Europe*, it purported to explain the European Community and the Maastricht Treaty to the general public. In fact it represented a statement of government policy:

The original Community treaties aimed at an 'ever-closer-union among the peoples of Europe'. The Government are committed to closer co-operation with our Community partners. This has brought political and economic benefits. But the Government don't want, and won't have, a United States of Europe.[21]

In negotiating the Maastricht agreements and in subsequent relations with Europe, the Major government moved steadily away from federalism towards a militant defence of national identities against encroachment from Brussels, a move that was driven by the disproportionately influential band of thirty or so eurosceptics led by Bill Cash. The Major administration proceeded to defend national interests through a variety of devices, such as:

- agreeing opt-outs from the Maastricht agreement;
- promoting the concept of subsidiarity;
- defending the national veto in the Council of Ministers;
- considering the possibility of multispeed European development.

Opt-outs and variable geometry

Having agreed the terms of the Maastricht Treaty, a number of member states negotiated protocols giving them exemptions from certain clauses in the treaty. Some of these were quite minor, as with France, Spain and Portugal, who all negotiated exemptions for those overseas territories such as the Canary Islands or the Azores, which are themselves unable to meet the EU's economic objectives.

A much more serious exemption, however, was granted to Britain over monetary union. Protocol 11 of the TEU states: 'The United Kingdom shall not be obliged or committed to move to the third stage of economic and monetary union without a separate decision to do so by its government and Parliament'. The most important effect of this opt-out is to preserve the independence of the Bank of England from moves to establish a European Central Bank. On the other hand, as was outlined earlier in this chapter, there is a contrary argument which says that the opt-out prevents Britain from having any say in the development and nature of the European Central Bank or on the form taken by an economic union that Britain may well have to join in the future.

The constitutional issue involved in economic and monetary union is that of economic sovereignty – meaning that the government, governor of the Bank of England and chancellor of the Exchequer surrender control of the British economy to central European institutions. The relevant issue as far as the public is concerned, however, is the far more emotional matter concerning whether a common currency would mean having to give up the pound and penny. In their pamphlet, ministers were reassuring in this: 'Britain is not committed to joining a move to a single currency. If we choose, we can stay out indefinitely.'[22]

The same exemption from the need to follow the other member states into economic union was granted to Denmark, on the grounds that Denmark could only enter into negotiations over economic union if required to do so by a referendum of the Danish people. It is to be noted that neither Britain nor Denmark see these opt-outs over economic union and the common currency as necessarily permanent; both countries retain the right to rejoin the process at a time which suits them best. The two countries are exercising their sovereignty to the extent of ensuring that any future pooling of that sovereignty will be done at the wish of the member country and at a speed set by the member country.

A more significant opt-out at the time was over the so-called Social Chapter, the programme for social protection in the workplace and elsewhere, which was accepted by all the other member countries. The British government claimed that the Social Chapter, particularly in its provisions for a minimum wage and legislation on maximum working hours, was potentially harmful to the competitiveness of British industry. As such, the British negotiators at Maastricht did not so much opt out of the agreement on social policy, as never opt in in the first place. In the final treaty, the Agreement on Social Policy is described as: 'Concluded between the Member States of the European Community with the exception of the United Kingdom of Great Britain and Northern Ireland'. As it happens, this was the very first Conservative amendment of the treaty to be swept aside by the Blair government after the 1997 election. Very little fuss was made about the reversal of policy. The press release issued by the IGC which reported to the European Council and formed the basis for the Amsterdam Treaty, states quite simply: 'The IGC has incorporated into the Treaty the Agreement on Social Policy which previously only applied to fourteen Member States'.

This approach – of only signing the parts of a treaty with which you agree – opened up the possibility known in EU jargon as 'variable geometry'. This was an option originally devised for applicant members in Eastern Europe, who might never become members if they had to wait until they had parity of economic strength and stability with the countries of Western Europe. Under variable geometry, member states would progress towards integration at a speed suitable for each individual state. According to Philip Lynch:

> The 'variable geometry' approach envisages European integration as a Chinese meal at which some diners take large portions of each dish but are left still wanting more, while the more sceptical steer clear of those bits they cannot stomach. This option may prove an attractive proposition for a British government eager to claim economic benefits without paying for them through further losses of national autonomy. But inherent in this is the danger of being relegated to Europe's 'second division'.[23]

This was the pattern John Major appeared to advocate during the 1994 European elections campaign when he claimed that the best way forward for Britain might lie in a multitrack, multispeed Europe. Those members who wanted it could proceed towards integration without involving those members who were less sympathetic to a federalist approach. In 1994 the French prime minister put forward just such a three-tier plan for a centre-core, fast-track integrated Europe consisting basically of France, Germany and the Benelux countries; a peripheral, slow-lane second-tier for the more reluctant members like Britain; and a third tier made up of other European countries that were not yet members. From what he had been saying it might have been expected that John Major would welcome the plan. Instead, he was the first to condemn it and made a major speech in the Netherlands in which he denounced any suggestion that Britain should not be 'at the heart of Europe'.[24]

Subsidiarity

The concept of subsidiarity was principally developed to counter British fears of what was seen as the committed pro-federalism of Maastricht. As we have seen, in Britain federalism was actually equated with centralism, giving rise to fears of a powerful federal administration in Brussels imposing its will on the member states, without regard to the wishes of national parliaments. What developed at Maastricht was the doctrine of subsidiarity, defined in the treaty itself in this way:

> In areas which do not fall within its exclusive competence, the Community should take action, in accordance with the principle of subsidiarity, only in so far as the proposed action cannot sufficiently be achieved by the Member States and can therefore, by reason of the scale or effects of the proposed action, be better achieved by the Community. Any action of the Community shall not go beyond what is necessary to achieve the objectives of this Treaty.[25]

At the time the Treaty was signed in February 1992, the British government felt that this definition of subsidiarity was inadequately expressed. The British presidency in the second half of 1992 presented an opportunity to strengthen and refine the principle, and much of the time at the Birmingham and Edinburgh European Councils was given over to the matter. The communiqué issued at the conclusion of the Edinburgh meeting stated in clarification that 'the Community [is] to act only when member states cannot achieve the desired goal themselves'.

The intention has been to ensure that an important role remains for national governments in the legislative process. Any proposed legislation in Brussels must now be first scrutinised for its subsidiarity. If action would be best dealt with by national governments, then the proposal must be passed down to the most appropriate authority.

It is here that the proponents of subsidiarity have made a rod for their own backs. Simply because a proposal is thought to be inappropriate for Community action does not necessarily mean that action by national governments is any more appropriate. It could well be the case that regional or local action might be even more suitable. The Committee of the Regions was established in 1994 to assert the rights of regions and districts within the member states. Subsequently, the Scottish Parliament and Welsh Assembly have both adopted the concept of subsidiarity with enthusiasm, insisting on direct negotiations with Brussels without an intervening English body over such matters as the beef crisis or regional funds. And the anomaly in the situation was that, although the Major government advocated subsidiarity to prevent centralisation in Brussels, that same government was very ardently centralist in its management of the affairs of the UK.

The veto

The use of opt-outs and the doctrine of subsidiarity are useful weapons for national governments in their fight to retain sovereignty, but their ultimate weapon, as proved by Charles de Gaulle in the 1960s or John Major at the Corfu Summit in 1994, is in the use of the national veto in the Council of Ministers. The original plan for decision making in the Council of Ministers was that there should be unanimity or the proposal would fail, thus effectively giving each member state a veto and the ability to block decisions approved by all other members. In the 1960s the use of the veto by de Gaulle not only blocked British accession on two occasions, but effectively stymied progress by the in any direction that did not suit French interests.

The reaction to de Gaulle's use of the veto was to move towards extending the number of areas that could be decided by majority voting instead of by unanimous decision. Because the smaller member countries were concerned that simple majority voting would disadvantage them in any confrontation with the larger countries, qualified majority voting (QMV) was introduced. This gave differential numbers of votes to the countries – roughly dependent on size – and required a coalition of around 30 per cent of the total number of votes in order to block a proposal. The figures were so arranged that it would take a coalition of at least three member states to prevent a decision from going through. It was on this basis that the use of QMV was steadily extended. Decisions requiring unanimity, and therefore subject to veto, were increasingly confined to major constitutional matters involving changes to the original treaties. QMV was becoming accepted as the norm until the mid-1990s, when the issue of voting and the veto became the sticking point for a Conservative government attempting to appear firm in its resolve to stand up for British interests, in order to allay the fears of eurosceptics on its own backbenches.

In 1994 the crisis over voting rights erupted because it was proposed to enlarge the EU by admitting four more countries to membership, these four countries being given weighted votes in the Council of Ministers in accordance with the rule of thumb previously applying: Austria and Sweden getting four votes each, and Finland and Norway three each. At the same time it was proposed that the blocking majority should be raised to twenty-seven, so as to remain at 30 per cent of the new total of ninety.

Britain at once objected, claiming that the change would weaken the position of the large countries within the EU. The argument that followed threatened to overthrow the timetable for entry of the new applicants, since the position of the British Conservative Party seemed to be that the veto in the Council of Ministers was the last remaining safeguard of national sovereignty. Ultimately, Britain had to agree to a compromise in which the blocking minority rose to twenty-seven (which became twenty-six when Norway withdrew)m but member countries retained a strengthened right to apply the veto if they could show that their national interests were threatened.

Only a short period later, Britain emphasised the importance of the veto by being the one country at the Corfu European Council to block the appointment of Jean-Luc Dehaene, prime minister of Belgium, as president of the Commission. As has been explained in chapter 2, it was a significant moment in Britain's relations with the EU because, by using the ultimate weapon of the veto for party political purposes, John Major had broken the unwritten rules of the EU. It was a crisis that was quickly resolved at the time, but its effects lingered on. It was originally intended that the issue of the veto would be settled by the IGC due to report at Amsterdam in 1997, but the crisis inspired by Major's actions delayed things considerably and the issue was included in Agenda 2000 for later resolution. The 'red lines' drawn by Tony Blair at Brussels in 2003–4 were much concerned with preserving the right of veto in key areas of policy (see pp. 68–9).

Accountability

Eurosceptics, in their criticism of Europe, often use the terms 'unelected' and 'undemocratic' in talking about the institutions of the EU and the need for Britain to defend its parliamentary sovereignty. At least the British Parliament can claim to speak for the British people, eurosceptics say, since it was the British electorate which elected that Parliament. The European Parliament, a traditionally weak body (albeit one with steadily growing powers), is also elected, although on the basis of a poor turn-out among Europe's voters. But for whom can the European Commission claim to speak, when its members are appointed rather than elected? To whom is the Commission accountable? This issue of the democratic deficit and possible solutions to it has already been discussed in chapter 3.

The ultimate device in ensuring accountability, however, is the referendum: much used in parts of the EU, where it is, indeed, required by constitutional law. The referendum is primarily used in those states where sovereignty is said to be vested in the people and where the constitution will often require that major constitutional changes can only be implemented with the approval of the people as shown in a popular vote. There are those in Britain who believe that changes in the British constitution, including those brought about by EU membership, should similarly be subject to referendum.

British parliamentarians have traditionally been opposed to referendums, which are seen as an alien device, antipathetic to representative democracy and liable to undermine the British constitution. When opposing calls for their use, the principle of parliamentary sovereignty is often evoked. This happened in ministerial replies to calls for a referendum on Maastricht. A similar line of argument appeared in the government pamphlet *Britain in Europe*, already mentioned:

> The British system is a parliamentary democracy: the Government is accountable to Parliament and Parliament is accountable to the electorate. The House of Commons approved the British negotiating stance before Maastricht and the results afterwards. Parliament will have a thorough and detailed discussion of the Bill . . . The Government believe that this is the right way to proceed in a parliamentary democracy.[26]

The reasons advanced for this position were expressed by the foreign secretary in the Commons debate as to whether to hold a referendum on Maastricht:

> As Parliament is sovereign it is clear that it could decide to hold a referendum, which it could either accept or reject. It could certainly choose, as it has before, to ask for advice from those who sent us here. But I return to the fact that we owe our constituents our judgment, and if we decline to exercise that judgment we are to some extent damaging the authority of Parliament.[27]

The expression 'as it has before' referred to the previous occasion on which the government had resorted to a referendum: indeed, the one and only instance of a national referendum for the whole of the UK. This was the referendum of June 1975, in which Harold Wilson's Labour government asked the British people to endorse the 'renegotiated' terms for continuation of British membership of the EC. On that occasion the British people had voted for membership two-to-one although, on a turn-out of 64 per cent, that meant that only 43 per cent of the electorate had voted in favour, as against 22 per cent of the electorate opposed to membership. There were special circumstances associated with the 1975 referendum. Harold Wilson was determined to keep Britain in Europe, but only kept his party with him by promising to consult the people of Britain before reversing party policy.

In 1993, at the height of the Maastricht debate, the issue of a referendum was brought up again by rebel eurosceptics in the Conservative Party. Led by Lady Thatcher – once one of the most scathing critic of referendums – the eurosceptics said that they would withdraw their opposition to the ratification of Maastricht if the government laid the issue before the electorate in a referendum. Naturally the eurosceptics wanted a referendum because they believed that the electorate shared their scepticism about the European project. But they acquired allies who were not opposed to Europe but were in favour of referendums, most notably the majority of the Liberal Democrats. However, a motion that a referendum must be held before the Act could take effect was defeated in the Commons on 8 March 1993 by 363 votes to 124. A similar motion in the House of Lords on 14 July 1993, for which Lady Thatcher and her friends pulled out all the stops, was defeated by 445 votes to 176.

The issue of a referendum did not go away and dissident voices in the Conservative Party were calling for a referendum to be held before Britain accepted the idea of a single currency. The logical conclusion to this was the formation in 1995 of the Referendum Party which attacked the failure of the Conservative government to allow a referendum on constitutional matters. In the event, the Referendum Party had little effect on the outcome of the 1997 election, except being yet another nail in the coffin of the Major government.

After the election, official government policy was that Britain would join the single currency 'when the time was ripe'. But both Blair and Brown agreed that Britain would only sign up to EMU and the euro after the public had been allowed their say in a referendum.

Collective responsibility

The referendum of 1975 was not the only breach of constitutional convention permitted by the Wilson government in the European cause. One of the oldest and most sacrosanct of conventions used to be that of collective responsibility, the premise of which is that all members of a government are collectively responsible for government policy. In the Cabinet and elsewhere ministers might argue all they like about government proposals, but once the Cabinet has reached agreement, and the proposal becomes official policy, even dissenting ministers must support that policy. If they feel unable to do so they must resign from the government.

In 1975, when Harold Wilson was proposing the referendum on Europe and it was decided that official government policy was to campaign for a 'yes' vote, the prime minister was faced with the serious prospect of about a third of his government being so opposed in principle to European membership that they could not in conscience keep silent under the rules of collective responsibility. At the same time the prime minister could not afford to lose so many prominent members of his government if they obeyed the logic of the doctrine and resigned. On the basis that it was only a convention and not a statutory part of a written constitution, Wilson simply suspended the rules and stated that the doctrine of collective responsibility was inoperative for the duration of the referendum campaign. This enabled politicians such as Peter Shore and Tony Benn to campaign vigorously against government policy, while remaining members of the government.

The suspension of the doctrine of collective responsibility was a pragmatic device to meet a specific dilemma, intended to be temporary. Once the referendum was over and the outcome decided, the rules of collective responsibility were reasserted. However, the significance of conventions within an unwritten constitution is that, if they are ignored once, they can be ignored again if it is seen as expedient to do so. In theory all members of a government are bound by collective responsibility but, in fact, if a minister is in conflict with government policy over an issue of principle, particularly over European issues, then that minister no longer feels so bound to silence as was once the case. In the post-Maastricht period, eurosceptical members of the Major government – most notably Michael Portillo – felt free to make anti-European statements despite government policy. That acceptance of collective decisions being flaunted followed the Conservatives into opposition. During the leadership of William Hague, prominent Tory euro-enthusiasts such as Kenneth Clarke and Michael Heseltine were quite ready to speak out against their party's position and even willing to share a pro-Europe platform with Tony Blair and leading members of the Labour and Liberal Democrat Parties.

Summary

There have been minor changes to the British constitution as a result of EU membership, such as the use of the referendum and the abandonment of collective responsibility. But the major change has been the fundamental loss of at least theoretical sovereignty caused by British acceptance – via the Treaty of Accession – of the primacy of Community law. Despite rearguard actions by the eurosceptics over issues such as the national veto, opting-out and variable geometry, the full and independent sovereignty of the British parliament has certainly been diminished. But some of that loss of sovereignty has less to do with British membership of the EU than the inevitable interrelatedness of modern economic life and the decline in the status of the nation-state.

Notes

1   A. Dicey, *Introduction to the study of the Law of the Constitution*, Macmillan, 1885.
2   D. Judge, *The Parliamentary State*, Sage, 1993.
3   D. Wincott, 'The Conservative Party and Europe', *Politics Review*, April 1992.
4   The Thatcher Bruges speech and Nicholas Ridley's comments are quoted by A. Watkins, *A Conservative Coup*, Duckworth, 1992.
5   P. Alter, 'A giant leap into the unknown', in V. Keegan and M. Kettle (eds), *The New Europe*, Fourth Estate, 1993.
6   J. Major, 'William and Mary Lecture', University of Leiden, the Netherlands, 6 September 1994.
7   D. Marquand, 'Heart of the matter', in V. Keegan and M. Kettle, as in 5 above.

8 British MEP Lord O'Hagan, as quoted in P. Norton, *The Constitution in Flux*, Martin Robertson, 1982.

9 Lord Thomas of Swynnerton, in a lecture calling for a written constitution for the EU, delivered to the Menendez Pelayo Summer School, Santander, 3 July 1994.

10 *The ABC of Community Law* (3rd edition), European Documentation Series, European Commission, 1991.

11 *The ABC of Community Law*, as in 10 above.

12 Factortame v. Secretary of State for Transport (No. 2) [1991], quoted in J. Alder, *Constitutional and Administrative Law*, Macmillan, 1994.

13 *The New Statesmen*, 10 June 1990.

14 Lord Bridges, quoted in A. Davies, *British Politics and Europe*, Hodder & Stoughton, 1998.

15 *The ABC of Community Law*, as in 10 above.

16 H. Wilson, quoted in P. Norton, *The British Constitution in Flux*, Blackwell, 1982.

17 P. Anderson and A. Weymouth, *Insulting the Public? The British Press and the European Union*, Addison Wesley Longman, 1999.

18 P. Norton, *Talking Politics*, Spring 1995.

19 J. Lodge, of the Centre for European Studies, University of Hull, quoted in 'Party divisions over unity', *Guardian Education*, 7 June 1994.

20 H. Young, *This Blessed Plot*, Macmillan, 1998.

21 Foreign and Commonwealth Office, *Britain in Europe, the European Community and Your Future*, HMSO Publications, 1992.

22 Foreign and Commonweath Office, as in 21 above.

23 P. Lynch, 'Europe's post-Maastricht muddle', *Politics Review*, November 1993.

24 J. Major, as in 6 above.

25 TEU, Title II (Amendments to the Treaty of Rome), Article 3b.

26 Foreign and Commonwealth Office, as in 21 above.

27 D. Hurd to the House of Commons, 21 April 1993.

5

Policy and the decision-making process

There are two categories of law in the EU. **Primary legislation** involves the body of law established by the founding treaties of the Communities, together with all later amendments and protocols attached to those treaties. **Secondary legislation** encompasses all laws passed by the institutions of the Communities in order to fulfil the aims and purposes of the treaties. As we have seen in the previous chapter, all this law is applicable to Britain, and Britain has its part to play in the formulation and implementation of that law.

Primary legislation

> Community law in this respect is provided by the three treaties, with the various annexes and protocols attached to them, and their later additions and amendments: these are the founding acts . . . Because the law contained in the treaties was created directly by the Member States themselves, it is known as primary Community legislation. This founding charter is mainly confined to setting out the objectives of the Community, establishing its mechanisms and setting up institutions with the task of filling out the constitutional skeleton and conferring on them legislative and administrative powers to do so.[1]

Primary law is therefore constitutional law, dealing largely with the relationship of the member states, both with Community institutions and with each other. On the other hand, primary law is the basis on which the European Court of Justice makes its judgements and, as in any legal system, the decisions made by judges and the precedents set by them form the basis for case law. And case law can apply to individual citizens, firms and organisations.

In the last chapter, we established the primacy of Community law over national law. Even more important for the individual are the judgements referring to what is called 'direct applicability'. This means that the rules laid down in the foundation treaties are applicable not only to the member states and institutions of the

Community but directly impose obligations and confer rights on the citizens of the member countries – without those rules having to be adopted and amended by national law.

The first important judgement on this issue concerned Article 12 of the Treaty of Rome, limiting the ability of states belonging to the EEC to impose or raise customs duties on goods circulating between members of the EEC. A Dutch transport firm, Van Gend and Loos, were importers of chemical products from West Germany and, in 1962 they went to court in the Netherlands protesting that Dutch customs had increased customs duties on the goods they handled, in clear breach of Article 12 of the EEC Treaty. At that time it was believed that laws contained in the treaty applied only to states and institutions, and could apply to firms and individuals only if adopted by national law. Now the Dutch court was being asked to rule that the Treaty of Rome conferred rights on individuals within member states.

Feeling that it was not competent to rule on Community law, the Dutch court referred the case to the Court of Justice. Naturally, any such decision had major implications for national sovereignty and many member states made representations to the Court. However, judgement was given in favour of the firm, the judges stating: 'Community law not only imposes obligations on individuals but is also intended to confer upon them rights'.[2] This judgement was taken as the criterion for direct applicability and the case law thus established set a precedent for all subsequent cases of this nature.

In May 1973 a young Dutch woman, Miss Van Duyn, was engaged as a secretary by the Church of Scientology in Britain. The Church of Scientology was regarded by the authorities as highly dubious. It was under investigation for practices by which young people were 'converted' and encouraged to join a community that took all their assets and forbade them to have any contact with family or friends. The church had therefore been declared 'socially harmful' by the British government, which was trying to shut it down. Because of her known association with an undesirable organisation, Miss Van Duyn was in effect declared *persona non grata*, barred from entry to Britain and refused a work permit. She immediately appealed to the British High Court on the grounds that Article 48 of the Treaty of Rome guaranteed freedom of movement for all workers within the Community. The High Court referred the matter to the European Court of Justice and received the judgement that 'Article 48 has direct effect and hence confers on individuals rights that are enforceable before the courts of a Member State'.[3]

We can therefore say that the importance of primary law in the EU is as follows:

- Primary law, as established in the treaties, has primacy over national law and, in these matters, the European Court of Justice has primacy over national courts.
- The provisions of primary law are as binding on the citizens of member states as they are upon the states themselves.

- The foundation laws of the Community are to be enforced by the national courts of the member states in exactly the same way as they apply national law.

The decisions of the European Court of Justice have created a new role for national courts. In the past, British judges have enforced and interpreted the laws of the UK: it has never been within their remit to question the validity of those laws. Now, it is very much the duty of a British judge to over-rule British law if it conflicts with Community law. Quite early in Britain's membership, in 1974, a senior British judge wrote that Britain was now 'part of a legal system which not only confers a right but imposes a duty on the Court in certain circumstances to invalidate legislation'.[4]

Secondary legislation

Secondary legislation refers to all those legal instruments devised and issued by the Community in order to administer policies laid down by the Community and achieve such aims and objectives of the Community as were established under primary legislation. Decisions made by institutions of the Community are passed to national governments for acceptance and implementation in the form of one of five different classes of legal instrument: regulations, directives, decisions, recommendations and opinions.

1 **Regulations**. Once issued, regulations become immediately effective as law within the member states without the need for any national legislation to endorse them. For the UK, the European Communities Act of 1972 gives authority for all subsequent EC regulations to have the same effect as UK domestic law approved by Parliament. Although regulations become law in the form that was agreed in Brussels, sometimes additional legislation is required in the member countries to make them more effective.
2 **Directives**. These are not as complete and detailed as regulations, but consist more of policy objectives. The results to be achieved are communicated to national governments and those objectives are binding on the governments. But the form and method in or by which those results are achieved is left to the discretion of the national governments.
3 **Decisions**. Unlike regulations and directives, decisions are not directed at all member states but are specifically directed at one country or a firm, organisation or individual within it. Because these decisions are specific, they are often administrative rather than legislative acts.
4 **Recommendations and opinions**. These are little more than suggestions or tentative proposals put out by the Council or Commission and are not binding on the member states in any way. Strictly speaking, they do not constitute Community legislation but are included here under secondary legislation because they may be taken into consideration by the Court of Justice when making a judgement about some other matter.

In any one year, several thousand legal instruments are issued. The number has declined in recent years with the completion of the drive towards the single market and an attempt to simplify and streamline EU procedures. The majority of these instruments are non-political, being routine administration and dealing with matters such as price levels in the CAP. Of those instruments that could be considered legislative, Commission figures indicate that in 2001 1,452 were regulations, 835 decisions and 122 directives. There were also 31 recommendations.

There are basically two sources of Community secondary legislation:

1 **Commission legislation.** This is made directly by the Commission and enacted under powers delegated by the Council. This legislation is largely made up of technical, trivial or routine administrative detail arising from legislation already agreed by the Council. However, the Commission can legislate without reference to the Council in certain areas, such as the granting of financial support from public funds.
2 **Council legislation.** Described more fully below, this involves consideration and consultation by the Council and EP of proposals formulated by the Commission.

The policy, decision-making and legislative process within the EU

As stated above, most administrative or regulatory legislation coming from Brussels takes the form of Commission legislation, drafted by the relevant directorate-general (DG) with the assistance of an advisory or management committee. With such routine measures there is little need for scrutiny or decisions by ministers, commissioners or national officials. On the other hand, when the regulations or directives to be issued are felt to be important or are likely to set a precedent or establish principles, then they are thought to need examination through the full Council legislative process. Traditionally described some time ago as 'a dialogue between the Council, representing national cabinets, and the Commission . . . acting . . . in the "interests" of the Community as a whole',[5] the European Parliament acts in little more than an advisory capacity in this process. It is known as the consultative or single reading procedure.

The passage of the Single European Act (SEA) and ratification of the Maastricht Treaty, and a growing awareness of the 'democratic deficit', pointed to the need for a greater involvement by the EP in the legislative process. For a range of important measures, specifically those relating to matters arising from the implementation of the SEA, a three-way process involving Commission, Council and Parliament was evolved, known as the co-operative or two-readings procedure. This was extended still further under Maastricht to give the EP the right to a final veto in certain circumstances. This extension of the co-operation procedure is known as the co-decision procedure and, under the provisions of the

Amsterdam Treaty, it has largely replaced the co-operation procedure in most matters relating to the single market.

The consultative procedure

1 **Initiation.** New policy initiatives are being put forward regularly and originate from a wide variety of sources. The suggestion may arise in the Commission, the Council of Ministers or in the EP: it may be the proposal of a member state, either through the Council or through the state's permanent representatives, or it may come from an outside body such as a pressure group. Whatever the source, a measure can only progress if and when it is adopted by the Commission, which is the only body with the power to draft legislation. Once a proposal is so adopted – a decision made at the highest level within the relevant DG – that same DG is set to work in framing the first draft proposal.

2 **Consultation.** The first draft is treated rather like a Green Paper in the British system. It is circulated to experts, national governments, committees of the EP, the Economic and Social Committee (ESC) and the Committee of the Regions (COR), and pressure or interest groups (see chapter 9), if they are involved. The views of these various bodies may or may not be considered when the draft is framed into a formal proposal. This proposal is passed by the DG to the *cabinet* of the responsible commissioner, from there to the *chefs des cabinets* and then, ultimately, to the College of Commissioners. The commissioners may accept, reject or amend the proposal, or they could just as easily refer it back to the DG for redrafting. The consultation process is very long-winded and it can take twelve months for the measure to move from draft to formal proposal.

3 **Scrutiny.** The formal proposal is passed to the Council of Ministers. It is also sent to the EP, the ESC and, if relevant, the COR for their opinions. As has been said, the EP has no legislative role here, its opinion being purely advisory, which the Council is free to accept or reject as it chooses. The EP does, however, have the means to delay legislation if it wishes, since the measure cannot proceed until the EP has given its opinion. If it wishes to delay matters until, for example, some change or amendment is made to the proposal, the EP can refuse to give its opinion until such time as it gets its way over the amendment, or at least until such an amendment has been considered. Nevertheless, however effective the delaying process may be as a tool of negotiation, it has to be stressed that the EP has no veto in the consultative procedure.

4 **Decision.** The proposal from the Commission is passed to the Council for a decision, work on the proposal often beginning in the Council before the EP and/or ESC have given their opinions. Preliminary work for the Council begins with a working party of national officials and representatives from the member states, who have the task of safeguarding national interests while reaching a common agreed text for the proposal. When the working

party has gone as far as it can, the text of the proposal is passed on to Coreper, which will attempt to reach final agreement. Any disagreements that Coreper cannot resolve can either be referred back to the working party for further negotiation, or can be passed to the Ministers in Council for a political resolution.

Only the ministers can make a legislative decision, either by unanimous agreement or by qualified majority voting. If no agreement can be reached at ministerial level the proposal can either be passed back to the Commission for the process to begin again, or the proposal can be referred to a future meeting in the hope that differences can be eliminated in the interim. In the event that agreement is reached in Council and the proposal adopted by the ministers, this marks the end of the consultative procedure.

The co-operative procedure

Brought in by implementation of the SEA, and extended by the Treaty on European Union (TEU), this procedure was an extension of the consultative procedure. It was introduced in an attempt to involve the EP in the legislative process, granting the EP powers over legislation that previously it had only possessed over the budget. Circumstances when the co-operation procedure is to be used have been prescribed by the relevant treaties and currently involve a large number of areas, including the European Regional Development Fund, research, the environment and overseas co-operation and development. The alternative name for the co-operation procedure is the 'two readings procedure' because it involves the proposal being presented twice to both the EP and the Council.

1 **First reading.** The initial stages of this procedure are very similar to the consultative procedure. In this instance, however, asking the EP for its opinion is known as the European Parliament First Reading and the EP is free to suggest its own amendments to the proposal, which are then forwarded to the Council after having been incorporated in the text of the proposal by the Commission. Under the Council First Reading, the Council of Ministers does not reach a decision but comes instead to a Common Position, usually by qualified majority voting, although unanimity is needed if the Council does not agree with the Commission.

2 The Parliament's second reading. The EP considers the Common Position of the Council over a maximum period of three months, although this can be extended to four months with the consent of the Council. At the end of this time it can act in one of three possible ways:

  i The EP can approve the Council's Common Position.
  ii The EP can reject the Council's Common Position, as long as it is by an absolute majority of all MEPs.
  iii The EP can amend the Council's Common Position, as long as it is by an absolute majority of all MEPs.

Whatever the decision by the EP, the matter is then sent back to the Council, except where the EP has proposed amendments. These must go first for further consideration by the Commission.

3 **The Commission.** Any amendments made to the Common Position by the EP must be considered by the Commission over a maximum period of one month, and one of two positions adopted:

i   The Commission can accept some or all the amendments made by the EP and incorporate them in the text of the Common Position. It is this amended text that is then sent to the Council.

ii The Commission may not accept some or all of the EP amendments, in which case they are not incorporated in the text of the Common Position. However, the Commission must send to the Council of Ministers even those amendments it has rejected, together with the reasons for that rejection.

4 The Council's second reading. The Council can follow a number of different courses of action, depending on what has happened in the EP or with the Commission.

i   If the EP has approved the Common Position, it can be passed without further discussion, and becomes a legislative act of the Community.

ii   If the EP rejected the Common Position by an absolute majority it can still be accepted by the Council, provided that action is taken within three months and that the Council decision is unanimous.

iii If amendments made by the EP have been incorporated in the Common Position by the Commission, the Council can accept the text by qualified majority voting.

iv   If amendments were not accepted by the Commission and not incorporated in the text, the Council can still override the Commission's objections and accept the amendments, but only by unanimous decision.

v   If the Council fails to act on an amended proposal forwarded by the Commission within three months of receiving that proposal from the Commission, the proposal is judged to have lapsed.

vi   If the EP failed to take any action during its second reading, the Council can choose to adopt the first agreed Common Position without any further procedures.

The co-decision procedure

This process was developed by the IGC reporting at Maastricht and is the subject of Article 189b of the TEU. It is intended to share decision making equally between the EP and Council and is meant to temper the right to veto legislation that had been given to the EP by the co-operative procedure.

Under the co-decision procedure a conciliation committee is formed, made up of equal numbers of MEPs and ministers from the Council, with the mediating presence of the Commission. This is done in the case of one of two possible situations:

1 if the EP has rejected an approved position of the Council
2 if the EP wishes to amend a Council proposal in a way unacceptable to the Council.

The conciliation committee will seek a compromise in the wording of the text that can be endorsed by both the Council and the EP. Because it comes after the second readings of the co-operation procedure, the co-decision procedure is sometimes known as the 'third reading'.

The procedure applies to a wide range of issues, but they specifically include the free movement of labour, consumer protection, education, culture, health and trans-European networks. Under the terms of the Amsterdam Treaty, the co-decision procedure largely replaces the co-operation procedure. It might be thought that the procedure would be long-winded, but an early assessment of TEU provisions (made by the Commission in May 1995) noted that the average time for a decision to be taken under the co-decision procedure was less than 300 days.

The assent procedure

This is not a legislative procedure but is nevertheless an important part of EU decision-making. The requirement that the assent of the EP was needed for any proposed enlargement of the EU was extended under Article 228 of the Maastricht Treaty to include such other constitutional matters as association agreements with third-world countries, the organisation and objectives of the structural and cohesion funds and the tasks and powers of the European Central Bank.

Decision making – the budget

In Britain, where the House of Commons has had control over the money supply since the fourteenth century, decisions taken about the Community budget are held to be very important. This was seen as especially true in the period 1979–84 when Margaret Thatcher was fighting hard to reduce Britain's overall budgetary contributions, as finally happened with the agreement on a rebate at Fontainebleau (1984).

Yet the Community budget is remarkably small in comparison with the budgets of even medium-sized member states. However, the outgoings of the Community, especially on the Common Agricultural Policy, have always been heavy and that expenditure continues to increase, despite reforms to the CAP, to the dismay of net contributors such as Britain and, even more so, Germany.

The Community sets a ceiling on revenue and expenditure which is expressed as a percentage of the gross domestic product (GDP) of all member states combined. The ceiling for the period 1993–97, which covered the implementation of the TEU, was fixed by the Delors Plan to 1.27 per cent of GNP. Part

Box 5.1
The British budgetary rebate

An agreement to resolve the British budgetary question was finally reached at Fontainebleau in June 1984 (see chapter 1 for details). As had happened since 1982, a special arrangement allowed West Germany – by far the largest net contributor – to pay a reduced share of what would otherwise have been a substantial proportion of the rebate, which in its first full year amounted to approximately £1 billion.

Subsequently the rebate has often been called into question at the time of any budget round, and periodically there is strong pressure for its abolition. Not surprisingly, British ministers are unwilling to yield on what they see as a good deal. They can accept being a relatively small net contributor to EU funds, but would find it difficult to sell any loss of the rebate to the British electorate.

During the Brussels talks in June 1994, preoccupied as British ministers were with the preservation of their 'red lines', they were also keen to see that the rebate was accepted for the foreseeable future.[6] They thought that it would be preserved, but shortly after the talks ended the Commission put forward a plan to operate from 2007–13 that the rebate (currently worth some £2 billion) should be shared among other more affluent member states. The effect of the proposal would be for Britain to become the largest net contributor, paying 0.51 per cent of its GDP into EU funds, compared with 0.35 per cent for Italy and 0.33 per cent for France – countries of similar size and wealth.

Some other states, including Finland publicly and others privately, are said to have called for the end of the rebate. The British are likely to resist strongly, knowing that any hope of winning a referendum on the EU constitution would be seriously endangered should the rebate be axed.

Table 5.1   *The value of the British budgetary rebate (£ million)*

Year	Rebate
1999	3,171
2000	2,085
2001	4,560
2002	3,099

of the eagerness for the enlargement of the EU in 1995 was that countries such as Austria and Finland would also be net contributors and would make a useful addition to swelling the hard-pressed budget.

On the other hand, the latest members (including Bulgaria and Romania, due to join in 2007) are in a very different position. They all look likely to be net beneficiaries of the EU budget. Taken together, they employ four times as many people in agriculture as the rest of the EU. The financial implications of extending even the current, semi-reformed CAP to these countries have long been recognised by the major contributors.

Revenue

Originally, the EC was financed by contributions levied on member states but this was found to be unsatisfactory and, since 1975, the budget has been financed through what are called 'own resources'. The components of these resources have changed over the years, but there are three principal forms of contributions made by member countries, as determined under the Delors budget package introduced post-Maastricht in 1992. These components of Community revenue are:

- a levy on the customs duties, agricultural dues and other premiums charged on imports from non-member countries;
- a proportion of national VAT revenue as the one consumer tax common to all EU member states;
- a direct charge on a country's gross national product (GNP) as the best indication of what a country can afford to pay – this charge was raised from 1.2 per cent in 1994 to 1.21 per cent in 1995 and to 1.27 per cent in 1997.

These three components were first introduced in 1988 and the proportions of EC revenue then represented by the three were: VAT – 59 per cent; customs duties, including agricultural levies – 28 per cent; GNP charge – 10 per cent (there was also about 3 per cent in miscellaneous revenue outside the three main headings). After 1993, the balance between the components was changed, because some of the poorer EU countries had a high consumption rate and therefore paid too much VAT in relation to the size of their economies. Accordingly, substantial reductions in the proportion represented by the VAT component were compensated for by increases in the GNP component. The figures in 2002 were respectively 35 per cent; 17.5 per cent; and 45 per cent (and 2.5 per cent miscellaneous).

It is apparent that all the revenue of the Community comes from levies on the revenues of member states. The Community, unlike any other form of government, has no tax-raising powers of its own. It is entirely at the mercy of the Council of Ministers, relying as it does on whatever levies the Council sees fit to grant, and out of which the Community must meet the expenditure commitments also fixed by the Council. It should be noted that only the EC has a budget, the other two pillars of the EU created by Maastricht being directly paid for by national governments.

Expenditure

The largest proportion of Community expenditure has always been devoted to the CAP, but reforms in the 1990s meant that this proportion was reduced to a figure below 50 per cent for the first time. (48.3 per cent in 2003). This reduction, however, is balanced by a whole new range of expenditure created by the Maastricht agreement. This new spending is divided between three main areas:

1 Increased aid to the Social and Regional Development Funds, to provide help for the poorer regions of the EU and to assist convergence of economic standards prior to monetary union. After the CAP, these funds are the largest recipient of EU expenditure, taking 34.3 per cent of the budget in 2003.
2 Money spent on increasing the competitiveness of European industry to reap the full benefit of the single market.
3 Increased foreign aid to countries outside the EU, especially to states in Eastern and Southern Europe that were formerly part of the Soviet bloc and which are now working towards making themselves acceptable for EU membership.

Table 5.2   *Contributions to and receipts from the EC, 2002 (€ million)*

Net contributors		Net beneficiaries	
Country	Amount	Country	Amount
Germany	5,896.9	Finland	−18.0
UK	3,985.0	Luxembourg	−791.0
Italy	3,038.9	Belgium	−1,474.7
Netherlands	2,876.3	Ireland	−1,581.1
France	1,928.7	Portugal	−2,685.5
Sweden	840.9	Greece	−3,356.9
Austria	255.1	Spain	−8,665.6
Denmark	215.8		

Note: There has been very little change in the countries to be found in either column since 2002, although of course the amounts involved are liable to fluctuate. The British figure allows for the rebate received under the Fontainebleau Agreement, June 1984.

Source: European Union Finance Team, HM Treasury.

The budgetary process

Each year's budget is different and there is therefore no typical format for the determination of the budget. But it is possible to detect a standard pattern for the process. It begins with the estimates of expenditure being sent to DGX1X of the Commission, which has responsibility for formulating the budget. These estimates arrive in the summer of the year prior to which the budget will apply. The likely revenue for the coming year is then calculated. The budget is then drafted in a preliminary form by the Commission before the first day of September, and submitted to the Council. The Council considers this document and sends its own revised version to the EP by 5 October. The EP debates the amended budget and proposes its own amendments, before returning it to the Council.

The proposals go back and forth between the Council and the EP, the two institutions that together form the budget authority. In the case of 'compulsory' expenditure (mainly the money spent on the CAP), the Council has the final word. In the case of other 'non-compulsory' expenditure (for example, on the size of the Social Fund), the EP has the final say and can modify expenditure according to conditions laid down in the treaties. The EP must not increase the overall budgetary expenditure beyond the ceiling devised by the Council.

There can be much conflict between the Council and the EP, who experience what Nicoll and Salmon call an 'uneasy partnership'.[7] The procedure can be slow, so that on occasions there is no settlement by the end of the year. In this case, the EU is allowed to spend each month one-twelfth of the provision made in the previous year's budget, so that the machinery of the EU may continue to function.

After difficulties over the budget in 1980, an attempt was made in the following year to improve the machinery. A Trilogue was created, comprising the president of the Budget Council, the president of the Commission (maybe with the relevant commissioner) and the president of the EP (maybe with the president of the Committee on Budgets). In 1988 it managed to bring about an agreement after a period in which deadlock had been reached.

It is the EP that ultimately adopts the budget and it has used its budgetary powers to the full in order to influence EU policies. This determination, together with the long-running threat that the EC budget might be stifled by a ceiling on 'own resources', explains why the budget procedure has often sparked off disputes between the EP and the Council.

All matters relating to the budget are closely scrutinised by the Court of Auditors, within which there are groups dealing with specific budgetary questions such as the CAP or the Regional Fund. Since Maastricht, the Court of Auditors has extended its activities from concern over financial rectitude to a wider monitoring of policy effectiveness. The Court not only checks that both revenue and expenditure observe legal regulations but also ensures that the Community is getting value for money by checking how far financial objectives have been met.

Scrutiny of EU legislation by the British parliament

By accepting the terms of the Treaty of Accession in 1972,[8] the British parliament accepted the primacy of EC legislation within the UK, with the exception of the need for some UK legislation to supplement regulations and implement directives. The Community legislation is not applied to the UK by any further

UK legislation, but is put into effect by way of statutory instruments or Orders in Council made under section 2 (2) of the European Communities Act 1972.

From the first, the House of Commons sought to overcome this breach of parliamentary sovereignty by insisting that when a proposal passed from the Commission to the Council, the British minister concerned did not approve the measure until it had been scrutinised by the relevant parliamentary committee. This reservation was expressed in a series of resolutions of the House from 1980 onwards, but its application to all proposals of the Commission was only formalised in what is known as the Scrutiny Reserve Resolution on 24 October 1990.

The Maastricht Treaty, which came into force in 1993, introduced the two new pillars of the EU – Title V, dealing with defence and security, and Title VI, dealing with justice and internal security. Since neither pillar involves legislation, there was a period when both escaped scrutiny by national parliaments and there were calls for this to be rectified. Then there was the introduction of the co-decision procedure in Community legislation, which meant that a third reading stage was introduced into the legislative process that was not covered by the UK Scrutiny Reserve. The Amsterdam Treaty required an increased use of the co-decision procedure, while the same treaty included a Protocol on National Parliaments (Protocol 13) which imposed a six-week delay between the point when legislative proposals or proposals under the second or third pillars were sent by the Commission to the EP and Council and the point when the decision was taken by the Council. This six-week period was ideal for scrutiny by national parliaments and it led to calls in Britain that the parliamentary scrutiny process be extended. This was duly done in a new resolution of the House of Commons adopted on 17 November 1998.[9]

The new resolution stated that 'no Minister should give agreement to any legislative proposal or to any agreement under Titles V or VI which is still subject to scrutiny or awaiting consideration by the House'. Definitions of agreement include:

- agreement to a programme, plan or recommendation for EC legislation;
- political agreement;
- in the case of a proposal on which the Council acts in accordance with the procedure referred to in Article 189b of the Treaty of Rome (co-decision), agreement to a common position, to a joint text, and to confirmation of the common position (with or without amendments proposed by the EP);
- in the case of a proposal on which the Council acts in accordance with the procedure referred to in Article 189c of the Treaty of Rome (co-operation), agreement to a common position.

It has to be said that the scrutiny process can do nothing to prevent the implementation of Community legislation; the committees involved can only concern themselves with prospective legislation. Parliament can advise ministers on the line to take in negotiation, but they cannot amend or revise legislation once it has been through the relevant legislative procedure.

Scrutiny by the House of Lords

Ironically, the House of Lords has always been more concerned with the workings of Europe than the House of Commons, a general belief having been established that the Lords had the time and ability to deal with non-legislative matters for which the Commons did not have time in its busy timetable. What is more, the Lords not only have more time to discuss Community policies on the floor of the House but members of the Lords appear to be more willing to serve on European committees than their opposite numbers in the Commons. Their interest is probably aided by the fact that, unlike the rules pertaining to Westminster parliamentary elections, members of the Lords are permitted to stand for election to the EP and several Tory peers, and more recently Liberal Democrat peeresses, have sat as MEPs over the years. Also in the Lords are many senior politicians who have served Europe in the past, such as the late Lord Jenkins, former president of the Commission.

With regard to the actual scrutiny process, a select committee, under the chairmanship of Lord Maybray-King, investigated possible procedures that could be adopted by the House of Lords and reported its conclusions in July 1973. Discussions arising from the Maybray-King Report finally resulted in the establishment of the Lords' European Communities Committee in April 1974. In 1999 notice was taken of changes introduced by the Treaties of Maastricht and Amsterdam and the committee changed its name to the European Union Committee. The committee is appointed for each parliamentary session only, but its renewal has always been as good as automatic.[10]

The actual size of the committee is not fixed, although it normally numbers about twenty. In 2004, it had nineteen members, each of whom served on one of the six sub-committees. These have the power to co-opt members. In all, allowing for permanent and co-opted members, some seventy peers are actively involved in the committee system (10 per cent of the membership of the House). Add to these those peers with a special interest or expertise on a given subject who are invited to take part, and those Lords who are MEPs and have an open invitation to attend, and it can be seen that there is considerable involvement by the Lords in the scrutiny of European legislation. To reflect the importance attached to this, the chair of the European Union Committee is appointed to be principal deputy chairman of committees and is paid a salary as an official of the House of Lords.

The six permanent sub-committees are labelled A to F and are:

A Finance, trade and external relations.
B Energy, industry and transport.
C Common foreign and security policy.

D Environment, agriculture, public health and consumer protection.
E Law and institutions.
F Social affairs, education and home affairs.

Sub-committee E is very important because it reflects the former status of the House of Lords as supreme court of the UK, having the special task of considering the legal implications of Community law on UK law. The sub-committee is chaired by a Law Lord and has access to expert advice from a counsel and a legal assistant. Sub-committee C is a fairly recent addition and was included after 1998 for the scrutiny of pillars two and three of the european union. Ad hoc additional sub-committees can be set up as needed; for example, in the immediate aftermath of Maastricht a number of sub-committees were set up to examine the implications and problems of monetary and political union.

The sub-committees meet once a week to hear and discuss evidence, from which they draw up draft reports. The reports are passed on to the full committee that meets once a fortnight. If the draft is approved it is published as a report of the select committee of the House. These reports also make recommendations as to whether there should be a debate on the report on the floor of the House.

Both committee and sub-committees have close relations with the EU Commission, the EP and the British permanent representative in Coreper, with visits to Brussels, Strasbourg and Luxembourg by the chairs, representatives and clerks of the various sub-committees. Officials of the Commission may also come to London to join in deliberations of the sub-committees. The select committee receives regular reports on European developments from Foreign Office ministers, particularly after European Council summits. The committee is also active in the Conference of European Affairs Committees of National Parliaments (COSAC).

Scrutiny by the Lords begins with a memorandum from the relevant ministry concerning the legal and political implications of a proposal submitted to the Council of Ministers. There are a large number of such memoranda, since about 800 EC documents are submitted to national parliaments each year. The Chair of the Lords committee must sift through these memoranda and decide as to which are worth consideration and which represent mere routine detail. About a quarter of the proposals submitted are considered worth discussion and these are referred to the relevant sub-committee.

Only about 10 per cent of these proposals are sufficiently important as to merit a report and only about half of the reports are debated in the House. A wide range of issues has been examined over the last three decades, examples including proposals to combat discrimination, the Convention on the Future of Europe, public access to EU documents, and fishing. Other than producing reports, the committee may set out its views on a matter in a letter addressed to the relevant minister and government department. The letter is then included in the committee's correspondence, which is periodically published in the form of a report to the House.

The scrutiny process is backed up by a 'scrutiny reserve' that states that the government cannot agree to any proposal in the Council of Ministers until it has been cleared by the committee. This arrangement was formalised in a Resolution of the House of Lords that was agreed on 6 December 1999 and allows the House of Lords the ability to influence the position the government will adopt in negotiating with the other member states of the EU.

Scrutiny by the House of Commons

In the Commons, the equivalent of the committee headed by Lord Maybray-King was the committee chaired by Sir John Foster, which reported in 1973 and which led to the formation of a select committee then known as the Committee on European Secondary Legislation, first appointed in May 1974. When Maastricht introduced two new pillars into the EU, both of them involved new categories of documents that the committee did not have the authority to scrutinise. The provisions of the Amsterdam Treaty, including Protocol 13, made for additional reasons for the scrutiny procedure to be reformed and modernised. Suggestions as to how this might be done were proposed in June 1998 and finally resolved in a resolution of 17 November 1998.

Three changes were made to the scrutiny process in the Commons:

1 the name of the committee was changed to the European Scrutiny Committee;
2 the remit of the committee included a new Scrutiny Reserve Resolution, discussed above;
3 existing standing committees considering European legislation were increased from two to five.

It was also recommended that:

• departmental select committees in the Commons should take an increased interest in European business;
• there should be more links between Westminster MPs and MEPs;
• a National Parliament Office should be established in Brussels.

New terms of reference for the committee included the scrutiny of documents that fell into one of six categories:

1 a proposal for legislation by the Council of Ministers, either alone or in co-operation with the EP;
2 any document which it is proposed should be submitted to the European Council, the Council of Ministers or the European Central Bank;
3 any proposal for action under Title V of the TEU which is to be submitted to the Council of Ministers;
4 any proposal for action under Title VI of the TEU which is to be submitted to the Council of Ministers;

5 any other form of document which is published by one EU institution for submission to another EU institution;
6 any other document relating to the EU, deposited in the House by a Minister of the Crown.

The committee has a membership of sixteen, with a quorum of five, but, unlike the session-by-session approach of the Lords, these are nominated for the life-time of a parliament. Like the Lords' committee, the Commons committee receives copies of proposals made by the Commission to the Council of Minis-ters, together with an explanatory memorandum from the relevant govern-ment department. The committee meets once a week to consider the various matters laid before it, producing a report together with recommendations for any further discussion or debate within the Commons.

Parliament is informed of Community developments retrospectively by six-monthly reports prepared by the select committee and published as White Papers under the title 'Developments in the European Community'. Originally debates on European matters took place late at night, with a one-hour limit on discussion, the whole heard before an empty and uninterested Commons chamber. However, in 1989, the whole system of scrutinising European legis-lation was examined by the Procedure Committee of the Commons, which rec-ommended that debates should be more forward-looking. As a result, there are now regular twice-yearly debates on EU matters, usually held just before the European Council meetings of June and December. Another recommendation of the Procedure Committee was that when the European Scrutiny Committee recommends that certain documents should be referred to the House for fur-ther discussion, discussion and debate should be moved from the floor of the House and into committee. The original proposal was for five standing commit-tees, which would differ from other standing committees in that, not only would they be permanent, but they would have no power to amend legislation.

In 1990 the Commons agreed to the setting up of the standing committees but modified the Procedure Committee's recommendation by saying that there should be just three. In the event insufficient interested MPs could be found to staff three committees and the system initiated in January 1991 provided for only two committees. However, the reforms of 1998 suggested that the system should revert to five standing committees and, in the event, a Commons Stand-ing Order established three European Standing Committees, each with thirteen members nominated for the duration of a Parliament. The chair is chosen from the Chairmen's Panel and may change for each sitting. The quorum is three, excluding the chair.

The three standing committees, with divided responsibilities, are:

A Agriculture, fisheries, forestry and food; environment and transport.
B Treasury, social security, Foreign and Commonwealth Office, Home Office, Lord Chancellor's Office.

C Trade and industry, education and employment, health, culture, media and sport.[11]

The committees meet on a weekly basis and their programme consists of a ministerial statement followed by two-and-a-half hours' debate. Any resolution reached is reported to the House by the committee's chair. That resolution is put before the House as a motion that is moved in the House a few days later, although this recognition by the full House is merely a formality and no debate is allowed on the subject.

As has already been said, although scrutiny of European legislation has been tightened up since Maastricht and Amsterdam, the only power over European legislation possessed by either House of Parliament is the resolution requiring ministers to await the scrutiny procedure before giving assent to measures coming before the Council of Ministers.

The role of the Civil Service

Unlike most other EU member states, Britain had neither a ministry for European affairs nor a specific minister charged with responsibility for European matters until the changes introduced by the Blair government in 1997. Before that, the tendency was for British governments to treat European policy as a branch of foreign policy, thereby leaving the operational aspects in the hands of the Foreign and Commonwealth Office (FCO). Margaret Thatcher tried to restrict the influence of the FCO, partly because she always distrusted the 'old-school-tie' type of links between the FCO and what she called the 'Tory Grandees', and partly because she detected pro-European sentiments in the teams of officials provided by the FCO for European Councils and other meetings with EU fellow-members. During her premiership, she actually contemplated the setting up of a separate department of state. However, she abandoned the idea when it was suggested to her that, because those Britons who had a close relationship with Europe – like Edward Heath or Leon Brittan – tended to 'go native', a European affairs department could prove to be a Trojan horse of Europeanisation in Whitehall.

The nearest thing that the Conservative administration ever had to a minister of Europe was during the British presidency in the second half of 1992. Tristan Garel-Jones, a minister of state at the FCO, was given the special task of coordinating the FCO's servicing of the many committees and working parties that Britain had to administer as president of the EC. In doing so he had the eager assistance of his FCO civil servants because, as has been written elsewhere, the FCO has always shown every sign of welcoming its work for Europe: 'Involvement in European policy has given the Foreign Office an interest in many areas of policy not usually associated with it; hence the powerful . . . [role] . . . of the Foreign Secretary . . . [in pressing] . . . for membership of the ERM'.[12]

Because the FCO has always claimed a leading role in anything to do with Europe it has within it two executive departments specifically designated to deal with European matters:

- the European Community Department (Internal), dealing with European matters in the UK;
- the European Community Department (External) dealing with British interests in Europe.

These arrangements are based on the FCO's view that relations with the EU are to be regarded first and foremost as facets of Britain's foreign policy, which should be dealt with exclusively by the FCO. Nevertheless, over the years, the FCO has been forced to cede work on European issues to the Cabinet Office and other government departments until, according to Cabinet Office statistics issued in early 1999, there were no fewer than sixteen separate British government departments dealing with specifically European policy issues.

A belief that the EU is essentially an aspect of British domestic policy rather than British foreign policy led government departments apart from the FCO to set up an alternative to the two European Community Departments of the FCO. This they did by establishing an important European secretariat in the Cabinet Office.[13] Through a weekly meeting with Britain's permanent representative in Brussels, this small secretariat, numbering no more than about twenty civil servants seconded from other departments, plays a major part in co-ordinating European matters. It:

- handles all those European matters likely to be included on Cabinet or Cabinet Committee agendas;
- helps to frame agreements on common responsibilities between departments where European issues are involved;
- briefs departmental civil servants on the present and future implications of British policy in Europe;
- oversees the scrutiny of European legislation by the European select committees of both Houses of Parliament, including the briefing of committee members on EU matters;
- checks that the UK complies to the full with any requirements demanded by the European Commission in the implementation of EU legislation.

Within Whitehall departments there is a great deal of work for civil servants in supporting those ministers who are carrying out their European role as members of the Council of Ministers; something which becomes a particularly onerous task during Britain's presidency of the EU. When ministers attend a Council meeting, they will be accompanied by a team of officials from the relevant department who act as advisers during meetings of the Council, as well as providing a secretariat to record the findings of the meeting and note the actions to be taken. This Council work for the Civil Service reaches far beyond actual Council meetings and includes regular contacts within and between national delegations over a period of several weeks in order to prepare the ground for the Council meetings. Council meetings are themselves so short that they rely on national delegations having reached a provisional conclusion on the final form of any agreement before the actual meeting takes place. As a result, ministers have comparatively little to do at Council meetings, merely concentrating on hammering out the final details while passing the main issues by the prior agreement established by the officials.

British civil servants in Brussels

British civil servants do a considerable amount of work for the EU without losing their place in the domestic structure of the Home Civil Service. This is especially true of civil servants seconded to work in Europe while themselves remaining part of the British Home Civil Service. Typical of this are those civil servants appointed or seconded for service with the UK Permanent Representation (UKREP) on the Committee of Permanent Representatives (Coreper).

At first a preparatory body set up to hammer out the details written into the 1957 Treaty of Rome, Coreper has developed into one of the most powerful groups of officials in the world. As we have seen in chapter 3, over the years the committee has come to comprise hundreds of officials, which split for convenience into two bodies, Coreper I and II, as long ago as 1962. Coreper II is the senior, its core membership comprising the fifteen permanent representatives, while Coreper I acts as a forum for their deputies. The two committees are responsible for:

- keeping EU institutions and the governments and bureaucracies of the member states informed of each others' work;
- ensuring that national and European policy are not at loggerheads;
- finding compromises so as not to undermine core national positions.

In practice, these different functions are difficult to separate and merge into the more general aim of keeping the EU working smoothly.[14]

The permanent representatives who make up Coreper are, of course, the equivalent of ambassadors to the EU; the British representatives are for the most part senior diplomats from the FCO, the UKREP having a regular staff of about forty officials plus ancillaries. The permanent representative in person is a career diplomat from the FCO, with the same status as a senior ambassador, ranking in seniority alongside the ambassadors to Washington or Paris. The UKREP staff in its entirety, however, is only partially provided by either the FCO or the Diplomatic Service, with as much as two-thirds of the staff in fact being from other Whitehall departments, including the deputy permanent representative who is traditionally from the Department of Trade and Industry. UKREP has three main functions:

1 UKREP officials provide advice, information and secretarial support in traditional Civil Service fashion for ministers and senior civil servants who are temporarily in Brussels or elsewhere in the EU on EU business.

2 The permanent representative and UKREP officials act to co-ordinate actions and liaise between the British government and EU institutions. UKREP will lobby the Commission and the EP on behalf of British interests, while the British government will be kept in touch by means of the permanent representative attending meetings with the Cabinet secretariat in London at least once a week.

3 As part of the EU legislative process, Coreper provides working parties which do developmental work on proposals put by the Commission to the Council of Ministers. These working parties are made up of officials and experts provided by national governments, either seconded directly or via the permanent representation. A member state such as Britain might have up to four of its nationals as members of any one working party, and since there may be anything up to ten such working parties operating at any one time, the contribution made by the national delegations can be quite substantial and significant.

Civil servants working within UKREP are the only British representatives permanently based in Brussels, although there are many temporary secondments of national officials to EU institutions. One major European duty that can best be filled by a senior civil servant is by secondment to the support team of one of the two British commissioners, since the members of a commissioner's *cabinet* are usually civil servants who have been seconded, either from the commissioner's own national civil service, or from another part of the EU bureaucracy. It is only natural that the convenience of familiarity means that it is not unusual for members of the *cabinet* to be fellow-nationals of the commissioner, even though convention expects at least one to be from another member state.

How to be a eurocrat

The Civil Service Management Code states quite clearly, under the heading 'Service with the European Institutions':

> Departments and agencies should encourage staff with potential to consider service with the European institutions as part of their developmental training. Work in the institutions should normally be regarded as experience which will be valuable to the department or agency on the officer's return.[15]

Recruitment for service with the EU bureaucracy is therefore encouraged by the Civil Service establishment and entry to service in Europe is by way of the normal recruitment channels of the Home Civil Service, even though successful candidates who are offered permanent service with the EU are required to retire from the UK Civil Service immediately upon appointment. There is a source of national pride for member countries in getting as large a number of their citizens as possible into service with the EU's institutions, competition for permanent places with the European institutions being very keen among would-be eurocrats from all member states.

However, permanent service is not necessarily the main aim of either the applicants in question nor the Civil Service establishment which has encouraged their application. It is equally as likely that, rather than seeking a permanent position, British applicants are looking for long or short-term secondments to work in Europe, either for a specific purpose or simply to gain experience with European institutions as a career-building move, experience that can be useful both to the civil servants themselves and to the departments or agencies which employ them and to which they return after their time in Brussels or elsewhere in Europe.

Summary

The EU has an established and complex procedure for the determination of policy making and legislation in which national representatives can take part and which involve all the institutions of the Community. Provisions of the SEA, TEU and Amsterdam Treaty are leading to a reduction in the democratic deficit through increased powers for the EP in an extended legislative process.

National involvement in the European process includes the scrutiny of European legislation by both Houses of Parliament, the work done in government departments and the interaction of British civil servants with their European counterparts. Possibly the greatest involvement of national interests is through pressure and interest groups and lobbyists of all kinds working in Brussels, a theme to which we turn in chapter 9.

Notes

1   *The ABC of Community Law* (3rd edition), The European Commission, (European Documentation Series), 1991.
2   Case 26/62, Van Gend & Loos [1963] ECR 1 (Nature of Community law).
3   Case 41/74, Van Duyn [1974] ECR 359 (Direct applicability – freedom of movement).
4   Lord Scarman, quoted in P. Norton, *The British Constitution in Flux*, Blackwell, 1982.
5   L. Lindberg and S. Scheingold, *Europe's Would-Be Polity*, Prentice-Hall, 1970.
6   As reported in *The Guardian*, 8 July 2004.
7   W. Nicoll and T. Salmon, *Understanding the European Union*, Pearson, 2001.
8   European Communities Act 1972, Section 2 (1).
9   *The House of Commons and European Communities Legislation*, Factsheet 56, Public Information Office of the House of Commons, originally published 1991 but amended and reissued May 2003.

10 *The House of Lords and the European Community*, Information Sheet 4, Journal and Information Office, House of Lords, originally issued 1993 but amended and reissued May 2003.

11 As far as European legislation is concerned, documents distributed to the three committees listed here are allocated according to the departmental responsibilities shown, even if those matters are also dealt with by the Scottish, Welsh or Northern Ireland Offices.

12 D. Watts, *Reluctant Europeans*, Sheffield Hallam University Press, 1996.

13 R. Pyper, *The British Civil Service*, Harvester Wheatsheaf, 1995.

14 Details of Coreper are taken from an article by A. Keene in *Europa*, a discussion journal published by the European Commission, 1997.

15 Cabinet Office, *Civil Service Management Code*, Machinery of Government and Propriety Division of the Cabinet Office (OPS), 1996.

6

EU policies and their impact on Britain

The Treaty of Rome alludes to three areas of policy as 'common' ones: agriculture (Article 43), commerce (Article 113) and transport (Article 74). In addition, there are other references to 'common policies', but it was in the later treaties that the term 'Community policy' began to appear. Initially, the emphasis on the Community was upon the development of a common market free of trading barriers, and this aspect is still of fundamental importance. The common commercial policy, competition policy and the Single European Act are all related to the promotion of what used to be called the Common Market, a label some people still employ when they refer to the EU.

Today, the EU is much more than a Common Market, for it was always the intention that close co-operation would extend into other sectors. Some of these are economic policies related to tackling wider issues than those of tariffs and their elimination. Others go well beyond the economic and financial spheres, and deal with matters ranging from foreign policy to immigration, from broadcasting to combating crime.

Just as the range of policies undertaken by the EU is a wide one, so is the degree to which the EU becomes involved in their management. In some areas, such as agriculture, industry and trade, many important decisions are now taken at European level, which is why the National Farmers' Union, the Confederation of British Industry (CBI) and the Institute of Directors (IoD) spend so much of their time on European policy. In others, including some of those dealt with in the second and third (intergovernmental) pillars of the Maastricht Treaty, EU involvement is increasing. This is also the case with many aspects of social policy, particularly those relating to labour relations, working conditions and employment practices more generally. In a few areas, there is little or no EU involvement in national policy. This is true of issues relating to policy on education, health and welfare. The position is summarised in Table 6.1.

The trend in recent years has been for Brussels to become more involved in many spheres, including some in which its role was once limited. On defence, foreign policy and the environment, the European machinery now has more of

Table 6.1   *The level of EU involvement in a range of key British policy areas*

Policy area	Much involvement	Joint involvement	Little/no involvement
Agriculture	*		
Fishing	*		
Trade	*		
Drugs		*	
Environment		*	
Regions		*	
Working conditions		*	
Foreign affairs and security[a]		*	
Education			*
Health			*
Housing			*
Welfare			*

Note: [a] Defence policy was not on the agenda a generation ago, but today there is limited involvement. In the whole area of foreign and security policy, the trend is towards greater EU interest.

a role than was the case even a decade or so ago, while many of the policies dealt with under the heading of justice and home affairs had only very limited Community involvement pre-Maastricht. The extent to which the adoption of the concept of subsidiarity involves any reversal of this broad trend has yet to become fully apparent, although so far few issues that have been within the competence of Brussels in recent years have ceased to be so.

The picture is then a patchy one, with the nature and extent of EU involvement in policy making differing from issues to issue. In some areas, national governments have been more willing to relinquish some of their capacity to determine policy than in others. The representatives of any country inevitably have to ask themselves what benefits are to be derived from a common approach and to balance possible gains for Europe as a whole against pressing national considerations. They also have to bear in mind what public opinion at home will stand.

Eurobarometer, on behalf of the European Commission, has regularly polled people across the EU to ascertain their views on which policy areas are best decided in Brussels and which are better handled by national governments. The findings usually indicate that people prefer Europe-wide decision making in those areas where the problems cross or go beyond national boundaries (the fight against drugs, the environment and overseas aid), and national action on issues where the decisions impact upon them more directly (education and health). Broadly, such findings are in line with the reality of existing practice, for the emphasis upon subsidiarity stresses that decisions are best taken at the most appropriate level. Those that require a co-operative approach tend to derive from Brussels, while those which can be taken closer to the citizen are made by national or in some cases regional governments.

In Eurobarometer poll 61, conducted early in 2004, it was found that of those interviewed 61 per cent across the EU thought it desirable for the EU to have a common foreign policy, 72 per cent thought it desirable to have a common defence and security policy. For Britain, out of the then fifteen members, the figures were the lowest, at 39 and 52 per cent. Of the issues that mostly concerned voters in the run-up to the European elections, employment, immigration and the fight against crime were seen as the most important, with the environment, citizens' rights, agriculture, defence and foreign policy trailing after them.

The effectiveness of EU action also varies considerably. Even where there is a substantial degree of Brussels involvement, it does not follow that the best policy is promoted. Part of the difficulty lies in deciding what is best for the EU and what is best for individual national states. Members have their own traditions and preferences and the fight to maintain and protect national interests in particular policy areas can make it difficult to achieve a genuinely co-ordinated and consistent EU approach. Nugent concludes that the pace, manner and effectiveness of advance depends on three factors:[1]

1 'The leadership given by the Commission.' Some presidents, such as Walter Hallstein (1958–66), Roy Jenkins (1977–80) and Jacques Delors (1985–94), imparted their own enthusiasms, imposed their own style on the Commission and were particularly effective in galvanising the Community into action, taking up new initiatives and seeing them through to implementation.
2 'The perceptions of the member states of what is desirable.' Representatives of national governments have to be convinced that there are significant gains to be made from acting together; gains not just for the EU as a whole but ones that coincide with a substantial measure of national self-interest. With the introduction and increasing use of majority voting, it is not necessary for all states to perceive the advantages.
3 'The individual and collective capacities of the member states to translate their perceptions into practice.' Even if there is a sympathetic response for a particular initiative, the ministers of that country may feel unenthusiastic about supporting it in the Council of Ministers. Domestic political pressures can make it difficult for them, so that any French of German government is going to think twice before it supports measures that could lessen the prosperity of its farmers, just as British ministers have been under enormous pressure from trawlermen over recent years to provide better protection for the domestic fishing fleet, Sometimes it is necessary for governments to concede, but negotiators need to show that they have earned some trophies in the negotiations before they yield to the pressure of other Council members.

In this chapter, we are concerned with the evolution and details of some of the better-known EU policies and their importance for Britain. We explore how Britain has played a role in modifying their development, the effects they have on British life and any issues that are problematic and/or currently under discussion. It is convenient to group the issues into three broad categories:

1 financial and economic policy;
2 social policy;
3 external relations.

Budgetary issues are relevant to the first category. The budget has been a cause of much controversy, and in Britain eurosceptics and europhobes often point to the costs of membership. Britain remains second only to Germany as a net contributor to EU funding and is likely to continue as a paymaster than a beneficiary (see p. 137).

The creation of the single market

The Treaty of Rome provided for the creation of a 'common market' based on the free movement of foods, persons, services and capital. But by the early 1980s a range of barriers to trade had developed – fiscal, physical and technical. Some of the obstacles were associated with enlargement. But they had also come about because, at a time of recession in the 1970s, member governments had subsidised firms and introduced regulations overtly designed to promote safety or consumer protection but which were in fact protectionist devices intended to protect their hard-pressed industrial sectors. Such obstacles prohibited the development of a genuinely free Community market.

The creation of a single market following the passage of the SEA marked a major extension of the original idea of a common market. It planned for an area without internal frontiers within which the free movement of people, services, goods and capital (the four freedoms) would be assured. The Commission's White Paper 'Completing the internal market' (June 1985) set a target date (1 January 1993) for the completion of the single market. The achievement of the programme required the enactment of nearly three hundred measures.

Pursuit of this programme was supported both by committed European federalists and economic liberals. As we have seen, Margaret Thatcher was distinctly unenthusiastic about most proposals aimed towards the further development of the EC, but she was a strong supporter of the 1992 programme, which she viewed as a massive exercise in deregulation – led as it was by a former member of her government, Lord Cockfield. Her government and subsequent administrations were committed to the deregulation and liberalisation of the European economy and wished to see it entrenched at European level.

Not every measure planned by Lord Cockfield was achieved by the set date of 1992, but the majority were implemented. Overall, Britain has a good record on compliance with single market requirements. Every two years, the Commission produces a list of compliant and non-compliant states: Britain, along with

---

Box 6.1

The main barriers to the creation of the single market

The fiscal barriers that the Commission wished to tackle concerned indirect taxation, mainly in the form of value-added tax (VAT) and excise duties, such as those on alcohol, petrol and tobacco. The Commission argued that wide variations in levels of taxation between the member states necessitated frontier controls to prevent the tax evasion brought about by individuals and firms importing goods from a state with a lower tax rate into one with a higher one. In this way, varying taxes represented a distortion to trade. The Commission favoured a harmonisation of VAT rates, but later compromised on a minimum general rate of 15 per cent, with lower rates for some specified items.

Physical barriers were those that confronted people or goods as they crossed frontiers, involving customs and immigration. A symbol of division in the EC, they also imposed heavy costs on business. For instance, lorries had to wait clearance at the EC's internal frontiers, sometimes for hours, or on occasion even for days. The costs of frontier checks on consignments of goods varied from country to country. The Commission wished to see them all removed.

Technical barriers included a range of regulations and standards. Regulations defined the specifications of a product to assure the consumer of its quality and safety, and standards were needed to ensure the compatibility of products. Plug compatibility was thought to be important in the areas of information technology. Guarantees of safety were not only required for products ranging from the bodywork of cars to the tyres fitted upon them, but also for articles of capital equipment and services such as banking and life assurance.

Belgium, Denmark, Finland, Spain, Sweden and the Netherlands, is among those that earns credit for strong progress, whereas states such as France, Germany and Greece score less impressively.

British governments have stressed the value of a single market for British industry. Indeed, this is one of the few areas on which ministers have sounded consistently sympathetic to the policies of the EU. They point to the extent of British trade with other members, currently approximately 58 per cent of total British trade. Indeed, seven out of ten top destinations for British exports and sources of imports are other EU states, enabling ministers to claim that much British production and income is linked to membership and that millions of jobs are dependent upon it.

These are benefits that derive from being a member of a Union in which British negotiatiors have a say in shaping Union policy. Opponents of British membership would argue that those benefits would accrue to the British economy whether or not Britain remains a member. Alternatives sometimes advanced are:

- membership of EFTA, whose member countries belong to the European Economic Area and gain all the benefits of the single market without – it is claimed – the disadvantages that accompany them;
- membership of NAFTA, as Iceland has had in recent years;
- 'going it alone', in the hope that Britain as a low regulation, privatised economy on the edge of the EU would become a magnet for private investment.

The Blair administration has been an enthusiastic supporter of the strategy agreed at the Lisbon Summit (March 2001) to create the most competitive and dynamic knowledge-based economy in the world by 2010, seeing this as the means of 'sustaining economic growth with more and better jobs, and greater social cohesion'.[2] In pursuit of this modernising agenda, Blair has been prepared to ally himself with right-of-centre governments in Italy and Spain in pursuit of the 'new economy' agenda, stressing the value of liberalisation for European firms and peoples.

Harmonisation and consumer protection

Although the bitterest arguments between eurosceptics and those in favour of European integration revolve around the issue of monetary union and the single currency, most misunderstandings about EU directives originate in the SEA and attempts that were made to apply the principles of the single market as from 1993. The problem initially was that each member country had its own national rules on health, safety and consumer standards. Because of this, products that satisfied the standards in one country might still offend the regulations of another. Similarly, products made in one country might not be accepted for sale in another, negating the principles of the single market.

Originally the solution was seen to be the standardisation of rules, replacing many different national regulations with a single set of rules common to the whole Community. But over the years a more realistic sense of what is practicable has meant that the emphasis has changed. Standardising or harmonisation has been replaced by a practice known as 'mutual recognition', meaning that whatever is legally produced in one member country is judged to be legally available for sale in any other member country: the consumer's interests being protected by stringent rules concerning labelling and consumer information.

The consumer in the EU is protected according to five fundamental rights:

1 The protection of consumers' health and safety – banning the sale of products that may endanger the health or safety of the consumer.
2 The protection of consumers' economic interests – involving regulation of misleading advertising, unfair contractual agreements and unethical sales techniques, such as those used in selling time-share.

3 The right to full information about goods and services offered, including all directives on the labelling of foodstuffs, textiles and medicines. Acceptable ingredients, additives and weights and measures are legitimised by e-numbers.
4 The right to redress – involving the rapid and affordable settlement of complaints by consumers who feel they have been injured or damaged by using certain goods or services.
5 Consumer representation in the decision-making process – usually meaning the Consumers' Consultative Council, which is a committee made up of consumer associations from the various member states together with five EC advisory bodies: the European Bureau of Consumers' Organisations (BEUC), the Confederation of Family Organisations in the EC (Coface), the EC Consumer Co-operatives (Eurocoop), the European Trade Union Confederation (ETUC) and the European Inter-regional Institute for Consumer Affairs (EIICA).[3]

Despite the flood of regulations and directives emanating from the Commission, most legislation on consumer affairs is the responsibility of national governments. Community legislation either fills in gaps left by national laws, or covers areas where the consumer in one member state has a complaint concerning another member state, as when a British consumer is the victim of dubious time-share sales in Spain. The guideline for EU legislation is: 'As little regulation as possible, but as much as is necessary to protect consumers'.[4]

Since the EU's first consumer programme was issued in 1975 there have been directives requiring national action on:

- the safety of cosmetic products;
- the labelling of foodstuffs;
- misleading advertising and doorstep selling;
- advertising aimed at children;
- comparative advertising;
- the selling of financial services;
- consumer credit and unfair terms in sales and service contract;
- guarantees and after-sales service;
- the safety of toys;
- the safety of building and gas-burning materials;
- an internal market in postal services.

One interesting facet of harmonisation suggested some years ago was that there should be a single European emergency number, whereby EU citizens would be able to call on the police, fire and ambulance services by dialling exactly the same telephone number in all EU member states. This has now been done, the European number having been established in parallel with recognised national emergency numbers. In the UK the citizen can choose between dialling 999 and 112.

Aiding the harmonisation of products and services across Europe in the interests of the consumer is the European Standardisation Committee (CEN). This is a body made up of national standards agencies and affiliated producer and consumer organisations from nineteen European countries. It is not an EU body, although the EU often gets the blame for its more wayward decisions from the tabloid press. In fact, many proposals pilloried by the British press as 'Brussels madness' turn out actually to have been suggested by the CEN rather than the Commission.

Competition policy

European legislation on competition in industry and commerce has been in existence for some time but gained greater importance after the establishment of the single market. As a former commissioner for competition policy has said: 'The continuing integration of the Community and the ever-present need for the protection of the consumer from competitive abuses, ensures that competition policy will always play a vital role in Europe'.[5] Competition legislation in Europe has had its effect on Britain in a number of spheres, including anti-monopoly and cartel legislation, selective distribution systems and action against restrictive nationalised industries.

Cartels

The aim of European legislation here is to prevent companies in various countries coming together to fix prices or rigging the market against the interests of the consumer. One area that has concerned Europe for years is the high fare structure on European airlines, where routes are assigned to specific companies and on which competing airlines are not permitted to fly. Prices have notably fallen on routes where competition from economy airlines like EasyJet or Ryanair has been introduced.

Selective distribution

This is where multinational companies prevent customers in one EU country from buying a product in another where the price is cheaper. The most noticeable example of this is in the car industry where the same model of car can be many times cheaper in another EU country. At one point, when British buyers had discovered that they could purchase a car in Belgium at anything up to 40 per cent less than they would have to pay in Britain, Ford was taken to the European Court because it was refusing to supply right-hand drive models for British use to Belgian dealers.

Removing national monopolies

The EU is interested in opening up national monopolies to competition when it is suspected that the monopoly is protecting inefficient practices. A principal target is the large state monopolies in the telecommunications field, for example Deutsche Bundespost Telekom or France Télécom. These cannot affect Britain domestically as the privatisation of British Telecom took place some time ago, but the removal of the state monopoly in the mainland EU does open up opportunities to British telecommunications companies. In the reverse direction, the Dutch post office, among others, is acting competitively to secure international mail services that the post office in Britain has been prevented from offering by the conditions applicable to the Royal Mail's monopoly

Economic and monetary union: the single currency

The IGC at Maastricht agreed a timetable for achieving economic and monetary union (EMU). This was to include economic convergence on inflation, interest rates and currency stability, the introduction of a single currency and the setting up of a Central European Bank. The programme set out at Maastricht envisaged a Stage 2 in this process that would begin in 1994 and end with the final Stage 3 of complete union in 1999. Britain had originally intended to be part of the EMU, albeit reluctantly on the part of many Conservative ministers. In September 1992, however, the events that culminated in the so-called 'Black Wednesday' led to Britain's withdrawal from the ERM and a negotiated opt-out for Britain from the EMU timetable.

Thereafter, thanks to the opt-out negotiated at Maastricht, the British government of the time chose to adopt the position that Britain would be free to join or not join the EMU according to what would be best for British interests. In the run-up to EMU and the single currency, British economic policy was naturally constrained by European factors such as the single market and the strength of the Deutschmark, but otherwise did not feel obliged to heed what the rest of the eurozone countries were doing. As the then chancellor of the Exchequer, Kenneth Clarke, said about the Commission's convergence statement in 1994: 'I'll wait to see what the Commission recommends. I'll follow it if I agree with it and not if I don't.'[6]

That position, of waiting to see what would happen while remaining on the sidelines outside the single currency, became official Conservative Party policy for the 1997 general election. And, after the election, something very similar was adopted as policy by the Labour government, although there was an acceptance in principle of the desirability of entry, Instead of 'wait and see', the position was 'prepare and decide'. As chancellor of the Exchequer, Gordon Brown argued for Britain to wait until it was absolutely clear that Britain had satisfied the five criteria laid down by he and his Treasury team for British entry. The criteria and his verdict upon them are outlined in Box 6.2.

Box 6.2
The Chancellor's assessment of his five tests for entry and his verdict

On 27 October 1997 Gordon Brown told the House of Commons that in principle he favoured British participation in the single currency. However, his assessment of the case for entry would depend on five factors. On 9 June 2003, he
delivered his verdict as to whether Britain had passed the five tests of entry that
he had laid down. In the light of his eighteen-volume Treasury assessment
dossier, he and his team concluded that only one of the tests had been passed and
that changes to the housing market, Britain's inflation target and the European
Central Bank were needed before Britain could safely live with the same interest
rates as the twelve existing members of the eurozone.

The original Brown criteria and the verdicts he delivered upon their fulfilment, were as follows:

1   Whether there was a sustainable convergence between Britain and the other
    EU economies.

Failed. The British economy has moved closer to the Euro-zone in the recent
years, but is not there yet.

2   Whether there was sufficient flexibility to cope with economic change.

Failed. Britain's markets are still too rigid to absorb the shock of joining the single
currency.

3   The effect on investment.

Failed. Admitting that becoming a part of the single currency would help business
by cutting transaction costs and that Britain's share of direct investment has been
falling since 1999, the Chancellor felt that the boost for British firms and inward
investment would only come about if the first two criteria had been passed.

4   The impact on the financial services industry.

Passed unconditionally. There could be additional benefits to the City, because of
the ending of transaction costs and exchange rate uncertainty.

5   The impact on growth, stability and employment.

Failed. The theoretical benefits of membership would only arise if the economy
were more closely aligned to Europe.

In 1999, eleven of the fifteen nations of the EU adopted the euro as their
common currency. From day one, the European Central Bank set a single interest rate for the entire Eurozone. Britain, Denmark, Greece and Sweden did not

join in 1999. Since 2002, other notes and currencies of the member states have disappeared. Europe's oldest currency, the drachma (first minted in about 650 BC) ceased to exist when Greece joined in 2002. The other countries continued to remain outside. Following the Fifth Enlargement, the ten new members are all committed to adopting the euro at some point, but first they must meet the convergence criteria. The Commission arranged Pre-Accession Economic Programmes to place their economies on the right course, but there is no fixed timetable and the states choose to wait until their representatives feel that their economies are compatible with membership. In any case, because of the way the criterion on exchange rate stability is worded, they cannot join euroland until 2006 at the earliest.

The merits and demerits of British involvement

The issues of the single currency and who makes the decisions affecting interest rates are of massive importance, for they have a key impact on the British economy and strike at the heart of the debate about national sovereignty. Not surprisingly, ministers in any recent administration have been reluctant to commit their country to an innovation in policy that could go seriously wrong, in the same way that British membership of the ERM provoked havoc in the money markets and initiated a fundamental rethink about the handling of economic affairs. On that occasion, the Conservatives paid a heavy price for getting things wrong, from which they never recovered in the years before the 1997 election, and arguably their policy has done damage to their reputation for economic competence ever since.

Advocates of the single currency portray it as being an obvious accompaniment of the drive towards a single market, began more than a decade ago. In their view, there is a limit to how much market integration can be achieved, as long as national currencies and economic policies differ. A single market functions more efficiently if there is one system of coinage employed throughout the trading area. They believe that the combination of the single market and the euro equip Europe as a solid and successful trading block, covering the majority of the twenty-five European countries and potentially a population of 450 million people.

More specifically, for private individuals and firms, a number of advantages in a single currency and monetary policy have been identified:

- The lowering of costs involved in cross-border business, ending the conversion costs involved in currency exchanges and thereby easing transactions between countries. It is easier to buy and sell in other euro-area countries, theoretically meaning more competition and pressure to drive down prices, so leading to cheaper goods and services.
- Greater certainty in the financial markets, as sterling ceases to be vulnerable to exchange rate fluctuations.
- Lower interest rates over a period of time.

Membership of the eurozone would provide the British government with a presence when currency and related issues are being debated in the Councils of the EU. As such, Britain would be playing a more important role within the EU, for there is a danger that exclusion from EMU and other policies may in time consign Britain to the periphery rather than allowing it to take a place 'at the heart of Europe'.

Those who doubt the value of membership do so on either constitutional or political/economic grounds, or both. Conservatives tend to stress the importance of the constitutional considerations, whereas those politicians of the centre-left are more influenced by the extent to which membership would adversely impact upon the British economy.

Opponents portray control of the currency as an indication of national sovereignty and dislike the idea of economic policy – and especially interest rates – being decided by a distant and unaccountable Central Bank in Frankfurt. They do not believe that what the Conservatives often describe as a 'one-size-fits-all' policy is in the interests of Britain, with its distinctive traditions and requirements. They emphasise the need for a country to retain flexibility to deal with national problems, such as a balance of payments difficulty. If a country is locked into EMU, it possesses no options; here the argument becomes political, for control over economic policy instruments is ceded by individual countries. British politicians and voters would lose all say in the difficult decisions that inevitably have to be made about the short-term trade-offs between inflation and unemployment, with ministers only retaining the power of persuasion over representatives of other member states.

Critics also question whether there can ever be genuine convergence between member states. Even if there does appear to be convergence, from a purely economic standpoint there are doubts about the timing of entry. Getting it wrong can prove costly, as Ireland found when it joined EMU at an exchange rate that was too weak. Critics also point out that Europe lags behind the flexible British economy in its pursuit of economic reform and that the European economy needs to come into line with the British, before the moment is appropriate.

More generally, for those who wish to resist the move towards an ever-closer union, critics see membership of the eurozone as a move that would further enmesh Britain into the process of integration. They fear that closer fiscal and economic ties might ultimately be associated with closer political ones, for in this way it is easier to make EMU function effectively.

Current attitudes to membership

The issue of membership has been considered by many organisations over recent years. In Britain, the City, business and the trade union movement are divided over the merits of entry. So, too, are the two main parties. Both have significant sections of opinion that do not agree with the views of the leadership. Further information regarding their current viewpoints is set out in Box 6.3.

Box 6.3
Party attitudes towards membership of the eurozone

Labour

The leadership wants to be seen as pro-European and is broadly sympathetic to entry, although there are varying degrees of enthusiasm among ministers and some MPs who doubt the whole enterprise. However, in spite of twice winning a large majority, he Labour government has not pressed ahead with its promised referendum which would follow any recommendation for entry.

For most of Labour, the case for and against is primarily a matter of economic considerations. It is felt that to go ahead when economic circumstances are not propitious, could be harmful, and the Treasury under Gordon Brown is charged with making the assessment of prevailing conditions. Widely portrayed as being less enthusiastic than Tony Blair about membership, Brown nonetheless made a declaration of principle in his June 2003 assessment: 'The potential benefits for Britain of a successful single currency are obvious in terms of trade, transparency or costs and currency stability . . . a successful single currency within a single European market would be of benefit to Europe and Britain'.

Conservatives

John Major had adopted a cautious 'wait-and-see' approach to the single currency, a stance partly determined by his wish not to lose the services of prominent pro-Europeans in his Cabinet. William Hague was not inhibited by the presence of euro-enthusiasts in his Shadow Cabinet, and after 1997 the bulk of the parliamentary party was hostile to the whole idea of entry into the eurozone and happy with the stance of rejecting entry for the lifetime of two parliaments. Hague made 'saving the pound' a key theme of the 2001 election campaign, in an attempt to establish 'clear blue water' between the Conservatives and other parties. Iain Duncan Smith was also strongly opposed to entry, and so was his successor.

Conservative opposition is a matter of sovereignty. Use of the single currency would involve the transfer of powers previously exercised exclusively by national governments to the ECB, including the right to authorise issues of currency and determine interest rates; the loss of national flexibility is therefore unacceptable to Conservatives.

Liberal Democrats

Liberal Democrats have long been supporters of British membership, but they stress the importance of joining at an appropriate time. The issue is less discussed in party speeches than it was in the days of Paddy Ashdown's leadership, but Charles Kennedy is committed to the goal of entry into euroland, subject to a 'yes' vote in a referendum.

According to opinion surveys, many people feel ill-informed about the issues involved. The majority seem to lack enthusiasm for entry, but suspect that Britain will eventually join (see Table 6.2).

Table 6.2   *Public reactions to the single currency (% rounded)*

If there were a referendum now on whether Britain should be part of a single European currency, how would you vote?	
In favour of a single currency	24
Against a single currency	62
Don't know	14

If the government were to urge strongly that Britain should be part of a single European currency, how would you vote?	
In favour of a single currency	27
Against a single currency	60
Don't know	13

Source: Results of a MORI poll, based on survey work conducted 28 October–3 November 2004.

The impact of the eurozone on British policy

Because of the decision not to join euroland, British policy is not directly affected by European monetary measures, just as Britain has ruled itself out from having any effect on EU policy. Yet it would be naive to think that Britain is totally unaffected by the policies followed by the monetary union. Once the euro became a reality, many politicians and commentators, as well as many members of the public, sensed that British involvement would at some stage become inevitable, because:

- Britain inevitably has to use and trade in the common currency and the London financial markets conduct an ever-increasing share of their business in the euro.
- The twelve members of the eurozone represent a trading bloc with which Britain conducts more than half of its trade.
- Even before the euro was introduced, firms such as British Steel, ICI and Marks & Spencer announced that they were ready to bill and be billed in euros by their suppliers.
- Even the apparent early 'failure' of the euro (which – to the delight of the eurosceptics – steadily lost value against the pound and the dollar) had an impact on the British economy. One result of the falling value of the euro was to make the pound overvalued in a market where Britain conducted much of its export business. When BMW pulled out of the Rover car com-

pany, two reasons given for Rover's poor performance were the overvalued pound and Britain's failure to join the euro.

The implications of EMU are far-reaching, for its creation was arguably the biggest step forward for Europe since the Marshall Plan laid the foundations for economic recovery in the aftermath of the Second World War. For the optimists, if all goes to plan, monetary union will lay the foundations for the renaissance of Europe after twenty-five years of underperformance, which saw the EU's growth rate drop from 3 per cent in the 1970s to 1.8 per cent in the 1990s. They believe that in an era of global economic forces, only the large and powerful can survive. For the pessimists, EMU represents a huge risk. They claim that the economies involved are not truly congruent, and that the criteria have been applied in some cases in a too liberal manner. They worry that the ECB will have a deflationary bias, that it will keep interest rates too high, will ultimately fail and in doing so imperil the European economy – and in so doing drag other countries outside euroland, such as Britain, down with it.

Regional aid

For Britain, regional policy represents the reverse side of the CAP coin. Whereas Britain is a net loser over agriculture, it is a major beneficiary of Europe's policy towards regions in need of regeneration and development, the more so because – until the latest enlargement – 20 million of the 50 million Europeans living in run-down industrial areas, are domiciled in the UK.[7]

There are significant inequalities and imbalances not only between the economies of Europe's member countries but also between different regions of the same country. The disparities may be due to the underdevelopment of some regions, economic decline or location at the periphery of the EU. In some countries the GDP for the country as a whole may equal or even exceed the EU average, but there are regions that fall well below 75 per cent of that figure. In Italy, for example, the GDP for the region around Milan is 137 per cent of the EU average, but that for Sicily is 68 per cent.[8]

In 1990 a survey of regional discrepancies and trends was conducted so that differences in wealth between one member country and another, and between one region within a country and another region of the same country, could be redressed ahead of the single market. The structural funds of the EC were reformed in 1989 and priority areas identified as objectives for financial aid. These were areas where there was evidence of real disadvantage, including inadequate infrastructures, run-down industries, social deprivation, poor-quality schools and high levels of unemployment.

Regional policy is concerned with the pursuit of two key themes:

1 **Financial solidarity**, aiming to benefit citizens and regions that are in some way economically and socially deprived compared to EU averages.

2 **Social cohesion**, recognising that there are benefits for everyone in the EU if the gaps in income and wealth, between the poorer countries and regions and the more affluent ones, are narrowed.

In the 1989 assessment the UK as a whole was judged to have a standard of living that was 100.7 per cent of the EC average, but that figure concealed a significant difference between the 121 per cent enjoyed by the South East and 74 per cent in Northern Ireland; at the time, only South-East England and East Anglia had a standard of living higher than the EC average. Large areas of the UK were able to lay claim to support from the regional funds of the EC, under one of three different types of regional aid.

Objective 1 regions

These are the weakest areas of the EU: countries or regions where the GDP is lower than 75 per cent of the EU average. Three countries are Objective 1 in their entirety – Greece, Portugal and Ireland, while so is most of Spain and the southern half of Italy. The problem of saying which regions qualify for Objective 1 status begins with EU officials who identify those regions whose economic output per head is less than 75 per cent of the average. The amount due to each region is calculated by a formula that matches the extent by which their performance falls below the 75 per cent mark with a number of other factors such as unemployment levels. Five sorts of projects are eligible for Objective 1 funding: business support, infrastructure, training, community development, and agriculture and fisheries.

Originally, the situation in the UK was judged to be less serious than elsewhere in the EC and it was only Northern Ireland that qualified for Objective 1 status for many years. But this was the fault of the UK government, which was reluctant to apply for this status on behalf of any British region, 'because they thought it would be interpreted as a signal of Britain's economic decline'.[9] Another handicap was the reluctance of the British government to put up any of its own money, despite it being a requirement that national governments should exactly match EC funds before Brussels loosens the purse-strings. Not that any money is ever actually received from Brussels: as a net contributor Britain simply subtracts the amount of funding due from Brussels from the amount Britain is due to pay into EU coffers.

In the summer of 1994 two regions of Britain, which had previously been treated as parts of larger regions, emerged as regions in their own right and recipients of Objective 1 funding. They were the Highlands and Islands of Scotland and Merseyside. The award of this status to Merseyside was delayed by the failure of the British government to satisfy Brussels that the Treasury would not take advantage of European money to withdraw British state funding for the area; the Merseyside Task Force bidding for European funds having to appeal to Europe directly over the heads of the British government. Apparently the Major government had wanted to use 40 per cent of the European money on schemes that would have manipulated the unemployment figures. The plan was rejected by Brussels, which requires the Objective 1 funding to be additional money; it is not to be regarded as replacing national funding and saving the money of national governments.

The reluctance of central government to provide money to match EU investment in the regions continued even after the 1997 election and the accession of a Labour government. In 1999 it was announced that Wales, Merseyside, South Yorkshire and Cornwall would qualify for £3.2 billion of Objective 1 funding in the six years between 2000 and 2006. At this point, however, problems arose because central government was reluctant to use money from the Regional Selective Assistance budget to match EU funds, even though the Brussels contribution doubled the annual £150 million of the regional budget to £300 million. The national government prefers to use these funds as sweeteners to encourage foreign companies to make any inward investment in certain areas.

Richard Caborn, a minister at the Department of Trade and Industry (DTI) with the task of sorting out the English regional claims, announced that the government was unwilling to match the entire £3.2 billion and that there would be a shortfall of £534 million. As a result, South Yorkshire, due to receive £780 million from the EU, was £300 million, or 38 per cent short in UK funding; Merseyside, due £844 million, was £150 million or 17 per cent short; and Cornwall missed out on £84 million, or 26 per cent of its expected funding. And, since the UK must hand back to Brussels any moneys that are not matched by national funding, that shortfall of £534 million can be doubled into a loss of more than a billion pounds. The situation was considerably worse in Wales, where the then first secretary, Alun Michael, only raised £25 million of a potential £1.2 billion total. In January 2000 the Liverpool MP Peter Kilfoyle resigned as a defence minister in order to speak out on the backbenches about what he saw as a government failure to secure European funding for North-West England. In early February his loss was followed by Alun Michael, who was forced to resign from leadership of the Welsh Assembly.[10]

In developing Agenda 2000 there was considerable concern that these problems should be resolved and the structural funds made more effective ahead of enlargement, because the average income in the applicant countries is only one-third of the EU average and it could well be that the entire new entry might qualify for Objective 1 under existing criteria. The Commission therefore proposed the following:

- The seven existing objectives should be reduced to three: Objective 1, concerned with improving competitiveness; Objective 2, promoting economic diversity; and a new Objective 3 for areas not covered by Objectives 1 and 2 but which need help in order to adapt and modernise their systems of education, training and employment.

- Management of regional funds should be simplified and decentralised by a new partnership involving the direct involvement of the regions with the Commission, possibly through the Committee of the Regions.

Objective 2 regions

This objective has the aim of providing economic diversification for areas formerly dependent on traditional heavy industries such as coal, steel or shipbuilding. Help is needed in these areas to attract alternative industries, to retrain the workforce and regenerate the environment. These regions have always received EU funds, especially areas which were badly hit when a dominant industry closed down: as with Consett in County Durham, a former steel town which was devastated by the closure of the steel works.

This assistance under Objective 2 has possibly increased under the reformed structural funds, because Britain, as the first industrialised country in the world, is suffering disproportionately in the post-industrial world. About 40 per cent of the total EU population living in Objective 2 regions is to be found in the UK. The regions concerned are the Central Lowlands of Scotland, West Cumbria, the North East including Tyne and Wear, Teesside and Cleveland, most of Yorkshire and Humberside, Greater Manchester, the West Midlands and South Wales.

Objective 5b regions

Objective 5 as a whole deals with rural areas. Objective 5a is given over to the modernisation of farms and has little relevance to much of Britain, except for a relatively few hill farms. Objective 5b is meant to make up for the decline in the importance of agriculture, replacing employment and income in areas where farming has been rationalised, and counteracting the drift of population away from rural areas. The objective is therefore to retrain and reemploy former agricultural workers, replacing an economy dependent on farming with a new economy based on small businesses or tourism. Regions of the UK most affected by Objective 5b are Dumfries and Galloway; North, Mid and West Wales (bar Clwyd); and Cornwall.

The impact of regional policy

Regional policy has had some notable successes. Ireland provides a good example: its GDP on accession was 63.8 per cent that of the EC, whereas today the figure is around 107 per cent. Yet many old inequalities in the EU remain to be eradicated and new ones have been added with the accession of the ten new member states from Eastern Europe and the Mediterranean. Their problems may be caused by longstanding handicaps imposed by geographic remoteness or by more recent economic and social change, or a combination of both. The

EU has tailored programmes of support for the period 2000–6, to assist them in taking advantage of EU membership. The aim is to carry out the goal set out in Article 158 of the Amsterdam Treaty, namely to 'aim at reducing disparities between the development of various regions and the backwardness of the least favoured regions or islands, including rural areas'. To help achieve that target, the UK is set to receive more than £10 billion from the structural funds between 2000 and 2006.

Agriculture

The impact of European agricultural policy upon the UK is measured more in terms of the controversy surrounding the Common Agricultural Policy (CAP) than in its implementation. From the very first days of Britain's membership, the CAP was a bone of political contention. It appeared to penalise the British taxpayer to the benefit of profligate foreigners, and politicians lined up to denounce its profligacy and waste, among other deficiencies.

The principles underlying the CAP were laid down in 1960:

- free trade within the EEC in all agricultural products;
- common guaranteed prices for most commodities;
- protective heavy levies placed on all imported agricultural products;
- purchase by the EEC of all commodity surpluses.

In its conception, the CAP had the worthiest of aims and objectives: attempting to make the EEC self-sufficient in food, while guaranteeing a good standard of living for those involved in agriculture. In the implementation of the CAP, however, some of the worthiness of purpose disappeared. Encouraged by the French, with an essentially peasant agricultural economy, the CAP provided a guaranteed intervention price for all agricultural products, significantly without any limit being put on production.

For critics of the EC, the second and fourth points together came to represent all that was wrong with the EC. The fact that the EC would not only pay guaranteed prices but would itself guarantee the purchase of any unsold surplus produce would not have mattered if the EC had also laid down limits on production. But the French held out for there to be no such limits and this represented an open invitation for farmers to produce more than could be sold on the open market, in the certain knowledge that the EC would buy any surplus at the full market rate. It is because of this that we began to hear about the 'butter mountain' and the 'wine lake'. It also led to two-thirds of the EC budget being swallowed up by the CAP and, in the 1980s, almost led to bankruptcy.

As a result the CAP could be claimed as both a success and a failure. By 1973 the EC had become self-sufficient in cereals, beef, dairy products, poultry and vegetables. In the years that followed, however, despite the increase in population brought about by enlargement, production increased into ever greater surpluses. By 1990 the countries of the EC were producing 20 per cent more cereals than they could consume, but continuing to pay the farmers more than the world price for all the cereal crops they could produce. The costs of the CAP increased at an even faster rate than production, since there was not only the cost of the support price to farmers but also the cost of storing the vast food surpluses.

There was also the non-financial cost, both in terms of the dubious morality that allowed expenditure of that extent for the benefit of the relatively small percentage of the EC population actually engaged in agriculture, and in the righteous indignation of the rest of the world which saw EC surplus production sold off at rock-bottom prices with what amounted to a massive subsidy. The repercussions of this last point nearly destroyed the Uruguay round of talks on the international agreement that was due to replace GATT.

For Britain the problem was that the CAP was devised before Britain was a member, and the ground rules laid down bore no relation to the needs of British agriculture. Britain's farmers were both fewer in number and more efficient than those of France and the feeling was that Britain was paying heavily to support inefficiency elsewhere. There was also a question of national taste. British farmers can produce large quantities of wheat for which the farmers are paid large sums under the CAP. But British taste does not like flour produced by British wheat, preferring hard wheat imported from Canada and elsewhere outside the EU; on which Britain has to pay the levy raised on all non-EU food imports.

Reform of the CAP became inevitable in the 1980s as the EC repeatedly failed to agree a budget and teetered on the brink of bankruptcy. In 1991 reforms began under the then commissioner for agriculture, Ray MacSharry, and switched the whole emphasis of the CAP away from support payments for unlimited production on to topping-up payments for farmers who restricted their production within strict quotas. At the heart of this reform was a 'set-aside' policy, by which farmers withdrew a percentage of their land from food production, a concession for which they were then compensated. For poorer farmers such as the hill farmers of Wales, Scotland and the Pennines, the emphasis of support moved out of the CAP and transferred to the programme of regional aid.

The impact of the reforms on the British environment was quickly seen in the extent of 'set-aside' land on British farms and the disappearance of the bright yellow of rape from the British landscape. But, in its own way, the new policy was just as controversial since farmers were now seen as being paid large sums of money to do nothing. Heavy subsidies of the order of £4–5 billion were being paid from the EU and British government to around 30,000 landowners, merely to keep the land out of production.[11]

The reforms of 1991–92 were judged to be successful in that they cut the product surpluses held by the EC without jeopardising a 4.5 per cent increase in farmers' incomes. Further reform was, however, rendered necessary by the potential impact of the enlargement of the EU eastwards, which could mean an increase of 50 per cent in the extent of agricultural land, not to mention a doubling in the size of the agricultural workforce. There was general agreement, however, that the main thrust of reform should be to move away from subsidising overproduction and turn instead to selective aid programmes.

Three areas where it was declared that reform was required were:

1 cereals, where it was projected that surpluses could rise to 58 million tonnes by 2005;
2 beef, where, despite BSE, stocks of surplus meat were due to reach 1.5 million tonnes by 2005 unless there was a change of policy;
3 dairy prices.

These were the problems tackled by Franz Fischler, the new agriculture commissioner, as soon as he took office in January 1999. Under the German presidency of the Council of Ministers three solutions were agreed:

1 Intervention prices for cereals would be progressively reduced by 20 per cent, with farmers receiving compensation payments for about half the drop in prices.
2 Subsidies to beef farmers would be cut by 20 per cent in three stages over seven years.
3 There was to be a 15 per cent cut in support for dairy prices, but implementation was delayed.

Agenda 2000 set out a programme for continued agricultural reform, the emphasis being on a new decentralised model that would allow countries to be more flexible in their application of CAP requirements, so that they could adjust implementation to suit sectoral and local conditions. Specific aims of the new programme were to promote:

- an agriculture which is competitive in world markets;
- production methods which are environmentally friendly;
- diversity in the forms of agriculture, product variety and rural development;
- simplicity in agricultural policy and sharing of responsibilities with the member states;
- greater food safety and quality.

Major reform was postponed to 2005, but a mid-term progress report pointed to the need to decouple direct payments to farmers from production, make payments more conditional on compliance with considerations such as environmental, food safety and animal welfare standards, and shift more money into rural development policy. All this was set against a background of increased concern to satisfy the consumer's demand for safe food of high quality and an awareness of the need to achieve the environmental goals of sustainability and improved animal welfare.

There is often discussion of further change, but fundamental departures from existing practice are hard to achieve, because governments of some states are determined to resist any innovations that threaten their electoral prospects. French sensibilities are a particular problem, for France has a strong agrarian lobby and a larger-than-average farming vote. Inevitably, Britain is on the other side to France in such discussions. For many years the majority of EU spending was allocated to agriculture, although its share of the budget is now around 48 per cent, some 15 per cent lower than fifteen years ago. As a net contributor to the EC, Britain was paying heavily towards the costs of sustaining what were labelled as 'inefficient French farmers'. The British did not benefit from the CAP to anything like the same extent. Agriculture is a much smaller sector of the economy than in all other EU countries, other than Belgium. In both cases, only 1.4 per cent of the workforce is engaged in the agricultural, fisheries and forestry industries. In the UK, agriculture now accounts for only 0.8 per cent of the total economy, as opposed to 2.9 per cent at the time it joined the EC. Moreover, unlike the situation in France or Germany, UK farmers – being relatively efficient – have needed the protection of guaranteed prices less than their European counterparts. Based on 2003 figures, the contribution towards the CAP in the UK was approximately £62 per head for every man, woman and child in the UK.

For years, British farmers with a large acreage benefited from the substantial subsidies they could derive from Brussels, and those who farmed intensively on vast stretches of land benefited from heavy set-aside payments. But over the last decade they have experienced a difficult period and farm incomes have fluctuated considerably, usually in a downward direction. Moreover, in that period British farmers have suffered from the crisis of confidence caused by BSE (see Box 6.4) and other food scares, before then being hit by the outbreak of foot-and-mouth disease shortly before the 2001 election.

Box 6.4
The beef ban crisis

In March 1996 the British government broke the news that there could be a link between bovine spongiform encephalopathy and a fatal human disease, Creutzfeldt-Jakob disease (CJD). BSE is an appalling disease in which the cow's brain turns to a spongy jelly, leading inevitably to death since there is no known cure. Although BSE only came to light in 1986, spongiform diseases have been known for some time and the human form most closely related to BSE – CJD – was first diagnosed in 1921.

For a long time no one suspected that a spongiform illness could be passed from one species to another, let alone that it could be passed from animals to humans. In 1988, however, a committee set up by the Ministry of Agriculture, Fisheries and Food (MAFF) discovered a link between BSE in cows and scrapie in sheep. As a result, a selective cull of BSE-affected cows began in 1989. Unfortunately most farmers failed to declare the full extent of the disease in their herds for fear of losing money and so the effectiveness of the cull was weakened. In early 1989 first Germany and then the USA banned the import of British beef.

In March 1996 a government research team in Edinburgh discovered a link between BSE and a more virulent form of CJD, which had been reported as affecting ten young people whose average age was 27. The connection between these worryingly early deaths and BSE was admitted by the then health secretary, Stephen Dorrell, in a statement to the public made on 20 March. The result could well be described as panic-stricken:

- beef sales to the public collapsed;
- the EU imposed a worldwide ban on the sale of British beef.

While the EU agreed to provide 70 per cent of compensation for the slaughter of infected beasts, this 70 per cent was offset against the British rebate from the EU and the true value of the compensation payments was probably nearer 25 per cent.

The government's strategy was to argue that there was nothing wrong and it summoned up teams of veterinary experts to argue the case with the European Commission for agreement to lift the ban. When that was refused, 'the government decided to attempt to shift the blame for what had happened on to the European Union'.[12] The British government announced a programme of non-co-operation in decisions of the Council of Ministers until the EU agreed to withdraw the ban: as a result, European business was disrupted for three weeks and 80 different European measures were blocked by a British veto. The anti-European actions of the government may have helped John Major with his own party, but it did nothing for Britain's status in Europe and it finally destroyed any willingness on the part of the Europeans to help Britain, 'The residue of ill feeling left by the British tactics was everywhere apparent . . . as they look to Europe's future, others have decided they can no longer accommodate their awkward island neighbours'.[13] Europe remained adamant in its refusal to lift the ban and there were many advisers who told the British government that, whether or not the threat from BSE was real, the public worldwide had lost confidence in British beef.

Early in 1997 the relevant committee of the EP produced a report that was extremely critical of the British government's handling of the situation and the BSE crisis stumbled on to the end of the Conservative government and beyond. The more conciliatory attitude towards Europe exhibited by the Blair government had its impact and there was talk of a relaxation of the ban, certainly as it related to the beef cattle of Scotland and Northern Ireland. Then, in December 1997, the situation worsened again when a ban was introduced within Britain on the sale of beef on the bone.

In the same month a new inquiry into the whole BSE affair was announced, the inquiry beginning its work in March 1998. Within a year the inquiry had made its report, giving British beef a clean bill of health, a conclusion shortly afterwards endorsed by the scientific committee of the EU which pronounced British beef to be as safe as any in Europe. After a vote by the Council of Ministers, in which the French abstained, the EU lifted its ban on the export of British beef as of 1 August 1999. Unfortunately, both Germany and France refused to lift the ban, although whereas the German ban was technically a procedural matter concerning the autonomy of the German Länder, France's refusal was because the French food agency did not accept the safety of British beef.

In late October 1999 the European scientific committee rejected the French case and the Commission instructed the French that they must lift the ban or be held as being in breach of EU law. France not only refused but retaliated by threatening to take legal action against the Commission for failing to protect consumer health. In the first week of the year 2000 the European Commission duly began legal action against France in the European Court of Justice. The food safety commissioner, David Byrne, who was spearheading the action against the French, also contemplated action against the Germans, but in the event Germany lifted its ban in early 2000. In December 2001 the European Court ruled in favour of the EU and ordered France to lift its ban.

The occurrence of BSE was not just a British problem. Incidences of infection had been reported in eleven out of the fifteen countries by the beginning of 2001, with significant increases in France and the Irish Republic. At that time there were still around thirty suspected cases being reported every week in the UK. By September of that year the total official number of cases in the EU stood at 181,946, of which 180,019 had occurred in the UK.

The Common Fisheries Policy

In 1973 the EC introduced the Common Fisheries Policy (CFP) in order to manage the industry for the benefit of both fishing communities and the consumer. The policy laid down regulations on fishermen's access to EC waters, quotas, measures for the conservation and management of stocks of fish which swim in the waters of member states, programmes to improve production and the conclusion of fishing agreements with non-EC countries, plus long-term security for the fishermen who depended on the EC for protection.

At the heart of the common policy is the principle that fish stocks should be managed on the basis of scientific advice, so that viable stocks can be maintained and stocks that have been seriously reduced can be replenished. Hence the need for a total allowable catch (TAC). Each year, a decision is made on the total catch that may be taken of each species without damaging the future of the stock. This total is then broken down by fishing areas and divided into quotas for each country.

In 1992 the earlier agreement was amended and extended, the main point of the revision being to provide for the Council 'to set . . . objectives and detailed rules for restructuring the Community fisheries sector with a view to achieving a balance on a sustainable basis between resources and their exploitation, taking account of possible economic and social consequences and of the special characteristics of the various fishing regions'.

A comprehensive review was undertaken in early 2003, for it was thought that the original policy emphasis was not adequately coping with the task of conserving fish stocks, matching fleet size to supply and providing consumers with quality fish at affordable prices. The purpose of the reformed policy is to ensure that that the EU has biologically, environmentally and economically sustainable fisheries. Conservation is a cornerstone of the CFP, with measures to regulate the amount of fish taken from the sea and to allow young fish to mature. It also protects other marine life, by requiring that fishing techniques minimise the number of dolphins and porpoises that get caught up in fishing nets. More and more, policymakers examine the environmental implications of their decisions – not only on fisheries and marine life, but on the whole marine ecosystem.

Britain and the CFP

Britain has the largest stocks of fish in the EU, so the opportunity to fish in British waters was a definite benefit for other member states, but not for British trawlermen. The consequences of the CFP have been serious for the British fishing industry, with fishing towns such as Aberdeen, Fleetwood, Grimsby and Hull adversely affected. The number of larger vessels still fishing from British ports has sharply declined, as has the number of smaller deep-sea boats. The trend has been for a diminishing number of fishermen to sail from smaller ports in shorter, but more efficient vessels.

The fate of the fishing industry has become politically contentious, for the issue touches on a number of concerns about the British relationship with the EU. Some critics, including the trawlermen, want Britain to withdraw f rom the CFP altogether, for they feel that livelihoods have been threatened by the events of recent years. The growing emphasis on conservation of stocks within the EU is at variance with the need for fishermen to make a living. They feel that the CFP was designed to allow continental fishermen the chance to cast their nets into Britain's rich fishing grounds, which are a 'common resource' within the EU. Spanish trawlermen have greatly benefited from their access to British waters, with Bulgarians, Poles and inhabitants of the Baltic states lined up to do so in the future. Countries whose fishing fleets are too large for their quotas can register their vessels as British, obtain European money and catch British quotas. According to the British fishing industry, some two-fifths of British hake and plaice are caught by such quota hoppers. In all, Britain provides three-quarters of the stocks of the EU, two-thirds of the waters, but receives a third of the catch and an eighth by value.[14]

When the EU agreed in December 2002 to major cutbacks in catch quotas for the North Sea fishing industry this was for many trawlermen and other workers in the fishing industry, the last straw. Boats catching the most endangered species had the number of days they can go out to sea each month reduced to a maximum of fifteen. Their owners are limited in the type of species they can fish. Cod quotas were cut by 45 per cent, haddock by 50 per cent and whiting by 60 per cent.

Critics argue that the largest fishing concerns and the fish processing industry will continue to make profits, but the losers are the thousands of small-scale owner-operators, their crews and the associated onshore workers, who are liable to suffer job losses. These critics claim that the CFP is destroying British fishing stocks and the British fishing industry, with British fishermen facing a bleak future, in the light of the quota cuts. Not surprisingly, they are disenchanted with government ministers of any party that sign up to agreements with other member states. Many accept that there is a problem of overfishing and that reform of the CFP is inevitably necessary, but they feel that the deal struck in 2002 produced the latest in a long line of regulations that hit northern countries and are especially damaging to British trawlermen. They would echo the words of Ruth Lea, then of the Institute of Directors, who described the system adopted as 'about the most rigid centralised system that could have been devised and one likely to exterminate small family enterprises'.[15]

The Conservative Opposition has seized upon EU policy in this area as an issue with which to attack the EU. Michael Howard has promised that under his leadership Britain would seek to withdraw from the CFP unless amendments to the present situation can be agreed.

The environment

At the Dublin Council of June 1990 the EC's commitment to environmental issues was confirmed in a declaration signed by all twelve heads of state or government:

> The environment is dependent on our collective actions; tomorrow's environment depends on how we act today . . . We intend that action by the Community and the Member States will be developed on a co-ordinated basis and on the principles of sustainable development and preventive and precautionary action.[16]

The EC was late in becoming involved with the environment. The Treaty of Rome contained a commitment to improve the quality of life for member states, but the possibility that this commitment might apply to the environment was not accepted until the late 1960s, and it was 1973 before the first action programme on the environment was announced.

In the 1980s came the realisation that the environment, and specifically the pollution of the environment, is very much a Community matter, because pollution pays no heed to national boundaries. Pollute the upper reaches of the Rhine and the pollution will affect France, Germany, the Netherlands and ultimately the seaboard of the North Sea. Similarly, air pollution in Britain can create acid rain over wide stretches of Northern Europe.

Concerns such as these led the EC to undertake an intensive programme of preventative measures, leading to a total of 280 environmental legislative measures, 200 directives, and four action programmes approved between 1973 and 1991. There was a change of emphasis in 1987, due to the work involved in setting up the Single European Act. Environmental requirements on factories and industrial plants, if it were left to national governments to administer them, could lead to differential costs and a loss of competitiveness in some national industries compared with others. There was therefore the need for a co-ordinated approach by all governments so as to provide a level playing field for the various member states involved in the single market.

Also in 1987 the World Commission on Environment and Development (WCED) produced the Brundtland Report, drawing attention to the way in which economic growth was leading to the destruction of finite resources. The WCED called for 'sustainable' growth. This, together with the institution of the single market, produced the communiqué of the Dublin Summit, the establishment of a European Environmental Agency in 1990 and the introduction of a fifth action programme, named 'Towards sustainability' which ran from 1993 to 2000. This was followed by a sixth action programme, 'Environment 2010: our future, our choice'. This charts the way forward to the end of the first decade of the new century and concentrates on four broad themes:

1 tackling climate change and global warming;
2 protecting the natural habitat and wildlife;
3 addressing environmental and health issues;
4 preserving natural resources and managing waste.

Under the plan, the European Commission has been given five important responsibilities:

1 improving the implementation of existing legislation, by making sure that laws are not just passed but actually put into effect;
2 integrating environmental concerns into other policies, ensuring that all policies are assessed for their environmental impact;
3 working more closely with the market, affording businesses and consumers a role in identifying solutions to environmental problems;
4 empowering private citizens and helping them to change their behaviour, by providing them with the information they need to make environmentally friendly choices;

5 taking account of environmental considerations in land-use planning and management decisions, thereby ensuring that natural habitats and land-scapes are preserved and urban pollution minimised.

The sixth action programme develops the earlier schemes and builds upon some thirty years of setting standards, laying down controls and countering environmental threats, and tackling issues from noise to packaging waste, from conservation to car exhaust fumes. Schemes are based on the 'polluter pays' principle, by which the firm that causes the environmental hazard either needs to pay through investing in special machinery (for example for recycling or disposing of waste), or via special taxes on using environmentally unfriendly goods. The emphasis today is not just on laying down specific controls, but on developing alternatives, whether they be in the form of safer chemicals or new technologies. The key theme is that development should be sustainable, so that it does not deplete resources in such a way as to impair the life of future generations.

Specific issues and the British response to them

The main targets of European environmental legislation have been pollution of the air, water and soil, together with the problem of waste, particularly toxic waste. Since the emphasis shifted to sustainability, the EU has laid great emphasis on issues such as the conservation of finite energy sources like fossil fuels, saving energy through insulation and other means, and the generation of energy from renewable sources like wind, sun and tide. There has also been a growing interest in the protection of wildlife, both flora and fauna; the EU has ruled that in future any major new engineering project must take into account its effect on the environment, particularly on the habitat of wildlife, before it is allowed to start.

Community directives have laid down emission standards for the release of pollutants into the air and water. Directives have concerned the release of sulphur dioxide (1980), lead in exhaust gases (1982), nitrogen dioxide (1985) and ozone levels (1992). There has also been a continuing programme curbing the emission of carbon dioxide, held responsible for global warming. Key directives have also been issued concerning the quality of drinking water, the pollution of rivers and waterways and the quality of bathing water at seaside resorts.[17]

A major environmental initiative was the 1992 Habitat Directive, based on a 1979 directive for the protection of birds and intended to preserve or restore the habitat for species of flora and fauna whose existence is threatened by intensive farming or pollution. In legislating for this directive, the British government joined proposals for wildlife habitat with the set-aside provisions of the reformed CAP to produce the Habitat Scheme. Launched by the then agriculture minister, Gillian Shepherd, this scheme sought to persuade farmers to restore the natural environment in three areas:

1 Any set-aside land which is managed for the nurture of endangered species of plants, butterflies, birds and so on would receive an extra subsidy.
2 Along the fringes of certain key waterways farmers would be paid to maintain a strip 20 metres wide from the water's edge within which farmers would not use artificial fertilisers and pesticides. This would allow safe areas for the colonisation by wildlife while preventing the pollution of the water by nitrates and other toxic substances, with their consequent effects upon fish life and the food chain of water-birds.
3 Certain areas of land reclaimed from the sea or marsh and maintained by expensive and potentially damaging coastal defence or drainage schemes would be allowed to revert to natural watermeadows, marsh or wetlands, with a subsidy being paid to farmers if the land in question was withdrawn from crop production.[18]

Environmental schemes are expensive and therefore tend to be unpopular with governments and industry. As a result there have been many disputes between national governments and the Commission about non-compliance with EC directives on the environment. In one major upset the British government's first attempts to privatise the water industry had to be abandoned because the EC refused to accept the suggestion that the privatised water companies should regulate themselves. It was only after the institution of the National Rivers Authority to police the activities of the water companies that privatisation could go ahead.

A long-standing dispute has been about the standard of bathing water on British beaches. This dates back to a directive of 1975 that demanded that national governments should designate bathing beaches that would be required to meet strict guidelines on water quality by 1985. This applied to some 391 beaches and nine inland bathing waters in the UK. The British government was first in trouble because it wanted to designate no more than twenty-seven beaches for this purpose; after discussion this number was raised to 446. The British government then pleaded for more time to comply with the set standards and was granted an extension until 1995. Yet a report by the National Rivers Authority in 1994 showed that fifty-five beaches in Britain could well fail to meet the required standards by the 1995 deadline and might still have waters unsafe for bathing because of raw sewage and other pollutants.[19] Progress has been patchy, with bad years as well as good, but by the turn of the century there were signs of a real improvement in the number of British bathing beaches judged to be safe for bathing. In 2002, 317 beaches in the UK were judged to be meeting appropriate standards of water quality and beach management. There has also been an increase in the number of beaches qualifying for EU Blue Flag status. To be considered, a beach must have attained the guideline standards of the Bathing Water Directive, before being assessed for twenty-four other criteria such as cleanliness, dog control and wheelchair access. In 2002 eighty-three beaches achieved the status, an improvement on the fifty-five of a year earlier.

Another high-profile dispute between Britain and Europe concerned a directive requiring civil engineering projects to have regard to the environment. In 1991 the then commissioner for the environment, Carlo Ripa di Meana, officially warned the British government that it was in breach of EC regulations in seven engineering projects, the most famous of which was the building of the M3 motorway across Twyford Down, an area of natural beauty and of historical and scientific interest near Winchester. The EC withdrew its objections to Twyford Down in 1992, but disputes over the government's road-building programme continued with major arguments over the Newbury bypass and proposals to widen the M25 across the Runnymede meadows where Magna Carta was signed.

Disputes between the EU and Britain have a high profile because environmental pressure groups such as Friends of the Earth learned very early on that the open nature of the European legislative process allowed for greater involvement of interest groups in decision making. And, while the Commission would not normally intervene on its own initiative, it was much more ready than national governments to respond to complaints. Over the years, the Commission has received more complaints about Britain than any other member state; in 1990, for example, there were no fewer than 125 complaints registered.[20] It is not only interest and pressure groups who intervene in this way. Local authorities, charged with the task of implementing environmental legislation, sometimes make direct contact with the EC. In July 1993 Lancashire County Council took the British government to the European Court of Justice for failing to clean up bathing beaches at Blackpool, Southport and Morecambe.

British membership of the EU has coincided with the era in which environmental politics began to interest the Community's policy makers. As the Community became more active in establishing environmental standards, ministers found themselves forced to respond to initiatives from the Commission. Hence, in Milton's phrase 'the most striking feature of the Government's policy on pollution is the extent to which it is dictated by EC directives'.[21] Some 80 per cent of environmental protection policy now originates in the EU, which can contemplate initiatives more easily because it is not subject to domestic electoral pressures.

Social policy

Most directives and regulations emanating from Brussels relate to economic issues and concern some aspect of the single market. The TEU introduced a comparatively new element in the emphasis it placed on social issues, specifically as they concerned employment policy. This was the so-called Social Chapter of the Maastricht Agreement, which regulated matters such as workers' health and safety, working hours and conditions, a minimum wage, rights to consultation through Works Councils and the rights of women in the workplace. The social dimension initiated by Jacques Delors was a policy of which Margaret Thatcher and her successor disapproved. In the words of Conservative MP and later minister, Michael Portillo: 'The government will not tolerate unwarranted interference in people's lives from Brussels which would put extra costs on employers, make firms less competitive and reduce the number of jobs. We have decided not to be part of the Social Chapter and that position will not change.'[22]

As a result of British objections, the Social Chapter was not integrated within the text agreed at Maastricht but was added as a protocol subscribed to, at the time, by eleven members, in other words by all members apart from the UK. The procedure demanded by this protocol meant that Commission proposals for social legislation would be vetoed by the UK but later reintroduced under the protocol as a measure applicable only to the Community minus the UK. This, for example, was the procedure adopted in September 1994 when Michael Portillo, as employment secretary, vetoed a proposal before the Council of Ministers to permit men to take three months unpaid paternity leave on the birth or adoption of a child. At the same Council meeting, Portillo gave notice that Britain would treat proposed legislation on the rights of part-time workers in the same way.

Three years later the Labour government under Tony Blair accepted all the terms of the Social Chapter and agreed to implement the measures already adopted under it by the other fourteen member states. At Amsterdam (1997) the Social Protocol was incorporated into the Treaty of Rome, so that there was a single framework for social plicy for all the member states. The promotion of jobs became an accepted goal of EU policy makers, subject to its pursuit not being a threat to competitiveness.

The implementation of the Social Chapter

By its 1997 manifesto, Labour was committed to signing the Social Chapter, noting that: 'An empty chair at the negotiating table is disastrous for Britain . . . We will use our participation to promote employability and flexibility, not high social costs.' The latter phrase indicated that there was a diminution of earlier enthusiasm, with the tone struck being significantly different from that of an earlier party leader, Neil Kinnock. He had claimed that the original British opt-out was not just bad for British workers but – contrary to what John Major was saying – actually liable to detract from Britain's competitive position. The rhetoric employed once in office emphasised that, by being part of the discussion, Britain could prevent potentially burdensome labour legislation from being imposed on it. The talk was about job creation and the merits of flexible labour markets.

By the time of the Amsterdam Treaty there were six directives either passed or being negotiated. They dealt with:

- European works councils (1994);
- parental leave (1996);

- burden of proof in sex discrimination cases (1997);
- part-time workers (1997);
- fixed-term work (1999);
- compulsory information and consultation procedures (national works councils) (2002).

These were now extended to the UK. During Labour's first administration (to 2001) several more legislative proposals were brought forward or transferred to the new Social Chapter.

The EU's social agenda remains controversial in Britain. Critics are to be found in the CBI, the IoD and some elements of the Conservative Party. The IoD is especially unhappy about the influence of the EU on UK employment, which is said to be 'very considerable'. It sees the heavily taxed and tightly regulated Social Europe model as discredited and instead would like to see European social policy more determined by reference to 'economic competition rather than outdated concept of labour market protectionism'. It would prefer policy to be based on the enterprise model in which employers are free to build up direct individual relationships with their employees.[23]

Within the Conservative party too, there has been unease about the British commitment to the Social Chapter. By 1999 Michael Portillo had undergone a change of view. He acknowledged that the dire consequences that had been forecast if Britain accepted the EU's social legislation had just not happened. He announced that if the Conservatives were returned to power, they would accept the Social Chapter as a given fact and he could see no reason why any future Conservative government should make any sort of attempt to overturn the legislation. Nevertheless, under the Howard leadership – and with Portillo no longer a relevant player in the debate – serious thought was given to negotiating an opt-out from the social provisions now written into the Treaty of Rome.

Trade union rights

In March 1994 the European Court reversed British anti-union legislation by finding that, in the privatisation of health service and local government services, the government had ignored a directive of 1977 concerning workers' rights when public enterprises are transferred to new ownership. Under the terms of the Court's ruling, the British government could be fined if it did not introduce legislation to reimpose collective bargaining on those privatised companies that had set up non-union agreements.

Equality for pensioners

Again in March 1994 the Commission took action against the British Treasury, which was proposing to issue grants for home insulation to old-age pensioners in order to offset the effects of VAT on heating bills. The Commission took action under sexual equality rules because, in Britain, men and women could not apply for these grants at the same age. The government was obliged to accept that sixty would be the age at which application for the grants could be made, even though men would not be pensioners until they were sixty-five. Later that same year a decision by the European Court against the Dutch government, but applicable to all member states, ruled that part-time workers should have equal pension rights to full-time employees, backdated if necessary. However, in order to gain that equality, British pensions for part-timers would be payable only at the age of sixty-five, for women as well as for men.

The real success for British pensioners, however, came when a case before the European Court ruled that it was unfair that men should have to wait until they were sixty-five before they qualified for free prescriptions, when women could receive free prescriptions at sixty. The British government had to concede the point and grant free prescriptions to all men and women over the age of sixty.

Women's rights

Perhaps the greatest beneficiaries of European social legislation or judgements are women. In the words of one writer: 'All the most progressive legislation on women's rights is coming from Europe. The British government is continually being pushed to act by European directives and court decisions.'[24] The cases with the highest profiles were women who were dismissed from the armed services when they became pregnant. As a result of a ruling from Europe, the British courts had to award substantial damages to the 5,000 or so women affected.

These rulings over sexual equality have little to do with the Social Chapter of the TEU. Most are as a result of Article 119 of the Treaty of Rome, which states the principle that men and women should receive equal pay for equal work. In 1984 the European Court ordered the British government to amend the Equal Pay Act so as to read 'equal pay for work of equal value', which meant that employers could no longer justify inequalities in pay by claiming that men and women were doing different jobs. In one case a female speech therapist claimed equality with a male pharmacist because they had a similar health service grade, although he earned very much more than she did.

European rules have also helped women in cases of equality of retirement, maternity benefits, compensation to pregnant women for unfair dismissal, invalid care allowances, sexual harassment in the workplace and so on. It is through actions such as these, from both the Commission and the European Court, that some measure of social legislation was forced on to the British government even during the years when the government was hostile to the social dimension and before British acceptance of the Social Chapter.

Internal security

One of the three pillars of the European Union instituted at Maastricht was a new deal on the policing of internal security through the Europol system, which would mean the abolition of border checks within the boundaries of the EU. The main advocate for the removal of internal borders was the Schengen Group – of France, Germany and the Benelux countries – which was so-called because of a meeting at the small Luxembourg town of Schengen in 1985. The five countries came to a formal agreement in 1990 and were joined by Italy (1990), Spain and Portugal (1991), Greece (1992) and Austria (1995). Occasionally the Scandinavian countries are reported to be thinking seriously about joining, but the UK and the Republic of Ireland resolutely remain outside the Schengen Agreement.

The reluctance of the UK and Ireland to agree to the removal of immigration controls for visitors entering one of the two countries from another EU country has a great deal to do with the problem of terrorism and the need to control the movement of terrorists and their weapons. But it has also a great deal to do with the insular nature of both the UK and Ireland and the two countries' lack of land frontiers. Both countries prefer to check thoroughly at the point of entry and then allow the visitor to move freely and unchecked within the country. In this way, the UK has in the past avoided the system of identity cards and residency permits demanded by most countries in the mainland EU, although discussion of ID cards is now firmly established upon the political agenda.

This drawing back from the removal of border controls is not unique to the British Isles. Many more states began to express doubts at the growing number of illegal immigrants, swollen by gypsies and others seeking political asylum; an influx which reached new levels in 1999 and 2000. Estimates made in the summer of 1999 put the numbers of illegal immigrants smuggled into the EU every year as 400,000, with the EU already containing nearly a million displaced persons, the highest level of stateless migrants since the post-war diaspora of 1945.[25] The Amsterdam Treaty, which came into force in August 1999, took note of the growing concern and made dealing with immigration an EU-wide responsibility rather than leaving it to individual countries. In October 1999 a summit at Tampere in Finland established the first moves towards creating a system of fingerprinting immigrants and maintaining an EU-wide computer database, as well as proposing measures such as repatriation, which could lead to problems with civil rights groups.

In January 2000 the principle of the Schengen Agreement was undermined when both Belgium and Luxembourg reimposed border controls to counter an expected increase in the number of illegal immigrants. The Belgian interior minister, Antoine Duquesne, insisted that it was a temporary measure lasting only a few weeks 'to dissuade illegal arrivals in our country and to combat effectively the mafia-style networks that exploit these people'. He also made it clear that a clause of the Schengen Agreement allowed member countries to opt out for short periods in the light of special circumstances. For British eurosceptics, however, the actions of Belgium and Luxembourg were final proof that the Schengen policy of a common EU external border had failed to control illegal immigration at a time when the sheer number of immigrants and asylum seekers was causing major concern in the UK.[26]

As far as asylum seekers are concerned, however, the EU member countries do not have as much freedom of action as might be thought and adjustments to the Schengen Agreement are a very minor factor in the equation. A statement by a British government minister in February 2000 made it clear that Britain's response to the refugee crisis had very little to do with directives from Brussels, stating that, 'far from being a European treaty, it is the 1951 United Nations Convention on Refugees – signed by more than 120 countries – that obliges the United Kingdom to assess every asylum claim on its merits'.[27]

One other recent aspect of asylum and immigration policy has been a side effect of the Fifth Enlargement. Unlike some other EU countries, Britain imposed no transitional controls on the free movement of citizens from the new countries of Central and Eastern Europe. The Conservative opposition and elements in the tabloid press urged action to prevent a mass influx of economic migrants seeking a better lifestyle in the more prosperous parts of the EU. Free movement of labour under EU rules is confined to people in search of jobs, not in search of benefits. Ministers did take late action to restrict benefits, but were prepared to argue their support for the open legal avenues available to economic migrants. The home secretary made it clear that blocking legal migration flows tends to encourage illegal migration and argued that any migrants from the accession countries would be welcome for the skills they could bring to a country with serious shortages of labour in the agriculture, construction, hotel and hospitality sectors.

In the event, the tabloid scaremongering proved to be unjustified. There was no massive immigration in the early days of May 2004 and within the first two months there were only 24,000 applications to the worker registration scheme that Home Office ministers had hurriedly brought in prior to enlargement. The idea of this transitional arrangement was to ensure that those who wished to migrate from their home country to the UK were able to work legally (and therefore pay taxes) rather than enter as non-taxpaying clandestine workers. Fears had been fuelled by elements of the tabloid press that there would be a flood of immigrants once the doors were opened. In the event, the majority of those who registered were already in the UK, with only 8,000 being new arrivals, mainly from Poland, Lithuania and Slovakia. Many of these were working in the hospitality and catering sectors, as well as in administration and management, and farming industries.

The issues of personal mobility, asylum and immigration, management of frontiers and cross-border co-operation all have implications for individual liberty. From the beginning, the EU has been based on respect for human rights and the rule of law. These values were enshrined in the Charter of Fundamental

Rights (CFR) adopted by EU heads of government at Nice (December 2000). In a single document, the Charter sets out the personal, civil, political, economic and social rights enjoyed by inhabitants of the EU, as well as addressing new issues raised by technological progress, such as bio-ethics and data protection. It was intended that this should become an integral part of the proposed constitution.

In Brussels (2004), a last-minute red-line issue was floated by the British government, because of the apparent threat to aspects of the trade union reforms of the Thatcher era, namely those concerning the imposition of secret ballots and the ban on secondary picketing. The issue raised the whole question of the status of the CFR, with some lawyers and judges anxious that the Court of Justice would see it as binding because the EU was set to acquire a new 'legal personality'. British ministers portrayed the CFR more as a political than a legal declaration of rights, but were able to ensure that the draft constitution did not enhance employment rights.

Defence and foreign policy

From the earliest days of post-war co-operation, there was always interest in the idea of developing Western security along the lines of the closest possible integration. The Preamble of the Treaty of Paris (1951) dwells less on the issues surrounding coal and steel, and talks in more grandiose tones of setting aside the rivalries of the past and safeguarding peace in the future, by a merging of national interests.

The states of Europe were aware of their military weakness, and keen to put the situation right. Co-operation with the USA through NATO was the route chosen, for the Six (soon to become the original members of the EEC) were all signatories of NATO. But the Americans were keen to see Europe strengthen its military capability, so that it would be a strong partner of the Atlantic Alliance between Europe and North America.

In 1950, in a speech to the Council of Europe, Winston Churchill put forward the outline of a plan for a unified European army which would act in concert with Canada and the USA. In the same year René Pleven, the French prime minister, put forward his proposals for a European Defence Community (EDC) and a European Political Community (EPC) was then proposed, each with their own institutions. The EDC involved the creation of a European army under the control of the political institutions of Europe, while the EPC was designed to be a complementary organisation that would add a political dimension to co-operation in defence policy. The EPC was also supposed to co-ordinate the external policies of the member states. The Pleven proposals were a key move in the attempt to integrate Europe rapidly and, as Jean Monnet – often, seen as the father of European integration – realised would have made 'the federation of Europe . . . an immediate objective'.[28] But the attempt was stillborn.

With the failure of this early attempt at common defence arrangements, Europe had no choice but to act as the junior partner of the NATO alliance. The only further attempt to create a European defence organisation was the development of the Western European Union (WEU), formed in 1955. Britain was a member, and the meetings of the WEU provided an opportunity for British representatives to meet with those of the Six to discuss common issues. But the scope of the organisation was quite unlike the Pleven initiative. The French proposal had embraced supranational thinking. The WEU acted on the basis that member states should act independently, but co-operate on an intergovernmental basis where this was feasible and desirable.

Progress towards the development of common policies

From the early 1970s there was a greater attempt to harmonise foreign policies within the EC, the process then known as European political co-operation (EPC). On some issues this was relatively successful, for after failure to act together in response to the oil crisis of the early 1970s there was a greater appearance of agreement in dealing with events such as the Iran hostage crisis and the Soviet invasion of Afghanistan. But over the Falklands War, after initial consultation, the fragile unity began to crack as countries began to think about their own national interests. The agreement on modest economic sanctions was far short of a common foreign policy.

For several years EPC was conducted on an intergovernmental basis outside the formal provisions of the Treaty of Rome. The passage of the SEA formalised the process of foreign policy consultation and co-operation between the member states, and brought it within the EC framework, although not actually into the Treaty itself. For some commentators this was 'the first step on the slippery slope to a common foreign policy and a federal Community'.[29] It was certainly the case that the cooperation in foreign policy received a new impetus. Ginsberg has drawn attention to the marked increase in foreign policy initiatives in the five years after the SEA was implemented (188, compared with 121 in the previous five years).[30] The trend towards developing a common and coherent approach to foreign policy was accelerating. Yet this was not the same as a common foreign policy, for it remained the case – and still does – that most member states intended to carry out their own external policy, with the backing of the EC if this could be obtained.

Dissatisfaction with Community policy was widespread within the EC by the late 1980s. Several states wanted to replace EPC with a more developed common foreign and security policy (CFSP). In the run-up to Maastricht, the issue of defence policy was hotly contested, the area being particularly difficult as it involved the wider issue of relations with the USA. The British suspected that the French were using the issue as part of their long-standing Gaullist strategy of separating Europe from American power and influence. The French believed that Britain's approach to defence matters reflected a more general ambiguity about its attitude to the development of closer ties with the continent.

Britain distinguished defence policy from the more general issue of security. For British ministers, defence was not a matter for the EC, for it is primarily a matter of how nations physically defend themselves when under attack. Besides, any new initiative might undermine NATO and prompt a US withdrawal from Europe. However, security policy involves a wider network of agreements to make war less likely, so that this could be an appropriate issue for Europe to handle – preferably at an intergovernmental level.

Pre-Maastricht, foreign policy again tested the ability of the EC to act on a common basis. Policy over the Middle East has long been an area on which a minority of members have had conflicting national interests with their EC partners. Over the Iraqi invasion of Kuwait (1990), it was not hard to agree that all EC citizens in that country should be protected and that sanctions should be imposed on Saddam Hussein. Beyond that, it was more difficult to move forward. It was left to the British and French to make their own individual approaches to avoid war breaking out. There was no effective Community approach in the run-up to and duration of the Gulf War.

Progress at Maastricht towards a common European foreign and security policy

At Maastricht, European political co-operation was taken further and placed within the wider conception of a common foreign and security policy. The CFSP was the second of the 'three pillars' of the new European Union. At the summit there was agreement that there should be closer co-operation on foreign and security policies to 'assert the Community's identity on the international scene'. Progress in these areas should build upon and develop existing forms of co-operation. National governments were still to be in the driving seat, although EC institutions such as the Commission and Parliament were able to express a view and have their recommendations take into account.

The treaty developed the position set out in the SEA. It was agreed that the new EU should 'define and implement a common foreign and security policy . . . covering all areas'. This was to include 'all questions related to the security of the Union, including the eventual framing of a common defence policy, which might in time lead to a common defence'. The procedure laid down involved regular co-operation between the states on matters of general interest. Where appropriate, the Council would – on a unanimous basis – define common positions to which the policies of member countries would have to conform. Majority voting did not extend to defence policy.

The WEU was given the role of elaborating and implementing 'decisions and actions of the Union which have defence implications'. It was to be developed 'as the defence component of the European Union' and as the means to strengthen the European pillar of the Atlantic Alliance. Defence was therefore to remain a matter for NATO, but the European arm would be strengthened. The WEU was to become the bridge between the two other organisations.

Recent developments

One of the problems in articulating a coherent European foreign policy is the lack of a single voice. No-one 'speaks for Europe'. Back in the 1970s, Henry Kissinger, the American secretary of state, was said to have asked: 'When I want to speak to Europe, whom do I call?'

There is no-one who can speak, let alone act, on Europe's behalf. Europe often seems to speak with different voices, and in response to issues such as the fighting in Bosnia in the 1990s or in Iraq more recently (see Box 6.5), there tends to be a lack of clear and agreed thinking. Alarmed at the dithering and squabbling in this field, Jacques Delors once spoke of 'organised schizophrenia'.

Box 6.5
Britain, the USA and Europe: the response to events in Iraq, 2003

The relationship between Britain and the USA

As we saw in chapter 1, in the years after 1945 Winston Churchill spoke of the three circles of British foreign policy: the relationship with the USA, the ties with the Commonwealth, and the association with the countries of Western Europe. It was the relationship with the USA that was seen as 'special', and this 'special relationship' has been the centrepiece of post-war British foreign policy.

Forged in the Second World War, the links between US President Franklin D. Roosevelt and Churchill were close and firm. The relationship worked well during the period of hostilities and in the period of Cold War that followed. It seemed in the mutual interests of Britain and the USA to stay closely linked. The ties of history, culture, language and friendship all served to cement the alliance. They continued after the Cold War ended, sometimes being particularly strong when the incidence of personality worked in their favour – as with the relationship between Margaret Thatcher and Ronald Reagan.

The Iraqi invasion of Kuwait brought the two countries into battle on the same side once more, acting as the world's policemen as they had once done over Korea forty years before. The terrorist attacks on the World Trade Center of 11 November 2001, again showed that a president and British prime minister can work very closely together, Britain being very supportive of the American position. The response of the British government showed that the USA could count on British support, and there was in the USA much admiration of the strong leadership given by Tony Blair.

Many Americans like the fact that Britain is a member of the EU, because they feel that the 'special relationship' means that they get a good idea about develop-

---

ments on the continent and an ally that might help them should there be problems over trade between the USA and Europe. If anything, Britain's influence in Washington is probably greater if it plays a full part in Europe. Americans tend to see a sympathetic British government as a useful bridge between the USA and the continent, because Britain is well placed to have strong links with both.

However, even before the events in Iraq, there was a developing unease among many people about Britain's proximity to the USA under its new conservative president, George W. Bush. It seemed to many people, particularly those on the centre-left in British politics, rather surprising that the Blair administration should be so close to the Bush White House. The prime minister had been on cordial personal terms with Bill Clinton and when the Democrats lost the presidency in November 2000, under somewhat questionable circumstances, there was some resentment at Bush, as the man who was 'illegitimately' in the White House.

Tony Blair likes to use a 'bridge' metaphor to describe the British stance in foreign policy. He portrays Britain as being the pivot at the axis of a range of international relationships. It is Britain's uniqueness, a position for which Britain is qualified by past history and circumstance. The thinking is that in this role Britain never has to make a choice between the USA and Europe: it is linked to, yet similarly distant from, both continents.

The build-up to the war over Iraq

In the build-up to the hostilities over Iraq, a rift began to develop and widen between Europe and the USA. Britain was unable to reconcile the two sides and had to make a choice. The divide could not be bridged by the prime minister's determined efforts to facilitate agreement. As de Gaulle had argued four decades before, when it came to decision time, Britain proved to be more Atlanticist than European.

Tony Blair understood the importance of obtaining a second resolution in the United Nations in favour of action against Saddam Hussein. The Spaniards and Bulgarians on the Security Council of the United Nations supported the British and American resolution, but the French and Russian governments were opposed, and other states could not be won over. In the event, Britain and the USA acted without that second resolution, and within the EU France and Germany led the opposition to the decision to press ahead with war against Iraq.

As on so many previous foreign policy issues, the EU found it hard to reach agreement. There was some support for the interventionist cause, notably from the Italians and the Spanish within the EU and from the governments of some of the Central and Eastern European countries waiting to join. But in March 2003 the Blair government found itself with few backers at the EU table. Critics of the British role could point to Britain's persistent isolation and unwillingness to act in concert with its European partners. They could paint a picture of a member that was never much loved, always a recalcitrant, awkward neighbour, constantly demanding concessions, and now behaving as a fifty-first state. Whereas once there was talk of Britain's leadership in Europe, now the Blair government was seen by its opponents at home and on the continent as being excessively beholden to and uninfluential upon the American government. These opponents were relatively united in their wish to contain American power, of which Britain was a supporter.

Britain was not without allies in Europe, particularly among the would-be entrants to the EU, many of whose peoples had had experience of living under a regime they viewed as tyrannous. But British influence in Brussels, Paris and Berlin had been struck a damaging blow.

On occasion, the immediate handling of issues has been the responsibility of a troika of the foreign minister whose country holds the Presidency, his predecessor and likely successor. At other times, the president of the Commission and the prime minister of the government which holds the Presidency of the Council have acted. It was because of this lack of an effective procedure that several calls have been made in recent years for a high-profile figure to represent the EU's agreed foreign policy to the world. Sceptics worry that such a supremo could easily become the master rather than a servant of the EU.

In the draft constitution, provision has been made for the creation of an EU foreign minister and a team of officials to assist the incumbent. The British government accepted the need to merge the two foreign policy posts then occupied by Commissioner for External Affairs Chris Patten and High Representative Javier Solana of Spain (a position created in the Amsterdam Treaty and backed by a Policy Planning and Early Warning Unit) into one single EU voice, strengthening the clarity of the presentation of EU policy where there is a shared policy. Britain would have preferred the term 'EU external representative', but the title proposed by the Convention was accepted.

In other respects, the draft treaty says that 'competence in matters of common foreign and security policy shall cover all areas of foreign policy and all questions relating to the union's security, including the progressive framing of a common defence policy, which might lead to a common defence'. It calls on member states to 'actively and unreservedly' support EU policy in what is called a 'spirit of solidarity', refraining from actions 'contrary to the Union's interests' or effectiveness. It also provides for greater military co-operation and arms procurement systems, as well as a terrorist 'solidarity clause', if attacked.

The British government felt able to accept these provisions, as long as within the treaty it was made clear that member states and the Council of Ministers – not the Commission – conduct foreign and security policy. Britain was concerned to ensure that NATO remains the mutual defence organisation for the Western Alliance of Europe and North America and resisted any inclusion of a defence structure that duplicated or weakened it.

Difficulties in achieving a common foreign and security policy

Matters of defence, security and foreign policy go to the very heart of the debate on political union. Until now there has been only limited scope for joint decision making on foreign policy matters, but many members would like to see the development of common policies, which would include the eventual framing of a common defence policy. In the eyes of many committed Europeans, the eventual goal of a common policy would be the creation of a European army (see Box 6.6 for details of the Rapid Reaction Force and why it is not a European army).

Box 6.6
Towards a European army? The Rapid Reaction Force (RRF)

In 1998 France and Britain launched an initiative at St Malo to strengthen the EU's capacity to respond to international crises, on the premise that the EU could only play a coherent and effective political role if it was underpinned by a credible military capacity. Their plan was adopted at the Cologne Council in June 1999. By May of the following year, the EU had operational capability across the full range of tasks, albeit one much limited and constrained by recognised shortfalls. By December 2003 it could – within 60 days – deploy some 60,000 troops with air and naval support, and sustain them in action for about a year. Of the troops in this Rapid Reaction Force (RRF), the UK was contributing some 12,500, in addition to 18 warships and 72 combat aircraft.

The crises that its creators had in mind included:

- humanitarian rescue work;
- peacekeeping;
- the tasks of combat forces in crisis management.

This military capacity is firmly rooted in NATO, which remains responsible for the collective defence of the West. NATO has and will retain the lead role in crisis management and the RRF will only act 'autonomously' when NATO chooses to do nothing. But there is a growing recognition in Europe that it should assume a greater share of its security burden and strengthen its military capability. The RRF is not a European army, even though it can be mobilised without NATO's approval, possesses a European command chain and draws primarily on European military resources. The troops are not members of a standing force and do not wear a common uniform; moreover, each country retains control over the number and deployment of its troops. Rather, it represents a pooling of national armies that remain under sovereign national command. It is a useful tool for EU policy-makers, which can be called upon as any situation requires. It represents what Bomberg and Stubb descsribe as a 'small but decisive step towards creating a European Security and Defence Policy'.[31]

This is an area of contention. As defence secretary, Michael Portillo told the Conservative Party Conference in 1996 that: 'We will not allow Brussels to control our defence policy. Britain will not be told when to fight . . . Britain is blessed with very brave soldiers, sailors and airmen, willing to give their lives – for Britain, not for Brussels'.[32] Many British people would echo his suspicions of any Europeanisation of defence policy, for it is considered to be too basic to British national interests.

In defence and foreign affairs, the same problems that delayed the evolution of common policies in the past have still yet to be resolved. They include:

- The lack of any shared vision about what the nature and objectives of a CFSP should be like.
- Divergences of opinion about the role of the EU in European security and as to whether co-operation should follow an integrationist pattern or – as Britain favours – remain intergovernmental.
- A lack of clarity about whether or not the enlargement of NATO or the WEU is a better route to developing European security in general and especially for the 'new democracies'.

The USA has been keen to see the Europeans develop a stronger role in looking after their own security, but in any burden-sharing it repeats its oft-stated position of 'three "no"s'. There should be no decoupling of the US from Europe, no duplication of American forces by the EU and no discrimination against the US, including in the area of arms purchases.

Member states know the issues and are aware of the difficulties. As yet, they are unclear on how to resolve them to the satisfaction of all members.

Summary

The rulings of the EC have had their effect on all aspects of life in Britain, even though some of the horror stories about interference from Brussels are little more than modern mythology. The impact of the CAP on both British farming and the British economy may not always have been beneficial, but at different times there have been benefits for the consumer and taxpayer, if not necessarily for the farmer. For many economically depressed parts of the UK, considerable assistance has come from regional aid.

The impact of environmental legislation has been most marked and environmental groups operating in Britain have found their causes considerably helped by the accessibility of the EU's legislative process and by the support of the European Court. It is true that Britain has, or has had, opt-outs on social, security and monetary issues, but one lesson that has emerged from the Community as it has developed is that it has become a community in all senses of the word and no member can be totally isolated from community actions.

Notes

1   N. Nugent, *The Government and Politics of the European Union*, Palgrave, 2003.
2   Strategic goal announced in a official statement of the European Council, 2000a:2.
3   *Consumer Rights in the Single Market*, European File Series, European Commission, 1993.
4   C. Scrivener, former EC Commissioner for Consumer Affairs, in *Consumer Rights in the Single Market*, as 2 above.
5   Sir Leon Brittan, then commissioner for competition policy, in *Competition Policy in the European Community*, European File Series, European Commission, 1992.
6   K. Clarke, at an informal council of EU finance ministers, Lindau, Germany, September 1994.
7   *Helping Europe's Regions*, European File Series, European Commission, 1992.
8   Figures produced by the EC in 1990. The GDP is expressed in PPS (purchasing power standard), which is a cost-of-living index based on a common 'shopping basket' of goods and services.
9   J. Carvel, 'Merseyside wins record Euro-grants', *The Guardian*, 13 July 1994.
10 Objective 1 figures for 2000–6 are taken from O. Morgan, 'Parsimony and red tape mean UK regions miss out on EU aid', *The Observer*, 13 February 2000.
11 R. Norton-Taylor and K. Cahill, 'This land is their land', *The Guardian*, 13 August 1994.
12 P. Dunleavy, A. Gamble, I. Halliday and G. Peele (eds), *Developments in British Politics*, vol. 5, Macmillan, 1997.
13 Report in the *Financial Times*, 24 June 1996.
14 A. Osborn, *The Guardian*, 21 December 2002.
15 R. Lea, 'The Common Fisheries Policy and the wreckage of an industry', Institute of Directors policy document.
16 *Protecting our Environment*, European File Series, European Commission, 1992.
17 S. Young, 'Environmental politics and the EC', *Politics Review*, February 1993.
18 Department of the Environment, *Protecting Europe's Environment*, HMSO, 1992.
19 P. Brown, *The Guardian*, 16 May 1994.
20 Reported in *The Guardian*, 16 May 1994.
21 K. Milton, 'Interpreting environmental policy', *Journal of Law and Society*, vol. 19, 1991.
22 M. Portillo, then employment secretary, commenting on the issue by the Commission of a six-year social programme, 27 Jult 1994.
23 R. Lea, 'Red tape in the workplace', Institute of Directors paper, 2003.
24 J. Grant of the National Alliance of Women's Organisations, reported by S. Rutherford, 'Europe, my Europe', *The Guardian*, 17 May 1994.
25 Figures quoted by I. Black, 'Refugees in Britain: special report', *The Guardian*, 27 March 2000.
26 E. MacAskill, 'Belgium restores frontier curbs', *The Guardian*, 10 January 2000.
27 B. Roche, junior minister at the Home Office, reported in *The Guardian*, 17 February 2000.
28 J. Monnet, *Memoirs*, Collins, 1978.
29 M Holland, *European Integration: From Community to Union*, Pinter, 1994.
30 R. Ginsberg, *Foreign Policy Actions of the European Community*, Adamantine, 1989.

31 E. Bomberg and A. Stubb, *The European Union: How Does it Work?*, Oxford Univesity Press,, 2003.
32 M. Portillo, quoted in J. Major, *The Autobiography*, HarperCollins, 1997.

Part III

Participation

7

Representation: elections to the European Parliament

Article 138 of the Rome Treaty included the following provision: 'The Assembly shall draw up proposals for elections by direct universal suffrage in accordance with a uniform procedure in all Member States'. The Assembly approved such proposals as early as 1960, but found itself frustrated by yet another requirement of Article 138, which gave the deciding voice to the Council of Ministers with the words: 'The Council shall, acting unanimously, lay down the appropriate provisions'.[1]

From this, it can be seen that it was always the intention that the Community should have its own democratically elected parliament. For twenty-two years, this objective was thwarted by the more intergovernmental members of the Council of Ministers, originally those representing France but thereafter those representing Britain and Denmark. The reason for these delaying tactics was the knowledge that direct elections would give increased legitimacy and credibility to the deliberations of the European Parliament; that such increased legitimacy would confer an improved status and authority on the EP: and that such an improvement could only be at the expense of the stature and authority of national parliaments. Those who valued parliamentary sovereignty wanted to ensure that the EP could be dismissed as being no more than an empty discussion chamber, with no constitutional purpose, legitimacy or authority.

After British entry in 1973, the UK was allocated thirty-six seats in the EP, with members of the British Parliament, both Commons and Lords, being nominated as MEPs and with the thirty-six seats distributed between political parties in proportion to those parties' representation at Westminster. This meant that all members of the EP had what is known as the 'dual mandate' in that they were, at one and the same time, members of both the EP and their own national parliaments. The main disadvantage of the dual mandate was that parties not represented in the national parliaments could not get representation in Europe, however large their support. In addition, critics of the EC were not represented in the EP because only euro-enthusiasts tended to put their names forward for nomination. Finally, there was the question of how effective members holding the dual mandate could be in either capacity, given the pressure of work the dual role laid upon them.

The dual mandate largely disappeared after the introduction of direct elections in 1979. In Belgium and Germany the dual mandate is no longer permitted, and other member countries – or parties within those countries – have rules restricting it. Indeed, this is the case with the British Labour Party, which does not allow its MPs to stand for the EP. However, even in cases where the dual mandate is permitted, there is another factor that inhibits members of national parliaments from seeking election to Europe. This is a ruling which says that ministerial office is incompatible with membership of the EP – any national member of parliament who was also an MEP would thereby rule themselves out of consideration for promotion to ministerial rank.

The Conservative Party has no members of the House of Commons holding the dual mandate, but it is not uncommon for members of the House of Lords to stand for election to the EP, and to be elected. In 1999 there was a feeling on the part of Conservative peers that forthcoming reforms of the House of Lords could mean a reduction in their political role in Britain and that they should now look to Europe for new fields of activity. In the European elections of 1999 and 2004 three Conservative peers (Lords Bethel, Inglewood and Stockton) were elected as MEPs, as were two Liberal Democrat baronesses (Sarah Ludford and Emma Nicholson).

The dual mandate still finds favour in Northern Ireland, where John Hume (and Ian Paisley to 2004) has been an MEP since 1979, as well as belonging to the Westminster Parliament. However, there is a history of the dual mandate in Northern Ireland: Ian Paisley was a member of the Northern Ireland Parliament at Stormont between 1970 and 1973, as well as being the Westminster MP for North Antrim.

Electoral systems

Although the Council of Ministers was forced to concede direct elections to the EP in 1979, the Council proved unwilling to grant the other provisions laid down in the Treaty of Rome that were meant to create a uniform procedure in all member states. For example, there is no common eligibility for candidature as an MEP, with the age qualification in the various member countries ranging from eighteen to twenty-five, and, as we have seen, some countries bar the dual mandate whilst others permit it. It is only since the 1994 elections that the EU's citizenship rules laid down at Maastricht made it possible to stand and vote in one's country of residence rather than one's country of national origin. Even here there is no uniformity, since Luxembourg, which has a very high proportion of non-nationals in its resident population, demands a five-year residency before allowing access to the electoral system.

EU countries cannot even agree on the day on which European elections should be held. The UK chooses to stick with Thursday, the day normally used for Westminster or local elections; this practice has been followed by other countries including Denmark, Ireland and the Netherlands. Most European countries, however, vote on Sundays, in both national and European elections. Since election results are declared simultaneously in all member countries, this divided practice means that voters in those countries which vote on Thursday have to wait until Sunday evening to find out whom they have elected, while officials have to ensure that ballot papers are securely locked away for the best part of three days.

The most serious failure in standardising the procedure for European elections concerns the choice of electoral system to be used. It was originally envisaged that all member countries would use the same electoral system, based on some form of proportional representation (PR). However, the UK resisted the arguments and insisted on retaining the British 'first-past-the-post' electoral system for constituencies in the UK. This system remained in use from 1979 until the elections of 1994. The Blair government, on assuming power in 1997, promised that, in line with other constitutional reforms, it would have a proportional system in place by the time of the 1999 elections. In accordance with that promise, the European Parliamentary Elections Act of January 1999 established an electoral system based on regional lists. It was first used in the elections of June 1999.

With the introduction of proportional voting, the UK still does not have a uniform system. Back in 1979, even the most diehard supporters of first-past-the-post recognised that the sectarian nature of Northern Ireland politics would cause considerable problems if a majority system of voting failed to give representation to the Catholic minority. Because of this, a single three-member constituency was established to cover the whole province, its three representatives to be elected under the single transferable vote system of proportional representation. That variation has continued in force, despite the 1999 act.

All member states are now united in using a proportional system of voting of some kind. Yet, because the UK set a precedent by breaking ranks in 1979, there has been a consequent general failure among the other states to agree on a common system of PR. Most countries use straightforward list systems, but others have a preferential vote element. The Republic of Ireland, like Northern Ireland and Malta, uses the single transferable vote, and Luxembourg, with six MEPs, has a system whereby each voter is entitled to six votes that can be split between the candidates as they wish.[2] In a number of countries that employ a list system of proportional representation there is a threshold – usually 5 per cent of the votes cast – that parties have to reach before they are granted representation.

There is a significant difference in the populations represented by MEPs in the various member states. As with qualified majority voting in the Council of Ministers, seats in the EP are allocated to member states for political reasons as much as for strict proportionality. Before 1994 Germany had the same number of MEPs (eighty-one) as France, Italy and the UK, despite having a much larger population. As from 1994, when the rise in population caused by German reunification made an increase in the number of EP seats necessary, the new distribution of seats meant that larger member states had one MEP for each 500,000 electors. At the other end of the scale, the smaller member states are probably over-represented in an attempt to prevent them being overwhelmed by the larger states in the decision-making process. Further changes were made to cater for the expansion of the EU in 2004. As a result, the UK lost nine seats and now has seventy-eight. The division of MEPs remains heavily weighted towards the smaller states under the new distribution, and is destined to continue to do so, as the figures in Table 7.1 illustrate.

Table 7.1   *Member states and present and future representation in the EP*

Member state	Population (millions)	MEPs to 2004	MEPs in 2004	MEPs from 2007	Population per MEP in 2007
Austria	8.1	21	18	18	450,900
Belgium	10.3	25	24	24	429,900
Bulgaria	7.9	–	–	18	–
Cyprus	0.8	–	6	6	133,700
Czech Republic	10.2	–	24	24	426,500
Denmark	5.3	16	14	14	383,100
Estonia	1.3	–	6	6	220,500
Finland	5.2	16	14	14	371,900
France	60.1	87	78	78	771,100
Germany	82.4	99	99	99	833,100
Greece	11.0	25	24	24	457,300
Hungary	9.9	–	24	24	411,500
Ireland	4.0	15	13	13	304,300
Italy	57.4	87	78	78	736,200
Latvia	2.3	–	9	9	256,300
Lithuania	3.4	–	13	13	264,900
Luxembourg	0.5	6	6	6	75,500
Malta	0.4	–	5	5	78,800
Netherlands	16.1	31	27	27	598,100
Poland	38.6	–	54	54	714,600
Portugal	10.1	25	24	24	419,300
Romania	22.4	–	–	36	–
Slovakia	5.4	–	14	14	385,900
Slovenia	2.0	–	7	7	283,400
Spain	41.0	64	54	54	760,400
Sweden	8.9	22	19	19	467,200
UK	59.2	87	78	78	759,600
Total		626	732	786	

Source: Facts Through Figures, Eurostat, Luxembourg, 1994.

The British system adopted for the 1999 elections: closed lists

There was a prolonged argument over the type of electoral system that should be put into place for The UK when proportional representation was finally introduced. Some commentators and politicians supported the single transferable vote because it was used in Northern Ireland. Others wanted a suitable variation on the additional member system, similar to that used for elections to the Scottish Parliament. However, it was decided that the list system generally used in the EU was preferable. This was the method in use in France, Germany, Greece, Portugal and Spain. As a result of these deliberations, the provisions of the European Parliamentary Elections Act are that:

- The United Kingdom is divided into electoral regions.
- England is divided into nine electoral regions, while Scotland, Wales and Northern Ireland each constitute a single electoral region.
- There are seventy-eight MEPs elected in the UK, of whom sixty-four are for England, seven for Scotland, four for Wales and three for Northern Ireland.
- The electoral regions in England and the number of MEPs elected for each are: North East (three), North West (nine), Yorkshire and the Humber (six), West Midlands (seven), East Midlands (six), Eastern (seven), South West (seven), South East (ten) and London (nine).
- Electors vote for a party list of candidates rather than an individual candidate (the 'closed list' system).
- Seats are divided between parties according to the proportion of the vote each has gained in the electoral region and are allocated to individuals according to their placing on the party list.

Variations on the proposed system were suggested. One of these was the use of party primaries, whereby it would be the party membership who would choose whose names went on to the lists. This was rejected on the grounds that, with local elections, European elections and elections in devolved Scotland and Wales, the electorate had already suffered a voting overload in 1999 without becoming involved in primary elections as well. A more serious suggestion was made that electors should be allowed to indicate preferences on the lists of candidates (the 'open list' system) rather than simply vote for the list as a whole. The case for this was argued hard and long, but was finally rejected, leaving many critics able to say that the European elections did nothing to reduce the Community's democratic deficit but represented yet another example of the party leader's patronage at work.

The party list method of elections created a great deal of controversy, and it almost had to be imposed by force on sections of the Labour Party. Critics regard the closed lists as undemocratic, in that – unlike in the countries using open lists (Austria, Belgium, Denmark, Finland, Italy, Sweden and the Netherlands) – there is no element of voter choice. Not only is the choice of candidates for the list entirely the responsibility of the party hierarchy, but the very same people also choose the order in which candidates' names are listed on the ballot paper, thus influencing the chances that named candidates have of being elected or not being elected. In other words, the party has complete control of the process, allowing not even party grassroots workers to have a say, let alone the electors. The Liberal Democrats did allow party members to determine the composition of their list; Labour did not, as we can see below.

The ministerial case as advanced by the then home secretary, Jack Straw, was that the closed list system was widely used on the continent and that, if employed in Britain, then some 70 per cent of MEPs would be elected in this way a move towards uniformity in the voting system. He also claimed that the method was a 'simple, straightforward system which takes individual candidates and allows the public to vote for particular parties. It still asks the electorate to put a single cross on the ballot paper'.[3] Above all, it was the best means of promoting gender equality and getting ethnic minority candidates on the list. He made the point that prior to the 1999 elections, there were 'no women north of the Humber, and in areas with quite a high ethnic minority concentration there are no ethnic minority members'.

Labour and its list

Sitting MEPs and would-be rivals who wished to be put on the Labour Party's regional lists had first to win an one-member-one-vote ballot within the existing Euro-constituencies, with rank and file members having their say, voting for one man and one woman. The crucial weeding out of 'unsuitable' candidates was done at the second stage by a joint panel of National Executive Committee (NEC) members and regional representatives. At this stage also was the even more important decision of ranking would-be MEPs in order on the list. Ken Livingstone, one of two left-wingers to vote against the formula endorsed by the NEC in January 1998, was anxious about any notion of a purge. As he put it: 'They are banning the voters from affecting the ranking and banning party members from affecting it too. So effectively the leadership will determine who gets in. This is exactly what Eric Honecker [the communist leader under the pre-unification regime] did in East Germany.'[4]

In spite of the strong denial of such considerations, there was a widely held view that the New Labour leadership wanted to exercise strong control over the Labour list. An open list would enable the voters to express a preference that might be for candidates who were on the left of the party and unsympathetic to the Blair approach. At the very least, it was certainly an attraction for the prime minister that here was a chance to reform and modernise the Labour contingent in Strasbourg. He believed that many of the existing members were out of touch with prevalent thinking in the country and party.

The effects of the new system

In spite of the use of the list method, the two main parties still received a bonus from the electoral system, at the expense of the smaller parties who might be expected to benefit from the use of proportional representation. Both Labour and the Conservatives received a higher number of seats than their vote entitled them to on a strictly arithmetical basis, although the victorious Conservatives would have been substantially more successful if the First Past the Post method had been employed. Other parties gained representation. The Liberal Democrats improved by eight seats on their meagre 1994 reward of two, although their share of the seats won was lower than the percentage of votes cast for them. The Greens (three seats) and UKIP (two) were for the first time successful in electing MEPs, and the nationalists in Scotland and Wales also won two seats.

As for gender representation, the use of proportional voting systems by all member countries has contributed to a better level representation of women at Strasbourg than is true of those legislatures that do not use such systems. Between 1994 and 1999, 27 per cent of MEPs were women, while between 1999 and 2004 the figure was 30 per cent. Sweden and Finland both have high levels of female representation in the EP, just as they do in their national parliaments. Overall, Protestant countries with a culture that is sympathetic to gender equality, fare well, whereas Catholic and Eastern Orthodox countries, where the prevailing view of the female role is more traditional (France, Greece and Italy), have the lowest proportions. The House of Commons elected in 2001 under the first-past-the-post system had 17.9 per cent women, but of the MEPs the figure is significantly higher at 25.3 per cent.

After the experience of the 1999 elections, some opponents of PR made the point that the low turn-out might be interpreted as evidence that voters did not understand or favour the new proportional system. Yet 'fair voting' is often seen by proponents of PR as a stimulus to voter turn-out, because it means that all votes actually count towards the outcome.

Turn-out and apathy

The low level of voter participation in European elections has always attracted a great deal of attention. In three countries – Belgium, Luxembourg and Greece – voting is compulsory and their turn-out figures can be regarded as respectable, with Belgium and Luxembourg managing a turn-out of around 90 per cent, while Greece averages out at about 70 per cent. In most other countries of the EU, the turn-out is little more than 50 per cent, while three countries in 1999 had turn-outs that were less than a third of the electorate. Of those three, a mere 24 per cent of the UK electorate took the trouble to vote. This was not only the lowest turn-out that the UK has ever managed in the European elections, but a record low figure for anything other than a local election.

There has always been a Europe-wide apathy towards the European elections, with turn-outs in the past ranging from a low of 56.8 per cent in 1994 to a high of 62.5 per cent in 1979. In 1999, however, the elections hit a new low of 49.4 per cent, meaning that less than half the EU electorate felt ready to vote for the EP, despite the increased powers given to the EP and the its heightened profile as a result of its disciplining of Santer's Commission. It does mean that the EU faces a problem of legitimacy in that it has been saying for years that something must be done to correct the democratic deficit, only to find that when something is done about it the outcome is spurned by the electorate.[5]

Many explanations are given for the disappointing figures across the EU. First, unlike the situation in general elections, there is no prospect of a change of administration and polling therefore does not generate excitement or interest. Second, campaigns are essentially national contests, 'but of a secondary sort . . . [having] little coherence or coordination'.[6] Finally, the politicians who approach national campaigns with enthusiasm do not exhibit the same tendency in European ones. Often, the 'big names' play a relatively minor part in campaigning. This may be because they wish to play down mid-term protest results that may are often disappointing for those in power.

As for the UK, it has always had a poor turn-out record for anything other than Westminster elections, and the level of voting in European elections is very much in line with the turn-out for local elections. It is worth noting that the abysmally low figures for the European elections in June 1999 followed closely on a fairly disastrous round of local elections in May. The two events are not unconnected. No matter what other reasons there may be for voting for one's Westminster MP, the main motivating factor for the voter is the chance to choose the government that will rule the country for the next four to five years: that vote matters. If even the important responsibilities of local councils are seen as being of no great matter in comparison with this, how much more irrelevant is an election which does not form a government, which does not select a legislature and which does not affect policy decisions? The British public does not understand the EP, does not see that it has any relevance to their lives, and therefore sees no reason why they should vote for it.

Thanks to the indifference of the British electorate to European elections, the people who ought to be working hard to overcome that apathy – the politicians, parties and the media – are equally indifferent. The media are only interested in what interests their readers, listeners or viewers and therefore display only limited interest in what apparently leaves the public cold. The parties are not going to devote precious resources to European politics when their resources are already limited for the more important field of national politics. And, with a few notable exceptions, politicians of ability and public appeal are not going to become involved in an activity so far removed from influence and power in the national arena.

The role played by European elections in the British political process is very similar to that assumed by local elections. The electorate does not look on

European or local elections in isolation but more as a reflection of national politics, the reasons for people voting as they do being founded on national rather than European politics. And this is not only true of Britain. Throughout Europe in 1999 there was evidence that the movement of votes from left to right in those member countries with a governing party of the left was very much to do with a general disillusionment with those governing parties. As was written after the 1994 elections: 'In effect the elections were fought as twelve different national votes with distinct domestic flavours, rather than on common issues or programmes'.[7]

The European elections 2004

The general scene

The 2004 elections were widely billed in the press as the world's first continental elections. Nearly 349 million adults in 25 countries stretching from the Atlantic to the border of Russia, from the Mediterranean Sea to Lapland, had the right to place their cross on a ballot form. The sixth direct elections to the EP were second in scale only to those in India.

In all, 14,670 candidates – of whom one third were women – were contesting 732 seats. Among the candidates was the usual diverse array of colourful individualists: a Nobel prize winner, an Oscar winner, a Eurovision Song Contest winner, a supermodel, a porn star, assorted TV celebrities and *Big Brother* finalists. Among the more serious candidates were six former prime ministers. Some of the politicians were trying to begin new political careers, others to revive flagging ones.

Despite the repeated pleas from Brussels, in virtually no country were the elections fought primarily on European issues. In most cases, they descended into little more than a referendum on the government of the day. Voters had the chance to cast a protest vote against those in office and to a lesser extent against the EU in general. In several contests, much of the running during the campaign was made by eurosceptic candidates and parties, noticeably in Denmark, Poland, the Czech Republic and the Netherlands.

Turn-out on polling day was generally low, with 45.5 per cent turning out to vote – over 4 per cent less than in the 1999 elections. Across the continent, the mood of the voters seemed to range from apathy to resentment. The findings of Professor Rose of the Swedish think-tank IDEA suggested that the gap between people voting in national and in European elections stood at 21.9 per cent in the fifteen pre-2004 member states and 29.1 per cent in the ten new member countries.[8] The latest recruits to the EU – whose voters might have been expected to be flushed with enthusiasm for their new common European home – had, in fact, the lowest turn-outs in the election.

Yet the broad decline in public involvement in recent European elections, as illustrated in Table 7.2, has not been matched by perceptions of its importance.

EU polls taken during the campaign were indicating that 54 per cent of European citizens trusted the EP, 46 per cent thought it had more power than their own national parliament, and 66 per cent felt the European elections were 'very important'.

Table 7.2　*The trend in average turn-out across the EU since 1979 (%)*

1979	1984	1989	1994	1999	2004
63	61	58.5	56.8	49.8	45.5

The elections revealed a pan-European anti-incumbency trend. Incumbent governments of the centre-left suffered (as in Germany's Social Democratic and Britain's Labour Parties), as did those of the right (France's UMP and Italy's Forza Italia). In all, in twenty-three out of the twenty-five member countries, the largest party in the national government saw its share of the vote slump. The two governments that escaped the trend – the Greek New Democracy party of the centre right and the Spanish Socialists – were still enjoying something of a honeymoon, having only recently been elected into office.

Although most votes appear to have been cast on national lines, they had European consequences. The election confirmed the centre-right as the largest group in the EP, followed by the Socialists, a new Liberal and centrist group based on the European Liberal, Democrat and Reform Party (ELDR) and the Greens. All four groups included many committed federalists within their ranks and those parties traditionally in favour of closer European integration formed the largest block in the EP.

However, there was also a pan-European trend towards increased support for eurosceptic parties, most obviously in Britain, but also in Austria, Sweden and the Netherlands. In Sweden a new party, the Junelist, took 14.4 per cent of the vote and won three seats. In Britain UKIP did even better. However, not all eurosceptic groups fared as well, for the Danish variety lost two seats and the French *souverainistes*, who have long campaigned against the transfer of powers to Brussels, suffered a sharp decline in their popular vote. The populist anti-European Polish Selfdefence Party that had been tipped to top the polls, came fourth, although a Eurosceptic League of Polish Families came second. Where the far right was in power, it did as badly as the left did in Germany and Poland.

Nonetheless, if some anti or lukewarm Europeans did less well than anticipated, it remained the fact that there was a larger 'awkward' squad in the new EP, with broadly eurosceptic parties comprising 10 per cent of all MEPs. The number who opposed the proposed constitution or whose rallying point in the campaign was corruption within the EU constituted a much larger group. Professor Rose estimated the number of 'euro-awkwards' to be around 200.[9] They are a diverse collection of people of many persuasions, including British Conservatives and Swedish Greens, far rightists and unreconstructed communists, nationalists and populists.

Table 7.3   *The political complexion of the EP, before and after the June 2004 elections*

Political grouping	Outgoing 1999 EP (including the May 2004 enlargement)	Incoming EP post June 2004
EPP (centre-right)	294 (37.4%)	276 (37.7%)
PES (Socialist)	232 (29.5%)	200 (27.3%)
ELDR (Liberal)	67 (8.5%)	67 (9.2%)
GUE/EUL/NGL (united left/communists)	55 (7.0%)	39 (5.3%)
Greens	47 (6.0%)	42 (5.7%)
UEN (nationalists)	30 (3.8%)	27 (3.7%)
EDD (radicals, eurosceptics)	17 (2.2%)	15 (2.0%)
Not affiliated	44 (5.6%)	66 (9.0%)

Note: The breakdown for political groupings post 2004 is provisional: some non-affiliated MEPs have negotiated to join other groups.

Source: European Parliament.

The British parties and the election campaign

What was conspicuously absent from the British 2004 campaign was any sustained campaigning by the major parties on European issues. They did not treat it as the primary issue and prominent spokespersons for the more obviously pro-European parties did not make the positive case for Britain in Europe unless they were pressed to so do.

Labour said little about Europe. Ministers relied heavily on making macho noises about the vigour with which they were defending their famous 'red lines' in the negotiations. They preferred to run their campaign on what was regarded as Labour's natural territory of government achievement in the area of public services. Tony Blair's most significant move on European issues came before the campaign, when he made his surprise pledge to hold a referendum on the proposed constitution. Although designed primarily to neutralise Europe as an election issue in 2005, the initiative took the wind out of Conservative sails in the European election campaign, for the Conservatives had intended to campaign hard for a referendum. Otherwise, the prime minister's role was so low key as to be almost invisible. He did not appear in any of the Labour broadcasts and the party contented itself with attacks on Michael Howard's record in office as a minister in the Thatcher and Major governments.

The Labour Party was always likely to receive a beating, although the impact of defeat might be minimised simply because of its poor performance in 1999 when it won only 28 per cent of the vote. Its position was weakened by the cut in the number of British MEPs, for four of the nine disappearing seats were ones that Labour held. It could only realistically hope to do not much more badly than it had done five years earlier.

The Conservatives adopted a middle stance between the Labour party, which they accused of selling out to Europe, and the United Kingdom Independence Party (UKIP), which was campaigning for British withdrawal from the EU. The strong UKIP challenge threatened to derail the Tory campaign, for the Conservatives were vulnerable to a UKIP advance as they were likely to lose more votes to the anti-European party than were Labour or Liberal Democrats. Many would-be Conservative voters were likely to be attracted by the idea of withdrawal and liked UKIP's idea of free trade agreements with the EU's remaining membership.

The Howard line, as set out in an election broadcast, was to stress that it was realistic to wish to stay in the EU without endorsing everything that it does: 'We'll make clear that not every country has got to sign up to everything that comes out of Europe'. The leader tried to take the shrillness out of the party's euroscepticism and unite party members of all shades around the construct of an open and flexible EU: a live and let-live association of member states. This was far less hardline than the Hague approach in the previous (1999) election, which had worked at the time but failed spectacularly in the 2001 general election.

The Liberal Democrats were keen to see the government held to account over its policy in Iraq and portrayed the contest as a chance for the voters to deliver their verdict on Blairite backing for George Bush. As the most avowedly pro-European party in recent decades, the Liberal Democrats had little to say about the British role in Europe or support for the euro. However, they tried to establish a link between ministerial policy over Iraq and its attitudes towards the EU, suggesting that when it came to making a choice Tony Blair and his colleagues had opted for Washington rather than Brussels.

Having done particularly well in 1999, mainly because of the introduction of PR, the target of the Liberal Democrats was to retain their ten seats and if possible pick up a few more in the North East, North West, London and the South West. But of course, as with the other parties, the chances of winning as many seats as they had previously done were threatened by the reduction in the number of available seats and consequent redrawing of boundaries, and by the risk of UKIP, whose strong showing in the polls threatened to push the Liberal Democrats into fourth place.

UKIP was the only party to campaign primarily on European issues. It stressed that it was not anti-European, but opposed to membership of the EU which – bureaucratic and corrupt – 'stifles our initiative and threatens our freedom' and is a drain on UK resources. It had a clear, unambiguous message – withdrawal from the EU – which made it a natural vehicle for eurosceptics and voters wishing to lodge a protest vote without changing the government. It portrayed itself as the only alternative to the eurozealots of the main parties. It also had well-funded celebrity support from the apolitical Joan Collins and long-time broadcaster on daytime television, Robert Kilroy Silk. It had high hopes of improving upon the three seats won in 1999.

Otherwise, the Greens hoped to improve upon their two existing seats, by capitalising on anti-Iraq War feeling and the rising tide of euroscepticism as a political force. The British National Party (BNP) hoped to win a seat in the North West, where its leader Nick Griffin was standing. It exploited unease about asylum policy with leaflets stoking up fears about immigration, a topic that also featured in some UKIP propaganda. George Galloway's Respect Coalition of groups including the Socialist Workers and the Muslim Association of Great Britain fought its first political battle, by tapping into the strength of feeling generated over Iraq. It hoped to fare well in London, by taking up other causes such as the scrapping of tuition fees and renationalisation of public services.

Turn-out

Turn-out in British European elections has traditionally been low, perhaps a reflection of geographical insularity from the mainland and a consequent feeling of remoteness from European institutions. It may also reflect the doubts of the British people about the value of the European enterprise, or more specifically the ambivalence of governmental attitudes to Britain's position in the EU and the lack of leadership on the issue. Certainly, the issues surrounding the EU and its future have failed to arouse the British electorate. In 1999 there was a general decline in popular participation across the EU, but in Britain the lack of interest was startling.

Many commentators were forecasting an even more dire figure in 2004, assuming that disillusion with the government and the EU had both significantly increased over the last few years. Anticipating a hammering over Iraq and allied issues, Labour had taken steps to shore up its share of the nationwide vote by experimenting with all-postal ballots in four English regions: the North East, the North West, Yorkshire and Humberside and the East Midlands. This was thought likely to boost turn-out in areas where Labour had much of its core support, making it easier for disillusioned party voters to offer their support. In the last few days of the campaign, there were many stories of undelivered ballot forms and serious electoral misconduct by candidates and their supporters. In the event, more than 85,000 votes were declared invalid in the four regions, with one defending candidate claiming that confusion over balloting might have cost her a seat in Strasbourg. However, investigations showed that the scale of fraud and other malpractice were in most cases broadly comparable to the pattern of previous years.

Contrary to expectations, the turn-out was higher than anticipated. Turn-out averaged out at 38.8 per cent, but varied across the regions from 36 per cent in the West Midlands to 43.4 per cent in the East Midlands. In the four areas of England with all-postal voting, the average was 41.9 per cent. In the other five English regions, it was 36.8 per cent. 41.4 per cent voted in Wales, 30.9 per cent in Scotland and 51.7 per cent in Northern Ireland.

Labour's decision to create a Super Thursday, on which voters could vote in local and London Assembly/Mayoralty elections at the same time as the European contests, had helped to create more interest in the outcome. So also did the rise of UKIP, whose campaign threatened to draw support from across the political spectrum. In addition, there were plenty of other parties and candidates for whom to vote. Public interest in political issues, especially the Iraq War, seemed to have politicised many hitherto disengaged voters. This time, there was a real choice, particularly on the European issue.

The outcome

Table 7.4   *British party performances in the European elections, June 2004*

Party	Votes (%)	Seats (%)	Seats	+ or – votes relative to 1999 (%)
Conservatives	26.7	36.0	27	−9.0
Labour	22.6	25.3	19	−5.4
UKIP	16.1	16.0	12	+9.2
Liberal Democrats	14.9	16.0	12	+2.3
Green	6.3	2.7	2	0
BNP	4.9	0	0	+3.9
Respect	1.5	0	0	+1.5

Note: In addition to the above parties, the Scottish Nationalists won two seats, and Plaid Cymru, the Democratic Unionists, the Ulster Unionists and Sinn Fein one each. The percentages for seats and votes are based on the performance in the 75 mainland European constituencies.

Labour, more than 5 per cent down on 1999, suffered its worst performance in a national election since 1918; its only comfort being that it avoided quite the same degree of humiliation in Scotland where voters delivered a damaging snub to the Scottish National Party (SNP). The Conservatives lost the equivalent of eight seats and an ever higher percentage of the vote than Labour, although they still emerged as the party with the most MEPs elected. The Liberal Democrats gained two seats and modestly increased their share of the vote, but were pushed into fourth place. All three parties benefited from the workings of the electoral system, winning a higher percentage of the seats than their votes entitled them on a strictly arithmetical basis. All of them found difficulty in attracting the support of less affluent and older men, many of whom were seduced by UKIP. UKIP gained ten seats and made strong inroads into Conservative support, but also inflicted damage on Labour and the Liberal Democrats. ICM polling data suggested that 45 per cent of UKIP's voters had opted for the Conservatives in the previous general election, as opposed to 20 per cent for Labour and 11 per cent for the usual 'third force' in British politics.

As in 1999, the use of a proportional voting system had ensured that seats were won by small parties, in this case UKIP and the Greens, as well as the nationalists in Scotland, Wales and Northern Ireland. Women were better represented than is the case at Westminster, with nineteen elected (25.3 per cent). As is usually the case in British elections, Labour fared better than the Conservatives in this respect (seven as against two MEPs), with six for the Liberal Democrats. Among the UKIP successes, Robert Kilroy Silk was one of two party candidates elected in the East Midlands, the party's strongest area for voter support (26.1 per cent).

The role of an MEP

Among the many aspects of the EP that are unknown to the average British citizen is any conception as to what an MEP actually does. As is the case with the British Parliament, one obvious assumption is that members spend most of their time in the debating chamber. But if this is far from the case at Westminster, it is even less true of Strasbourg or Brussels. Even when commissioners are summoned before the EP to answer for their area of responsibility or to make a policy statement, very few turn up to listen or question them. An interesting example of this is provided by Matthew Engel's description of Sir Leon Brittan's appearance before the Parliament in 1994, to announce the new world trade agreement that would replace GATT:

> In the whole vast near-circular debating chamber there were, officials and flunkeys aside, only a dozen people. The press gallery was almost empty . . . This was not a particular comment on Sir Leon or his subject . . . It is always like this. No one goes to debates, except to speak. No one listens except the interpreters.[10]

The point about interpreters is important, as there are eleven official languages in the EU. It is very hard to make an impact with a speech when one's words cannot be understood directly by most of the people present; even the finest speech-making cannot survive the neutral intermediary of an interpreter. As Engel says, 'oratory, rhetoric and invective all fall flat'.

In the EP, as in the US Congress, all the detailed and most important work is done in committee, more so than is the case at Westminster. All MEPs serve on at least one of the committees, the membership of which is proportional not to national representation but to the political groupings in the EP. The committees are very much bound up with the Community legislative process, spending up to nine months on items of legislation entrusted to them and ensuring that more than one-third of all legislation originates from the EP. Maastricht gave MEPs a considerable say in certain policy areas related to the SEA, such as education, culture, public health, consumer protection and action programmes on the environment. The EP's involvement in legislation was increased by the Amsterdam and Nice Treaties, both of which extended the areas of co-decision. As Bomberg and Stubb point out: 'Under this procedure, no text can be adopted without the formal agreement of both the Council and Parliament. The Council knows it must listen and accommodate the EP, which means many more Parliament amendments now find their way into EU legislation.'[11]

Few of the British MEPs are known to their electorates. They are, in the words of *The Economist*, 'unloved and obscure'. However, its researchers noted

---

Box 7.1
The committee structure of the EP

There are seventeen specialist committees within the EP:

- Culture, youth, education, the media and sport;
- Citizen's liberties and rights, justice and home affairs: dealing with all aspects of human rights and also concerned with the internal security pillar of the EU, including Europol;
- Legal affairs and the internal market: covering both Community law and co-ordinating aspects of national legislation;
- Agriculture and rural development;
- Fisheries;
- Budgets: including not only the annual Community budget but all aspects of the financial framework of the Community;
- Industry, External trade, research and energy;
- Women's rights and equal opportunities;
- Regional policy, transport and tourism;
- Environment, public health and consumer policy;
- Development and Co-operation: largely concerning help for the Third World, including the Lomé Convention;
- Budgetary control: which basically means auditing Community expenditure;
- Employment and social affairs;
- Constitutional affairs: now largely concerned with enlargement;
- Foreign affairs, human rights, common security and defence policy;
- Economic and monetary affairs;
- Petitions: to receive and analyse petitions received from EU citizens.

In addition, as a result of the Maastricht Treaty, ad hoc, temporary committees of inquiry may also be set up by a vote of the parliament (the BSE crisis is a typical example of the sort of issue calling for an ad hoc committee).

---

that just a few had managed to attract media coverage. Labour's Glenys Kinnock, the Liberal Democrat Chris Huhne and the Green's Caroline Lucas achieved more than 100 mentions in the national quality press in the five years of the 1999–2004 Parliament. According to the database search, the vast majority received less than half that number and more than a quarter managed only single figures, two scoring zero.[12] Such a survey is inevitably flawed, not least because MEPs in remoter parts of Scotland and Wales find it easier to obtain a mention in local papers than in London-based national papers. But the impression remains that some members are indolent and the work they perform is too specialised or uninteresting to capture the interest of journalists and therefore of their readerships. Several MEPs have been known to complain that even in discussions of the work concerning life in the Strasbourg Parliament, the media prefer to feature Westminster MPs than its representatives.

MEPs are paid the same salary as members of their own national parliaments, although they can choose the currency and country in which to receive that salary. These salaries are constantly changing, but the lowest paid representatives at the time of the Fifth Enlargement were the Finns and the Spanish, who received less than one-third of the salary paid to the Italians (just under £100,000), who were by far the best rewarded contingent. East European members earned significantly less than their Western counterparts. British MEPs came more or less exactly in the middle, those elected in 2004 having a salary of £55,000. MPs enjoying the dual mandate as a member of a national parliament as well as the EP receive their normal parliamentary salary for their work at home, plus one-third of that salary for their work as an MEP. Because there are such wide variations in salary between MEPs of different nationalities, the Amsterdam Treaty laid down the aim of moving towards a common statute for all MEPs in order to remove disparities.

Expenses and allowances are the same for all MEPs and are often very much better than national allowances. Subsistence and travel allowances are particularly favourable, since they have to cater for the considerable amount of travelling MEPs must do, not only between Brussels, Strasbourg and Luxembourg but also between the EP and their home country. The figures agreed, as of 1 January 2004, are:

- **General expenditure** (office and communication costs etc.): €3,700 (halved in the case of members who, for no valid reason, do not attend half the number of plenary sessions).
- **Travel allowance** (to cover cost of travel undertaken by members within the EU, in order to attend official meetings of the EP; also covers associated expenses such as accommodation, meals and taxis): economy class air fare, or train/car allowances per km (€0.67 per km for first 500 km and €0.28 for rest of journey), plus distance allowance.
- **Travel allowance** (for travel throughout the world when on parliamentary business, including hotel costs): maximum €3,652.
- **Subsistence allowance**: €262 for attending meetings within the EU (covers both accommodation and meals); €131 per day on top of actual bed-and-breakfast costs for attending meetings outside the EU.
- **Secretarial allowance** (arising from the engagement or employment of one or more assistants): up to €12,576.

There are frequent complaints about the amount of money paid out to MEPs and the comfortable lifestyle they are said to enjoy, with the tabloids making great play of the 'Brussels gravy-train'. The pressure of complaints led to the introduction of sanctions by which MEPs may have their allowances cut by half if they do not attend at least 50 per cent of plenary sittings of the EP. Despite any such sanctions, however, it has been claimed that a perfectly honest MEP can, without fiddling the system, bank a six-figure sum for every session they spend as a member of the EP.

The alleged profligacy derives primarily from the generous flat-rate travel allowance that bears no relation to the expenses incurred in travelling to Brussels or Strasbourg. Members, aware of the need to shed the gravy-train image, bowed to public pressure on the issue and in December 2003 voted to abolish the lax expenses regime. Under the terms of the proposed deal, they would have had to provide receipts and their salaries would have been liable for national tax on top of a special low rate of EU tax. As a quid pro quo for accepting tougher limits on the perks, MEPs were to receive a hoist in salaries that in future were to be standardised across the EU. The standardisation would have granted a British member a 30 per cent rise to around £72,000 a year. However, although the EP had supported the deal, the last word rested with member states' foreign ministers who, in January 2004, balked at picking up the tab for salary reforms, thus blocking moves to crack down on abuses of expenses.

For all the complaints and accusations, it has to be said that the costs of the EP, even with its heavy expenditure on interpreters and translation, are less than half of what is spent in the USA on the House of Representatives.

One area where some suspicion lingers after the corruption scandals in the Brussels Commission, as well as in various national parliaments, concerns the extent of payments that are made to MEPs by lobbyists and interest groups. To counter this there is a register of interests on the British pattern that is supposedly completed by MEPs, copies of which are kept in Brussels and Luxembourg. But the register is not kept very assiduously and very few MEPs are particularly scrupulous in declaring their interests. Only the Dutch and British representatives seem to make any serious attempt to declare all their external earnings and allowances.

Political groupings

Members of the EP do not sit or associate as national groups but as members of a variety of political groupings based on an approximation of ideological similarity. The largest of these groupings form transnational federations for mutual assistance at election time, creating propaganda and campaigning material based on an agreed manifesto. None of these federations and few of the other groups have the cohesiveness or discipline of national political parties, but there is certain feeling of common interest. The groups have more influence than individuals or small national groupings would have and they receive financial support from the EP for administrative and research purposes, dependent on their size.

According to the EP rules of procedure adopted in 1999, a group must have a membership drawn from more than one member state. It requires a minimum of twenty-three MEPs if the members come from just two states, eighteen if they come from three, and fourteen if they come from four or more. In any Parliament, there are usually between seven and ten groups, there being seven in the 2004 Parliament. Their respective strengths in each member country are illustrated in Table 7.5

There are two major groupings or party federations in the EP. For a long while, the larger and more cohesive of the two was the Party of European Socialists (PES). It is still the more cohesive, although its position as largest grouping was lost in the elections of June 1999 and 2004. It includes twenty-eight parties from the twenty-five EU countries and represents the broad left in European politics. The PES group ranges ideologically from the traditional state interventionists of the hard left to the more moderate Social Democrats of the centre-left. Its major aims are to:

Table 7.5   *Party groupings in the 2004 EP*

Country	GUE/EUL/ NGL	Greens/ EFA	PES	ELDR	EPP	UEN	EDD	No affiliation	Total seats
Germany	7	13	23	7	49				99
UK		5	19	12	28[a]		12	2	78
France	3	6	31		28			10	78
Italy	7	2	15	9	28	9		8	78
Poland			8	4	18	7		17	54
Spain	1	5	24	1	23				54
Netherlands	2	2	7	5	7		2	2	27
Belgium		2	7	5	7			3	24
Czech Republic	6		2		11			5	24
Hungary			9	2	13				24
Greece	4		8		11			1	24
Portugal	2		12		7	2		1	24
Sweden	2	1	5	3	5			3	19
Austria		2	7		6			3	18
Denmark	2		5	4	1	1	1		14
Finland	1	1	3	5	4				14
Slovakia			3		8			3	14
Ireland		1	2		4	4		2	13
Lithuania			2	3	3			5	13
Latvia		1		1	3	4			9
Slovenia			1	2	4				7
Cyprus	2			1	2			1	6
Estonia			3	2	1				6
Luxembourg		1	1	1	3				6
Malta			3		2				5
Total in EU	39	42	200	67	276	27	15	66	732

Note: [a] Conservative total includes one Ulster Unionist.

Source: European Parliament.

- strengthen the position of the socialist and social democratic movement in the EU and throughout Europe;
- to develop common policies for EU adoption and a common manifesto.

On the centre-right, the European People's Party and European Democrats (EPP/ED) replaced the PES as the largest grouping in 1999 and remains so today. It is the only grouping to have representation in every country of the enlarged EU. In origin this group was made up of Christian Democrats and the full title of the group still contains the words 'Christian Democrat' in parentheses. In this respect, it is the direct heir of the tradition established in the 1950s by Robert Schuman, Konrad Adenauer and Alcide de Gasperi. However, the great days of Christian democracy seem to have been replaced by a wider but still moderate centre-right approach.

UK Conservatives and the sole Ulster Unionist MEP are associated with the EPP, but very loosely since the British parties find the strongly pro-federal approach of the party hard to live with. After the June 1999 elections there were weeks of negotiations before the Conservatives announced that they would only join the EPP on the basis of a deal which had been arranged whereby the EPP would drop all federalist references from its constitution, replacing the word 'federalism' with the words 'decentralisation and subsidiarity' wherever it appears. The EPP also added the name of the European Democratic group to its own. Until 1992 this had been a group of almost exclusively British Conservative MEPs, together with two anti-Europe Danish MEPs. It was only after the departure of Margaret Thatcher in 1990 that the Conservatives felt able to join the EPP, finally affiliating in May 1992. As we see on p. 240, there are still doubts in the minds of many British Conservatives over the merits of membership of the EPP.

All other political groupings in the EP are smaller and less influential. The largest of these groups is the European Liberal, Democrat and Reform Party (ELDR). Despite the presence of some Liberal members with leftish tendencies, the Liberal parties of mainland Europe are still very much rooted in the laissez-faire liberalism of the nineteenth century and the ELDR as a whole is much more a party of the right than its British component. After the 1999 elections it did a deal with the EPP involving support for each other's candidates for the presidency of the EP.

The European Free Alliance (EFA) and Greens, formed in 1999, comprises supporters of greater regional autonomy and a variety of Green members with very diverse approaches, some having a background on the left, others being of no fixed ideological attitude.

Firmly on the left of the EP is the Confederal Group of the European United Left/Nordic Green Left (GUE/EUF/NLG) whose members largely represent the remnants of former communist parties. Also affiliated to this loose structure of the Left are the Nordic Greens.

Also on the right is the Union for Europe of the Nations Group (UEN), an assortment of convinced nationalists reluctant to join up with the one of the more established centre-right groups. It currently includes nationalists from Italy and Fianna Fáil representatives from Ireland. A more recent grouping, formed after the 1999 elections, is the Group for a Europe of Democracies and Diversities (EDD). It includes radical eurosceptics such as the UKIP contingent. Many of its members are more anti-EU than those of the UEN. They pride themselves on their commitment to maintain national and cultural identities in their native countries.

The remaining sixty-six MEPs are regarded as independents, not attached to any of the foregoing groupings because those groupings fight shy of association with parties that are too openly on the far right. Members range from the French Front National of Jean-Marie Le Pen, the Austrian Freedom Party of Jörg Haider, the Italian Alleanza Nazionale and the Democratic Unionist from Northern Ireland.

The use of referendums

In two countries, Ireland and Denmark, it is a requirement of the constitution that constitutional changes should be put to the people in a referendum. Both countries referred the question of accession to the EC in 1972, 71 per cent of the Irish voting and a massive 90 per cent of the Danes. Twenty years later, both countries held referendums on the ratification of the Maastricht Treaty, the Danes most famously having to hold a second referendum in May 1993, after voting 'no' the first time. Since then, there have been several other referendums, either to ratify a new treaty or in the case of new countries, to approve their decision to join the EU (for example, the Austrian and Finnish referendums in 1994). Most of the recent batch of entrants who collectively made up the Fifth Enlargement held referendums to confirm their decisions.

Britain has had one referendum on European matters, which was called by Harold Wilson's government in 1975. This was the first and only time on which the issue of Britain's place in the EC has been opened up for popular discussion. With clear advantages deriving from the financial support of big business and the political backing of a majority of government ministers, the umbrella organisation 'Britain in Europe' won a handsome victory on a 64.5 per cent turn-out.

The future is likely to see the question of referendums becoming a much more important part of British relations with Europe. In 1997 there was broad agreement between the three main parties on the need for a referendum prior to entry into any single currency. The Referendum Party went further and wanted a more general vote to give people a chance to register their protest at the way in which – as a result of successive treaties – there was a developing momentum in the process towards European integration. Since then, the Conservatives have made it clear that they do not favour membership of the single currency in the foreseeable future. Labour and the Liberal Democrats are both committed to putting the issue of a single currency to the electorate before any decision on participation is taken.

British entry into the eurozone appears to be unlikely in the near future, so that the question of whether or not to participate is not one that the voters will have to decide. However, they have been promised a vote on the European constitution, as agreed in Brussels (June 2004).

The difference in participation between referendums and elections for the EP shows that people appear to be more willing to vote in referendums over a matter that they can see as being important to themselves than they are to vote in elections to a parliament that seems to have no direct effect on their lives.

Summary

Despite the growing democratic powers of the EP, the elections of 2004, just like those of ten years earlier, seem to show that the people of the EU as a whole are less enthusiastic about Europe than many of their leaders. Turn-out in European elections has always been poor in the UK and reached an all-time low in 1999. However, five years later voters turned out in much greater numbers and the discrepancy between the British and other European figures was markedly less than on previous occasions.

Overall in 2004 the figures for turn-out were unimpressive, with clear evidence of a serious decline in the long-established member states and even worse performances in the countries that joined the union in the Fifth Enlargement. Even when people do vote, they are hardly acting out of any sense of belonging to Europe, but rather tending to vote on domestic rather than European issues, mostly in order to show their displeasure with national governing parties.

The electorates of the EU tend to show more interest in referendums than in elections for the EP, perhaps precisely because they are being asked to respond to specific questions that they see as more important in their lives than the abstraction of a distant parliament.

Notes

1   N. Nugent, *The Government and Politics of the European Union*, Palgrave, 2003.

2   The source of this information is the directorate-general for information and public relations, Central Press Division of the European Parliament, as circulated through the UK Office, 2 Queen Anne's Gate, London SW1H 9AA, and now also to be found on the Internet at www.europarl.eu.int/uk.

3   J. Straw, speech in House of Commons, 17 July 1997.

4   K. Livingstone, quoted in *The Guardian*, 19 January 1998.

5   M. Walker, 'Voters indifferent to MEPs' new powers', *The Guardian*, 14 June 1999.

6   N. Nugent, as in 1 above.

7   P. Lynch and S. Hopkins, 'Europe decides', *Politics Review*, September 1994.

  8   R. Rose, 'Voter turnout in Western Europe: a regional report', International Institute for Democracy and Electoral Assistance, 7 June 2004.

  9   R. Rose, as in 8 above.

 10   M. Engel, 'Parliament of snoozers', *The Guardian*, 25 January 1994.

 11   E. Bomberg and A. Stubb, *The European Union: How Does it Work?*, Oxford University Press, 2003.

 12   *The Economist*, 5 June 2004. The database search was conducted by Factiva.com and based on a review of nine daily and Sunday quality papers in Britain, plus the *International Herald Tribune* and the *Wall Street Journal*.

8

British political parties and Europe

The area of British political life which has been most affected by membership of the EU is, without doubt, that of the fortunes and policies of the political parties. The Labour Party split over the question of Europe in the early 1980s, while the Conservatives followed suit in the 1990s, having lost a leader over the issue in the process. In the development of British political parties the argument over Europe and European integration has assumed the same importance as the repeal of the Corn Laws or Home Rule for Ireland did in the nineteenth century. It has been a contentious issue that has dominated the political agenda and redrawn the political map.

Yet although European integration has proved to be a disruptive issue in British politics, it does not hold much fascination for the British public. In a MORI survey in June 2001 it ranked tenth among the issues that most interested the public, a finding that makes the Conservative decision to highlight the euro in the general election campaign all the more surprising.

The Liberal Party and its successors

Of all the parties, the Liberals, followed by the Liberal–SDP Alliance and, latterly, the Liberal Democrat Party, has been the most consistent in its attitude to Europe. Membership of what was then still known simply as the Common Market was the policy of the Liberal Party in the early 1960s and it remained consistently supportive of a pro-European policy throughout the successive applications and rejections of the 1960s, even while the Conservative and Labour parties blew hot and cold over the matter.

The 'Gang of Four' who formed the Social Democratic Party (SDP) broke away from the Labour Party over a number of issues, but it was Labour's policy on Europe that was the match to the powder keg and the SDP was solidly pro-European from the first. It could hardly be anything else since one of the four – who became the SDP's first leader – was Roy Jenkins. He had resigned from the deputy leadership of the Labour Party in 1976 in protest at Labour's negative stance on Europe, had led the 'Britain in Europe' campaign during the 1975 referendum and had been president of the European Commission between 1979 and 1981. Indeed, the formation of the SDP and its alliance with the Liberals was the product of ideas first put forward in the Reith Lecture given by Jenkins on his return from the Commission presidency, a lecture which advocated not only a strategy that would 'break the mould' of bi-partisan British politics but one which would involve increasingly closer integration with Europe.

The Liberal Democrat Party, in deference to its antecedents, is wholeheartedly pro-European. Indeed, it has sometimes been said that its leadership has been too uncritical and starry-eyed in its attitude towards Europe. According to this view, the party will accept without question policies emanating from Europe that perhaps ought to be questioned. Critics within the party have suggested that sometimes it has sacrificed possible tactical advantage, for fear of compromising pro-European credentials – as over its backing of the 'paving motion' for the Maastricht Ratification Bill (November 1992). On that occasion, it rejected the opportunity to vote with Tory rebels and Labour, even though there was a real prospect of bringing about a governmental defeat and resignation. But a vote against the Maastricht provisions could have been interpreted as a vote against Europe and the Liberal Democrats were unwilling to risk that. As one commentator wrote at the time: 'The Liberal Democrats, though opponents warned them that they might save the life of an unpopular government, declared that the cause of Europe ought to come first, and voted with the Conservatives'.[1]

The Liberal Democrats were heavily criticised by the Labour Party and others for their part in that critical vote. But the point made by their first leader, Paddy Ashdown, was that sufficient damage had already been done to Britain's place in Europe by the actions of the two major parties. Britain could no longer afford to send ambiguous messages to Europe by appearing to reject a pro-European measure.

As leader, Paddy Ashdown's enthusiasm for the EU was firmly apparent. But he was aware that people across Europe are 'in the dark' about an organisation increasingly responsible for decisions affecting their lives. He was critical of its language, that 'inscrutable, acronym-laden, bureaucratic-speak which so much dominates communication in the EU'. As part of his solution, he committed his party to support for a written constitution for the EU, formulated from the bottom up, a radical departure for a body which has long been run from the top down, as the exclusive preserve of the great European elites. He favoured the writing of a written constitution, contained in a single document, clear enough to be understood by everybody and short enough to be easily carried around, as a means of 'stripping away the mystique of the EU . . . In an instant, it would seem less faceless and less out of reach, and more like a human-made creation that can be moulded and unchanged.[2]

Under the leadership of Ashdown's successor, Charles Kennedy, the party devoted around 5 per cent of its space to Europe in its 2001 manifesto, making the topic its twelfth priority in terms of word count.[3] It adopted a less overtly pro-European tone and even the leader jested that the topic was tucked away 'in the sports pages' towards the rear of the manifesto.[4] The case for a constitution was reiterated, although it was put in terms of 'defining and limiting [the Union's] powers'. Similarly, there were other indications of a hardening of party attitudes, notably in the importance attached to maintaining the veto in areas of vital national interests. These were widely drawn, covering the constitution, defence, 'own resources', budgetary and tax matters and regulations on pay and social security. Moreover, the party preferred not to talk too much about its traditional enthusiasm for a federal Europe.

Although that same manifesto emphasised the party's 'firm support' of the EU and stressed the need for Britain 'as a core member' to engage positively in its activities, several commentators have detected a definite shift of emphasis in the rhetoric on Europe. Kennedy has admitted to giving a harder edge to policy on the euro, saying that his party must adjust its attitude and become a 'candid friend' of Europe.[5] He is aware that in the past the impression has been given that Liberal Democrats have sometimes given the impression of abandoning their critical faculties on EU matters and has drawn a parallel with his approach to membership of the House of Commons: he disagrees with many of its procedures, but this does not prevent him from participating.

In making such pronouncements, Kennedy is no doubt aware that Liberal Democrat policies are coming under more scrutiny as his party advances at Westminster and in the country. Some repositioning in his view is desirable and necessary. He recognises the need to gain support in constituencies held narrowly by the Conservatives and to retain seats in areas such as the South West, rural Wales and Scotland, which are not 'hotbeds of pro-European sentiment'[6]. He is also aware that the general lack of enthusiasm for 'things European' among the electorate is shared by many of his party's members. There has often seemed to be a mismatch between the euro-enthusiasm of the Liberal/Liberal Democrat leadership and parliamentarians and the greater scepticism of the rank-and-file, a point confirmed by the findings of Bennie *et al.* who conclude that party members are 'scarcely more pro-European than the electorate as a whole'.[7]

Nonetheless, the Charles Kennedy emphasises his personal and party commitment to the EU, observing that: 'I am absolutely down the lines a firm supporter of Europe and of us developing an enlarged European Union, but that is not to say a massive organisation is without its faults'.[8]

Such backing was reaffirmed in the 2004 European elections when the party secured twelve seats (an improvement on its 1999 position) but was forced into fourth place by UKIP. Again, there was the same reluctance positively to sell the case for Europe. Rather, the emphasis of campaigning was on the government's handling of the war against Saddam Hussein's Iraq, the link being that the prime minister chose to give the 'special relationship' with the USA priority over any commitment to working in concert with Britain's European partners.

The nationalist parties

The Scottish National Party (SNP) was once bitterly opposed to Europe, campaigning vigorously against membership during the 1975 referendum. Its attitude at that time was that a party campaigning for independence for Scotland could hardly advocate yet another level of government to which Scots would be subjected. However, since 1983 the position of the SNP has changed to one of advocating a strong EU. The reasoning now is that it makes sense for an independent Scotland to be a full member of an effective and integrated EU, thereby eliminating any control of Scotland from Westminster, and replacing domination by London with direct relations between Brussels and Edinburgh.

The European dimension also helps to reduce the doubts about economic viability that used to be advanced against full Scottish independence. After all, with an electorate of 3.8 million, Scotland is many times the size of Luxembourg, a third as large again as Ireland and about the same size as Denmark. The SNP can justifiably point to the success of small states in the EU, and argue that the EU provides them with a greater influence than would otherwise be possible. Moreover, 'Scotland in Europe' would be the likely beneficiary of EU funding to help promote modernisation of the country's economic and social infrastructure, and regional development. Accordingly 'An independent Scotland within Europe' has been the slogan of the SNP in recent years.

In its literature, the SNP stresses that it is a pro-European party, while at the same time advocating reform to bring the EU closer to its citizens. It has anxieties about the impact of the Common Fisheries Policy on Scotland and argues for a constitution that clearly states that the EU should be a confederation of nation states that choose to share sovereignty rather than a federal organisation. It offers broad support for the euro (subject to popular approval for its use, as expressed in a referendum), seeing exclusion from the eurozone because it places Scottish exporters at a clear disadvantage.

For a long while, the SNP was the only minor party in mainland Britain to have had a representative in the EP since the start of direct elections: Winnie Ewing won the Highlands and Islands constituency in 1979 and held it until she retired in 1999. As a result of the 2004 European elections, the party still had two seats, although its share of the popular vote in Scotland declined from 27.0 to 19.7 per cent, well behind Labour.

The position adopted by the Welsh nationalists, Plaid Cymru, mirrors that of the SNP, the party having moved from initial hostility to the EC to the current enthusiasm for Welsh independence within Europe. As with the Scottish situation, the approach of Welsh nationalists was reinforced by seeing the favoured position accorded in Brussels to the regions of other member states.

According to its website, Plaid aims 'to promote the constitutional advancement of Wales with a view to attaining full national status for the country within the European Union'. After the 2004 elections it had one MEP who, like the two SNP members, sits as part of the European Free Alliance (EFA), a group of left-leaning regional and national parties, and Greens.

In Northern Ireland the Unionist parties are largely hostile to Europe: Ian Paisley's Democratic Unionist Party (DUP) more so than the official Unionist Party (UUP). This has not stopped the unionists in either group from campaigning vigorously in the interests of the province, most notably in pursuit of a special dispensation from the beef ban for Northern Irish cattle. Both parties have a seat in the Strasbourg Parliament, the DUP having comfortably topped the Northern Irish poll in 2004, with the UUP slipping back into third position, well behind Sinn Fein. The Social Democratic and Labour Party (SDLP) has been more supportive of Europe than the unionist parties, in part because the EU offers a way in which republican Northern Ireland politicians can work alongside those of the Republic of Ireland within a European context. In 2004 the SDLP lost its seat in the Strasbourg Parliament, Sinn Fein taking the republican vacancy.

All these minor parties have maintained a united policy front on Europe throughout the period of direct elections, even if that policy has changed over the years, as it has done with the SNP and Plaid Cymru. When we turn to the two major parties, however, it is a very different story. For both parties the relationship with Europe has been turbulent, with major and potentially fatal divisions in both parties over their European policy.

The mainland anti-European parties

Three British parties have stressed their opposition to Europe in recent years, two of them making it their main campaigning issue. The Referendum Party was formed in advance of the 1997 election by the multimillionaire, Sir James Goldsmith. He employed his personal wealth to support 546 other candidates who backed his own views on the European issue. He wanted a referendum not just on the issue of the currency, but on the much broader question of the degree of Britain's entanglement with the EU. He argued that people had not been able to express their views on the development of the EU for more than twenty years and that – given the direction it had taken – they should be given the chance to show their acquiescence or disapproval.

Outwardly the Referendum Party was not anti-European – after all, Goldsmith was half French by birth, retained French nationality, lived for part of the year in France and was an MEP for a French constituency – but it claimed to want no more than to permit the British people a say through a referendum that had been denied them by the traditional parties. As Goldsmith said at the press alunch of the party on 27 November 1995, 'we are not politicians and our only aim is to secure a referendum'. Yet his election literature was openly opposed to the EU, with statements such as 'unelected Brussels bureaucrats will soon be handed almost total control of our lives'. The explicit aim of the party was the referendum, but its implicit purpose, hardly hidden and understood by the electorate, was to achieve Britain's withdrawal from Europe.

In the event, under a million voted for the Referendum Party, an average of 3.1 per cent of the vote in those constituencies where its candidates were standing. David Butler and Dennis Kavanagh calculate that although the presence or absence of an anti-European candidate clearly made a difference to the performance of the Conservatives, 'only a handful of their losses can be blamed on the intervention of the Referendum Party which was not so much a cause of the Conservatives' difficulties as a symptom'.[9]

Of greater significance, because it is still not merely alive but actually flourishing, is the United Kingdom Independence Party (UKIP). Formed in 1993, it was outperformed by its rival in capitalising on anti-European sentiment in the 1997 election, averaging only 1.2 per cent of the vote in the 194 constituencies where it stood. But in 2001, as the sole vehicle for the anti-European cause, it fared better than the other small parties, averaging 1.6 per cent. It did best in those constituencies:

> whose social profile is most commonly associated with euroscepticism (that is, those with an older age profile) and least well in those with a relatively younger population. It also tended to do rather better in seats with a low proportion of people with degrees, away from the most urban constituencies, and in the southern half of England outside of London.[10]

UKIP wants to see Britain regain its alleged lost independence. It believes that successive treaties have given the EU more powers and particularly laments the loss of the veto in key policy areas. It also points to the high cost of membership of the EU. Its conclusion is clear: in every sense, Britain would be better off outside the EU. Here then, is one party offering a distinctive message on Europe, as compared with the broad pro-Europeanism of the main parties: namely that Britain needs freedom from the EU.

UKIP's message found clear support from some voters in the 1999 European elections, for under the proportional voting system it gained three representatives in the EP. In 2004 it did markedly better, winning twelve seats and gaining more than 2.6 million votes (nearly 200,000 more than the Liberal Democrats). Its MEPs, members of the loose alliance known as the Europe of Democracies and Diversities (EDD), played little part in the 1999-2004 Parliament. Its rising star, Robert Kilroy Silk, elected in the East Midlands after nearly topping the poll ahead of the Conservatives, immediately promised to 'wreck' the proceedings in Strasbourg, 'to expose it for the waste, the corruption and the way it's eroding our independence and our sovereignty'.[11] On further reflection, Nigel Farage, one of its three re-elected UKIP MEPs, attached greater priority to working to establish a strong block of eurosceptic members, including Czechs, Danish, Dutch and Polish MEPs, within the EDD. As members of a large grouping covering at least five countries, they would gain financial advantages, qualifying for paid staff and funding.

UKIP's success in 2004 served to neutralise thee impact of the anti-European British National Party, which substantially increased its share of the vote but was denied by UKIP of the seat in the North West region for which it had high hopes.

The Labour Party

The hostile phase

Historically the Labour Party was opposed to Britain's membership of the EC. Originally the attitude of the Labour Party was governed by the 1945 Labour government's attempts to make major changes to British society through a programme of nationalisation and the introduction of the Welfare State. To bring about what it saw as necessary changes, the government needed to be in full control of the British economy and social legislation. In this way, it could act as a true reforming government, without fearing any pressure to dilute its programme through the need to co-operate with other countries. For many on the left of the party, the EEC, as it was established in the mid-1950s as a business-orientated Common Market, was little more than a capitalist club, membership of which was inimical to socialist principles.

The Marxist Tom Nairn, writing about Europe at the time of Britain's accession to the EC, pointed out that Labour's opposition to membership was not solely ideological.[12] There is, in fact, an old-fashioned strain of British nationalism in grassroots Labour thinking and a strongly xenophobic, vaguely jingoistic attitude underlying working-class values. It was that nationalistic thread which split the party over what its attitude should be towards the Macmillan government's first application to join the EEC in 1961. Most of the party was bitterly opposed to the idea, but no one could be certain as to the attitude of the leadership. In the summer of 1962 the Labour leader, Hugh Gaitskell, seemed to define his own stance, claiming that to join Europe would mean that Britain had to throw out 'a thousand years of history for the sake of a marginal advantage on the price of a washing machine in Düsseldorf'. Yet, only a few weeks later, in replying on television to a talk by the prime minister, Gaitskell seemed to hedge his bets, saying that he would wait to see the terms of entry before he committed himself. Macmillan had great fun at Labour's expense, telling the 1962 Conservative Party Conference that Labour's policy on Europe reminded him of the old popular song:

She didn't say 'yes', she didn't say 'no',
She didn't say 'stay', she didn't say 'go',
She wanted to climb but dreaded to fall,
So she bided her time and clung to the wall.[13]

Shortly after this Macmillan's application was rejected by de Gaulle and Labour's scepticism seemed to be vindicated.

It was Gaitskell's successor, Harold Wilson, who initiated Britain's second application to join the EEC in 1966. Having in the election struck a note of deep euroscepticism (at one point ridiculing Edward Heath for, on receiving one encouraging gesture, rolling 'on his back, like a spaniel'), Wilson soon shifted to a more sympathetic stance. He was always a pragmatist and he weighed the ideological and nationalistic objections to Community membership against the penalties of being excluded from the then economic success of the six EEC members. He noted the thinness of alternatives to membership, such as the Commonwealth, and the difficulties for Britain of trying to maintain a global role east of Suez. He was also acutely aware of Britain's economic weakness. With the backing of his new foreign secretary, the pro-European George Brown, he concluded that Britain must engage more fully with the countries within its own region and that ideally membership of the EEC was desirable.

The second rejection of Britain by de Gaulle dented Wilson's confidence and he publicly reverted to a position critical of Europe. However, he had become convinced of the need for Britain to be involved in the development of the EC, and this would inform his thinking after Labour's re-election in 1974.

Renegotiation and referendum

When the Heath government negotiated the terms for Britain's entry into the EC in 1971 it was decided that Labour would oppose the government in the motion accepting the principle of EC membership. But Wilson was still playing it canny by avoiding outright condemnation of membership itself. The Labour stance was that the terms negotiated by Heath's team were wrong for Britain and would have to be renegotiated before Labour could accept them. In a free vote of the House of Commons the principle of EC membership was passed by 356 votes to 244. Significantly, in the light of future divisions, thirty-nine Conservatives voted against the government motion, and sixty-nine Labour MPs went against party advice to vote with the government.

Wilson's main concern was to keep his party united despite the deep divisions that had opened up over Europe, so, to avoid giving offence to anyone, he gave no clear guidance as to the leadership's stance on Europe. The party entered the first general election of 1974 with senior members of the party advocating at least three different approaches. These were:

- the party should accept membership now that Britain was in the EC and the party's energies should be devoted to getting the best possible deal for Britain out of the EC (Wilson's private position);
- an immediate withdrawal from the EC and the full restoration of British parliamentary sovereignty;
- Britain should probably stay within the EC but that the terms needed to be renegotiated (Wilson's public position).

The Labour Party made no attempt to paper over these cracks, but rather chose to flaunt them, as when it decided to devote its last party political broadcast before polling day to the issue of Europe.

> About half the team then talked about the Common Market. Michael Foot claimed British housewives were paying high prices in the shops to subsidise French farmers; Shirley Williams said Labour would re-negotiate the terms of Britain's entry and Denis Healey added 'we can get out altogether if we don't get what we want'.[14]

Between the February and October elections of 1974 Harold Wilson, at the head of his minority government, determined his strategy for dealing with divisions within the party. The device adopted by Wilson to keep all shades of opinion in his party sweet was to fight the October election with the manifesto promise that membership terms would be renegotiated and that the government would take no further action until the public had given their verdict in a referendum.

At a European Council meeting in Dublin in March 1975 the British government formally requested a revision of the terms agreed in 1971. By June 1975 James Callaghan was able to announce changes in the terms which were cosmetic rather than substantive, but which were sufficient for Wilson and Callaghan to be able to endorse them when placing the matter before the electorate in the referendum. The referendum itself was so worded as to encourage a 'yes' vote, the question put being 'Do you think the United Kingdom should stay in the European Community (the Common Market)?'

The referendum campaign was not fought by the political parties but by two all-party umbrella groups: 'Britain in Europe' supporting a 'yes' vote and the 'National Referendum Campaign' in favour of a 'no' vote. Wilson wanted to remain aloof from the campaign but he was left with the problem of a deeply divided cabinet, all eager to take part in the campaign but with sixteen ministers wanting to support a 'yes' vote and seven wanting to advocate a 'no'. To escape his dilemma, Wilson took the unusual step of suspending the convention of collective responsibility so that prominent ministers, such as Barbara Castle, Peter Shore, Tony Benn and Michael Foot, could campaign against government policy while remaining members of the government.

At first Wilson tried to prevent cabinet ministers on opposing sides from appearing on the same platform or on the same television programme. But this was relaxed towards the end and the *Panorama* television programme was allowed to screen a head-to-head confrontation between Roy Jenkins and Tony Benn. Wilson maintained his neutrality but his preference for a 'yes' vote was known and may have been influential in persuading 66 per cent of the electorate to vote in favour of membership. Certainly Tony Benn thought so when he said 'I regard it as the third election in which the Labour Party was defeated and Wilson won'.[15]

Renewed hostility

The defeat of Labour in 1979 led to a resurgence of anti-European thinking in the party. The left, as exemplified by Tony Benn, blamed the Conservative victory on a lukewarm attitude towards socialism in the Labour leadership, and advocacy of European policies was seen as one of the hallmarks of that lukewarm attitude. With the hard left in control of many constituencies and exercising its influence on Conference, Labour policy began to move leftwards towards an uncompromisingly anti-European stance.

In 1981 the party finally split, with David Owen, Shirley Williams and Bill Rodgers joining Roy Jenkins to form the 'Gang of Four' which issued the Limehouse Declaration and brought the SDP into existence as a party which felt very strongly about Europe: the Labour MPs who followed the Gang of Four into the SDP comprised the most pro-European sections of the Labour Party. Their departure, combined with the leftward drift of the party, led to a renewed rejection of and sustained opposition to European integration.

In the run-up to the 1983 general election, under Michael Foot, the Labour Party adopted the alternative economic strategy (AES):

> The AES assumed that it was possible to revitalise the ailing British economy through a programme of socialist economic expansion which would include domestic reflation and the use of import controls. An essential prerequisite was full economic sovereignty. In other words, a potential Labour government would need to have full control of the British economy. This was not deemed to be possible with continued membership of the EC.[16]

The Labour Party fought the 1983 election committed to a policy of complete withdrawal from EC membership, which was the most extreme position ever to be adopted by Labour in opposition to Europe. At the time it seemed that Labour had rooted itself in an anti-EC position and that nothing was likely to change; in 1984 two distinguished political commentators wrote, 'It is quite possible that a future Labour government will want to take Britain out of the EEC, or demand such fundamental structural changes as the price of staying in, that withdrawal becomes inevitable'.[17]

The change of direction

Since those words were written the Labour Party changed so fundamentally that it could be described at the start of the 1990s as 'the more European of the two major parties'.[18] Yet the change was slow in coming, only really beginning in 1987 when Neil Kinnock set up a review of the party's policy following the election defeat of that year. There are those cynics who say that Labour's change of direction was little more than a political device to counter the direction taken by the Conservatives, but Labour's change of heart was more deep-seated than a mere search for electoral advantage. It was based on a number of premises that needed rethinking after Labour's third successive general election defeat:

- The economists in the party recognised the interdependence of economic processes in the modern world and came to doubt the viability of the AES in isolation from the powerful economic blocs such as the EC.
- There was a realisation that the continued success of Margaret Thatcher and the Conservatives meant that, while there was no scope in Britain for advancing the policies of the left, those policies were still prominent in Europe and that it was possible to introduce social policies into Britain via the EC – what Thatcher called 'socialism by the back door'.
- Exposure of the faults in the British political system by groups such as Charter 88 made advocacy of parliamentary sovereignty less acceptable, removing one of the props from the nationalistic arguments against Europe.

The real turning point was the visit to Britain in 1988 of the president of the Commission, Jacques Delors. Delors came to Britain to address the Trades Union Congress and received a standing ovation for a speech in which he laid out his thinking on a social charter for Europe, which guaranteed certain minimum standards for pay, working conditions and social benefits across the whole Community. This was so much in line with Labour thinking that the party enthusiastically endorsed the direction being taken by Delors and the Commission. Labour's change from an anti-European to a pro-European stance is therefore due to a change in the nature of the EU. When the EC was seen as little more than a trading area for the benefit of commercial interests, the Labour Party felt obliged to oppose it; when the EC was seen as promoting improved social and environmental standards, then it became natural for Labour to support it. It is, in many ways, a mirror image of the change in Conservative attitudes to Europe.

To a Labour Party denied any hope of power in Britain since 1979, Europe seemed a logical way by which the social policies desired by Labour could be introduced into Britain, despite even a Conservative government, and the acceptance of a pro-European stance was adopted successively by Neil Kinnock, John Smith and Tony Blair. The modernising tendency in the party associated with the rise of Tony Blair and known as New Labour was made up of virtually all pro-Europeans. It was ironic for Labour to see Neil Kinnock, who had campaigned against Europe in 1983, accept the post of European commissioner in 1994, be promoted to deputy president of the Commission in 1999, and all in a Brussels where his wife was meeting in the EP's committees as a prominent MEP.

Labour – the pro-European of the two main parties

As we saw in chapter 2, New Labour has been a pro-European party. However, it has not been naively enthusiastic about the EU, recognising its faults such as the CAP. Neither has it shared the interest of some continental socialists in creating any kind of federal Europe. Its language in the 1997 election was not markedly different from that of the Conservatives, as was apparent in the stated preference for 'an alliance of independent nations choosing to co-operate to achieve the goals they cannot achieve alone'.

Four years in dealing with the EU leaders were inevitably a chastening experience, for they illustrated the difficulty of trying to be a key player in EU affairs while at the same time firmly standing up for British interests on matters such tax harmonisation, the euro and common policies on security and foreign affairs. What had emerged by the time of the 2001 election was that, like its predecessors, Labour preferred the intergovernmental approach; rejected integrationism; had an economic liberalisation agenda that stressed the value of flexible and dynamic labour markets, rather than the social welfare model preferred by some continental socialists; and was determined to retain a strong link with the USA. The Blairite equivocation over the euro indicates that while the party wants to stay ahead of the Conservatives by stressing its pro-europeanism, the prime minister recognises that he operates in a country whose enthusiasm for the EU is muted and sometimes grudging. Membership is often seen as a necessity rather than a cause for celebration.

There was an undoubted continuity in some aspects of New Labour's approach to European policy. Tony Blair appeared to be more comfortable with other European heads of government than some of his Conservative predecessors and he employed more obviously pro-European rhetoric. But the two strands already apparent in 2001 remain significant, namely the emphasis on intergovernmentalism and the value attached to the 'special relationship' within the Atlantic Alliance. The preference for co-operation between nation-states co-operating for their mutual benefit has been reinforced by the latest EU enlargement, offering the prospect of support from new entrants for the British outlook in a wider and looser EU. As for the relationship with the White House, it was evident from the early days of the Blair premiership that Bill Clinton and the prime minister, were personal as well as political friends. What is more surprising is that the special relationship survived the change of personnel in the Oval Office.

Under Tony Blair, Britain removed firm and steadfast as the USA's strongest ally in Europe, to an extent that troubles many in the Labour Party. When

George Bush was elected, many Labour supporters were uneasy about co-operating with a leader whose election was widely portrayed on the left as fraudu-
lent and illegitimate. But his relationship with the prime minister was a strong
one, based on a good personal rapport as well as the perceived common interests of the countries they represent. The terrorist threat exemplified by the
events of September 2001 and the build-up to, conflict in and outcome of the
war against the Saddam Hussein regime in Iraq, meant that the two leaders
were united by events. Traditional Labour and New Labour preferences for co-
operation with the Democrats have been cast in doubt, to such an extent that
the fate of the Labour leadership became intertwined with that of Republican
President Bush.

In choosing to follow the USA, rather than ally Britain with Jacques Chirac
and Gerhard Schroeder, New Labour in office made a clear choice. It has shown
that when there is a potential conflict, British governments tend to see the
special relationship as paramount. Speaking to the Foreign Office Conference of
British ambassadors on 7 January 2003, Tony Blair outlined the British stance
unambiguously:

> First, we should remain the closest ally of the US, and as allies influence them to
> continue broadening their agenda. We are the allies of the US not because they
> are powerful, but because we share their values . . . For all their faults and all
> nations have them, the US are a force for good; they have liberal and democratic
> traditions of which any nation can be proud . . . there are not many countries
> who wouldn't wish for the same relationship as we have with the US and that
> includes most of the ones most critical of it in public.

However, he then went on to add that:

> Britain must be at the centre of Europe . . . To separate ourselves from it would
> be madness. If we are in, we should be in wholeheartedly . . . For fifty years we
> have hesitated over Europe. It has never profited us . . . The [two] roles reinforce
> each other . . . We can indeed help to be a bridge between the US and Europe and
> such understanding is always needed. Europe should partner the US and not be
> its rival.

The Blairite position of acting as a 'bridge' rejects the extremes of both isola-
tionism and euroscepticism. But the fissure between Britain and other most
other EU leaders over Iraq showed how difficult and exposed a position the
British one can be, attempting as it does to balance two of Churchill's three
circles in foreign policy. But this is the pragmatic position that New Labour
adopted in office.

Whatever the difficulties, Blair would claim to have transformed British relations with Europe for the better. The main thrust of what he said in a speech in

November 2000 is often echoed today. After extolling the virtues of 'enlightened patriotism', he stressed that: 'If we want to stand up for Britain then we have to be in Europe, active, constructive, involved all the time. We have to negotiate tough and get our way, not stand aside and let other European countries make the decisions that matter to us'. Elaborating on the theme that Britain gains from closer European co-operation, he went on to say that: 'It is patriotism, it is national self-interest, to argue for Britain's full engagement as a leading partner in Europe. It is a betrayal of our nation and our future constantly to obstruct every fresh opportunity for cooperation.'[19]

The outlook of Labour MPs today

The battle for pro-Europeanism within the Labour Party has been won. The majority of MPs and party members accept that the best position for Britain is to be firmly situated in the EU. The old divisions on the issue have disappeared, although there are tensions about the extent of the British commitment. Anti-European attitudes rarely rear their head. Many MPs view Europe as a force for progress, helping to achieve better social and employment protection. They go along with the views of what Baker *et al.* refer to as 'open regionalism', involving the acceptance of major changes in the global economy that diminish the sovereign authority of state and which means that 'traditional goals of national economic management are now best pursued at the collective level of the EU, rather than left to the nation state alone'.[20]

But the enthusiasm of many parliamentarians and others on the left is less than wholehearted. They are aware that there is only lukewarm support for or interest in the EU among British voters. This makes many of them cautious about pushing too hard for adoption of the euro (even if they support British membership of the eurozone), knowing as they do that there is a referendum to be fought and won. At a time of governmental difficulty on several fronts in the aftermath of the Iraq war, there is an understandable reluctance to embrace another unpopular cause.

Similar doubts about the direction of European policy have surfaced over the proposed constitution. A number of MPs (and maybe some ministers, but more discreetly), primarily but not exclusively on the left, have professed their unease about the contents of the document. Some are not natural allies, but others are long-term eurosceptics who were united in their opposition to the EC at the time of the 1975 referendum. For a few of them, their anxieties centre on the issue of protection of workers and enhancement of their rights. They note the failure of the Blair government to back the Charter of Fundamental Rights and worry about any seeming preference for a 'bosses' Europe'. Others are troubled by the thought of any more integration that makes it easier to take powers away from the Westminster Parliament. Labour's eurosceptics have formed themselves into a group entitled 'Labour Against a Superstate'.

The Conservative Party

In the period in which the Labour Party has moved from antagonism to support in its attitude to Europe, the Conservatives have moved in the opposite direction, from support to a situation where some members of the party can advocate withdrawal from the EU. The trigger for this change was the same for both parties – the belief that Europe should be something more than just a mere club of trading partners. But, whereas the Common Market aspect of Europe was the aspect that Labour originally found most objectionable, for many Conservatives that remained the sole justifiable reason for membership. Once the single market was established, the European Community had served its purpose and senior Conservative politicians became determined not to let the movement towards European integration proceed any further.

Back in the 1960s and 1970s the Conservatives had been dedicated to British membership of the Community. Edward Heath, as the prime minister who took Britain into the EC, became and has remained an enthusiast for European integration. While Heath remained leader, opposition to Europe within the Conservative Party was muted. The only prominent party member to raise his voice against the policy was Enoch Powell, who urged fellow Tories to vote Labour in 1974 as an anti-European gesture.

From the first, Margaret Thatcher was more critical of Europe, but her criticisms were more to do with operational matters such as the CAP rather than the basic principle of membership. She was particularly concerned about the influence of the Commission, which she referred to dismissively as the 'Eurocracy', possessing what she saw as a marked tendency to overregulate economic activity through devices such as the CAP, at the expense of the free operation of market forces.

Until the creation of the single market, the prime minister was seen by her European colleagues as being bloody-minded and confrontational, but yet working in her own idiosyncratic way towards some vision of Europe. This was not the case. It was the appointment of Jacques Delors as president of the Commission that began the chain of events that culminated in Thatcher leading an increasingly vocal eurosceptical movement within the Conservative Party and inspired Labour to move in the opposite direction.

The impression created by Lady Thatcher was one of single-minded dedication and undeviating steadfastness of purpose. Yet in reality her views were an uncomfortable marriage of two contradictory nineteenth-century ideologies – nationalistic conservatism and economic liberalism. The economic liberal could take pride in the creation of the single market but the nationalist in her reacted against the consequences of that act, namely the imposition of a single currency, the creation of a European Central Bank and the initiation of a social dimension to the Community as part of the Delors Plan.

Thatcher believed that under Delors the EC would introduce socialism by the back door. She was particularly vitriolic in her attacks on the 'social dimension' of the EC, whether in the form of the Social Charter or the social chapter discussed at Maastricht. In her 1988 speech in Bruges Thatcher argued that she would not allow the frontiers of the state to be rolled forward by the EC when she had spent nine years rolling them back in the UK.[21]

The Bruges speech led to the formation of the Bruges Group and an identifiable faction within the Conservative Party opposed to any suggestion of European federalism, political or monetary union, or any measure that might lead to any further diminution of British sovereignty. As discussed in chapter 1, the attitude towards Europe adopted by Thatcher was one of the major factors in her downfall and resignation. Freed from the restrictions of her position and operating from the upper chamber, Lady Thatcher became the leading voice and propagandist of the eurosceptical tendency, a tendency that began to assume the characteristics of a party within a party. In Parliament there were several Conservatives of ministerial rank who were unable to criticise Europe too openly because of the constraints of their position. But a sizeable group of eurosceptical backbenchers grew up under the unofficial leadership of Bill Cash, MP for Stafford.

Maastricht and after

From the moment John Major became prime minister he was plagued by trouble from his backbenchers, as the eurosceptics in the party shifted their position. Until then, Conservative attacks on Europe had centred on centralism in the Community, or were directed against 'creeping socialism'. Now the main line of attack switched to one of outright nationalism in defence of British sovereignty. 'Federalism' became the 'f-word' that was not to be mentioned in polite society.

In negotiations leading to the Maastricht Treaty, John Major succeeded in cutting out the word 'federal' where it had appeared in the draft treaty as well as negotiating opt-outs for Britain on both EMU and the Social Chapter. Major may therefore have felt he had done enough to satisfy the eurosceptics with the deal he had negotiated, but in fact the most bitter debate within the party was about to follow, in which the prime minister suffered from one major disadvantage. In the 1992 election the overall government majority had been reduced to twenty-one, while there were known to be at least thirty eurosceptics ready to vote against the party line. The government had become very vulnerable to any backbench rebellion.

During the process of Maastricht ratification after the election the Major government was beset with difficulties. Events conspired against ministers, whether it was the Danish rejection of the Maastricht Treaty, Black Wednesday and the withdrawal from the ERM, the withdrawal of the party whip from eight persistent rebels or the dispute with the EC over the handling of the BSE episode.

The ratification process was particularly tumultuous. Rebellions were regular and much debated in the media, often as a result of interviews willingly given by the champions of a more eurosceptic position. Some of them were members of the Cabinet, the people denounced by Major as 'bastards' in an unguarded moment at the end of a television interview when he thought he was 'off the air'. On the opposing side were prominent europhiles, notably the chancellor of the Exchequer, Kenneth Clarke, and Michael Hesetline, the deputy prime minister. In the middle was John Major, trying to perform a balancing act to keep the show 'on the road'. His was an unenviable position.

The eurosceptics, active at all levels in the party, had some strong financial backing from wealthy patrons. They were well informed about every aspect of the Maastricht Treaty and the potential threat that iT posed to sovereignty. By contrast with their organisation and obsessive concern with detail, the response of the europhiles was often more general in tone, supportive of the broad drift of the EC and stressing the importance of British membership for the British economy. The confession by Kenneth Clarke that he had not read the treaty was portrayed by eurosceptics as deeply shocking on an issue that mattered so much to the country's future.

The government did get Maastricht ratified (23 July 1993), but at a price. Thereafter, eurosceptics seized every opportunity to air their views. The bitter divisions aroused spread to other areas of policy and resulted in a leadership battle in July 1995 that the prime minister won. But his victory was in some ways a pyrrhic one, for in the contest more than a third of the parliamentary party had denied backing for his leadership. These divisions continued to damage the government's reputation, with John Major making occasional anti-European gestures in a bid to fend off his critics. His wish to place Britain 'at the heart of Europe' was undermined and Britain became seriously isolated in European diplomacy. At home, he paid a heavy political price in the 1997 election.

The 1997 general election

The issue of EU membership came to dominate the 1997 general election to the detriment of most other issues and not necessarily to the benefit of those members of the Conservative Party who insisted in bringing the matter to the fore. The main subject of debate and controversy was the question of EMU and the acceptance of a single currency, but, for many of those involved, arguments over EMU were just a coded way of opposing European unity and advocating British withdrawal from the EU.

As the economy improved, it looked as though Britain might easily satisfy the Maastricht criteria for membership of the eurozone. There were those – even in the Tory government – who began to contemplate the possibility of Britain joining EMU in the first wave. Yet the official position of ministers was that set out by the strongly pro-European chancellor, Kenneth Clarke. This was that it was doubtful whether Britain would join in the first wave of entry in 1999, but that it would nevertheless be foolish to rule out the possibility. There was a chance to play some part in the negotiating process, if British options were kept open. And so was adopted a policy of 'wait-and-see', the approach proclaimed by the prime minister in spite of considerable hostility from sections of his party.

The mere prospect of possible entry in the distant future made the euroscep-tical wing of the Conservative Party ever more strident in their demands that government and party must rule out membership of EMU at any time and under any conditions. To make matters worse for John Major, he faced another source of opposition over the issue. The formation of the Referendum Party in 1996 was an indication of a growing opposition to Europe. To put pressure on the Tories to adopt a more sceptical approach, its leader (Sir James Goldsmith) claimed in his election material that his party would fight 'every seat where the leading candidate has failed to defend your right to vote on the future of this nation'. Faced by such growing antipathy to Europe and the electoral danger posed by the Referendum Party, even left-of-centre Tories like Stephen Dorrell moved to a eurosceptic approach. One senior Tory spoke of some 'Dorrelling away, pretending to hold views that they don't'.

The European issue kept resurfacing during the 1997 campaign. John Major insisted that the manifesto adhered to the agreed position of 'waiting and seeing, prior to deciding'. But the stance took a sustained battering in the tabloid press, from the two anti-European parties and from sections within the Conservative Party. Some candidates, including junior ministers, issued election statements that rejected British participation in a single currency at any time. The prime minister was provoked into one of his more memorable utterances of the campaign: 'Whether you agree with me or disagree with me, like me or loathe me, don't bind my hands when I am negotiating on behalf of the British people'[22].

John Major took the view that, armed with the Maastricht opt-out, it was unnecessary for Britain to decide definitely to reject a policy that might still not get off the ground. He could see no national interest in closing the door. Rather, there was a danger that this might harm inward investment and be interpreted by some people as meaning never at any time. Such a once-and-for-all rejection could seem tantamount to withdrawing from the EU.

The prime minister clearly had a major problem, for his party was seriously divided and some of its members – including some in office – were unwilling to compromise. In that situation, any policy decision could seem unconvincing and the incumbent of Number 10 was open to the charge of lack of leadership. The intense media interest in Conservative divisions was bound to be damaging – and it was not just the tabloids who were exposing deep schism. *The Daily Tele-graph* published a regular update on candidates who were breaching the official line, coming to a final judgement that of 385 candidates whose election state-ments were analysed almost half were against any adoption of the single cur-rency (see Table 8.1).

The arguments over Europe in the 1997 campaign were not about Europe alone, but a reflection of wider internal disagreements and personality issues within the Conservative Party. Nonetheless, the issue of Europe was for many

Table 8.1   *Conservative MPs and their attitudes to the single currency, 1997*

Against the single currency	190
Anti-European, but not specific	26
Anti-Brussels tone, not specific	52
Neutral	2
Supportive of the official position	57
No indication given	51
Pro-European	3

Source: Daily Telegraph, 17 April 1997.

MPs and party members a defining one, for as the prime minister himself pointed out the issue of EMU was 'the single most important decision that any government has been asked to make for generations'. On this matter, there could be no reconciliation of differing outlooks and some members were not particularly interested in seeing one. As one prominent Tory politician, Lord Whitelaw, later put it: 'The reason they got into trouble was over Europe. If they can't work together they won't achieve anything.'[23]

The outcome of the election indicated that there was no evidence that the British people were as europhobic as the right-wing of the Conservative Party thought they were. An element in the population may be wary of foreigners, particularly the Germans; they do not like the idea of 'losing the pound' and they can get very annoyed with the more futile bureaucratic measures from Brussels. However, abstract arguments over concepts such as national sovereignty come a poor second to bread-and-butter issues like taxation or education. On polling day, eurosceptics and europhiles alike suffered defeat, as the electorate delivered a harsh verdict on the recent Conservative performance in office.

Overall, the mood of the voters was for change after a prolonged period of Conservative hegemony. That change would lead to a more positive approach on European issues.

The Hague leadership

In the last years of the Major leadership it was evident that party opinion was hardening over the currency issue and generally moving towards a more eurosceptic position. Few Conservatives would ever launch a convincing defence of the EU and its work. More often, they took every opportunity to pour scorn on what the EU stood for and seemed to want to see Britain fighting a rearguard action to stave off European influence in British political decision making.

William Hague, chosen as the new leader of the party a few months after the election, was noted for his euroscepticism. Leading a party whose 164 other MPs were generally at best cool on the EU and in many cases hostile to it, he found it easier to unite the party. There were few pro-European challengers to the official line of euroscepticism and the bulk of Conservative parliamentarians saw value in putting the European divisions behind them. On the single currency, the party leadership made it clear that it would not be supporting membership for the present or the next parliament, a position put to party members in a ballot and overwhelmingly endorsed in October 1998 by 85 to 15 per cent. Hague had succeeded in opening up 'clear blue water' between the main parties in a way that John Major had been unable to do.

In the 1999 European elections the slogan 'In Europe, but not run by Europe' had been adopted and this summarised the broad approach taken by the Conservatives on European issues. Most MPs accepted the fact of British membership of the EU but were resistant to any moves towards further integration. Indeed, they wanted to roll back the frontiers of EU influence, with some members of the Shadow Cabinet talking about the need to 'repatriate' powers surrendered to Brussels by recent treaties such as Amsterdam (1997). The broad approach was one of 'picking and choosing' those parts of EU policy that Conservatives favoured and arguing for opt-outs of those of which they disapproved. This was applied to areas where there were agreed common policies already in existence, such as the CFP, from which any withdrawal would be difficult without raising the issue of continued British participation in the EU. Not being in office made it easier to unite around such a eurosceptic stance, for the leadership did not have to react to new EU initiatives and could afford to advance positions that seemed unreal and – if effected – would place Britain consistently in opposition to its continental partners.

Many of the Hagueite fears and some of his policy positions were expressed in his remarkable 'foreign land' speech delivered to the party's spring forum in early March, 2001. In it, he took the audience on a journey to the 'foreign land' that Britain would be should there be a second Blairite victory at the polls. The voters would not be merely voting for the next administration, but rather haing 'to decide whether our people will remain sovereign in their own country'. Expressing his determination to renegotiate the 'outdated and failed' CFP and CAP, he went on to appeal to people 'who may not have voted Conservative before, but who believe in an independent Britain'. He urged them to 'lend us your vote. Vote for us this time, so that your vote will mean something next time, and the time after, and the time after that'.

Apart from such scaremongering, the developing emphasis of Conservative policy was on the need for Britain 'to shun the allegedly high-cost and over-regulated continental European economies' and instead create a deregulated, low-cost Hong Kong-type alternative.[24] There was also an expressed interest in strengthening Atlantic ties, possibly by linking up with the North American Free Trade Area and by showing a new regard for Britain's traditional global role as a partner of the US government.

Above all, however, the Hague approach was characterised by a clear and overriding rejection of the tide towards integrationism in Europe. The EU was portrayed as a monstrous superstate, moving dangerously and rapidly in a federal direction. As was his style, Hague put the issue in humorous terms when – a few months before the election – he advanced his elephant test to determine whether or not the EU as at present constituted was a superstate of the sort he and his colleagues so frequently denounced. His view was that if an animal looks, smells and walks like an elephant, then it must be one. So, too, if an organisation has got a president and laws, a currency, a passport and an anthem, and is likely to have a constitution, then it must be a state.[25]

In the 2001 election campaign the Conservatives took the bold decision to make Europe an issue, hoping that this would be a popular policy. Most members of the party machine realised that their chances of victory were slim, so the temptation was to adopt policies that would please the core Conservative support and win backing from that section of the electorate which liked populist gestures on asylum, crime and Europe. This was easier to achieve than developing alternative policies on the key issues of education and health, on which voters seemed willing to give government ministers a further chance to achieve lasting benefits. Moreover, the eurosceptical – at times euro-bashing – approach was one that came naturally to William Hague and his supporters, for they were Thatcherite Conservatives who had always regarded the EU with some misgivings, particularly when it moved towards deeper integration and seemed to threaten the British national identity.

The high profile of Europe as an election issue was of more interest to party MPs and candidates, and political commentators and journalists, than it was to the voters. Voters wanted to hear what the party was proposing on the future of the public services and little was said about this. The ever-more-desperate messages of 'ten days to save the pound' and other doom-laden references to the dangers posed to the British way of life did not match the public mood. As the *Daily Express* had noted back in the 1997 campaign, Europe was an issue that made 'the parties swoon and the voters yawn'.

Defeat inevitably followed on polling day and the Hague strategy was undermined. As Andrew Geddes remarks: 'the Conservatives appeared to be a single-issue party that was talking to itself and trapped in the debates that had bedevilled it during the 1990s'.[26] It was time for a new figure to assume the mantle of leadership.

Beyond 2001: the Duncan Smith and Howard approaches

On Hague's resignation, the new leader was a surprise choice who was unknown to many people beyond the Conservative party and to quite a number within it until the leadership campaign got underway. He was Iain Duncan Smith, a one-time hard-line Maastricht rebel, and a regular thorn in the flesh of John Major nearly a decade earlier. Duncan Smith was a dedicated eurosceptic, perhaps in those Maastricht days perhaps better described as a europhobe. He was then willing to contemplate British withdrawal from the EU, a position later downplayed.

In his new role as leader, the ex-Thatcherite included another opponent of the EU, Bill Cash, within his shadow team. There was no reason to anticipate any broad change in the Conservative position, but once the election was over there was equally no reason for Duncan Smith to raise the European issue to prominence. With his party broadly united in its euroscepticism, he could concentrate on a bid to learn the lessons of the second successive defeat and widen the party's appeal.

Yet there were stories that the new leadership was moving to sever party links with the mainstream group of centre-right parties in the EP, the European People's Party, after the 2004 European elections.[27] The leadership at Westminster felt that the EPP – of which Conservatives were members – was too keen on further political integration and that the British eurosceptic views were being drowned out. In particular, they were seeking to forge an alliance with prospective Eastern European members on the centre-right, with whom there had been close ties ever since Margaret Thatcher had given support for democracy in the region after the fall of the Berlin Wall.

There were also suspicions that other members of the Shadow Cabinet were voicing Iain Duncan Smith's true feelings, in their anti-European pronouncements. At one stage, the shadow agriculture minister, John Hayes, launched a ferocious attack on the EU, in particular the CFP. He spoke of possibly using the 'nuclear option' should talks on CFP reform fail, emphasising that this would mean withdrawal from the EU.

Generally, however, actual and potential difficulties over European policy were contained and the leader's problems were more about his personality and his failure to create interest in the party and raise its ratings in the polls than they were about Britain's role in the EU. These failings led to his defeat in a leadership election in November and Michael Howard's assumption of the role of Leader of the Opposition.

The Howard approach: Conservative attitudes today

Michael Howard had a reputation as an inveterate eurosceptic when he took over the reins. According to Norman Lamont, the then chancellor of the Exchequer, he had threatened to resign if John Major had embraced the Social Chapter.[28] In the 1997 election he had told the BBC's *Election Call* (21 April) that 'the Amsterdam Summit . . . would indeed put our survival as a nation-state in question'. But he was not elected as leader because of his euroscepticism, which was now widely shared within the party. Rather, party supporters were looking for a display of effective, professional leadership from a deft and heavyweight politician who might damage the reputation of Tony Blair.

Yet as part of a general repositioning of Conservative policy and a softening of the party position on a range of issues, it emerged that there would be no withdrawal from the EPP after the 2004 European elections. Moreover, the new leader gave a thoughtful speech on Conservative attitudes to Europe in early 2004, when he spoke in Berlin.[29] His words were clearly expressed and well received by a number of continental politicians, some of whom in the past had despaired of the party's approach. Like a number of other prominent British politicians in either party, he was willing to strike a markedly more positive pro-European tone when addressing a continental audience, than when talking to the voters back home.

In that speech, Howard first chose to remind his European audience that his party:

> [had] been at the forefront of Britain's engagement with Europe. It was a Conservative government which first applied for membership in the 1960s. It was a Conservative government which took us into the European Economic Community in 1973. It was a Labour government which threatened to withdraw from Europe and held a referendum on that issue in 1975. It was the Labour party which stood on a manifesto of withdrawal from the European Community in 1983, a manifesto on which Tony Blair was first elected to Parliament. Three years later, in 1986, it was Margaret Thatcher who was one of the leading forces behind the Single European Act which established the single European market.

He then set out a Conservative vision of Europe, assuring his audience that he wanted Britain to 'remain a positive and influential member of the European Union'. But he did not want that Union to be:

> a one-way street to closer integration to which all must subscribe . . . Forcing common standards upon them will mean that Europe as a whole falls further and further behind as each member state tries to put its own costs onto its neighbours . . . In areas which serve their own national interest, individual member states [should] be able to decide whether to retain wholly national control or whether to co-operate with others.

Alasdair Jones proposed a typology of divisions in the Conservative party of William Hague at the time of the European elections in 1999. In his survey he identified six different groupings within the party on the European issue.[30] Bearing in mind the limited turnover of seats achieved in the 2001 election, things have changed little since:

- **Anti-marketeers.** These make up a group which is totally opposed to membership of the EU. Some anti-marketeers, like Teddy Taylor, have been opposed from the days before British entry. These long-term opponents were later joined by those like Norman Lamont who began his European journey in a mood of euroscepticism and ended in complete opposition and calls for withdrawal.
- **Gaullists.** This group claims to be pro-European, but theirs is a Europe in which all the member states preserve their national identities as part of what de Gaulle termed a 'Europe des Nations'. This is the group favoured by Lady Thatcher who was proudly patriotic and claimed she did not wish to see British, French or German characteristics submerged so as to become what she called 'identikit Europeans'.

- **Tory modernisers.** Largely made up of those involved in trade or commerce like Michael Heseltine, this group wishes to protect British interests by taking a more active role. On the euro, for example, it believes that Britain should belong, if only so as to have a voice on the committees developing and regulating the single currency.
- **Free-market neo-liberals.** This group is proudest of all of the single market. Free-market neo-Liberals are pragmatists in that they want what is best for Britain and are willing to sacrifice some aspects of sovereignty in return for the triumph of market forces. John Major typified their attitude.
- **Federalists.** The goal of a united Europe was once a common belief in the Tory party but it is now definitely a view held only by a small minority of MPs. Tory MEPs, under the federalist influence of the EPP, were once more disposed to this viewpoint, but few current MPs or MEPs would describe themselves in this way.
- **Commonsense Europeans.** These are europositives, described by Kettle as 'people who are basically in favour of the Euro-project but who do not want to endorse change indiscriminately'.[31] Once a majority in the Conservative Party, the group is shrinking rapidly in the face of the scepticism and hostility exhibited by recent leaders and many party activists.

Table 8.2   *The position of the main parties on European issues*

Issue	Labour	Conservative	Liberal Democrats
Recently used slogan Europe of nation-states or a federal Europe?	Britain 'a leading player in Europe' Europe of nation-states, with strong British role in the Council of Ministers; use of 'red lines'	'In Europe, but not run by Europe' Intergovernmentalist like Labour, but mphasis increasingly eupon a 'flexible Europe', not a ' one-size-fits-all' Europe	'Freedom through Europe' More federalist, although the word is little used in propaganda. Keen on strong EU institutions and integration, but balanced by subsidiarity
The draft constitution	Not keen on a constitution originally, but came to accept it as a useful tidying-up exercise, necessary in the light of enlargement. Use of 'red lines' to prevent unwanted measures	Opposed to any constitution, which is seen as unnecessary: 'states have constitutions'. Fear that Court of Justice will interpret document in an integrationist manner. Wishes to renegotiate some past treaties and 'repatriate' powers to Westminster	Long-term supporters of an EU constitution, believing that this will clearly define and establish the extent of EU authority and clearly set out the powers of the main institutions. See such a document as necessary in light of enlargement

Enlargement	Committed to enlargement, recognising that new entrants might help to weaken Franco–Germany hegemony and prove useful supporters of a looser, more flexible and intergovernmentalist EU	Keen supporter of enlargement over recent years. Has long stressed that Europe means more than the traditional member states of Western Europe. Welcomes new entrants, as likely allies of vision of a flexible Europe	Strong supporters of enlargement, especially to include 'new democracies' from Central and Eastern Europe'
Single currency	In principle, favours entry into the eurozone, subject to the five economic conditions and a positive referendum vote	Rejected for the lifetime of the 2001 Parliament, but most members of the Shadow Cabinet would never join	Long tern supporters of entry; in favour, subject to the outcome of the referendum
Tax harmonisation, social security and workers' rights	Opposed to tax harmonisation (Jack Straw: 'tax matters are a key component of national sovereignty') and EU intrusion into national social security policies or issues of workers' rights: 'red line issues'	Opposed to any concessions on tax harmonisation and EU interference on welfare matters or labour laws. Especially keen to see Thatcherite labour provisions upheld	Also accept that there should be no concessions on tax harmonisation and support use of national veto to maintain present position
Foreign and security policy	Willing to co-operate with other states in Council of Ministers where a foreign policy can be agreed. Sees British role as forming a bridge between Europe and the USA, but leans to Washington when conflicts arise. Supports common European defence under NATO umbrella and willing to contribute to a European Rapid Reaction Force	Strongly resists any notion of a common foreign and security policy, beyond working together where interests coincide. More Atlanticist than European, leadership broadly supportive of Americans over Iraq. Stresses importance of NATO role	More European than Atlanticist, especially over Iraq. Happy to accept common policies in foreign and security matters, but feel that any defence element should not be at the expense of NATO alliance

Source: 2001 (general) and 2004 (European) election manifestos, and the writings and speeches of the party leaderships.

The divided parties

Originally, Labour was the party most divided on the European issue. The party has gone through many different phases in the post-war era, but finally found a form of unity in the 1990s, managing to keep itself a step ahead of the Conservatives. Its rhetoric today is pro-European, as is indicated by the marked difference of language between William Hague and Tony Blair in the run-up to the 2001 election. Whereas the one man spoke of his fear of the 'foreign land' that Britain might become, the prime minister was criticising the 'gross misjudgements' of past British policy towards the rest of Europe over half a century and stressing the 'huge opportunity' ahead for Britain and Europe.[32]

This is not to say that the Labour Party is totally united on this issue. It, too, has its anti-European campaigners still, as typified by Tony Benn and Dennis Skinner. If there were to be a move to join the eurozone, divisions might be publicly exposed. But New Labour – as led by Tony Blair, and with a whole host of spin doctors to manipulate opinion and create an effective image – has been a lot better at masking dissent within the party than the Conservatives.

The Conservatives, once the cautiously pro-European party, have moved in the other direction. By the 1990s they were experiencing the same sort of difficulties that troubled Labour in the Wilson years and it was difficult to convey any impression of possessing an effective European policy. If Labour's disunity was more concerned with the issue of membership, the Conservatives have been more troubled by the extent of the British commitment to the EU. Most Conservatives accept that membership is desirable and inevitable, but they worry about the intrusion of Europe into areas best reserved for the action of British ministers.

In either case, what has been remarkable is not just the longevity of schism within the main parties, but rather its sheer intensity. Europe is an issue that has proved remarkably difficult for British politicians to handle. As they have tried to cope with internal divisions, the temptation has been to flirt with short-term solutions that meet the immediate need and get them 'off the hook'. But as Blair said in the address referred to above, this has involved 'mistaking what we wanted to be the case with what was the case; hesitation, alienation, incomprehension, with the occasional burst of enlightened brilliance which only served to underline the frustration of our partners with what was the norm'. As Simon Bulmer has observed: 'It is this mixture of divisions between and within the two main parties that has characterised the European "fault-line" in British party politics'.[33]

Notes

1   D. McKie (ed.), *The Guardian Political Almanac 1993/4*, Fourth Estate, 1993.
2   P. Ashdown, speech to Centre for European Reform, 16 July 1998.

3   J. Fisher, 'The Liberal Democrats' in A. Geddes and J. Tongue (eds), *Labour's Second Landslide*, Manchester University Press, 2002.

4   *The Guardian*, 22 March 2001.

5   *The Times*, 15 March 2003.

6   A. Geddes, *The European Union and British Politics*, Palgrave, 2004.

7   L. Bennie, J. Curtice and W. Rudig, 'Liberal, Social Democrat or Liberal Democrat? Political identity and British centre politics' in D. Broughton, D. Farrell, D. Denver and C, Rallings (eds), *British Elections and Parties Yearbook 1994*, Frank Cass, 1995.

8   C. Kennedy, as in 5 above.

9   D. Butler and D. Kavanagh, *The British General Election of 1997*, Macmillan, 1997.

10 D. Butler and D. Kavanagh, *The British General Election of 2001*, Palgrave, 2002.

11 R. Kilroy Silk, press release, 12 June 2004.

12 T. Nairn, *The Left Against Europe?*, Penguin, 1973.

13 The exchanges between Gaitskell and Macmillan are quoted in M. Cockerell's volume on relations between broadcasters and politicians, *Live from Number 10*, Faber and Faber, 1998.

14 M. Cockerell, as in 13 above.

15 M. Cockerell, as in 13 above.

16 B. Rosamond, 'The Labour Party and European integration', *Politics Review*, April 1994.

17 B. Jones and D. Kavanagh, *British Politics Today*, Manchester University Press, 1984.

18 S. George, *Britain and European Integration since 1945*, Blackwell, 1991.

19 T. Blair, annual foreign policy speech to City audience at the Mansion House, 31 November 2000.

20 D. Baker, A. Gamble and S. Ludlam, 'The parliamentary siege of Maastricht 1993: conservative divisions and British ratification', *Parliamentary Affairs*, Vol. 47, No. 1, 1994.

21 D. Wincott, 'The Conservative Party and Europe', *Politics Review*, April 1992.

22 J. Major, *The Autobiography*, HarperCollins, 1999.

23 J. Major and Lord Whitelaw, quoted in 22 above.

24 A. Geddes, 'Europe' in A. Geddes and J. Tongue, as in 3 above.

25 W. Hague, public speech, 8 December 2000.

26 A. Geddes, as in 24 above.

27 *The Guardian*, 20 December 2002, and *The Times*, 28 October 2003.

28 N. Lamont, *In Office*, Warner Books, 1997.

29 M, Howard, speech to Konrad Adenauer Stiftung, Berlin, 12 February 2004.

30 A. Jones, 'UK relations with the EU, and did you notice the elections?', *Talking Politics*, Winter 2000.

31 M. Kettle, 'A leader lost amid the phobes and sceptics', *The Guardian*, 19 March 1994.

32 W. Hague, speech to Conservative spring forum, 4 March 2001, and T. Blair, speech to Polish stock exchange, Warsaw, 6 October 2000.

33 S. Bulmer, 'Britain and European Integration' in B. Jones, D. Kavanagh, P. Norton and M. Moran (eds), *Politics UK*, Prentice Hall, 1998.

9

Pressure groups in the EU

Pressure groups have always been active in the EU, playing a significant role in its political development and policy making. In the early days, agricultural interests were especially influential, so that in the evolution of the CAP many agrarian interests were active in lobbying EC institutions. The issue of price support for farmers was particularly contentious and when Commissioner Sicco Mansholt proposed to cut price levels in order to force inefficient farmers off their land his plan was denounced by the main farming groups, some of whose members resorted to staging a major riot in protest at what was being contemplated. In the words of George and Sowemimo: 'The Council of Agricultural Ministers . . . were accompanied to Brussels by 80,000 demonstrating farmers, who hung Mansholt [the commissioner] in effigy, burned cars, tore up street signs, broke windows, killed one policeman, and injured 140 more of the 3,000 deployed to restrain them'.[1]

Business groups that had also been active in the EC from its formation assumed even greater importance in the 1980s. The passage of the Single European Act and the drive towards the completion of the single market was a goal they had long urged upon EC leaders. As Greenwood explains:

> In the shape of the ERT (European Round Table – a select group of the leaders of Europe's largest firms), they helped provide the blueprint and much of the impetus for the single market, and, where member states faltered or showed signs of a loss of nerve, business was there encouraging, prodding, or, if necessary, threatening removal of investment.[2]

Farmers and businessmen have always been well represented and carried political clout in the councils of the EU, but over the last two decades lobbying from other sectors of the economy has markedly increased at the European level; so, too, has that of professional associations, as well as many cause groups. Not surprisingly, in their study of group activity in the EU, Mazey and Richardson have concluded that: 'It is no longer possible to understand the policy process in . . . the member states of the EU – and especially the role of pressure groups in that process – without taking account of the shift of power to Brussels'.[3]

The growth of lobbying in the EC/EU

The lobbying of EU institutions by interest and other groups has dramatically increased since the 1970s, both in range and in numbers. Research by Gray (1998) and Wessels (1997) has attempted to track the overall number of trade associations, interest groups, regions, national associations, think-tanks and other campaigning organisations operating within the EU.[4] Their findings suggest that the 400 or so bodies involved in the 1970s have today quintupled. There are now estimated to be more than 500 eurogroups whose existence is officially or semi-officially recognised, over a thousand advisory committees working with the Commission, and over 3,000 full-time, professional lobbyists working in Brussels. In numbers, the lobbyists in existence probably match the numbers of Community officials involved in the policy-making process.

In substantial part, the increase derives from the impact of successive treaties and enlargements. In particular, the SEA and the Maastricht Treaty served to deepen and widen Community responsibilities. The SEA was not just of interest to business and commercial groups. It had implications for many professional associations who found that the commitment to free movement of labour and harmonisation of professional qualifications meant that their members might work in the EC and require protection. In other areas too, such as the environment, cohesion, and research and technology, new initiatives in policy making meant that decisions taken in Brussels were bound to have an effect on national groups. In the same way, Maastricht included a protocol covering the Social Chapter, and the TEU spelt out the rights of employers' organisations and trade unions to be consulted by the Commission on social policy. Given the enlargements of the 1980s and 1990s, there were of course more national groups who became involved. Before the Maastricht Summit, the policy on cohesion and the growing decentralisation of power in several states meant that the representation of regions and local authorities was becoming more important. The decision by the summiteers to establish the Committee of the Regions opened up new opportunities for involvement in the affairs of the EU by lobbyists representing the different areas of the EU.

As we have seen, there have always been interests active within the EC, especially in agriculture, the coal and steel industries, and commerce. National umbrella groups have long had offices in Brussels, keeping an eye on new proposals and the ways in which policies were being implemented and how they were working. But until the mid-1980s the scope of EC competence was limited, so that many national groups had little interest in its policy processes. Prior to the passage of the SEA much lobbying was done via national governments, as groups relied on their country's ministers to stand firm in defence of national interests in the Council of Ministers. However, the development of qualified majority voting over some sectors of policy meant that no longer could group activists rely on such robust ministerial action, for the veto no longer applied. Accordingly, it was prudent to become involved in EC policy making at an earlier stage and to seek to build coalitions of support with other like-minded groups across the Community.

Moreover, institutions such as the European Commission have become more accessible and receptive to lobbyists. In part, this was because the expansion of responsibilities under the SEA and Maastricht Treaty meant that bodies such as the Commission found that they required the knowledge, understanding and expertise that well-informed groups could provide. The Commission maintains a large register of interested bodies, which it will regularly consult on matters of policy development.

The range of groups operating in the EU

- **Manufacturing industry.** Examples range from the powerful pan-European eurogroups (see pp. 254–5 for a discussion of such groups) such as the Union of Industrial and Employers' Confederations of Europe (UNICE) to smaller ones such as the Hearing Aid Association, from associations with influential members such as those operating in the chemical industry to the bodies of increasing importance who represent the food and drink or the audiovisual and publishing sectors. In addition, many multinational businesses, such as Philips and IBM, now have well-developed public relations departments that lobby on their own behalf, sometimes assisted by one of the growing number of professional lobbying agencies.
- **Labour.** Examples include eurogroups such as the European Trades Union Confederation (ETUC); the major national umbrella groups such as the French Confédération Générale du Travail (CGT); as well as individual trade unions across the member states.
- **Agriculture.** Examples vary from the powerful eurogroup, the Committee of Professional Agricultural Organisations in the EU (COPA), to groups representing more specialised sectors of agriculture, such as wine-growers or organic farmers.
- **Professions.** Examples include eurogroups such as law firms and law, medical and veterinary associations.
- **Public interest bodies.** Pursuing non-economic aims, these range from think-tanks such as the European Policy Centre to organisations such as the European Blind Union, from protection/environmental bodies such as the World Wide Fund for Nature (WWF) to Greenpeace, and from the European Consumers' Organisation (BEUC) to Human Rights Watch and the European Youth Forum.

- **Government.** Governmental organisations include 167 accredited non-EU embassies and delegations, such as the important United States Embassy and that representing Albania. The category also comprises regional governments such as the German Länder and local authorities representing large cities.

British groups involved in lobbying Europe

The activity of British pressure groups in the EU has developed significantly in recent years, as lobbyists have come to understand the need to protect and promote the interests of their organisations. Many decisions affecting key areas of British national life are now taken in Brussels. Some 80 per cent of British laws derive from regulations and directives of the Commission, so that 'in some sectors the bulk of new regulatory activity now takes place not in Whitehall but in Brussels'.[5] Not surprisingly, Mazey and Richardson have concluded that: 'Any British pressure group which continues to rely exclusively on lobbying Whitehall and Westminster is now adopting a high-risk strategy, because on a large range of issues policies are now being determined in Brussels'.[6]

On topics ranging from food hygiene to the movement of live animals, from fishing to the outbreak a few years ago of BSE, the actions of British governments are much affected by what is laid down in the Commission. Of the 300 or so measures adopted in preparation for a single internal market, 60 had animal health and veterinary control implications. Others affected the veterinary profession, having implications for such things as the freedom of movement and rights of establishment of veterinary surgeons. The British Veterinary Association and the Royal College of Veterinary Surgeons were inevitably going to be interested in such initiatives, while some of them were of relevance also to the Royal Society for the Prevention of Cruelty to Animals (RSPCA), the National Farmers' Union (NFU) and the Eurogroup for Animal Welfare.

In recent years, a multiplicity of British interest and other groups have operated in Brussels. Grant has estimated that the number of employees of groups engaged on work in Brussels doubled to more than 10,000 between the late 1980s and the mid 1990s.[7] The increase indicates the growth in importance that pressure groups have attached to Europe, particularly as:

- the pace of development towards greater integration intensified and activists increasingly understood the importance of the EU in decision making affecting their organisations;
- lobbyists have gained more knowledge and experience of the decision-making process within the Union and have been able to take more advantage of lobbying opportunities.

The range of EU lobbying by British groups

The British groups most involved within the EU are business/trade organisations, and those representing trade unionists, farmers and environmentalists. In
his survey of 100 or so business, labour and cause groups, Baggott found that
12 per cent of them had offices based in Europe, but more than 75 per cent had
become a member of a European-wide pressure group, defending their cause or
interest at this level. He noted that the business groups had been especially active
in employing both strategies.[8]

The pressure groups at work on Brussels-based activity largely fall into one
of five types: national economic and professional interest groups; multinational and national companies; regional local authorities; national promotional groups; and eurogroups.

National economic and professional interest groups.

The major British interest groups have traditionally spent much of their time
and energy on lobbying in Whitehall. As key insider groups, they have access
to the corridors of power and can offer their expertise and co-operation to ministers in exchange for the opportunity to influence the making of decisions. But
from the early days of British membership of the EC, several organisations
recognised the value in adopting a European as well as a national strategy in
their lobbying activity. The interest groups most affected by European developments include those concerned with business and finance, farming, fishing,
trade unionism and the professions.

The Confederation of British Industry (CBI) quickly recognised the importance of the European dimension in furthering the interests of its members, and
established its Brussels office before Britain had actually joined the EC. In the
last two decades it has placed even more emphasis upon developing its contacts
with Europe, as its understanding of the EC and how it works has increased (see
Box 9.1).

Farming features more largely in the economies of several European countries than it does in Britain, although some British farmers have benefited from
the gains secured by the powerful agrarian lobbying carried out by their French
and German counterparts. But on occasion the interests of British agricultur-
alists have conflicted with the rest of Europe, particularly when British exports
of beef were to banned following the BSE outbreak in the mid-1990s (see pp.
171–3). The NFU co-operated with government ministers in a bid to get the ban
lifted. It represents the interests of UK farmers and growers in all matters of EU
policy. To achieve this, it is active in fortifying the government's resolve in
Whitehall, especially at times when the Council of Agricultural Ministers is due
to meet. Otherwise, it works with other bodies via COPA, and lobbies the Commission directly via its permanent office in Brussels (the Bureau de l'Agriculture Britannique). It was similarly one of the first groups to recognise the

---

Box 9.1
Business interests in the EU

Big business has been broadly sympathetic to British membership of the EU, the single market, the single currency and some other steps in the direction of closer integration. The Confederation of British Industry (CBI) was one of the first organisations to see the importance to industry of membership and its leadership has consistently articulated a pro-European viewpoint, even though more recently some of its members have shown scepticism about the alleged benefits of the euro. The amount of the CBI's workload deriving from Brussels is huge, and although staffing in its Brussels office does not usually exceed six, more than half of the seventy or so executive staff in London spend up to half of their time on European matters. It also lobbies via UNICE, the eurogroup for manufacturers.

Among the business groups, the Institute of Directors (IoD) is also much involved in watching EU developments. Like the CBI, it is an umbrella group that defends the interests of mainly medium to large-scale-businesses, as represented by its 38,000 members. Unlike the CBI, it is wary of the Social Chapter, the single currency and other integrationist tendencies, but nonetheless recognises that membership of the EU has a considerable impact on issues of much concern to its members, affecting British trade and manufacturing. Much legislation affecting companies now originates in Brussels. Accordingly, the IoD lobbies via its office there, and through UNICE. It sees the Commission as its prime target, although it also seeks to win the support of groups of MEPs and the EP's committees, as well as working through UNICE.

Founded in 1958, UNICE is the main employers' group within the EU. Indeed, its membership extends to thirty-two national organisations and across twenty-five countries, so that it can proudly claim to be 'the voice of European business and industry'.

Another pro-business Euro-group is the European Round Table (ERT), sometimes described as the 'rich man's club', since it comprises forty-six chief executives from top multinational companies. Since its creation in 1983, it has regularly produced position papers on issues of concern in the world of manufacturing.

---

relevance of the Community to its work, as its lobbyists appreciated just how many key decisions were taken in Brussels under the CAP.

Fishing interests operate under the limitations imposed by the CFP (see chapter 6). Groups representing British trawlermen co-operate with European trawlermen in lobbying on areas of common concern, including the levels of fish stocks, subsidies for some sectors of the fishing industry and regulations regarding the ways by which the fish are caught. But as with British farmers, British trawlermen sometimes find themselves in competition with the fishermen of other countries.

Controversies arise over the distribution of fish quotas and the activities of Dutch and Spanish trawlermen in British waters.

Unions and consumer organisations were slower to respond to the EC and it was not until the late 1980s that their European activities gained a higher profile (see Box 9.2). Many individual unions, such as the RMT (the National Union of Rail, Maritime and Transport Workers) came to see the advent of a

---

Box 9.2
British trade unionism and the EU

Trade unionists discovered the value of the EC as an outlet for their campaigning rather later than manufacturing organisations such as the CBI. It was the visit of Jacques Delors to the TUC Conference (1988) that made the TUC realise the possibilities of achieving valuable protective legislation via the Social Chapter. As a socialist, Delors understood that the way to win the support of working people for the EC was to make the single market attractive to them, by conferring benefits. In his words, 'one does not fall in love with a single market' – the rewards needed to be more tangible.

Delors' commitment to a social dimension to the EC was especially welcome to both the political and industrial wings of the British labour movement at a time when unions found themselves being cold-shouldered by a government that was systematically depriving trade unionists of rights they had secured in the postwar years. Ron Todd, then the T&GWU, saw the general picture. As he told that same TUC Conference: 'The only card game in town at the moment is in a town called Brussels, and it is a game of poker where we have got to learn the rules and learn them fast'.

In addition, and especially after the signing of the SEA with its move towards the creation of a single market, some individual unions were finding that they had an important interest in decisions taken in Brussels. Occasionally, their own members might work in the EC or, more often – as in the case of T&GWU members – find themselves travelling across the continent.

In recent years, most trade unions have been generally supportive of British involvement. The EU has shown itself to be sympathetic to workers' rights, promoting such issues as working hours, holiday entitlement, pension rights, health and safety, part-time workers' rights and women's equality. British unions press the Commission directly for sympathetic legislation. The General, Municipal, Boilermakers' and Allied Trades Union (GMBATU) maintains a one-person office in Brussels. As with other unions, it also works with fellow European colleagues in ETUC, the pan-European group.

As an umbrella body, the TUC employs two representatives in Brussels and works closely with ETUC, whose current general secretary is John Marks, who previously held that position with the British organisation.

European transport system and the Social Chapter as of immense importance to them, as did other unions, such as the Transport and General Workers' Union (T&GWU).

Professional organisations developed their interest in the EC following the passage of the SEA, for the harmonisation of professional qualifications and regulations concerning date protection were of much concern to their members. The Law Society has members working temporarily or permanently in the EU. Its office in Brussels acts as a servicing post for such personnel, as well as a base from which to represent the interests of the profession to the Commission and – to a lesser extent – to the EP. The British Medical Association (BMA) similarly adopts a high profile towards Europe, having campaigned there on matters ranging from employment rights for pregnant women to the hours of junior doctors, and from environmental matters with a health connection to the banning of advertising of cigarette smoking.

The effectiveness of contact with the European decision-making process is particularly relevant for groups whose aims may not be sympathetic to the government of the day, such as trade unions and big business organisations. The recognition that an increasingly large number of decisions are now being made in Brussels has forced interest groups to move at least some of their operations across the Channel and to co-operate with their counterparts in other member states.

Multinational and national companies

EU directives can have an immense influence on business activities within the EU, either directly through tariff-control, taxation or competition legislation, or indirectly through employment policy or measures of consumer protection. The Ford Corporation was one of the first to seek representation in Brussels in response to worries about competitiveness in the motor industry. Since then, many other companies have followed its example, particularly those such as the major Japanese corporations who are looking for the most effective form of inward investment. Philip Morris, GlaxoSmithKlein and Six Continents (formerly Bass) are leading British companies with strong European leanings. All have felt it worthwhile to establish offices in Brussels to monitor and influence decisions that affect their fortunes and their workforces.

Regional and local authorities

The UK has tended not to be strongly represented in this sphere, but regions such as Wales have long felt it worthwhile to maintain a promotions office in Europe and this has proved even more true – for Scotland as well as Wales – since the introduction of devolved government in the UK. Some local organisations feel that they can negotiate better directly rather than through national bodies. Merseyside, for example, had direct contact with Europe in its campaign to get Objective 1 funding for the area. According to Harry Rimmer, a former Labour leader of Liverpool City Council, Whitehall was never keen on the Objective 1 campaign because the status was gained over ministers' heads via a direct appeal to Brussels.[9]

Birmingham, too, has been active in seeking out European funding for its major projects of civil renewal. Working through its European and International Division, members of the City Council are keen to build upon the city's recently secured European and wider international profile and are active in pursuit of lobbying opportunities. The Council was active in helping to establish the Eurocities Association that now brings together more than a hundred cities in the EU and serves as a vehicle for promoting a common urban agenda across Europe. Birmingham City Council also uses its connections with the EP, via the West Midlands MEPs and its involvement in the Committee of the Regions, to have a voice in influencing and shaping policy and legislation within the EU.

National promotional groups

Mazey and Richardson point out that the 'EC decision-making process provides greater access to what in Britain would be considered "outsider groups", not normally influential in the inner circle of Whitehall-group contacts'.[10] This is especially true of environmental groups, which sometimes find that they receive a more sympathetic hearing than that given by British governments over the last two decades. They recognise that environmental problems do not usually recognise national borders and in many cases operate on a European (sometimes global) basis. By influencing European legislation, environmentalists can hope to see benefits throughout Europe, not just in a single member state. The kind of issues on which Friends of the Earth and Greenpeace have taken action relate to genetically modified foods, coastal waters and river quality, species conservation, emissions and nuclear safety. Groups specialising in matters of animal welfare similarly have a European dimension to their activities.

Eurogroups

These are interest groups that represent sectoral interests within several, if not all, the member states of the EU. These federations of like-minded national groups operate across the EU. The 700 or so eurogroups are obviously most active in areas that are of the greatest concern to the EU; something like 150 lobby represent the diverse range of agricultural interests. This reflects the fact that the growth of the CAP within the EU has meant that decisions on agricultural policy are increasingly taken in Brussels rather than at national level. As Neill Nugent says, 'Pressure groups usually go where power goes'.[11]

These umbrella groups have advantages and disadvantages. They can claim to represent more members than can any single group working alone. They also derive strength from speaking on behalf of a broad spectrum of European opinion. Just as COPA can claim to be more representative than the UK NFU, so too can ETUC make the same case in comparison with the TUC. However, eurogroups suffer from certain disadvantages in the Brussels setting:

- Often they are limited by lack of resources, of which staffing is but one problem. Many are small-scale operations with only a handful of permanent staff, and become active only when an issue of relevance to them becomes important. The research of Butt Philips suggests that very few groups have the resources to compaign over a long period.[12] They find communication with their many different members time-consuming, which is especially problematic for those groups with meagre funding and personnel.
- Eurogroups represent such a range of interests that they can lack cohesion and fail to present a united front. Disagreement often represents national differences that are difficult to reconcile. Such was the scale of disunity within the Committee on Common Market Automobile Constructors that it collapsed in 1990. Because there can be internal tensions and disagreements, the temptation is to water down proposals so that they command as wide an area of assent as possible. In this process, their effectiveness can be diminished.
- Eurogroups are often not specific to the EU but generally European, so that the ETUC, for example, represents over thirty trade union bodies in twenty different European countries.

The most important eurogroups are the umbrella organisations, each representing an entire sector such as agriculture, industry or commerce (see Table 9.1).

How British groups lobby the EU

Broadly, there are two routes for groups wishing to lobby the EU. They can adopt a 'national' or a 'European' strategy. The national approach involves attempts to influence EU decisions by persuading national political leaders to take up their cause in the Council of Ministers or to amend or delay EU laws. The European approach, what we might call the 'Brussels' strategy, refers to attempts to influence EU decisions by lobbying the EU's institutions directly or via membership of a eurogroup.

The national strategy

This strategy involves an attempt to influence the position taken by British ministers in EU discussions and also to influence the implementation of EU directives. For some groups this is the most effective form of lobbying, because:

Table 9.1   *Examples of leading eurogroups*

Group	Date founded	Membership	Committees and working groups	Other information
BEUC (European Bureau of Consumer Unions)	1973	36 members across 28 countries. Not EU specific	No permanent working groups: groups established on ad hoc basis	Main voice of the consumer associations. Smallish staff to cover whole range of EU issues
COPA (Committee of Professional Agricultural Organisations in the EU)	1958	29 members across 25 countries. EU specific	More than 50 specialist sub-groups and working parties, e.g. on milk and tobacco	Main agricultural group, seeking to represent most types of farmers on most types of issues. Very well resourced: more than 50 full-time officials
EEB (European Environmental Bureau)	1974	143 members across 31 countries. Not EU specific	No permanent specialist groups, but working groups established on ad hoc basis	Lacks resources of more powerful umbrella organisations
ETUC (European Trades Union Confederation)	1973	74 members across 34 countries. Not EU specific		Main trade union association. Sometimes seen as less influential because of its lack of concentration on EU
Fédération Bancaire (Banking Federation of the European Union)	1960	More than 4,000 banks across 28 countries. EU specific	15 permanent committees and specialist groups	Main voice of the commercial banks in EU
UNICE (Union of Industrial and Employers' Confederations of Europe)	1958	36 members across 29 countries. Not EU specific	5 main policy committees and other working groups as necessary	Main employers' group, very well resourced

- it is less expensive for groups than lobbying directly in Europe on their own;
- if they belong to a eurogroup then they may find that their counterparts from other countries do not share their viewpoint.

British insider groups with a European interest will seek to build upon this channel of influence. The hope is that as a result of meetings with senior officials and junior ministers in Whitehall, the secretary of state will be persuaded to advance their arguments and defend their cause in the relevant Council meetings. The national farmers union finds it helpful to meet senior civil servants in Whitehall when the issue of reform of the CAP rears its head, in the anticipation that when the minister goes to Brussels meetings, he or she will resolutely defend the position of the agrarian community back home. (Representatives of the NFU also try to influence deliberations in the Council by lobbying Coreper. Backed by its working parties, Coreper resolves most issues before the relevant ministers meet.) Of course, as Butt Phillips reminds us, 'the national pressure groups will be very much in the hands of government officials once the Council of Ministers' negotiations begin'.[13]

Many British groups pursue a national strategy, and writers such as Greenwood have drawn attention to the fact that relationships between groups and national governments are 'stable, well-developed and reliable'.[14] Moreover, most groups carry more weight with their own government than with European institutions, so that the impact of their lobbying is therefore maximised by focusing on Whitehall and Westminster. However, for the larger organisations such as the Institute of Directors, this avenue is used in conjunction with others, the emphasis being on that which is most likely to be effective in a particular case.

The European strategy: working via eurogroups

As we have seen, many British groups belong to eurogroups European-level federations of national groups. More than a decade ago, Baggott's findings showed that three-quarters of them were members of such a body.[15] Several eurogroups have operated from the early days of the original EC, often being based in Brussels, although some are to be found in Amsterdam, Cologne, London and Paris. The best-organised eurogroups are those concerned with representing the interests of big business. In the Butt Phillips survey, the largest number represented employers, closely followed by those groups representing agricultural and food interests. Other significant sectors dealt with issues such as consumers, labour, animal welfare and the environment.[16]

These groups can be useful to national groups in several ways, for example strengthening the case they wish to promote, putting pressure on the government of other EU countries to modify their position, and influencing counterpart organisations elsewhere in the hope that they might lobby their own government. They are a strong means of lobbying the EU: a two-way channel representing national groups to the European institutions and a means of keeping national groups informed of EU proposals and initiatives. But as we have seen, their weakness is often their lack of resources, of which staffing is but one problem. Many are small-scale operations with only a handful of permanent staff and limited means for sustaining a long campaign. However, some are very powerful and well-resourced, among them those featured in Table 9.1.

The European strategy: direct contact with EU institutions

Most national groups will have some form of communication with the machinery of the EU, particularly the Commission. Direct lobbying can be done in the home country by phone or in writing, perhaps by talking to a British commissioner but more often with the local MEP. It can involve visits to the EP to meet a group of elected representatives or journeys to Brussels to meet members of the Commission or a committee of Parliament.

A much smaller number of groups will also have an office in the EU to further their interests and enable them to keep a close eye on key developments within the EU. Such lobbying is usually a complement to that done in London, rather than a substitute for domestic action. As we have seen, Baggott found that 12 per cent of groups in his 1992 survey had established a Brussels office.[17] The number has grown, so that today the CBI, at least 25 companies, the TUC, the GMBATU, the NFU, the Law Society, Amnesty International, Greenpeace and Friends of the Earth all have such outlets. For wealthy insider groups that can afford it, there are many advantages in having an office, for as Coxall observed: 'Brussels has been called "an insiders town" in which it pays to have a presence'.[18] For many other groups, the cost of setting up an office is prohibitive. Very under-resourced groups have to rely on meetings with their MEP.

The institutions targeted by those who wish to lobby within the EU

Whatever the strategy adopted, the targets for lobbyists in the EU machinery are many and diverse, not just the obvious bodies such as the Commission, Council and the EP. Decision-making in the EU is 'a complex, multi-level process',[19] so that lobbyists need to be prepared to seek influence at more than one level. They have to decide where they think that the power resides in the resolution of particular types of issue.

Although the Council of Ministers is the most powerful institution within the EU, it is not the usual focus for most pressure groups. They find it difficult to obtain access to its members when they are assembled and the Council usually operates in a secretive manner. Anyone wishing to influence its proceedings normally does so via pressure at the national level (in the British case, in Whitehall) or through the permanent representations in Brussels such as Coreper or UKREP. An alternative approach, in the days of QMV, is for members of a national group to persuade their counterparts in a eurogroup to place pressure on their national government representative in the Council, the hope being that this will create a blocking minority to thwart a proposal they dislike.

Usually, the Commission is the prime target for pressure group activists. As a relatively open bureaucracy it welcomes approaches from interested parties. It maintains a list of several hundred bodies whose spokespersons it automatically consults on matters relating to technical legislation. In particular, it has dealings with several eurogroups that are favoured because they represent a wide span on opinion. Underresourced itself, it values the specialist knowledge and expertise that groups can provide. Its regard for such consultation is evident from a passage in its 2001 White Paper on 'Governance' which suggests a strengthening of the partnership between itself and civil society, comprising as it does the myriad of voluntary associations and group activity that characterise modern life.

The Commission has formalised its relationship with the lobby groups by setting up recognised channels of communication:

- There are a large number of advisory committees specifically created so that they can brief and advise the Commission at the start of the policy-making process.
- The so-called 'Social Dialogue' set up between the Commission and both sides of industry involves regular meetings between the Commission, ETUC, UNICE and the European Centre of Public Enterprises (CEEP).
- Commissioners and directors-general receive delegations and documentation from interest groups of all kinds and are in regular telephone communication.
- Representatives of the Commission attend meetings of the larger eurogroups.
- Commission representatives will travel to member countries to meet national interest groups as well as national governments.
- The Commission will participate fully in conferences and seminars set up by interest groups to investigate policy areas.

Commission officials in the directorates-general are in great demand. Most are willing to meet representatives of various groups, although they have to balance the consultative aspect of their work with the need to complete other tasks. Bomberg and Stubb quote one official who observed that:

> Sometimes people want to see the new text [of a proposal] every time a comma is changed in a draft directive. That is unrealistic. The one big problem with consultation is that it lengthens the process. You need to balance efficiency witih respect for democratic values . . . If we can get the consultation structured and put draft documents on the Internet, then everyone should benefit. It is also important that other organisations should be able to see who is in contact with the Commission.[20]

Communication with individual commissioners is relatively infrequent, for it is usually seen as less useful than regular dialogue with the officials engaged in the development of policy. Of course, all commissioners have a small *cabinet* of officials serving them and lobbying can be done with the *chefs de cabinet* who meet prior to the weekly meetings of the Commission.

In recent years, eurogroups and other groups have begun to attach more importance to the EP and its committees. Its influence and legislative powers have increased considerably as a result of recent treaties such as the SEA and Maastricht, thereby enhancing its attractiveness to pressure groups. Although still much less significant than the Commission, groups representing animal welfare interests, environmentalists and consumers have come to recognise its developing importance. They actively lobby one of the most powerful of the EP's nineteen standing committees, that covering the environment, public health and consumer protection.

People in the world of sport and entertainment have also come to appreciate the increased significance of the EP. The music industry used The Corrs, an Irish pop group, to lobby MEPs over copyright legislation, laying on a special concert for elected representatives and other EU officials. Sir Alex Ferguson and other dignitaries from the football world similarly lobbied them over the impact of EU competition policy on the transfer market. Such lobbying may yield a receptive hearing from European parliamentarians, but this is not the same as having access to people who exert a genuine leverage. This is why business groups tend to concentrate their fire on the Commission. Parliament is the obvious focus for those who lack such ready access.

Grant has pointed to the way in which MEPS belonging to Intergroups are much lobbied by groups representing a wide variety of interests. Intergroups operate across the boundaries of the different party groupings and member states, and espouse a range of diverse causes. There are some sixty of them, 'covering subjects such as financial services, pharmaceuticals, defence industries and small and medium-sized enterprises'.[21] Other examples range from the Federalist Intergroup for European Union and the Friends of Israel to the Animal Welfare Group and the Media Intergroup.

The Court of Justice, too, is of growing significance, given its role of interpreting and enforcing EU legislation. British environmental groups have in the past lobbied its members in connection with the quality of drinking water. Women's groups have used it to win supportive rulings on equal pay, as in 1998 when several thousand NHS female employees gained a decision in their favour. So, too, have trade unions who benefited from a judgement against governmental policy on the Working Time Directive. As a result of the decision, some four million British workers gained extra holiday benefits. The National Union of Mineworkers and the Law Society have taken up causes such as pit closures and legal aid. Finally, individual firms in the airline and car industries have taken cases to Luxembourg in protest against regulations that adversely affected their interests.

As we have seen, some groups use a number of different avenues when lobbying Europe. They may use a professional agency (see pp. 263–5), tackle their own national officials and ministers, and also adopt a Brussels/Strasbourg/ Luxembourg strategy.

Recent trends in EU lobbying

The most obvious recent trend has been in the growth in the number and influence of organised interests operating within the Union, as already outlined. Bomberg and Stubb have noted that 'different types of interests have congregated in Brussels in a series of waves', reflecting 'the deepening and widening of the European Union itself'.[22] In the 1960s the dominant actors represented commercial interests and agriculture. Employer, and later labour and consumer, interests followed, and by the 1980s more public interest organisations had European representation. Trade associations and remaining professional associations became more active in Europe after the passage of the SEA with the prospect of a single market. Some large companies also began to open their own offices in Brussels and take an interest in its decisions.

Particularly significant in recent years has been the increase in the lobbying carried out by regional and local governments, ranging from the German Länder to the Scottish and Northern Irish Executives and the Welsh Assembly. The development of cohesion under the SEA and the formation of the Committee of the Regions under the Maastricht Treaty both pointed to increased EU concern for Europe's regional diversity and discrepancies. Representatives of such authorities have their eyes firmly set on the prospect of special funding for their pet regional and social projects, but they are also interested in environmental policies and EU programmes for social inclusion, support for business and cultural and tourism activities. The Brussels delegations of regional and local authorities maintain close links with all institutions, working closely with appropriate commissioners or staff of the directorates-general and with sympathetic MEPs. The Committee of the Regions has estimated the number of delegations representing regional and local autorities at around 190.

Think-tanks have also increased in number, although their numbers are more modest and their resources more limited than many of those operating in Washington DC, London or several other capital cities. Other areas of growth include environmental, animal rights, public health and human rights groups, reflecting growing EU interest and responsibilities in these areas.

In addition to the proliferation of groups, groups have also targeted a wider range of institutions, making more use of the EP and Court over the last decade or so. The Committee of the Regions, the Economic and Social Committee and other bodies provide other formal routes for the lobbyist. The greater understanding by group activists of how the EU actually functions means that they recognise that informal approaches can be worth pursuing. Key personnel in issue and policy networks are also worth cultivating; these policy communities function in areas dominated by major producer groups, as in the chemical,

Box 9.3

Findings of a 2004 questionnaires on lobbying in Europe

In 1993 a survey was made of twenty British pressure groups to find out more about the European dimension to their activities. These same groups were contacted again in 2004 to find out just how important this aspect of lobbying has now become to their overall work.[23]

Of the sixteen groups that responded in 1993, in 2004 two no longer existed as separate entities. Of the remaining fourteen, twelve replied to the questionnaire. The groups covered important areas ranging from manufacturing to labour, farming to the environment, and animal welfare to the law. A brief summary of the findings is to be found in Table 9.2.

All the respondents agreed that the impact of the EU had grown significantly over the last ten years, although in most cases they pointed to the development of the single market as the major impetus to their involvement in matters European. The representative of the Transport and General Workers' Union drew attention to the increasing amount of relevant legislation in recent years in the area of working conditions, notably that relating to hours of work, and the conditions of part-timers and young people.

The officer for the Law Society also noted an increase in EU legislation of interest to its members, and the effect of an establishment directive that set out the conditions under which lawyers of a home country can practise elsewhere in the EU. Beyond that, she pointed to the EU's increasing legislative competence in certain areas of civil and criminal law, which affects the advice British solicitors give to their clients.

Not surprisingly, the two environmental groups – Friends of the Earth and Greenpeace – also felt that the EU was more important in their work than ever before. Friends of the Earth has recently been much involved with submissions on waste, while Greenpeace has taken up issues of emission levels and illegal logging.

The policy officer for the Society of Motor Manufacturers and Traders (SMMT) confirmed the growing impact of EU measures on national pressure groups. He drew attention to the way in which the number of interest group offices established in Brussels has grown steadily and how the timing of these creations has broadly coincided with the acquisition by the EU of new responsibilities covering a range of policy areas. In particular, he stressed the importance for the motor industry of environmental measures such as the REACH Chemicals Review, emission standards for new cars, and safety issues such as pedestrian protection. He provided other explanations for the growing attraction of the EU for interest groups, already implicit in what we have said in regards to EU institutions. He referred to its 'multi-level architecture', meaning that there are many opportunities to influence legislative outcome compared with some national arenas – for example in the early drafting stage in the Commission, in the Council via national governments and in the EP. He also referred to the EU's consciousness of its perceived 'democratic deficit' and its recognition of the need to become 'closer' to its citizens. He noted that the Commission is taking an increasingly pragmatic approach to consultation. Its officials realise that there is little point in passing 'unworkable' legislation with which member states will have little interest in complying.

In the last few years, the SMMT has made increasing use of e-mail as a means of communication. It has also developed its programme of holding seminars and staging events in Brussels. Otherwise, it continues to employ a dual strategy in its lobbying programme. On the one hand it holds regular meetings with UK ministers and officials in key departments, such as the Department for Environment, Food and Rural Affairs, the Department of Trade and Industry and the Department for Transport, in the hope that its concerns are taken into account both when formulating the UK negotiating position for the Council of Ministers and working group meetings, and in transposing EU directives into national law. It also works through two eurogroups based on national automotive associations, as well as having a more general input into manufacturing policy via its membership of the CBI, itself a member of UNICE.

Overall, of the twelve respondents, all of them lobby the national government in seeking to influence EU policy. All of them belong to eurogroups and engage in direct lobbying of EU institutions from Britain (for example via approaches to MEP, or by contacting officials in EU institutions). Only two of them (the CBI and Law Society) have their own offices in Brussels, although the RSPCA has a base at the Eurogroup for Animal Welfare's headquarters. The survey of the RSPCA and its operations provides a fuller example of how one British group goes about its task of 'lobbying Europe'.

pharmaceutical and technology industries. Coxall has drawn attention to the role in Brussels of the policy network that discusses agricultural policy away from the public gaze. It is 'dominated by DGV1 of the Commission, member states' ministers of agriculture and farmers' groups, based on a consensual desire to increase both production and farm incomes, and with consumer and environmental groups excluded'.[24]

Another main development over the last decade has been the increased professionalisation of lobbying. The Commission values well-presented, highly specialised information and lobbyists need to demonstrate their expertise and carefully tailor their data and advice. Increasingly, they make links with other like-minded lobbyists, and establish alliances and networks across institutions and nationalities. E-mail has been used to develop and sustain dialogue with Commission officials and parliamentarians. It is used extensively by eurogroups, as they seek to maintain contact with their wide and highly dispersed membership.

Table 9.2　　*Findings of the 2004 questionnaire: lobbying methods employed*

Name of group	Via British government	Via eurogroup	Direct lobbying of EU institutions, from Britain	Direct lobbying of EU institutions, via Brussels office
Confederation of British Industry	*	*		*
Engineering Employers' Federation	*	*	*	
Institute of Directors	*	*	*	
Society of Motor Manufacturers and Traders	*	*	*	
National Union of Rail, Maritime and Transport Workers	*	*	*	
Transport and General Workers' Union	*	*	*	
Trades Union Congress	*	*	*	*
Law Society	*	*		*
British Veterinary Association	*	*	*	
Royal Society for the Prevention of Cruelty to Animals	*	*	*	
Friends of the Earth	*	*	*	
Greenpeace	*	*	*	

Bomberg and Stubb quote one much-lobbied MEP who told them that he felt that the art of lobbying has been much developed in recent years: 'Now, we have far higher skills and standards in the lobbying industry. You very rarely get the utter fool you would have encountered some years ago.'[25] Lobbying has certainly become more specialised, with the individuals concerned becoming more expert in:

- preparing a specialist brief;
- tailoring and targeting their knowledge;
- creating alliances or networks across national frontiers and between members of Union institutions;
- knowing when and where to intervene at different stages in the decision-making process: the Commission at the drafting stage, the EP and the national governments later on.

In the last few years there has also been a marked growth in the employment of professional lobbyists at the EU level. For a substantial fee, lobbying firms will monitor developments in particular areas of policy, and suggest possible contacts, arrange meetings and generally help groups which themselves may lack the right connections to put over a powerful case. Many firms and groups combine their own lobbying with the use of such professional agencies.

Finally, it is worth noting the growing significance of policy communities and issue networks (see Box 9.4), as Peterson's research has indicated. In his words: 'as the European Union has become a more important tier of governance in Europe, EU policy networks have become a more important link between states and societies. A considerable amount of EU decision-making now occurs within policy networks'.[26] This development is associated with the vagueness of some intergovernmental agreements that left the Commission and the groups with whom it had dealings a role in 'filling in the gaps'.

Box 9.4
Policy communities and issue networks

The concept of policy networks has attracted much attention in recent years. Policy networks describe the different kinds of relationships between groups and government. The term is a generic one, denoting a continuum from close and stable policy communities to looser, more open and discontinuous policy or issue networks.

Whereas American commentators traditionally used the term 'iron triangles' to describe the relationship between interest groups, congressional committee chairmen and government departments, elsewhere there was talk of 'policy communities'. Such communities involved a high degree of interdependence between insider groups and government, without the involvement of committee chairmen in the legislature. They were characterised by close, mutually supportive ties, based on a stable relationship between the participants and a high degree of contact. The idea of policy communities fitted in well with Grant's classification of insider and outsider groups, the former having close involvement in decision-taking.[27] In Britain, policy communities were formed around subjects such as food and drink policy, technical education and water privatisation.

In the last two decades policy communities have begun to decay in most democracies as other players have become involved in discussion of a policy area, including the research institutes and the media. Commentators now often speak of 'issue networks'. These are wider and looser, and are characterised by a more open style of policy making. The impact of any particular group may vary from time to time, issue to issue, partly depending on the expertise it possesses. There are more participants in issue networks than there were in policy communities, relationships are not continuous or particularly close and there is less interdependence.

Policy communities and issue networks in the EU

As a means of organising the policy-making process, policy communities and issue networks are just as useful within the EU as they are in individual countries. But Martin Smith points to the paradox that the very characteristics they possess that make them an asset in the EU can also make them harder to establish.[28] They are useful because EU policy making is complex and multilevel, but they are difficult to establish because of:

- the vast range of conflicting interests that come from a wider range of countries
- the relative smallness of the Brussels bureaucracy compared to national bureaucracies
- the degree of openness of European institutions such as the Commission.

Such networks exist in almost every policy area, the most well-known policy community covering agricultural, chemical and technology policy-making. In other policy areas, such as the environment, issue networks also operate, and are characterised by numerous players, constantly changing membership and conflictual rather than consensual relationships. Such issue networks became more important from the late 1980s onwards, as the EU enlarged its area of competence.

The influence of pressure groups within the EU

What distinguishes the EU from most national governments is the apparent openness of EU institutions to those promoting sectional interests and the willingness of officials to talk to any lobbyist beyond just a few favoured groups. As Mazey and Richardson observe: 'The very willingness of officials to talk to groups and individual firms means that the market for policy ideas is much more broad and fluid than in the UK'.[29]

Lobbyists from well-resourced groups who are armed with an expert brief are inevitably likely to be more effective than those who represent underfunded organisations. Mark Aspinwall has lamented this unequal distribution of resources and argued that it is damaging to EU policy making if wealthy private interests are at an advantage over smaller, public bodies that cannot afford to employ professional agencies or commit extensive funding to their activities.[30] But against this viewpoint others claim that at least the EU provides another channel through which lobbying may be conducted. Organisations that do not have much access to decision makers on the national scene may find that the European outlet offers alternative scope. The studies of Wallace and Young (1997), and Peterson (1997) have both suggested that lobbyists concerned with environmentalism, consumerism and women's rights have all had more opportunity to pursue their cause at the European level, perhaps by forging informal alliances with members of the Commission, EP or Court.[31]

Inevitably, in any discussion of pressure groups there is invariably discussion of their merits or otherwise, the question being asked as to whether they are a hindrance or a help to the workings of the democratic system. Whatever the verdict, their growth in number and range was inevitable, the more so as the EU expanded its area of competence. It is inconceivable that there can be any return to the days before lobbying took root on such a vast scale, for a myriad of national and eurogroups see the EU as an arena in which to exert their influence and/or proclaim their views.

Against the lobbyists, critics stress the imbalances referred to above, with some groups more powerful than others: the voice of producers often proving more influential than that of consumers – most obviously in the agrarian sphere. Critics also point to the time taken up by meetings between officials and group representatives, a problem that develops with the proliferation of campaigning bodies and with successive enlargements. Either the meetings become shorter and less valuable or there is less time for officials to spend on the development, administration and implementation of EU policies.

In their favour, lobbyists provide specialist information to those who develop EU policy. There are now few topics within the EU's area of responsibility on which expert advice and data are not available. As a result, the views of the European peoples are conveyed to the policy makers, allowing a healthy channel of communication between the voters – many of whom feel 'left out' and alienated from EU institutions – and ensuring that policies that finally emerge are broadly in step with popular opinion. This may seem a healthy antidote to the elitism that characterised the early growth of the EC, when decisions were made 'top-down' rather than 'bottom-up'.

Summary

Interest groups have played an important role in the processes of the EU ever since its foundation. Agricultural and business interests were later joined by consumer and labour ones, and interest groups have been joined by promotional ones. The intensification of group activity came about as a result of the passage of the SEA that much extended the scope of policymaking by the EC and changed the nature of decision making in ways that provided more opportunities for lobbyists to conduct their operations. Some groups take the national route, others the European route. Most target the Commission, but the Council of Ministers, the EP and Court of Justice are all useful access points for those who wish to convey their views. The choice of target largely depends upon which seems to be the most appropriate for the particular issue involved.

Notes

1 S. George and M. Sowemimo, 'Conservative foreign policy towards the European Union' in S. Ludlam and M. Smith (eds), *Contemporary British Conservatism*, Macmillan, 1996.
2 J. Greenwood, *Representing Interests in the European Union*, Macmillan, 1997.
3 S. Mazey and J. Richardson (eds), *Lobbying in the European Community*, Oxford University Press, 1993.
4 O. Gray, 'The structure of interest group representation in the EU: some observations of a practitioner' in P. Claeys, C. Gotinne, I. Smets and P. Winard (eds), *Lobbying, Pluralism and European Integration*, European Interuniversity Press, 1998, and W. Wessels, 'The growth and differentiation of multi-level networks: a corporatist mega-bureaucracy or an open city?' in H. Wallace and A. Young, *Participation and Policy-Making in the European Union*, Clarendon Press, 1997.
5 B. Coxall, *Pressure Groups in British Politics*, Pearson, 2001.
6 S. Mazey and J. Richardson, 'Pressure groups and the EC', *Politics Review*, September 1993.
7 W. Grant, *Pressure Groups, Politics and Democracy in Britain*, Harvester Wheatsheaf, 1999.
8 R. Baggott, *Pressure Groups Today*, Manchester University Press, 1995.
9 H. Rimmer, quoted by P. Hetherington, *The Guardian*, 13 July 1994.
10 S. Mazey and J. Richardson, as in 3 above.
11 N. Nugent, *The Government and Politics of the European Union*, Palgrave, 2003.
12 A. Butt Phillips, 'Pressure groups in the European Community', occasional paper, University of Bath, 1985.
13 A. Butt Phillips, as in 12 above.
14 J. Greenwood, as in 2 above.
15 R. Baggott, 'The measurement of change in pressure group politics', *Talking Politics*, autumn 1992.
16 A. Butt Phillips, as in 12 above.
17 R. Baggott, as in 15 above.
18 B. Coxall, as in 5 above.
19 B. Coxall, as in 5 above.
20 E. Bomberg and A. Stubb, *The European Union: How Does it Work?*, Oxford University Press, 2003.
21 W. Grant, as in 7 above.
22 E. Bomberg and A. Stubb, as in 20 above.
23 D. Watts, *Talking Politics*, Autumn 2004.
24 B. Coxall, as in 5 above.
25 E. Bomberg and A. Stubb, as in 20 above.
26 J. Peterson, 'States, societies and the European Union', *West European Politics*, vol. 20, no. 4, July 1997.
27 W. Grant, as in 7 above.
28 M. Smith, *Pressure Politics*, Baseline Books, 1995.
29 S. Mazey and J. Richardson, as in 3 above.
30 M. Aspinwall, 'Collective attraction: the new political game in Brussels', in J. Greenwood and M. Aspinwall (eds), *Collective Action in the European Union*, Routledge, 1998.
31 H. Wallace and A. Young, as in 4 above, and J. Peterson, as in 26 above.

Part IV

Concluding thoughts

10

Britain and the EU:
past, present and future

Europe has been a problem area of policy for British politicians for many years. Sometimes it has become a political football in the party battle, with those who exhibit signs of pro-European attitudes and policies facing a barrage of adverse media criticism in the tabloid press at home. David Butler and Martin Westlake make the point that euroscepticism has a long history:

> If there is a European 'problem', it is not restricted to one British political party, but more generally diffused throughout the British political and administrative establishment . . . In truth, virtually every postwar British prime minister has been in a similar position and played a similar role, from Attlee to Churchill and Eden, from Macmillan to Wilson, and from Callaghan to Major and Thatcher.[1]

Leaders from Attlee to Major have been tested by European 'problems'. Their difficulties relate to the problem of leading parties whose composition reflects the ambivalent attitudes of many British people to the post-war position. Britons are caught between the desire to hold on to their country's past greatness and traditions (what former Foreign Secretary Douglas Hurd has called 'punching above its weight'), and yet also to keep apace with the modern world. Although most MPs and many British people recognise that the country has a European future, a number of them do not enthuse about the prospect. Other countries, lacking the same traditions and attachments as Britain, do not experience the same feelings, or at least not to the same extent. As one former Conservative MP, Sir Anthony Meyer, put it: 'For France, Europe offers a chance to extend its influence; for Britain, Europe is a damage-limitation exercise'.[2]

Most Britons recognise that the country cannot separate itself from the European fold, but within it ministers seem to find it difficult to make the EU work to the national advantage. By seeming to resist the initiatives that other nations want in so many areas, it then becomes harder to achieve those goals that really matter to Britain. Yet by going along with other nations' initiatives, ministers risk having their actions savaged in the eurosceptic tabloid press. It is difficult for even a pro-European administration to be a constructive, if distinctive, actor on the continental stage.

Britain's reduced circumstances in the world

In 1945 Britain was still a 'great power', although its strength even then can be overstressed. As a result of this status, change seemed unnecessary. For a long while the British allowed their awareness of the historical and cultural differences between Britain and Europe to predominate over their political judgement. Hugo Young has written perceptively about popular attitudes at the time:

> The island people were not only different but, mercifully separate, housed behind their moat . . . They were also inestimably superior, as was shown by history both ancient and modern: by the resonance of the Empire on which the sun never set, but equally by the immediate circumstances out of which the new Europe was born, the war itself. Her sense of national independence, enhanced by her unique empire, absorbed by all creeds and classes and spoke for by virtually every analyst, could not be fractured.[3]

Since 1945 Britain's declining economic fortunes have meant that it has not been able to sustain the position it once held. It has been hard to come to terms with that situation. Managing national decline is not a glorious role for politicians, and it is one that arouses little popular enthusiasm. Some people still hanker after the world leadership that was possible in their parents' generation. Many more concede that Britain's capacity to influence events has been much weakened, but are unconvinced that the logic of events should drive the country more closely into the embrace of its continental partners.

For years, Britain still attempted to preserve its global role. Churchill expressed his view of the competing claims on British foreign policy, in a speech he made in May 1951:

> Where do we stand? We are not members of the European Defence Community, nor do we intend to be merged in a Federal European system. We feel we have a special relation to both, expressed by the preposition 'with' but not 'of' – we are with them, but not of them. We have our own Commonwealth and Empire.[4]

Smilarly, Sir Anthony Eden spoke for many of his countrymen when he gave his reasons for not signing up for membership of the EDC. Speaking a few months later, and with the authority of a foreign secretary, he observed:

> Britain's story and her interests lie far beyond the Continent of Europe. Our thoughts move across the seas to the many communities in which our people play their part, in every corner of the world. These are our family ties. That is our life;

without it we should be no more than some millions of people living on an island off the coast of Europe, in which nobody wants to take any particular notice.[5]

Not surprisingly, the country that 'won the war' felt that with such a worldwide role and importance it could win the peace. It did not need to tie itself in to any commitments with the countries it had defeated or which had been overrun in the hostilities of the Second World War. Britain felt that it could afford to remain aloof from Europe. It was not ready to recognise or admit its increasing weakness.

Such an attitude had deep roots in the British psyche, and it may be considered understandable in the circumstances of the time. However, it was combined with an inability to appreciate the enthusiasm and dedication of other nations to closer integration in pursuit of 'the European Idea'. Consistently, British politicians then and in more recent years have underestimated the strength of this determination, and have assumed that carefully constructed measures of intergovernmental co-operation would be a substitute for their more visionary approach.

In 1963 Dean Acheson, a former American secretary of state, observed that: 'Britain has lost an empire, but not yet found a role'.[6] The comment wounded British pride, but some politicians recognised that it contained more than a little truth. Among them, there was a growing belief that Europe might provide the theatre in which Britain would have the best chance of influencing events and opinions in the world at large.

As it became clear that Britain's capacity to influence the outcome of events had become much curtailed, Conservative Prime Minister Macmillan found it expedient to apply for Britain to join the EEC in 1961. Neither the Commonwealth nor the American connection seemed any longer to count for as much as had been assumed a decade or so before. But not until the retirement of General de Gaulle was British membership welcome to the whole Community.

Eventually, Britain joined the EEC in 1973, fifteen years after it began its operations, and twenty years after the Six had pioneered the path to unity. Whereas other late entrants seem to have made the adjustments in attitude required to make a success of membership, this has not been the case for many British people and some of their elected representatives. The British have found it hard to adapt, hence their reputation on the continent as 'reluctant Europeans'. Perhaps this reflects a long-lasting national difficulty in coming to terms with Britain's reduced circumstances in the world.

Wolfram Kaiser offers an interesting explanation from a continental perspective of the British predicament in Europe. He notes the lack of British experience of working as equal partners:

It is not only . . . a matter of having lost an empire without finding a role. More fundamentally, Britain had little experience of multilateral relationships conducted on equal terms. Its key external circles of influence after 1945 were characterised by clear hierarchies: Britain led the Commonwealth and Empire, and it was led by the United States. There was no clear European hierarchy, and the Foreign Office remained fixated by an outmoded 'balance-of-power' mentality which failed to take account of the strengthening Franco–German alliance.[7]

Apart from a committed band of ardent Europeans, it would be hard to detect widespread enthusiasm for the prospect of entry to the EEC in 1973. However, there was a fairly general feeling that the changes on the world scene and the need for access to the large continental market made accession desirable, even necessary. When the chance came for the British people to express their view in the referendum of 1975, they showed a strong backing for membership, for once the country had committed itself it was recognised that it might be a cold world outside should it prematurely depart.

Yet there never was popular excitement in Britain about belonging the Community. It was appreciated that it was probably wise and necessary for Britain to work with our new partners, for the alternatives did not look very promising. The point was well made by Northedge:

> [The] important thing about British entry into Europe was that it had almost every appearance of being a policy of last resort, adopted, one might almost say, when all other expedients had failed. There was no suggestion of it being hailed as a brilliant success . . . the impression remained that it was brought about in humiliating circumstances, and when other options in foreign policy had lost their convincingness.[8]

Hugo Young has written similarly of British motives:

> For the makers of the original 'Europe', beginning to fulfil Victor Hugo's dream, their creation was a triumph. Out of defeat, they produced a new kind of victory. For Britain, by contrast, the entry into Europe was a defeat: a fate she had resisted, a necessity reluctantly accepted, the last resort of a once great power, never for one moment a climactic or triumphant engagement with the construction of Europe. This has been integral to the national psyche, perhaps only half articulated, since 1973. The sense of the Community as a place of British failure – proof of Britain's failed independence, site of her failed domination – is deep in the undertow of the tides and whirlpools [of Britain's relations with the other European countries].[9]

The point is a fair one. Eurobarometer, the EC's polling organisation, has consistently found that the majority of British respondents favoured closer cooperation in Europe in some form, and accepted the inevitability of further steps along the route to unity, on the right terms. But they are unsure about any move to further integration, for by choice they would never have been in the position of needing to take the European journey. British attitudes were noted by Geoffrey Martin, the head of the European Commission office in London: 'The British have not seen Europe as an opportunity. They regard it as somewhere between an obligation and a mistake.'[10]

British politicians – even those who are seen as among the more pro-European – have often expressed a coolness towards their counterparts on the continent. It was Harold Macmillan who wrote to Whitehall officials (shortly before the first British application to join the EEC) that the problem with the European Commission was that it was run by 'the Jews, the planners and the old cosmopolitan element'. He went on to state his fear that the Community would be 'dominated in fact by Germany and used as an instrument for the revival of German power through economic means', which amounted to 'really giving them on a plate what we fought two wars to prevent'.[11]

Members of Macmillan's party have subsequently taken a more overtly anti-European (or they might say anti-Community/Union) stance. In the era of Conservative government after 1979, there was a developing toughening in the approach to relations with Europe, at times a distinct frostiness. The author of *Using Europe, Abusing the Europeans*, shows that the 'British tradition of using Europe [as an instrument of policy] and abusing the Europeans [for failing to get its way]' has a long history.[12] The tactic intensified during the era of Conservative rule after 1979. As we have seen (p. 54), John Major, usually regarded as more sympathetic to Europe than his predecessor, was aware after the Maastricht ratification that enthusiasm among the Conservatives had distinctly cooled on matters European. Under pressure from eurosceptics in his cabinet and party, he sought to limit its competence, delay making any decisions that bound Britain more closely to the other member states and resorted to obstruction accompanied by accusations of bad faith. At that time, the Thatcherite ex-minister and arch eurosceptic Lord Tebbit was moved to describe the EU as 'a bunch of liars and cheats'.[13]

When Tony Blair entered Downing Street in 1997 there were many optimists who hoped that the sometimes icy relationship with Europe would thaw. There could be a fresh start, with an internationalist, pro-European government in office. The process of building support for the EU might begin. As prime minister, Blair attempted to strike a more positive note. In a speech in Paris during the first British presidency of his premiership, he reassured his audience of his pro-European credentials: 'I happen to share the European idealism. I am by instinct internationalist . . . Britain's future lies in being full partners in Europe'.[14]

After several years of Blairite leadership, there were growing doubts about the extent of British commitment to playing that more positive role. There has long been some sympathy among European leaders for Britain's position over the euro, but doubts have nonetheless been expressed as to whether the prime minister was really willing to start developing a more pro-European constituency. The rhetoric from London is generally more *communautaire* – supportive of the EU – but there have been suggestions from some continental leaders suggesting that Tony Blair has been unwilling to try and sell the European cause – and particularly the single currency – to the electorate. Also, even before the war against Iraq, critics pointed out that when issues such as the handling of Saddam Hussein (Iraq) or Slobodan Milosevic (Serbia) emerged, the Blairite reflex was to turn to the Americans rather than to consult with and rally European opinion. There may have been good reasons for acting as he did, but in continental eyes it sometimes seems as though he should prove his European credentials in action as well as in words. Doubters noted that he regularly revealed a preference for Washington over Brussels, and that his relationship firstly with Bill Clinton and latterly George W. Bush seemed to be more important than his ties with European leaders such as Jacques Chirac and Gerhard Schröder.

That Tony Blair exhibits a greater enthusiasm for Europe than all of his predecessors other than Edward Heath is difficult to challenge, although the claim is not a particularly remarkable one. But as Geddes observes, Blair's dilemma is that 'whilst he has been able to make the case for Britain in Europe . . . he has not been able to make the case for Europe in Britain'.[15] It is one of the ironies of recent history that the leader who has the reputation of being pro-European was 'an umpire not a player' in May 1998, when eleven members of the EU took the field and pledged to complete their economic and monetary union. 'He chaired the meeting, but did not sign the pledge'.[16]

The British approach: lines of continuity in recent decades

British ministers – especially during Margaret Thatcher's premiership – sought to fashion the EC along the lines set out in her Bruges speech of September 1988. Rejecting any form of European superstate, she reminded her listeners of Britain's contribution to the liberation of Europe in 1944–45 and offered a description of how the EC might develop in the future. Her remarks cast her firmly in the Gaullist mould, for she made it clear that it was neither possible nor desirable to 'suppress nationhood and concentrate power at the centre of a European conglomerate'. She favoured 'willing and active co-operation between independent states' and wanted to see Europe speak with a more united voice. But this must be done in such a way that it 'preserves the different traditions, Parliamentary powers and sense of national pride in one's own country'. It was apparent that she had little or no sympathy with talk of a European Idea. She was no utopian, but took the view that Europe could be made to work to Britain's advantage – as long as British leaders made a firm stand against EC interference and regulation, and were determined to concentrate attention on developing a deregulated market in Europe.[17]

While Conservative leaders were concerned to stress and expand the role of the EC as a free trade area, their continental partners often had a different long-term agenda. Their vision was of a Community in which the degree of union became ever closer, and this was written into the small print of the treaties. For several years, these implications of membership were not fully realised in Britain. Even those who were involved in the negotiations, and signed up for the next stage in the road to unity, sometimes had an inadequate grasp of the detail contained therein. This was particularly the case with Margaret Thatcher, who by supporting the SEA committed Britain to what has been described as 'a milestone on the federalist road'.[18]

Margaret Thatcher – in office and subsequently – has been a strong exponent of intergovernmentalism. She accepted the EU in as much as she believed membership of the EU conferred practical economic advantages upon Great Britain. But she had grave doubts about the way in which it operated, disliked many of its policies and was never a committed European in the way that her predecessor, Edward Heath, had been. She shunned the integrationist road, her preference being for an enlarged EU – one that was broader and looser. She always remained a firm Atlanticist, seeing merit in the 'special relationship' that her government developed with President Reagan during the 1980s.

Her successors as Conservative leaders – Major, Hague, Duncan Smith and Howard – have shared a similar set of views. In the early–mid 1990s Duncan Smith introduced a bill in the House of Commons 'to provide . . . for the disapplication within the United Kingdom of judgements, rules and doctrines propounded by the European Court', in so doing describing it as a 'purely political court'.[19] In his view, Parliament must reclaim its lost sovereignty over legislation, an approach that would involve amending the 1972 Act of Accession from which the threat to sovereignty had originated. His anti-Europeanism was toned down after he became leader in 2001, for the party was anxious to unite around its position of broad euroscepticism.

The Howard approach, as outlined in chapter 8, has clear similarities with the Bruges speech, if modified by the development of events in the intervening decade and a half. He, too, has stressed that countries 'approach European integration from a perspective shaped by their history . . . different histories, different institutions and different traditions'. In the light of the 'historic connections with our Commonwealth partners and with the United States', it is necessary to accept that Britain is a global trading nation. It is also right to develop for a flexible EU that does not seek to 'impose a rigid straitjacket of uniformity from Finland to Greece, from Portugal to Poland'.[20] Margaret Thatcher had thought that 'it would be folly to try to fit [member states] into some sort of identikit European personality' and urged that Europe should 'be a family of nations, understanding each other better, appreciating each other more, doing more together, but relishing our national identity no less than our common European endeavour. Let us have a Europe which plays its full part in the wider world, which looks outward not inward, and which preserves that Atlantic Community.'

As we saw in chapter 8, there have been echoes of the Thatcherite approach in the Blair period. However, there are differences, and not merely ones of rhetoric. Blair has shown more interest in joining the euro, having no overriding constitutional objections to so doing. He took Britain into the Social Chapter and he has supported moves towards a more integrated European military capability. But he is no federalist, preferring an enlarged and looser EU to the organisation envisaged by those who dreamed of European integration after the Second World War. At Nice and in the constitutional talks he was concerned to ensure that national interests were strongly defended, as part of a vision of strong countries co-operating for their mutual advantage. The new Europe created as a result of the Fifth Enlargement provides him with allies likely to be solid in their support for the battle against the Franco–German push for more political integration, and in favour of a free-market vision of independent nation states.

Box 10.1
Fears about the creation of a European superstate

Several British parliamentarians, particularly but not exclusively Conservatives, have an often-expressed fear that Britain is in danger of being dragged into some European monstrosity – a form of superstate. In the Labour Party, such a view surfaces less frequently, although it was evident in the discussions over the desirability of a European constitution.

However, it was the Conservative William Hague who described those feelings in the most vivid tones, in the speech in which he outlined his 'elephant test'. Simplistically expressed, his view was that if it looks, smells and sounds like an elephant, then it is an elephant you're dealing with. Applied to the emerging shape of the EU, he discerned the characteristics of a future superstate, among them a proposed president, a parliament, a court and a single currency. Recognising the possibility of such a state being created without remedial action, a *Mail on Sunday* writer expressed the more extravagant view that this outcome would 'be worse than Stalin's Soviet Union'. Pro-European Labour ministers clearly operate in a hostile climate.

According to the Oxford English Dictionary, a state is 'the political organization or management which forms the supreme civil rule and government of a country or nation . . . the sphere of supreme political administration . . .a community of people occupying a defined areas and organized under one government: a commonwealth, a nation'.

Academics, constitutional experts, diplomats and European officials are divided in their views about what form the EU will eventually take, but the general view is that the Union will fall far short of being a superstate.[21] For Julia Smith of the Royal Institute of International Affairs, two key tests can be applied:

- Will there be a single European defence force, a real European army?
- Will there be a single tax regime throughout Europe?

They are in her view unlikely to happen and Britain's 'red lines' are all about ensuring that they will not do so.

Historian Eric Hobsbawm points out that the idea of the nation-state which is sovereign, independent and with which no-one interferes – the nineteenth-century idea – no longer corresponds to the reality of the world today. There is one such state – the USA – and perhaps Japan and China also qualify. But in the rest of the world we are subject to the influence of the international markets, global corporations, and bodies like the World Trade Organisation, which were up by treaty or convention and affect all our lives. We live in a world where more and more states are banding together – whether in Europe, the Americas or Asia – to make policies that benefit the member states. That does not mean new super-states are being created, rather that we are living in a world where layers of governance overlap in many different ways.

Historian Norman Davies points out that what is evolving is something of an in-between situation, rather than one of either of the extremes sometimes presented. On the one hand, Europe is not going to be the Common Market created by the Treaty of Rome – a free-trading area designed to maximise economic advantage. Neither is it going to be, on the other hand, a classic supersate 'which would have a head of state, an executive in permanent session, a legislative assembly to whom it is answerable and its own individual judiciary'. In his views, we are seeing a new kind of polity emerge, but still one in which the Council of Ministers, rather than the European Commission, has the final say: 'those ministers represent their national interests, not the interests of a superstate.'

At Nice, heads of government were keen to take control of the way in which decisions are taken; rather than expanding the power of the Commission or the EU itself, they wanted to limit it. They wished to retain their national identities within Europe. Again, while talks were proceeding in Brussels over the constitution, there was much discussion in the press and among eurosceptical politicians as to whether the act of devising a constitution was in itself an indication that a superstate was being created. Opposition foreign affairs spokesman Michael Ancram saw it as 'a gateway to a country called Europe'. Others see the EU not as a country, but a collection of twenty-five nation-states who choose to pool some of their sovereignty. The constitution says that countries confer competences upon the EU, not the other way round.

Finally, the point has been made by an Oxford don, Larry Siedentop, that it is hard to imagine any superstate in which the size of the budget was limited by treaty to 1.27 per cent of the member states' GDP: 'No large state uses less than 30 per cent'.

In his attitude to the issue of Britain's position in the world and the special relationship with the USA, Tony Blair has tried to perform a balancing act. As a self-confessed committed European, fault-lines appeared in that approach when he strongly backed the American-led coalition in the war on terrorism and against Iraq. His vision of Britain's role is that it should be act as a bridge across the Atlantic, linking the USA to the continent of Europe. Many would see this as a position that makes good sense, in view of Britain's past attitudes and traditions, and present realities. But bridges can be uncomfortable places on which to be located, when the going gets rough and the pressure builds up from either side. There are times in which there is a clash of interest, and on those occasions even the most dexterous of leaders cannot ride two horses without experiencing problems and upsetting one partner or the other.

Also, from a European perspective, it has sometimes seemed as though the old British habit of lecturing the Europeans has continued even under a more pro-European administration. At an early stage in his premiership, Tony Blair urged his pragmatic and free-market variety of social democracy as the best way forward for the EU. Some saw as arrogance the fact that they were being lectured by a new arrival in the Union club, even if the speaker was one of the more charismatic and genial politicians on the European stage.

British parties in office – whatever doubts they may have had in opposition – seem to be clear about the desirability, and many would say necessity, of membership of the EU. They have seen clear economic advantages for Britain in belonging to a club that believes in free trade and the market economy, and whose remit covers such a substantial area of the continent. But whether the government is of the left or right, and led by a pro-European or eurosceptic, two key strands have been characteristic of the British approach to European policy adopted ever since the Second World War:

- an emphasis upon the importance of Britain's transatlantic ties as a central tenet of foreign policy;
- a preference for intergovernmentalism over integrationism – a belief in the central role of national governments that renders any federalist notions as out of the question for British ministers.

The bonds between Britain and the USA as expressed in the Atlantic Alliance are in line with the broad preferences of many British people. Hugo Young has suggested that Britain needs to shed its 'Anglo Saxon' identity and its preference for things American and embrace more fully its membership of the European family.[22] Yet for reasons of history, geography and language, the British do not naturally identify with Europe. As Geddes remarks:

A holiday in Tuscany or an appreciation of French wines does not necessarily translate into full-hearted enthusiasm for the Euro . . . they can enjoy a cappuccino, sip a glass of Chianti, book a holiday to Spain or cheer or the English or Scottish national football teams coached respectively at the time of writing [2003] by a Swede and a German. Yet these positive images of Europe can effortlessly be countered by the ubiquitous presence of American brands such as MTV, Starbucks, Nike and McDonald's . . . when the question 'Is Britain European?' is asked, then the answer must be 'Yes, but not only'[23]

Jacques Delors, more of an admirer of things British than many people in Britain ever thought possible back in the 1980s, has described the British aversion to many things European as 'a great mystery of history'.[24] For him, it is not just about the special relationship with the USA, although that is important. As he put it: 'Asking Britain to distance itself much from the US is like asking someone to cut off an arm or a leg'. He claimed that 'there's just something in the people, the product as they are of a great and proud history'.

The EU of the future and Britain's role within it

Whereas Monnet and his fellow pioneers believed the intergovernmentalism of the OEEC to be 'the opposite of the Community spirit' and favoured the creation of 'new functional authorities that superseded the sovereignty of existing nation states' rather than 'more cooperation',[25] British governments have traditionally doubted the wisdom or desirability of the drive towards an ever closer and deeper union. From Dalton to Brown, chancellors have not wanted to see their hands tied by policies initiated in Brussels, and issues such as tax harmonisation have illustrated the determination of ministers to cling on to the British veto and resist the plans of those who want to advance the pace of progress towards greater unity.

Britain has not been the only country to have doubts about the nature and pace of advance within the EU. The Danes have often been an ally, while one reason for the support given by British administrations to enlargement has been the hope that the new members would wish to see a looser and wider EU. Indeed, by the very act of enlarging, British politicians have often assumed that their preference would ultimately triumph. Yet past history has shown that some of those countries committed to enlargement have also been determined to maintain their commitment to strengthening the bonds of membership.

The process of integration in Europe has not been smooth. On several occasions there have been conflicts between national interest and the interests of Europe as a whole. Yet the direction of movement has always been towards greater integration, a term which the Oxford Dictionary describes as 'the harmonious combination of elements into a single whole'.

Widening, deepening and enlargement: possible ways ahead

As we have seen, the argument over deepening or widening the EU usually occurs in the discussion of enlargement and the benefits it may confer. There have always been some commentators and politicians who believe that enlarging the EU has been the greater imperative and that further action to strengthen the bonds between existing members can be an impediment to enlargement, given the obligations laid upon all new members to accept the *acquis communautaire* – the range of laws, obligations, policies, practices and principles that have developed within the EU. On the other side are those who stress that enlargement will make the EU more heterogeneous and institutionally unwieldy, so that the deepening process must at least accompany, if not precede, enlargement, if progress towards an ever closer union is to be maintained. Depending on which side of the fence the observer is sitting, enlargement can either be used as the pretext for slowing down or quickening the process of integration.

Substantial enlargement has now been achieved, with the further prospect of two new entrants (Bulgaria and Romania) in 2007, eventually taking the EU to at least twenty-seven. In spite of the deliberations that took place in the Convention and subsequent agreement on the proposed constitution for Europe, some of the details relating to the functioning of an enlarged EU have not yet been agreed and in other cases much will depend on how the Court of Justice chooses to interpret the final document. But most observers agree that a union of twenty-five nations cannot easily operate in the way that a much smaller one has done. It remains to be seen what attitude will be taken by new entrants to the future development of the EU, although early indications suggest that there may be a sturdy defence of national interests.

The issue of how to ensure that an enlarged EU functions cohesively and effectively, while yet allowing for the defence of important national 'lines in the sand', is one yet to be resolved. The intergovernmental character of much of the Maastricht Treaty, allowing further pillars to be added to the Union structure, is one approach, having the merit of being flexible enough to allow for the worries about loss of sovereignty that are particularly troublesome to some member states. But many supporters of the process of integration are uneasy about any possible dilution of EU objectives and achievements that such an approach may involve. They feel that the EU should move ahead together and at one pace. In recent years, there has been much discussion of schemes that allow for differing rates of progress.

Variable geometry

To overcome the many problems associated with progress for the EU, compounded on one side by the economic weakness of some new members and on the other by the reluctance of larger states such as Britain to surrender part of their sovereignty as represented by the national veto, the idea of variable geometry has re-emerged in recent years as a desirable possibility. Sometimes it is known by an alternative name of 'enhanced co-operation' (*coopération renforcée*).

Originating in the plan for a series of concentric circles (see below), the term refers to models of European integration which allow member states the choice as to whether they wish to participate in or stand aloof from new initiatives – accepting of course that there will always be a number of 'core activities' in which all states are involved. The approach allows for a greater flexibility in the evolution of the EU, involving a tiered system whereby groups of countries at different levels of development would be enabled to move at different speeds within certain policy objectives.

The first reasoned argument for the variable approach was produced by the then French prime minister, Edouard Balladur, in August 1994. Balladur called for a three-tier Europe that he preferred to describe as three concentric circles.[26] There would be:

- a strong central core of France, Germany and perhaps the Benelux countries, united politically, economically and militarily;
- a middle tier made up of the other EU countries, unable or unwilling to join the political and economic union at the centre;
- an outer circle containing the other European countries, which are not part of the EU but which have economic and security links.

Balladur claimed that only such an arrangement could prevent paralysis of the EU by the problems inherent in enlargement. Two days later, the German Christian Democratic Union published a policy document designed 'to strengthen the EU's capacity to act and to make its structures and procedures more democratic and federal'.[27] At the heart of this aim was the need to establish a form of constitution for the EU which would create a federal structure according to the principle of subsidiarity. Recognising that movement towards union would be impossible if all countries progressed at the speed of the slowest, the Germans repeated the Balladur suggestion that there should be a fast-track central core of countries, which they proposed should be France, Germany and the Benelux countries, since 'they (together with Denmark and Ireland) are the ones which come closest to meeting the convergence criteria stipulated in the Maastricht treaty'. Two years later, the then German chancellor, Helmut Kohl, was insistent that the pace of European integration should not be set by those who wanted to advance more cautiously, or not at all. As he put it: 'The slowest ship in the convoy should not be allowed to determine its speed. If individual partners are not prepared or able to participate in certain steps towards integration, the others should not be denied the opportunity to move forward.'[28]

John Major had made great play of a 'multispeed and multilayered European Union' during the European elections of 1994. But now that the mechanism for creating such a layered institution was being suggested, he began to express reservations. He feared that such a solution would relegate Britain to some second-class outer circle. In September 1994 Major made a speech in which he reiterated British adherence to the European ideal: 'Britain is irrevocably part of Europe', he said, 'but it must be the right sort of Europe'. And the right sort did not include an inner and outer core of member states. There was a wide range of policies within the EU and member states should be allowed to adopt differentiated approaches to these policies, as Denmark and the UK had adopted a different approach to monetary union. The key word was flexibility, which was 'essential to get the best out of Europe'. Major concluded by attacking the idea of federalism and reasserting Britain's belief in the nation-state, seeing the EU as an association of nation-states, co-operating but each at their own speed and in their own interest.[29]

British ministers in the 1990s increasingly spoke of a Europe in which they could pick and choose the parts they favoured: a Europe 'à la carte' in which they sought allies with whom they could achieve those things that mattered to them. The difficulty was that when so many items on the agenda were unacceptable to London, then leaders in other capitals were likely to hesitate before agreeing to such an approach. They feared that if one or more countries such as Britain opted out of nearly all major initiatives, the result would be a 'two-speed' or 'two-tier' Europe in which some countries moved ahead to integration at a rapid pace, while others, which did not wish to go so far or so quickly, trailed behind.

Many suggestions have been put forward for a future based on some kind of 'variable geometry' model. The underlying idea in all of them is that all states would normally take part in a core of essential areas, but they would be free to move at a different pace on others. The phrase sometimes used by British ministers a few years ago was 'flexible integration' – a more diplomatically worded variant of some prevailing ideas.

Any model of concentric circles, with an inner circle committed to the fast track and an outer one to slower progress, has disadvantages, not least for Union solidarity. It would also call into question the rights of all member states to have equal status in decision making, and could have budgetary implications as well: the inner few might be reluctant to finance those states who were unwilling to move ahead at the faster rate. For Britain the danger of any approach based on different rates of progress is that Britain will be in the slow lane on all key issues. The fear is that if Britain does not belong to the advance guard, it will be sidelined, and lose any ability to influence events in Europe. Britain would not be 'at the heart of Europe'.

The Blair government claimed that it did not wish to be left behind, and it has shown less enthusiasm for any variant of variable geometry. Its rhetoric implies that the intention is to join the euro 'when the time is right', and that it will seek to co-operate in other fields unless essential interests are at stake. But as yet, in spite of two large majorities in the House of Commons, 'the time has not been ripe' for the euro. Moreover, Britain has found itself resisting the thrust of integration in other areas favoured by the powerful Franco–German alliance, which is usually in the vanguard of further progress.

After the talks over the constitution, Blair conceded that in order to preserve his red lines it was necessary to agree that other states could be allowed to forge ahead with integration, including a common tax policy. Some states, particularly from the former Soviet block, had shared his approach, indicating that what is beginning to emerge is a complex patchwork of alliances that form and reform over different issues, and come and go with changing governments. The outcome is likely to be a looser union, in which the integrationists form a core group who will drive things forward, with other nations choosing how and when they will participate, as national interests and pressures permit.

Conservative leader Michael Howard recognised how Europe has been developing in recent years, in his speech to a German audience in 2004:

> So far, everyone has had to move forward together, with individual countries negotiating specific opt-outs. This has caused tremendous tension . . . But since 1998, there has been a new procedure within the treaties to allow some member states to go ahead with further integration in a specific area, without involving every other member state . . . known as enhanced co-operation. It means that, instead of individual member states having fraught negotiations to opt out of a new initiative, those that support it can simply decide to opt in . . . it suits the integrationists, it suits the non-integrationists . . . let's use it . . . it would [then] not be necessary for them to drag Britain and quite possibly some other member states kicking and screaming in their wake . . . I am not talking about a two-speed Europe. That implies that we are all agreed on the destination and differ only about the speed of the journey. I don't want to reach the destination that some our partners may aspire to.[30]

Increasingly today there is talk among some European politicians not committed to the older, integrationist model of a more flexible Europe in which member nations would in future be able to decide whether to retain wholly national control or whether to co-operate with others. In effect, this would create a series of overlapping circles, with different combinations of member states pooling their responsibilities in different areas of their own choosing.

The real debate – stay or go?

During all the debates on the future of the EU – on federalism versus pragmatism, the nature and pace of advance, the cost of British membership or the iniquities of the CAP – there has been one constant. Even the most eurosceptical of critics have generally seemed to accept that withdrawal was not an option and that for several reasons Britain should remain a member of the EU:

- With the single market in operation British trade and industry is part of a very large internal market. Very few members of Britain's commercial and industrial community are ready to retreat from that, with the possible threat of European tariff barriers being raised against British goods and services.
- Britain has received a great deal of inward investment from the USA and elsewhere by firms who wished to set up a manufacturing base within the EU so as to avoid the external trade tariff. Withdrawal from the EU would mean the loss of these companies, with a consequent loss of investment, tax revenue and jobs.

politicians and people never fully willing to commit themselves to a European road.[32] A case for the 'awkwardness' of Britain from a continental point of view is easy to outline. It might start with the failure to join early supranational organisations such as the ECSC and the EEC; point to the early renegotiation of the terms of entry, once Britain was a member of the EEC; note the divisions that the issue of European membership and the extent of British commitment to the Community/Union has caused division and strife within the main parties and provoked ministerial resignations: draw attention to the hostilities aroused over policy crises such as BSE and problems such as the CAP and CFP: mention the low degree of interest in European affairs by the British people and their reluctance to vote in European elections; and conclude by commenting on the preference shown for the American stance in the Iraq war and its aftermath, over Europe.

In fairness, there are other nations, too, that have expressed some reluctance to embrace the EU and its works. The Swiss rejected membership of the EEA, and the Norwegians did the same in regards to the EEC and later EU. The Danes have often shown a preference for intergovernmentalism over integration, and like the Swedes have decided against participation in the eurozone. Even the normally pro-European Irish at first rejected the Nice Treaty. And if critics of British administrations argue that they 'missed the European bus' after the Second World War and have consistently had a record of joining up with their continental partners too belatedly and when ministers could not have a say in the original negotiations, then a defence can be mounted that perhaps this is not altogether surprising – given the country's unique global role and responsibilities. Moreover, there is an element of hindsight in such a viewpoint. It was not so obviously apparent in the 1950s that the ECSC and the EEC were going to be as successful as they turned out, nor that the supranational structures constructed at the time were destined to work as well as they did.

However, whatever the defence that can be mounted against the George thesis, few would argue that for most of the post-1945 era Britain has been on the periphery of the broad thrust to European integration, at times more and at other times less willing to co-operate effectively with its European partners. In some areas, ministers have been willing to engage more fully; in others there has been a much greater degree of reluctance.

The implications of membership of the European Community, later Union, have become more apparent in recent years: not just the impact upon our constitutional arrangements but also upon the attitudes of parties and the fortunes of politicians. Many British people have been confirmed in their doubts about British membership, the fact of which they may accept as inevitable – but they do not particularly like the experience. The lack of enthusiasm and commitment in Britain confirm its reputation on the continent as a country that always wants to slow down the pace of advance, that always says 'No, no, no!'. In the eyes of many people in Britain and beyond its shores, British politicians and people remain 'reluctant Europeans'.

Notes

1   D. Butler and M. Westlake, *British Politics and the European Elections 1994*, Macmillan, 1995.

2   Sir A. Meyer, quoted in H. Young, *This Blessed Plot*, Macmillan, 1998.

3   H. Young, as in 2 above.

4   W. Churchill, speech in House of Commons, May 1951.

5   Sir A. Eden, quoted in S. Greenwood, *Britain and European Cooperation Since 1945*, Blackwell, 1992.

6   D. Acheson, speech at the Military Academy, West Point, 5 December 1962.

7   W. Kaiser, *Using Europe, Abusing the Europeans: Britain and European Integration 1945–63*, St Martin's Press, 1996.

8   F. Northedge, *Descent From Power: British Foreign Policy 1945–1973*, Allen & Unwin, 1974.

9   H. Young, as in 2 above.

10 G. Martin, quoted in A. Davies, *British Politics and Europe*, Access series, Hodder & Stoughton, 1998.

11 H. Macmillan, quoted by A. Adonis, *The Observer*, 17 November 1996.

12 W. Kaiser, as in 7 above.

13 Lord Tebbit, quoted in H. Macmillan, as in 11 above.

14 T. Blair, speech to French National Assembly, October 1998.

15 A. Geddes, *The European Union and British Politics*, Palgrave, 2004.

16 H. Young, as in 2 above.

17 M. Thatcher speech, quoted in M. Thatcher, *The Downing Street Years*, Harper Collins, 1993.

18 A. Adonis, as in 11 above.

19 I. Duncan Smith, speech in House of Commons, April 1996.

20 M. Howard, speech to Konrad Adenamer Stiftung, Berlin, 12 February 2004.

21 The information in this box is based on an assortment of views expressed in a special report for *The Observer*, 10 December 2000.

22 H. Young, as in 2 above.

23 A. Geddes, as in 15 above.

24 J. Monnet, *Memoirs*, Doubleday & Co., 1978.

25 J. Delors, interview in *The Guardian*, 17 January 2004.

26 E. Balladur, interview in *Le Figaro*, 30 August 1994.

27 CDU/CSU policy paper, presented on 1 September 1994, but not approved by the then Christian Democrat Chancellor Kohl.

28 H. Kohl, speech in Cologne, February 1996.

29 J. Major, 'William and Mary Lecture', University of Leiden, the Netherlands, 6 September 1994.

30 M. Howard, as in 20 above.

31 N. Lamont, speech to Selsdon Group of Conservative Party, Bournemouth, 11 October 1994.

32 S. George, *Britain and the European Community: The Politics of Semi-Detachment*, Oxford University Press, 1992.

Further information about the EU

Books

Much of the writing on the EU is academic and specialised. There are few accessible and authoritative accounts of Britain's place in the EU, although in recent years some have appeared that are more geared to the school and college market. There is also a growing recognition of the European perspective in general textbooks. The following are particularly useful as more detailed, follow-up sources of reference.

The EU in general

E. Bomberg and A. Stubb, *The European Union: How Does it Work?*, Oxford University Press, 2003.
J. McCormick, *Understanding the European Union: A Concise Introduction*, Palgrave, 2002.
W. Nicoll and T. Salmon, *Understanding the European Union*, Pearson/Longman, 2001.
N. Nugent, *The Government and Politics of the European Union*, Palgrave, 2003.

Britain and the EU

A. Geddes, *The European Union and British Politics*, Palgrave, 2004.
S. George, *An Awkward Partner: Britain in the European Community*, Oxford University Press, 1998.
H. Young, *This Blesssed Plot*, Macmillan, 1998.

On the web

A vast amount of information is available on the internet. General sites include:

- **ww1w.europa.eu.int** A truly massive site that is a valuable starting point for further reference, offering in all languages of the EU direct access to the home pages of EU institutions, basic information about the EU and its policy areas, enlargement, official documents, etc.

- **www.cec.org.uk** The UK office of the European Commission.
- **www.europarl.en.int/uk** The UK office of the European Parliament.

Other than the Europa site, current issues are aired via several think tanks, notably:

- **www.ceps.be** The Centre for European Policy Studies.
- **www.cer.org.uk** The Centre for European Reform.
- **www.theepc.be** The European Policy Centre.

Index